Elite Conflict in a Plural Society:

Twentieth-Century Bengal

Elite Conflict in a Plural Society:

Twentieth-Century Bengal

J. H. BROOMFIELD

UNIVERSITY OF CALIFORNIA PRESS
Berkeley and Los Angeles 1968

University of California Press
Berkeley and Los Angeles, California

Cambridge University Press
London, England

Library of Congress Catalog Card Number: 68-13822
Printed in the United States of America

For Jenni

PREFACE

THIS IS NOT an exhaustive (nor, I hope, an exhausting) study of Bengal politics in this century. My main concern has been with institutional politics, particularly the politics of the legislature, and I have concentrated on the decade and a half, 1912 to 1927, which witnessed crucial developments in communal relations. An introductory chapter provides an outline of events leading to the reunification of Bengal in 1912, and an epilogue carries the story down to the partition of 1947, but no special claim of originality is made for these sections.

The research extended over a seven-year period, including three visits to India and Pakistan, and one to the United Kingdom. The sources were both written and oral. I interviewed approximately fifty old politicians and administrators, among them Maulvi Fazlul Huq, Dr B. C. Roy, Hemendra Prasad Ghose, Sir Percival Griffiths, B. P. Singh Roy, Maulana Akram Khan, Sir Khwawja Nazimuddin, Professor N. K. Bose, and Nawab Khan Bahadur Musharruf Husain. The interviews were invaluable for the insights which they gave into personality, and they often suggested profitable new lines of enquiry. Where possible, however, I did not rely upon them for facts, always attempting to document any details I was given. Consequently the reader will find relatively few references to these interviews in footnotes.

The most important documentary sources for the research were the official records of the Government of Bengal and the Government of India. Their main depositories are the West Bengal Government Record Office, Calcutta, and the National Archives of India, New Delhi. The East Pakistan Government Record Office, Dacca, has duplicates of some of the pre-partition records of the Government of Bengal, and it also has files concerning Eastern Bengal Districts unavailable in Calcutta.

Among the provincial Government's records are the *Reports on Native Papers in Bengal*, weekly compilations of political and social comment from the vernacular and English-language press, prepared by the British administration to keep its officers informed of current opinion. Translated into English from a variety of languages, arranged by subject and indexed, this is an invaluable research source. Complete files of even the leading Bengal newspapers and periodicals are difficult to find. The National Library of India, Calcutta, and the India Office Library, London, have the most extensive holdings. The West Bengal Secretariat Library, the Indian Association, and the British Indian Association have much good material, and fragmentary files of smaller publications can be unearthed by a search through libraries in the Calcutta suburbs and mufussil towns. For more than sixty years before his death in 1963, Hemendra Prasad Ghose, a Calcutta journalist and politician, maintained books of press clippings, with his personal comments penned in the margins. I am greatly indebted to him for giving me access to these.

Among my other documentary sources, the following were the most important:

Indian Association proceedings, Indian Association office, Bow Bazar, Calcutta

British Indian Association proceedings and correspondence, British Indian Association office, British Indian Street, Calcutta

C. F. Andrews papers, Rabindra Sadana, Visva Bharati, Santiniketan

Sir Tej Bahadur Sapru papers, National Library of India, Calcutta

Satya Kinkar Sahana Vinyavinode diaries, Ananda Kutir, Kenduadihi, Bankura

Fazlul Huq speeches, 466 page typescript collection in possession of Azizul Huq, Dacca

Of the relevant published materials, the National Library of India, Calcutta, the West Bengal Secretariat Library, Calcutta, and the India Office Library, London, have the best collections. I extend my sincere thanks for the assistance rendered me by the directors, librarians, keepers of records, and other officers of the various depositories in which I worked.

A note on my system of transliteration might be helpful. When using words which are frequently heard in Indian English (e.g., zamindar, mufussil, pandal) and which would be less easily recognised by the reader if they were transliterated strictly according to their Bengali form, I have used what I consider their most common English spelling and have left them unitalicised. For all other Bengali words I have employed a regular though simplified scheme of transliteration, with only one diacritical mark to distinguish long 'a' from short 'a' (e.g., *hartāl*). In spelling Indian personal names I have consistently adhered to the form used by the individual himself when signing in Roman script.

My research was made possible by financial assistance from the following institutions: Australian National University, American Council of Learned Societies, Social Science Research Council, Rackham School of Graduate Studies and Center for South and South-East Asian Studies of the University of Michigan, and American Institute of Indian Studies.

I have many individuals to thank for their help and succour during the years of the book's gestation. My heaviest debt of gratitude is to my wife, Jenni, who was involved with every stage of its production, as unpaid research assistant, unpaid typist, unrelenting critic, and constant companion. In India my way was always smoothed by Dr Ajita Ranjan Mukherjea, formerly Secretary of the Bengal Legislature, scholar and friend of scholarship. The study would have been impossible without his help. In Canberra I was extremely fortunate to have the guidance and enthusiasm of Professor Anthony Low and Dr Bruce Graham, my doctoral supervisors, and the cheerful companionship of Dr Peter Reeves, whose experience made easier my early days as a raw recruit to South Asian studies. In America I have benefitted from the advice of Robert I. Crane, Duke University, Stephen Hay, University of California, Santa Barbara, and Warren M. Gunderson, City College of New York, who were all so generous as to give time to the reading and criticism of my drafts. For their research assistance I am indebted to Mrs Nancy Van Loo Mate, Mr Niranjan Sen Gupta, and Mr Michael Pearson, and for her cartography to Miss Karen Ewing, Department of Geography, University of Michigan.

Ann Arbor,
August 23,
1967

JHB

CONTENTS

PREFACE vii

KEY TO ABBREVIATED REFERENCES xiii

INTRODUCTION

PART I: BENGAL AND THE BHADRALOK 1

PART II: THE BHADRALOK AND THE BRITISH 21

CHAPTER I · A MAN WITH A MISSION 42

II · 'TALL TALK AND LOW PERFORMANCES' 82

III · THE VOTE OR VIOLENCE 113

IV · THE INTERREGNUM 131

V · THE MODERATES' FAILURE 169

VI · HE WHO RIDES A TIGER 204

VII · REAPERS OF THE WHIRLWIND 244

EPILOGUE · THE TRAGIC DECADES 282

CONCLUSION 316

GLOSSARY 333

INDEX 335

MAPS

MAP 1. Bengal, 1912–1947 xvi
MAP 2. Bengal, Rivers and Railways, 1921 xvii
MAP 3. Partitioned Bengal, 1905–1912 28
MAP 4. Partitioned Bengal, 1947 314

TABLES

TABLE 1. Composition of Bengal Legislative Council under Indian Councils Acts, 1861 and 1892 19
TABLE 2. Composition of Bengal, and Eastern Bengal and Assam Legislative Councils under Indian Councils Act, 1909 38
TABLE 3. Composition of Bengal Legislative Council and Electorate under Revised Regulations of 1912 54
TABLE 4. Composition of Bengal Legislative Council and Electorate under Government of India Act, 1919 128
TABLE 5. Composition of Bengal Legislative Assembly and Council and Electorates under Government of India Act, 1935 292

Key to Abbreviated References

*	When appended to the title of a newspaper, indicates that the original was seen. The source of all other newspaper references was *Report on Native Papers in Bengal*
Andrews	B. D. Chaturvedi and M. Sykes, *Charles Freer Andrews, A Narrative* (London, 1949)
Andrews MSS	C. F. Andrews papers, Rabindra-Sadana, Visva-Bharati, Santiniketan
Azizul Huq collection	Speeches of A. K. Fazlul Huq, typescript copies in the possession of Azizul Huq, Dacca
BIA	British Indian Association, Calcutta
BLAP	Proceedings of the Bengal Legislative Assembly
BLCP	Proceedings of the Bengal Legislative Council
Carmichael	Lady Mary Carmichael, *Lord Carmichael of Skirling. A Memoir* (London, 1929)
Coupland	Reginald Coupland, *Report on the Constitutional Problems in India* (London, 1942–1943)

DIB	C. E. Buckland, *Directory of Indian Biography* (London, 1906)
DNB	L. Stephen et al. (eds.), *Dictionary of National Biography* (London, 1937–1959)
Essayez	Lord Zetland, *Essayez* (London, 1956)
GB	Government of Bengal
GI	Government of India
IA	Indian Association, Calcutta
IAR	N. N. Mitra (ed.), *The Indian Annual Register* (Calcutta, 1921–1947)
Indian Struggle	S. C. Bose, *The Indian Struggle, 1920–1934* (Calcutta, 1948)
Jayakar	M. R. Jayakar, *The Story of My Life* (Bombay, 1958–1959)
Montagu	E. S. Montagu, *An Indian Diary* (London, 1930)
Nation in Making	S. N. Banerjea, *A Native in Making* (London, 1925)
N. C. Banerji	N. C. Banerji, *At the Cross-Roads, 1885–1946. The Autobiography* (Calcutta, 1950)
NP	*Report on Native Papers in Bengal* (Calcutta, ?1876–1947)
PP	Parliamentary Papers, Great Britain
Pundits & Elephants	Lord Lytton, *Pundits and Elephants* (London, 1942)
Reading	Lord Reading, *Rufus Isaacs, First Marquess of Reading* (London, 1942–1945)
Reformed Constitution, 1927	*Reports on the Working of the Reformed Constitution, 1927* (Calcutta, 1928)

Sahana diaries	Diaries of Satya Kinkar Sahana Vidyavinode, Ananda Kutir, Kenduadihi, Bankura
Sapru papers	Tej Bahadur Sapru papers, National Library of India, Calcutta
Simon Commission	*Indian Statutory Commission. Report* (London, 1930)
Subhas Chandra	H. N. Das Gupta, *Subhas Chandra* (Calcutta, 1946)

STANDARD FORM OF REFERENCE TO GOVERNMENT FILES:

Government of India:		*Department /*	*Branch /*	*Proceedings number /*	*Date*
Example	GI,	Home,	Public,	B64–66,	Mar. 1903.

Government of Bengal:		*Department /*	*File number /*	*Proceedings number /*	*Date*
Example	GB,	Police,	6P–18(1–10),	A10–19,	Apr. 1919.

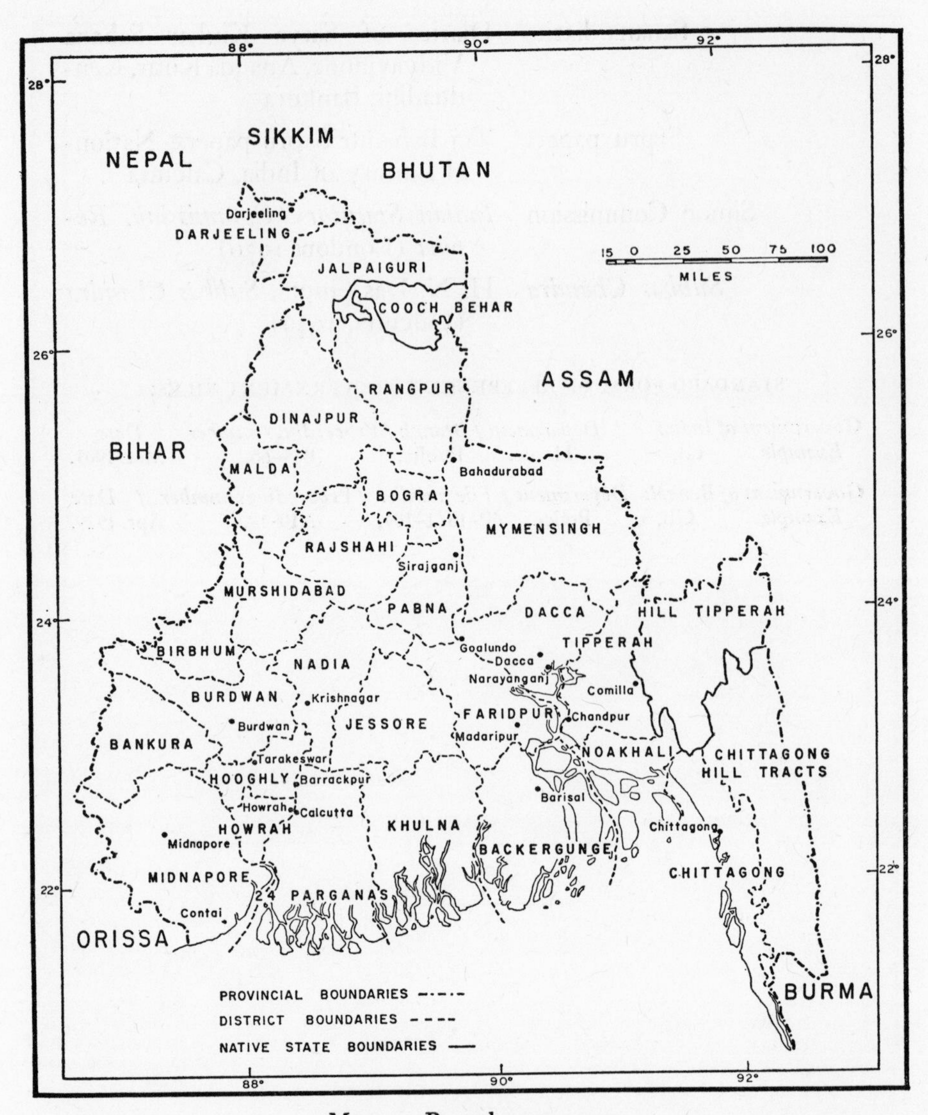

Map 1. Bengal, 1912–1947

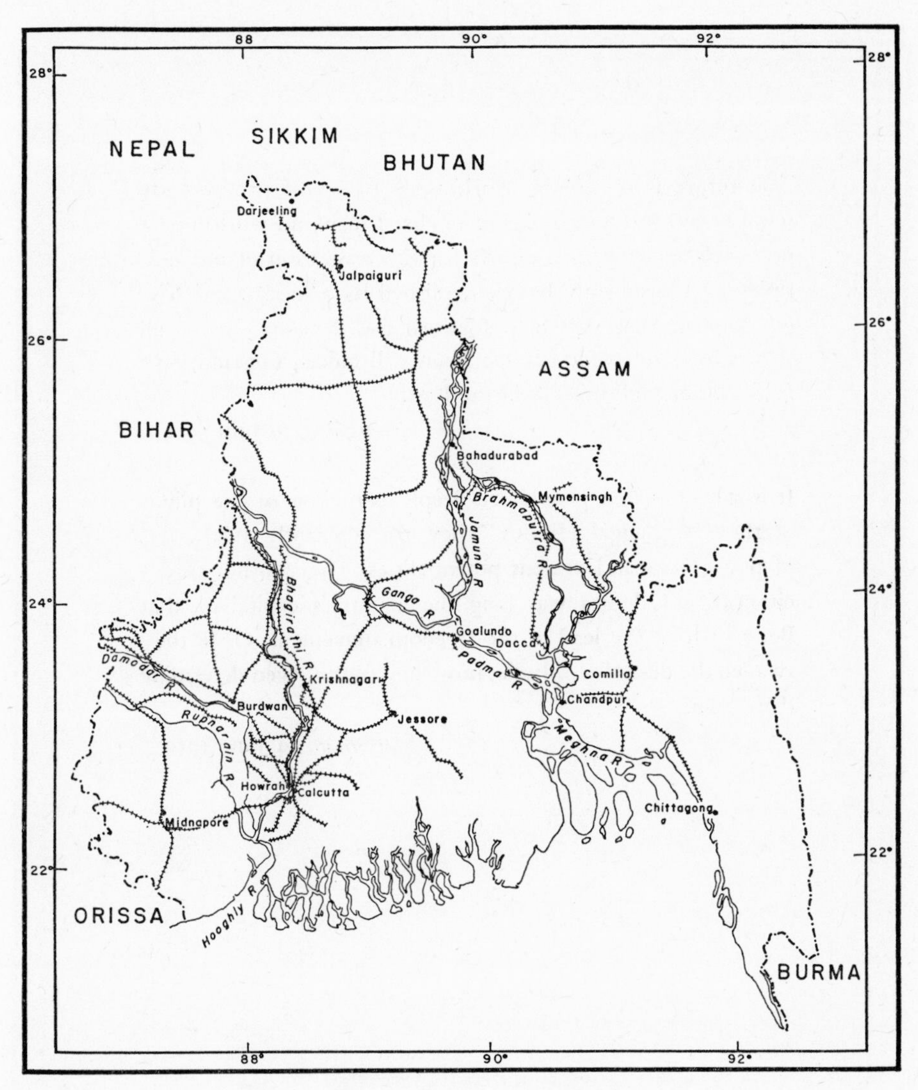

Map 2. Bengal, Rivers and Railways, 1921

The future is ours. The world-wide forces of progress are with us and the sympathies of civilized mankind will support us in our constitutional efforts for the realization of our destinies which can only be accomplished by a measure of self-government that will help forward the development of all that is best and noblest in us. Then will indeed England have fulfilled her high mission in the East.

Bengalee, 19 July 1912

It is not only that people are deeply conscious of the plight of the East Bengal Hindus. They are constantly aware also of past glories and present potentialities. They do not forget either that Calcutta was long the country's capital or that Bengalis took the lead in the freedom movement. Once they swayed the destinies of India; now they cannot even determine their own.

Statesman, 24 June 1950

Introduction

PART I: BENGAL AND THE BHADRALOK

CALCUTTA

Of all the cities of the British Empire, only London was greater than Calcutta at the opening of the twentieth century. With more than a million people, it towered above the surrounding villages and puny district towns. It had no rivals closer than Madras and Bombay, both distant by a thousand miles and neither of them three-quarters its size. It was, as it always had been, a city of migrants, drawn in a never ceasing flow by its opportunities of wealth and distinction, education, or more simply, employment.

Its economic strength rested on the broad stream of the Hooghly River, which brought the commerce of Europe and Asia by steam and sail 80 miles up from the sea to the wharves along Strand Road on its left bank, and the rich natural products of the valleys and deltas of the Ganga and Brahmaputra Rivers to the warehouses and markets of this great entrepôt. The power of the British banking and agency houses on Clive Street was felt along the whole maritime fringe of Asia and, together with the Indian merchants of Burra Bazar, these latter-day nabobs controlled virtually the entire trade of eastern and northern India. They had financed a network of canals and railways radiating from Calcutta that distributed European manufactured goods to the densely populated tropical hinterland and brought back raw materials, the most profitable of which were jute, coal, indigo, and tea. Around the railhead at Howrah on the right bank of the Hooghly and for 20 miles north along both sides of the river there were workshops and mills that processed the raw materials for local consumption and export.

Calcutta's fame as a port and jute-milling centre was matched by its fame as the capital of India and Bengal. Two imperial vice-consuls held court in spacious, colonnaded eighteenth-century residences at either end of the Maidan. In Government House, with regal lions proudly guarding its gateways, the Governor-General and Viceroy with his six Councillors ruled a fifth of the world's population, the three hundred million people who inhabited the British Indian Empire.[1] In its vaulted durbar hall representatives from all provinces of the subcontinent and Burma assembled for the sessions of the Imperial Legislative Council, which legislated for India under the delegated authority of the British Parliament.

From Belvedere, an older and more elegant mansion above whose entrance stalked a lithe Bengal tiger, the Lieutenant-Governor of Bengal administered a territory half again as large as the United Kingdom, with twice as many people. Apart from Bengal proper, his province included Bihar, Chota Nagpur, and Orissa. Unlike the Viceroy and the Governors of Madras and Bombay who were usually British parliamentarians, he was a senior member of the Indian Civil Service, the elite cadre of 1200 gentlemen professionals who held all the superior posts in the Indian administration. He had the assistance of a Legislative Council but, again unlike his counterparts in Madras and Bombay, he had no Executive Council. This is, as it was intended to be, a measure of his subordination to the Governor-General, in whose shadow he always stood.

His Secretariat and that of the Viceroy, together with a host of minor functionaries of both Governments, occupied a maze of offices in the mile square between Clive Street and Government House: a vast and ponderous bureaucracy which was the despair of many an eager young officer in the mufussil. Flanking the administrative district on the southwest was the Calcutta High Court, which had superior jurisdiction over all of eastern India, making Calcutta India's principal legal as well as administrative centre.

For many, however, Calcutta's first attraction was not its courts and offices, but its schools. From every district of Bengal and places far beyond, young men flocked to the city's colleges to prepare for the university examinations that were the exclusive entrée to

[1] *Census of India, 1901*, Vol. I, pt. 1, p. 13. All figures on Calcutta and Bengal in this Introduction, unless separately footnoted, are from Vol. VI, pt. 1.

the clerkships and professional appointments to which they aspired. Calcutta University itself, approaching its half centenary, and the older and equally distinguished colleges around it in the heart of the crowded Bengali residential area of North Calcutta were the focus of a stimulating cultural life. For the educated elite there were learned societies, theatres, museums, art galleries, libraries, and a flourishing book-publishing industry; for the general literate, who were more numerous here than anywhere else in India, there was the daily press, appearing in four major languages: English, Bengali, Hindi, and Urdu.

The heterogeneous composition of Calcutta's population reflected its varied opportunities. At the pinnacle of political and economic power stood 13,000 British, one of the largest and most exclusive European societies in the East. Closely associated with them but never allowed to presume to social equality were the Anglo-Indians, 16,000 Eurasians whose loyalty to the Raj assured them of reserved positions on the railways, the telegraphs, and other vital communications services. Sharing with the British businessmen the profits of the inland trade were small groups of Armenians and Jews, Bengali Hindus of the banking and trading castes, Gujerati Hindus and Muslims, and the Marwaris, Jain migrants from Rajputana whose communal collaboration and speculative flair was just beginning to make the impact on Calcutta commerce that was to change its face in the subsequent forty years.

Personal service and labour for industry, transport, and construction were supplied by men from the poorer rural areas of Bihar, the eastern United Provinces and Orissa. These men left wives and families in their villages and crowded into tenements or insanitary bustees, creating immediate problems of public health, and, for twentieth-century Bengal, long-term problems of political control.

These outside groups made up slightly less than half the city's population.[2] The remainder were Bengalis. Some, as we have noted, were bankers and traders; some were fishermen and market gardeners, subsisting on the swampy eastern and northeastern fringes of the city and supplying produce for its markets; but the great majority were in professions or clerical service, for it was the Bengalis who supplied the army of white-collar workers which daily trooped into the offices, the banks, the courts, the consulting rooms, the schools, and the colleges of the metropolis.

[2] *Ibid.*, Vol. VII, pt. 3.

For many of its residents, Indian as well as non-Indian, Calcutta was a cosmopolitan enclave in a foreign land; but for the Bengali majority there was an intimate relationship between the city and the country around it. For them Calcutta was Bengal's city.

BENGAL

Bengal lies astride the tropic of Cancer. It has a monsoonal climate with an adequate and reliable rainfall. Bounded on the north by the Himalaya and on the south by the Bay of Bengal, it encompasses the linked deltas of the Ganga and Brahmaputra Rivers, a lowland of 'new mud, old mud, and marsh'[3] interlaced with distributaries great and small, which annually inundate vast areas for the four months of the monsoon. Everywhere the rivers and their vagaries have shaped the pattern of human activity. The staple diet is fresh-water fish and rice, and the main cash crop is jute which shares with paddy a propensity for wet feet. For the human inhabitants who prefer to go dry-shod the unruly rivers forced settlement onto levees or mounds, with the consequence that here the distinct, compact villages of the Gangetic Valley give way in most places to straggling lines of individual homesteads, half-hidden in clumps of palm and bamboo.

The inconvenience of the annual flood has its compensation: a regular deposit of rich silt which maintains the land's high fertility. As a consequence, Bengal can support a large agricultural population. At the beginning of the twentieth century it had 43,000,000 people, of whom 95 percent lived in the countryside at densities between 300 and 1700 to the square mile. The less heavily settled areas were in west Bengal where the rivers had silted up in the nineteenth century, impoverishing the land and leaving stagnant backwaters and marshes that were the source of a devastating fever. Its worst ravages were in the 1860's and 1870's, but even at the turn of the century the rate of population growth had barely recovered; compared with that of eastern Bengal, where the rivers had continued to give faithful service, it crept along at a snail's pace.

This differential between population growth in eastern and western Bengal was having a marked effect on another important statistic: the relative size of the Hindu and Muslim communities, which together made up 98 percent of the province's total population.

[3] O. H. K. Spate, *India and Pakistan: A General and Regional Geography*, 2nd ed. (London, 1957), p. 524.

Twenty years earlier the two religions could claim almost equal numbers of adherents, but by 1900 Muslims outnumbered Hindus by 10 percent (22 to 20 million), and the Muslim population was growing twice as fast as the Hindu. The main reason was one of location. Almost four fifths of the Muslims lived in the healthier and more prosperous areas of eastern and northern Bengal, while 60 percent of the Hindus lived in the declining western and central districts.

These figures may give the misleading impression that Muslims and Hindus lived separately in clearly demarcated areas to east and west, but in fact there were few places in Bengal where there was not a sizeable minority of one or other community. In eastern Bengal the Hindus were one in three, in western Bengal the Muslims were 13 percent of the total population, while in the centre the two communities were equally balanced. Another striking fact about their relative distribution was the higher proportion of Hindus in towns. Even in Dacca and Chittagong, two urban islands in a predominantly Muslim countryside, Hindus were in a majority, and in all of Bengal they contributed 60 percent of the townspeople.

A glance at the province's urban structure immediately reveals the overwhelming dominance of Calcutta. Of Bengal's total urban population of 2,500,000, Calcutta had half; Dacca was the only other city with more than 35,000 people. Whereas in Bombay, the Punjab, Madras, and the United Provinces a significant fraction of the population lived in small towns,[4] in Bengal, Bihar, Orissa, and Assam not more than 30 in every 1,000 people were to be found there. In Bengal and the provinces tributary to it, there was one great city, a few towns, and innumerable villages.

THE BHADRALOK

At the beginning of the twentieth century Bengali rural and urban society differed in many fundamental respects, yet they shared at least one feature: a common dominant elite. In city, town, and village there was one group of Bengalis who claimed and were accorded recognition as superior in social status to the mass of their fellows. These were the *bhadralok*, literally the 'respectable people', the 'gentle men'. Thy were distinguished by many aspects of their behaviour–their deportment, their speech, their dress,

[4] *Census of India, 1901*, Vol. I, pt. 1, pp. 24–26.

their style of housing, their eating habits, their occupations, and their associations–and quite as fundamentally by their cultural values and their sense of social propriety.

The basic and most rigidly maintained distinction between *bhadra* and *abhadra*, between high and low, the respectable and the others, was the bhadralok's abstention from manual labour and their belief in the inferiority of manual occupations. This stigma attaching to physical labour was a long-enduring proscription of the three upper castes of Bengali Hindu society, Brahmin, Baidya, and Kayastha, from which so many of the bhadralok were drawn that the term bhadralok was frequently used in the late nineteenth century as a synonym for high caste. For many centuries there appears to have been an unusually wide gap between the high and low castes in Bengal, for there were few of the respectable intermediate castes that existed in other areas to act as a bridge. Unlike the high castes of some parts of India, those of Bengal did not till the soil. If they were engaged in agriculture they employed others to work their fields, for manual labour was considered degrading.

Land ownership as distinct from land cultivation was not objectionable, however, and high-caste men had shown alacrity in investing in landed property when the opportunity to do so was provided in the late eighteenth and early nineteenth centuries by British experiments with new forms of land revenue settlement and land tenure. Few of the great hereditary zamindaries survived this profoundly disturbing period of innovation, and in the nineteenth century the place of the old Muslim and Hindu aristocratic landholding families was taken by a host of lesser parvenus, mostly high-caste Hindus, who valued landed property for the superior prestige and security resulting from its possession. As the population grew, the ambition of increasing numbers of people for land ownership could be satisfied only by a division of holdings or shares of rent, and the result was a complex subinfeudation of tenures. Although this progressively reduced the economic return from individual estates, it did permit an extraordinarily large number of families to share in landholding. At the turn of the century there were in fact few bhadralok families (for these parvenus were the bhadralok) without an interest in landed rents, and the group as a whole regarded itself as 'landed'. No matter how small their holdings or how unproductive their share of rent, the bhadralok still drew a hard and fast line between themselves and those who tilled the soil.

In some parts of India there was another dividing line between landholders and the professional middle class, but there was no such dichotomy in late nineteenth-century Bengal. The same bhadralok families who were in receipt of rent supplied sons to Government service and the learned professions.

In the eighteenth century, as the British had extended their trading activities in Bengal and then had become involved in administration, they had had to recruit increasingly large numbers of Indian associates. Some of these were Hindu bankers and traders,[5] but most were from the Bengali upper castes (Brahmin, Baidya, and Kayastha) which had previously supplied administrators and entrepreneurs for service in the Mughal province and the local Hindu rajadoms. Throughout the first three quarters of the nineteenth century opportunities for such employment under the British had continued to expand. As the Imperial armies marched triumphantly westward through central and northern India they were followed by administrators and judges. Indian assistants and clerks were needed. As courts, hospitals, and schools were established, there were openings for lawyers, doctors, and teachers, and the construction of the railways created demands for accountants and more clerks. The Bengal bhadralok were quick to grasp these opportunities, and from hundreds of villages throughout Bengal ambitious men stepped onto the road that led to Calcutta and beyond to all parts of India.

To set foot on that road, however, the young Bengali had first to learn the tongue of the new rulers and, if he wished to go far, he had to have an advanced English-language education. Lal Behari Dey, recalling his father's reasons for taking him from their Burdwan village in 1834 to find a place in a Calcutta school, wrote:

> A knowledge of English education, he [my father] said, was necessary to enable a man to earn a competence in life. People ignorant of English no doubt got berths, but berths to which only paltry salaries were attached. He felt his want of English every day, and was therefore resolved to remedy that defect in the education of his son.[6]

[5] Of the Bengali banking and trading castes, the Subarnabaniks and Gandhabaniks were particularly successful during the nineteenth century in securing English-language education and profitable British associations. Educated men from these two small castes were freely admitted to bhadralok society.

[6] Quoted in B. T. McCully, *English Education and the Origins of Indian Nationalism* (New York, 1940), p. 44.

There were many fathers in Bengal equally ambitious for their sons, and they displayed remarkable initiative in financing English-language primary and middle schools in the districts, and high schools and colleges in Calcutta. By judicious pressure on the British authorities, they secured government funds for education, and with their approval these were chiefly expended on the development of higher and intermediate English-language instruction. The establishment of the University of Calcutta in 1857 put the coping stone on the structure, for it provided an administration to coordinate all aspects of higher education and a convocation to register and reward superior achievement.

These developments had profound consequences. The enthusiasm with which the Bengal bhadralok accepted and promoted English-language education, in marked contrast to the response of the landed elites in the surrounding provinces, gave them the lion's share of the new opportunities for professional, administrative, and clerical employment throughout eastern and northern India. They were justly proud of their achievement in creating the educational system that was the key to this success, and the maintenance and development of that system became one of their main preoccupations. Most men of consequence in the community in the late nineteenth century were involved with educational administration, whether in a rural district, a mufussil town, or in Calcutta; and educational politics, particularly the politics of Calcutta University, assumed extraordinary importance for the bhadralok as one of the few avenues of constructive public endeavour open to them in their circumscribed colonial society.

Education itself became the hallmark of bhadralok status. Not every individual who considered himself a bhadralok could obtain an education. Not every bhadralok family could afford the education it desired for all its sons. But the ideal was generally accepted: an education, preferably in the English language, leading to a university college in Calcutta and white-collar employment. For the elite: the Presidency College, an English university or the Inns of Court in London, and success in the I.C.S. (Indian Civil Service) examination, at the Bar of the Calcutta High Court, or in one of the other learned professions of the capital. 'The school', observed a Bengal Government report in 1928, 'is the one gate to the society of the *bhadralok*'.[7]

[7] *Simon Commission*, Vol. VIII, p. 24.

This points to another characteristic of the group: membership was not wholly ascriptive. For a low-caste Hindu or for a Muslim it was difficult to enter the charmed circle of the respectable, but it was not impossible and education was the means. If one could obtain urban professional employment through an English-language education, and if one were willing to adopt the cultural values and style of life of the educated, high-caste men among whom one worked, one might gain acceptance as a bhadralok–ultimately even in the village.

There were, however, formidable difficulties to be overcome. To the normal initial handicap of cultural deprivement, common to lower-class children in all societies, was added the problem of competing for an English-language education with boys from English-literate upper-caste families, many of whom had received their elementary education from private tutors. Places in schools, especially in primary schools which were mostly private, were difficult to obtain, for provision had been made for the elite, not the masses. The educational system was costly and exclusive. It was controlled by the bhadralok primarily in the interest of the bhadralok. And for those non-bhadralok who did get the necessary education, there was still the formidable task of securing employment and reasonable promotion in offices under the regime of high-caste *bara bābus* (chief clerks), for whom the exercise of patronage or outright nepotism was the accepted rule.[8]

[8] The extent to which the high castes dominated education and the professions in Bengal can be judged from the following figures (*Census of India, 1901*, Vol. VI, pt. 1, pp. 297–303, 486, and 506):

	Total population	Brahmin	Baidya	Kayastha	Subarnabanik	Gandhabanik	Muslim
Male literacy percent	10.0	63.9	64.8	56.0	51.9	51.0	6.8
Male literacy in English, percent	0.9	15.7	30.3	14.7	26.8	17.5	

'Amongst the lower castes, who form the great bulk of the population, there are practically none who are acquainted with English' (p. 303):

From education, which had given the bhadralok their command of the professions, came another of the group's most distinctive attributes: a passionate attachment to Bengali language and literature. From the early nineteenth century under the stimulus of European contact in Calcutta bhadralok intellectuals had refashioned Bengali as a rich literary language, freely borrowing forms and techniques from English to enable them to grapple effectively with the intellectual issues introduced to their society by the European cultural intrusion. To the existing body of fine religious poetry, they added secular writing in a variety of forms: prose essays, histories, novels, short stories, dramas, and new styles of poetry. The publication of journals and newspapers flourished, and Calcutta became a major book-publishing centre. The development of elegant, literary Bengali, *sādhu bhāshā*, was parelleled by an enrichment of the colloquial language through coinages, adaptations and extensive borrowings from European and other Indian vernaculars, and, at the same time, the Calcutta dialect, which was most directly influenced by these innovations, won acceptance with the bhadralok as *chalit bhāshā*, the standard colloquial form. The seal was set on this process when, in the latter half of the century, literary radicals began using *chalit bhāshā* in prose writings.

When viewed from 1900, these trends had had three apparent effects. One was the increasing divergence between bhadralok and non-bhadralok speech, as the former strove to avoid dialect and *apabhāshā*, unrefined diction. The second was the bhadralok's common pride of achievement in Bengali linguistic and literary creation, which had its clearest expression in a universal veneration of the major poets and authors. The third was the bhadralok's conviction that they had a vital role to play as guardians of a great cultural tradition.

	Appointments in covenanted and statutory civil services	High government appointments		Percentage of total population
		Number	Percentage of total	
Brahmin, Baidya, Kayastha	22	1104	80.2	5.2
Lower-caste Hindus	0	131	9.5	41.8
Muslims	3	141	10.3	51.2

The bhadralok as a group had gained a new sense of cultural identity from their nineteenth-century experience in adapting local traditions to the challenging demands of their rapidly changing society. The Bengal Renaissance, as this process has come to be known, was the product of a small group of intellectuals from the Calcutta colleges who, whether attracted or repelled by European values, had felt a compulsion to reexamine the philosophic basis of their culture. These men had spread an intellectual ferment through educated Bengal. From the third decade of the nineteenth century English studies had flourished. Bengali had been enriched. The rational philosophy of the West had been weighed against Indian traditionalism. An acquaintance with European scholarship had awakened an historical consciousness, and the rediscovery of the great Hindu scriptures had brought a new appreciation of the Indian past. Under the influence of Christianity, and often in protest against it, reform movements had been attempted in Hinduism. The structure of society had been subjected to critical scrutiny and there had been experimentation with new institutions. Every stage of this process had been marked by intense and often bitter debate; but despite enduring disagreements, the cumulative effect was the creation of a new and distinct cultural synthesis.

This new bhadralok culture was the product of the urban environment of Calcutta but it did not remain an exclusively urban phenomenon, for the bhadralok had their roots deep in the soil of rural Bengal where they held the land they prized so highly. The men who went to the city came back with new ideas and new habits, and the wives they took from the village imposed a restraint on their unorthodoxy.

The interchange between urban and rural bhadralok society was sustained by a variety of formal and informal institutions. The most fundamental was the extended joint family, maintaining a village home for a number of generations of kin, and pooling income from landed rents and the salaries of its professionally employed members. Many men whose work took them to a district headquarters or Calcutta preferred to leave wives and younger children in this village home, and even those who moved to town lock, stock, and barrel returned regularly for religious and family celebrations. Retirement usually brought them back to spend their last years in the comfort and security of village society.

Bhadralok who lived in a high school or college centre customarily provided board and lodging for the sons of relatives and rural friends for the duration of their schooling. Where this facility was unavailable, as was often the case in Calcutta, students could find accommodation among bhadralok youths from their home districts in privately organized messes, or in larger hostels attached to a college or a religious institution.

The Students' Associations, which gave an institutional focus to the activities of the adolescents during these formative college years when they were freed briefly from the constraints of the joint family, set a pattern of voluntary association which for most bhadralok lasted a lifetime. Consequently, we find in late nineteenth-century Bengal a network of loosely connected bhadralok organisations facilitating communication between town and country. There were Landholders' Associations in each district and in the capital. There were Peoples' and District Associations in the mufussil towns, and Ratepayers' Associations in the Calcutta suburbs. These, together with the District Bar Associations which provided a forum for the members of that most popular and overcrowded profession, the law, were the watchdogs of local bhadralok interests and the arenas for local faction fights. There were libraries, reading rooms, and literary circles in every Bengal town, supported by bhadralok money and managed by bhadralok committees as centres for educated gathering and discussion. There were social welfare and religious societies, run by members of the same community and operating primarily within the community.

The importance to the bhadralok of participation in educational administration has already been stressed, and this had its parallel in the institutions of local self-government. Local bodies in Bengal had been developed from the 1860's, and the bhadralok had shown such enthusiasm and aptitude for this new area of political activity that by 1900 they dominated all levels of the system from the District and Local Boards, to the Calcutta Municipality, and beyond to the provincial Legislative Council, which had been opened to them only in the preceding decade.

STATUS GROUP

We now have a picture of the Bengal bhadralok at the beginning of the twentieth century: a socially privileged and consciously superior group, economically dependent upon landed rents and professional and clerical employment; keeping its distance from the masses by its acceptance of high-caste proscriptions and its command of education; sharing a pride in its langauge, its literate culture, and its history; and maintaining its communal integration through a fairly complex institutional structure that it had proved remarkably ready to adapt and augment to extend its social power and political opportunities.[9]

In this study the term 'bhadralok' is used as an analytical category. There are two difficulties in its usage which are recognised and which must be accepted. The first, which is inherent in the definition of any perceived social group, is the fact that there will be, at any given time, marginal areas of disagreement in individual contemporaries' uses of the term because of differing social experience or differing social ethics. The second is that it is impossible to give the exact number of bhadralok. Figures are available on caste, landholding, occupation, education, and literacy on which estimates can be based,[10] but there is no quantitative evidence on other equally important bhadralok qualities such as style of life, cultural values, or pride of language.

The advantage in the use of the Bengali word 'bhadralok' is that it emphasises the attribute which was most important to the members of the group themselves: their social honour. The use of the word underlines the cardinal fact that this was a status group (in Max

[9] The best English-language sources for a picture of late nineteenth century bhadralok society are: *Bengal District Administration Committee, 1913–1914. Report* (Calcutta, 1915); N. K. Bose, *Modern Bengal* (Calcutta, 1959); and 'Social and Cultural Life of Calcutta,' *Geographical Review of India*, Vol. XX, Dec., 1958, pp. 1–46; N. S. Bose, *The Indian Awakening and Bengal* (Calcutta, 1960); R. Carstairs: *The Little World of an Indian District Officer* (London, 1912); *Census of India*, 1901 and 1911, Bengal and Calcutta volumes; N. C. Chaudhuri, *The Autobiography of an Unknown Indian* (London, 1951); S. Gopal, *The Permanent Settlement in Bengal and Its Results* (London, 1949); A. C. Gupta (ed.), *Studies in the Bengal Renaissance* (Calcutta, 1958); J. C. Jack, *The Economic Life of a Bengal District: A Study* (London, 1916); B. T. McCully, *English Education and the Origins of Indian Nationalism* (New York, 1940); R. C. Majumdar, *Glimpses of Bengal in the Nineteenth Century* (Calcutta, 1960); B. B. Misra, *The Indian Middle Classes. Their Growth in Modern Times* (London, 1961); *Report of the Land Revenue Commission, Bengal* (Calcutta, 1940); P. Sinha, *Nineteenth Century Bengal. Aspects of Social History* (Calcutta, 1965).

[10] In 1900 the bhadralok may have been 3 to 4 percent of Bengal's population, i.e., between 1,300,000 and 1,700,000 people.

Weber's sense of the term),[11] not an economic or occupational class. A man did not become a bhadralok simply by achieving a given level of wealth or securing certain employment. Nor did impoverishment or unemployment automatically deprive one of bhadralok status, provided certain values were maintained and certain social proprieties observed.

It is particularly important to distinguish between the terms 'bhadralok' and 'middle class'. If by 'class' status group is meant (in the manner of Talcott Parsons), then the bhadralok were upper, not middle, class. If 'class' is used in its Marxian sense of an economic group, then the bhadralok will be seen to have excluded many middle-class men, for example, merchants and prosperous peasants, and to have included some persons from classes both higher and lower. The bhadralok fishpond of the late nineteenth century, like that bourgeois fishpond of late eighteenth century France described by Alfred Cobban, included 'a few big fish, many of moderate size, and a host of minnows, who all knew that they swam in the same element, and that without the pervasive influence of the social hierarchy and the maintenance of individual and family property rights . . . their way of life . . . would come to an end'.[12]

AN OPEN OR CLOSED ELITE?

In his definition of status group, Max Weber distinguishes between the 'open' and 'closed' group, admission to the latter being determined solely by birth. By this definition and our own evidence the bhadralok were an open status group, for entry was possible through education as well as birth.

[11] 'What is a "status group"? "Classes" are groups of people who, from the standpoint of specific interests, have the same economic position. Ownership or nonownership of material goods or of definite skills constitute the "class-situation". "Status" is a quality of social honor or a lack of it, and is in the main conditioned as well as expressed through a specific style of life. Social honor can stick directly to a class-situation, and it is also, indeed most of the time, determined by the average class-situation of the status-group members. This, however, is not necessarily the case. Status membership, in turn, influences the class-situation in that the style of life required by status groups makes them prefer special kinds of property or gainful pursuits and reject others. A status group can be closed ("status by descent") or it can be open'. (H. H. Gerth and C. Wright Mills (eds.), *From Max Weber: Essays in Sociology* (New York, 1958), p. 405).

[12] A. Cobban, *The Social Interpretation of the French Revolution* (Cambridge, 1964), p. 173.

We have, however, observed that there were serious difficulties in the path of aspiring entrants; and it is clear that despite repeated pronouncements by their public figures on the social advantages of extended educational opportunities, there was little practical bhadralok effort to remove the stumbling blocks. Although bhadralok intellectuals and politicians were pleased to describe their community in the currently popular European term of 'educated middle class' (in Bengali *sikshita madhyabitta*) with its progressive overtones, they found it easy to recognise fellow upper-caste men as class members and extremely difficult to admit any but the highest achievers among the lowborn. Their frequently heard boast that the social reform movements of the nineteenth century had weakened caste distinctions in Bengal overlooked the fact that it was the barriers between the three upper castes that had been lowered, while the great gulf between upper-caste Hindus and the mass of the community, Hindu and Muslim, remained unbridged. When a Government committee in 1915 described Bengali society as 'a despotism of caste, tempered by matriculation',[13] it was tactless but not wrong.

What we observe here is a point of critical significance: profound bhadralok uncertainty on the crucial issue of whether their society should be open or closed. If we look carefully at the subjects of social and political discussion at the turn of the century we find that this was the fundamental issue underlying bhadralok debates. Should Bengali society be dominated by a caste elite, drawing its authority and its strength from the great tradition and organic unity of Hinduism, or should free access to the elite be provided for able individuals of all classes through an expansion of the utilitarian institutions that had been developed in the nineteenth century in contact with Europeans?

Revealing themselves the children of a common culture, the protagonists on both sides of this debate used the same intellectual tool, historical analysis, and they began by confronting the same historical fact, the foreign conquest of India. They agreed that this was a result of Indian decadence, but they offered radically different recipes for an Indian renaissance.

One school asserted that the key to revival could be found only within the Indian tradition, or more particularly the Bengali tradition, for society was an organism which could be regenerated

[13] *Bengal District Administration Committee, 1913–1914, Report* (Calcutta, 1915), p. 176.

only from within. For modern Bengal to rise again, it must recapture the genius of the golden age of classical Brahminism, an age in which a strong and able elite had acted as the intellectual mentors of the people, the guardians of the social order, and the leaders of the creative struggles with inferior alien cultures which had secured the cohesion and integration of Hindu society. Decline had come with the quietist doctrines of Buddhism and the emotional popular cults of medieval Hinduism, particularly Vaisnavism, which had emasculated a mighty people.[14] The great traditional virtues of intellectual initiative and rational self-assertion had been neglected, and the degradation of the Muslim and British conquests had been a natural consequence.[15]

This myth had a number of advantages. It explained foreign conquest as the result of internal errors—and rectifiable errors at that—rather than as the outcome of any inherent Indian inferiority. It conceded the need for internal reform but demonstrated that rational change was a traditional Hindu virtue. It justified a hierarchical ordering of society and, to a long-subjected people, it gave a pride in a great past which could be the inspiration for a great national future.

The myth had other implications for Bengal. In a society where the mass of the people were Muslims and Vaisnava Hindus, and where only a section of the Hindu upper castes were Saktas, worshippers of the Mother Goddess as the embodiment of strength, this was an exclusive myth which reduced popular Hindu beliefs to

[14] 'That is the Vaishnavism of Chaitanya Dev. The Vaishnavism which was the outcome of the atheistic Buddhist religion—nonviolence is its sign. The sign of true Vaishnavism is the suppression of the wicked and the salvation of the world. . . . The Vaishnava religion preached by Chaitanya Deva is not the real Vaishnava religion, it is only half a religion. The Vishnu of Chaitanya Deva is Love incarnate. But God is not only Love incarnate, He is also infinite Power'. (Bankim Chandra Chatterjee: *Anandamath* (trans. by Aurobindo and Barindra Kumar Ghosh, Calcutta, n.d.), p. 97. *Anandamath* was first published in 1882).

[15] Apart from the writings of Bankim Chandra Chatterjee, who was the most influential thinker of this school (*Bankim Rachanabali*, 2nd ed., Calcutta, 1960), see: Swami Vivekananda, *From Colombo to Almora* (Madras, 1904); H. Mukherjee and U. Mukherjee, *Sri Aurobindo's Political Thought, 1893–1908* (Calcutta, 1958); B. C. Pal, *Writings and Speeches* (Calcutta, 1958); S. Sen, *The Political Thought of Tagore* (Calcutta, 1947); B. B. Majumdar, *History of Political Thought, From Rammohun to Dayananda, 1821–1884, Vol. I, Bengal* (Calcutta, 1934); A. C. Gupta (ed.), *Studies in the Bengal Renaissance* (Calcutta, 1958).

the level of degraded survivals of medieval cults, and which gave an obvious sanction for continued high-caste Hindu dominance. In its chauvinism it classed all non-Hindus as inferior, and inculcated the virtue of struggle against aliens and alien cultures. In thus identifying foreigners and their cultures as a threat to Hindu integrity, it provided an argument for the rejection of the imported, liberal institutions–the educational, legal, bureaucratic, and legislative structures–that were threatening to create an open society in Bengal.

The other school would not accept this ethnocentric argument. For modern India to shut her windows upon the outer world, they asserted, would be to repeat the mistake that had led to the decay of her ancient civilization. Indians had as much to learn from European as from Indian history, and they had to accept the universal truths of rationalism, liberalism, and secularism. For Bengal and India the ideal of a Hindu nation was inadequate. Only the European nationalist ideal of a secular state, transcending religious and regional differences, could weld together the plural society. Accepting the utilitarians' evaluation of nineteenth-century developments in education, law, and administration as an unparalleled achievement in social engineering, this school praised India's good fortune in sharing these benefits; and accepting the Whig historians' myth that the progressive development of elective institutions guaranteed stable and ordered political progress, they espoused a parliamentary system for India. Their Whiggery carried them further. By the logic of its Imperial history, they maintained, Britain was obliged to develop parliamentary institutions in India, and, through these institutions, to concede the equality and self-government which Indian national development demanded.[16]

This myth, like the other, had the advantage of explaining 'The Fall' in terms of an error (in this case, insularity) for which amends had since been made, but, unlike the other, it provided a justification for the pragmatic acceptance of the European institutions that had assumed such importance for the bhadralok. While the opposing school took refuge in the mystical notion of a natural Hindu unity and the romantic ideal of creative struggle to purge the body politic

[16] See S. N. Banerjea, *A Nation in the Making* (London, 1925); A. C. Majumdar, *Indian National Evolution* (Madras, 1915); P. C. Ghosh, *The Development of the Indian National Congress, 1892–1909* (Calcutta, 1960); B. B. Majumdar, *History of Political Thought* (Calcutta, 1934); *Proceedings of the Indian National Congress*, from 1885.

of aliens and their institutions, this school offered a practical programme for the creation of an integrated plural society through the extension of existing structures. It had a prescription for political action—the reasoned representation of needs and grievances couched in the language of universal rights—and a determinist faith in British justice which could be an embarrassment to the Imperial rulers.

At the same time the myth had two serious limitations. It gave no sanction for continued high-caste dominance, and it demanded too many concessions to the British and their ideals to satisfy a burgeoning national pride.

INSTITUTIONAL OPPORTUNITY

At their purest these two ideologies were diametrically opposed, and the issue at stake was fundamental: an open or closed elite for Bengal. This issue was to dominate Bengal politics throughout the first half of the twentieth century, and these ideologies competed for the bhadralok's allegiance. The competition was keen and decision was difficult, for both ideologies were attractive and the outright acceptance of either demanded sacrifices from the bhadralok. In these circumstances it should come as no surprise to discover ambivalent thinking and action. On the one hand it was reasonably easy, with a little romanticism or imprecision of thought, to reach some intellectual accommodation between the two doctrines and, on the other, there was a good practical reason for desiring such an accommodation. The bhadralok valued their caste status *and* their liberal institutions equally, and they had little desire to dispense with either. Moreover, so long as high-caste men maintained their commanding position in education, law, and the civil services there was no compelling reason to apply abstract judgments to these institutions.

This was equally true of the elective local bodies which had become an integral part of the local bhadralok power structure, but it was not so true of the legislative councils. Bhadralok involvement in these institutions was a fairly recent phenomenon. The Imperial Legislative Council and the Bengal Legislative Council, both of which sat in Calcutta, had included occasional Indian members since 1861; but it was not until 1892 that representation had been introduced and Indian Members had gained some parity in numbers with the British (see Table 1). The bhadralok filled most of the

TABLE 1

COMPOSITION OF BENGAL LEGISLATIVE COUNCIL UNDER INDIAN COUNCILS ACTS, 1861 AND 1892

1861[a]	
Ex officio member:	
Lieutenant-governor	1
Nominated members:	
European officials	4
Indian officials	2
European nonofficials	4
Indian nonofficials	2
Total	13
1892[b]	
Ex officio member:	
Lieutenant-governor	1
Nominated members:	
Officials, maximum	10
Nonofficials, minimum	3
Recommended members:	
Calcutta Corporation	1
Municipalities	2
District boards	2
Bengal Chamber of Commerce	1
Calcutta University	1
Total	21

[a] PP, 1890 (42), vol. LIV, pp. 106–107.
[b] PP, 1894 (86), vol. LVIII, pp. 656–662.

seats in the Bengal Council, and they displayed for this new sphere of activity the same aptitude that had brought them success in their other ventures. But the British kept tight control of this institution, emphasising that its purpose was simply to provide legislative and consultative aid to their bureaucracy.

The councils were small and it was not yet clear how they would be developed; but they could not be disregarded, for in their power to legislate, which already gave them control over other institutions, they possessed a potential means of reshaping the social structure. For that reason, as for the additional reason that their model was so patently exotic, the legislative councils offered a direct challenge to the ideals of the 'Hindu revivalist' school; this challenge was made explicit by the opposing school's identification of them as prototypes of the parliamentary institutions which were to be the basis of their ideal pluralist state of the future. With a grand disregard for official disclaimers, the 'secularists' declared that the British had led India into the first stage in the development of parliamentary self-government.

The legislative councils were new and as yet unencumbered with bhadralok vested interest; their potential was unmeasured, and to the ideologues of both persuasions their existence involved clear questions of principle. They were thus a natural ground for the battle of ideals.

In that battle the arguments and personalities of the contestants would have some influence on the bhadralok's decision to accept or reject the councils, and on their underlying choice between an open or closed elite; but in the long run, more practical considerations would be decisive. A firm bhadralok commitment to a legislative system would be assured only if it were developed in such a way as to give the group the same sense of possession as it enjoyed in its other recently adopted institutions. To be fully accepted, the councils would have to become the instruments of bhadralok power. They would have to provide for a dynamic and ambitious elite enlarged opportunities and responsibilities to measure and extend its growing political capability. They would have to satisfy in some degree its new nationalist aspirations.

That the legislative councils stood a good chance of gaining bhadralok approval was a fair inference from the success of other imported structures in Bengal; and that the partisans of both schools were right in their belief that involvement with these new institutions would remould bhadralok ideals was also a reasonable expectation in view of the liberalising effect of the other institutions. At the beginning of the twentieth century the development of the legislatures seemed to offer a creative opportunity for influencing elite ideals in Bengal.

Introduction

PART II: BHADRALOK AND THE BRITISH

THE LIBERAL IDEAL

It was the British who held this opportunity. In 1900 they were free to mould the legislative councils into any shape they wished, consistent with their perception of their role in India and their relations with the Indian elites. On these basic questions there were two distinct bodies of opinion within the senior ranks of the I.C.S. in the last quarter of the nineteenth century.

One group believed that the British Indian administration could further its constructive purposes by encouraging and directing the aspirations of the westernised elites throughout India. In the social and political ambitions of these elites, particularly in their concern with affairs of state as expressed in their nationalism, this group perceived a progressive force which should be provided with constructive outlets through a diversification of institutions and the adaptation of administrative procedures. In the early 1880's men of this opinion, most notably William Wedderburn, A. O. Hume, George Yule, and Henry Cotton, assisted the leaders of the westernised elites in the formation of regional political associations and the organisation of an annual all-India convention, the Indian National Congress, which from 1885 was the main platform for the advocacy of liberal, secular ideals.

This movement had been given an impetus by the Viceroyalty of the Liberal Marquess of Ripon, who had been sent out by Gladstone after his electoral victory in 1880 to reverse the Earl of Lytton's policy of aggressive imperialism. Ripon was convinced of 'the hourly increasing importance, nay I will say the necessity, of making the educated natives the friends, instead of the enemies, of our rule'.[17] To this end they should be given a share in administration and provided with an opportunity to influence legislation. Ripon argued that it was 'not only bad policy, but sheer waste of power, to fail to utilize' the new 'intelligent class of public spirited men'.[18] In the preceding quarter century there had been a spectacular extension in the activities of government in India, accompanied by an equally profound change in concepts of the proper spheres of governmental responsibility. The regular agencies of administration were overtaxed, and to Ripon it seemed no more than common sense to take advantage of the able nonofficial assistance that was now being offered by English-educated Indians. 'We have made them, let us use them for their good and our own'.[19]

With this in mind he urged the provincial governments to transfer a large share of the work of local government to elected nonofficial committees. In his now famous resolution of 18 May 1882 he emphasised that his aim was not primarily to improve the administration but to foster 'the small beginnings of independent political life'.[20] Earlier he had also suggested the inclusion of a few elected Indian members in the legislative councils as a development in 'extended freedom and cautious confidence',[21] but his proposal was not favoured in Calcutta or London, and it was left to his successor, Lord Dufferin, to frame a scheme for the reform of these institutions.

Prior to 1857 there had been a single legislative council in Calcutta legislating for all of British India, and it was composed wholly of official British members. As a result of the shock of the Mutiny, the system had been reformed to provide the Government with a means of consultation with leading Indians, so that it might avoid 'the perilous experiment of continuing to legislate for millions of people, with few means of knowing, except by rebellion, whether the laws suit them or not'.[22] In 1861 separate legislative councils

[17] Ripon to W. E. Forster, 19 May 1883, quoted in S. Gopal, *The Viceroyalty of Lord Ripon, 1880–1884* (London, 1953), p. 84.

[18] PP. 1883, Vol. LI, p. 27.

[19] Ripon to Lord Kimberley, 10 July 1883, quoted in S. Gopal, *op. cit.*, p. 84.

[20] Quoted *ibid.*, p. 92.

[21] Ripon to J. Bright, 19 July 1882, quoted *ibid.*, p. 84.

[22] Sir Bartle Frere, minute, 16 March 1860, quoted P. Sharan, *The Imperial Legislative Council of India, 1861–1920* (Delhi, 1961), p. 24.

were set up in the three presidencies—Bombay, Madras, and Bengal—and a few nominated Indian members were included in these bodies and in the Imperial Legislative Council.

In 1886, Dufferin suggested the extension of this consultative system to give the new class of educated Indians a greater opportunity to influence policy formation. He recommended to the Home Government that the councils be enlarged to include representatives chosen by local bodies and public organisations, and that their members be given wider powers of discussion.[23] The result was the reforming Indian Councils Act of 1892.

The liberal sympathies of men such as Wedderburn, Cotton, Ripon, and Dufferin gave hope to Indian intellectuals of the secularist school and sustained their Whig conviction that the British in India would act true to their historic ideals. But these liberals were not representative of the main body of British administrators in the last quarter of the nineteenth century, and their vision of Indian political development was not generally accepted. The main trends were toward authoritarianism and centralisation. This can be understood if we appreciate the nature of the British sense of imperial mission.

THE PATERNALIST IDEAL

Of all the traditions of the Indian Civil Service none was stronger than its paternalism. It saw itself as a wise and benevolent body of rulers, keeping the peace between the irreconcilable races, religions, and castes of a huge subcontinent; a corps of dedicated men giving their knowledge and their energies to improve, however slowly, the material well-being of an ignorant but warm-hearted and grateful people; protecting the weak and the downtrodden against the strong, minorities against majorities—a faction of order (as one officer wrote) in a factious society.[24] This was a tradition which newcomers to the service inherited from their predecessors and upon which the years in their first districts—healthy, exciting, and impressionable years of youth—put the stamp of personal conviction. They learned of the hardships of Indian village life; the sufferings that followed natural calamities, so often made worse for the poor by the oppression of landlord, money-lender, or priest. They saw the misery that could be inflicted with

[23] *Ibid.*, pp. 107–108.

[24] R. Carstairs, *The Little World of an Indian District Officer* (London, 1912), p. 162.

the sharp weapon of social boycott. They enjoyed the gratitude that rewarded their efforts to free a peasant from an illegal tax or to provide good drinking water for a village. They believed that they were meant to rule and they were confident that they ruled wisely, for they knew India and Indians 'at least as well as any body of men in the country'.[25]

Paternalism was an admirable tradition for an all-powerful service of foreign autocrats, but it prevented most I.C.S. officers from seeing imported institutions as anything other than instruments of their own efficient administration. In general, I.C.S. concepts of structural development were simplistic. They could see that transplanted institutions worked some degree of change in the society that received them; but they could not admit as a corollary the proposition that in the process of acceptance these institutions should, and inevitably would, be remoulded by the developing needs of the indigenous groups who were associated in their working. How far from gaining general acceptance was the idea that enlarged political responsibilities should be provided for the westernised elites through institutional diversification and adaptation, can be gauged from the frequency with which senior British officers in the late nineteenth century exhorted their colleagues to beware of Indian 'misuse' of European ideas and institutions. There were constant warnings of the danger of 'native influences' subverting institutions from their original or 'real' purposes.

Underlying this concern to preserve institutional chastity was a general distrust in the British Indian administration of the elites, like the bhadralok, who had such an immoderate appetite for European institutions. For many British officers the bhadralok and their ilk were simply the representatives in modern dress of those exploiting castes and classes against whom, in the interests of Indian social justice, the British had waged a long and as yet indecisive battle. What the publicists of these groups meant by extended political opportunities, the Civilian asserted, was greater freedom to exploit the peasant. Explaining the reluctance of his fellow officers to develop local self-governing institutions in the 1880's and 1890's as Ripon had urged, a Bengal Civilian wrote: 'Considering . . . that the Government had now for twenty years been endeavouring, so far in vain, to untwist the fingers of the landlord from the tenant's

[25] Sir Andrew Fraser to a District Officer, 12 Dec. 1907, in A. H. L. Fraser, *Among Indian Rajahs and Ryots* (London, 1911), p. 29.

throat, it was not unnatural to suspect that he might use any local body we appointed as an instrument of oppression.'[26]

If the spokesmen of the westernised elites were not malevolent, they were certainly ill-informed. When the bhadralok protested in 1892 against his proposal that trial by jury should be restricted in Bengal, the Lieutenant-Governor, C. A. Elliott, wrote in exasperation:

> . . . these people talk and talk themselves into a belief quite opposed to the truth, and are led away by newspaper phrases about 'Judges of an alien race'. It is very pitiful, for the stream is poisoned at its source, and the people who ought to be leaders of society and sources of information to us, know less of the country and its wants and wishes than we do.[27]

To most of the British in India it was axiomatic that the bhadralok and their kind had lost touch with the people—the 'real Indian people'—because they had become cultural hybrids. In 'aping the West' they had destroyed their cultural integrity, and created a 'stucco civilization' which had made them a 'laughing-stock'.[28]

> Such are the town Bengalis, of whom disparaging opinions are expressed [wrote the Australian politician, Alfred Deakin, after an Indian visit in 1890–1891]. The Baboo produces nothing but words. The country people, though debased by the tyranny of iniquitous landlords under an iniquitous law, are of a better type; they are the cultivators, the irrigators, and the producers, and they are cared for as much as possible by European officials, who protect them as far as lies in their power.[29]

CURZON AND PARTITION

To a large majority of officers in the I.C.S. it was absurd to suggest, as Ripon had done, that the problems of their overburdened administration could be relieved by the delegation of

[26] Carstairs, *op. cit.*, p. 172.

[27] Elliott to Lord Lansdowne, 24 Nov. 1892, item VII, Vol. 8, pt. A, No. 386, Lansdowne Papers, India Office Library MSS Eur. D 558.

[28] W. S. Lilly, *India and Its Problems* (London, 1902), p. 123.

[29] A. Deakin, *Irrigated India* (London, 1893), p. 85. The verbose, unmanly and ineffectual westernised Bengali was a familiar stereotype in English literature in this period. See A. Greenberger, *The British Image of India, 1880–1960: A Study in the Literature of Imperialism* (University of Michigan, Ann Arbor, Ph.D. dissertation, 1966).

responsibilities to the westernised elites. The problem of over-burdening was not denied, but the I.C.S.'s answer was to strengthen central authority in order to increase governmental efficiency.

To this ideal Lord Curzon, Viceroy from 1898 to 1905, lent the weight of his office and the force of his considerable personality.

> . . . what I have been engaged upon since I came to India [he explained in 1903, has been a process] of raising the standard of administration all round. For this purpose the initiative has had to spring from the Supreme Government—because there is no other fountain of initiative in India. I am not exaggerating when I say that in nine cases out of ten it has had to spring exclusively from myself.[30]

Curzon saw two main obstacles to the rigorously efficient system he wished to create. One was antiquated bureaucratic procedures, and the other was the proliferation of secondary political structures, which were threatening to choke the roots of the British administrative oak in a mass of tangled native undergrowth. It had been Ripon's object to encourage this second growth, but Curzon, with the passion of a tidy gardener, was determined to prune it back.

He started with Bengal, his headquarters province and by all admissions the most politically overgrown. A bill to reconstitute the Corporation of Calcutta was under consideration by the Bengal Legislative Council when he arrived in India. It seemed to him inadequate, so he brushed aside the provincial Government and drafted a new measure, under which the elected element on the Corporation was reduced and executive functions were entrusted to a committee with a British majority. These reforms, he declared, were essential for efficient local government.[31]

He believed that the Indian university system was in similar need of an overhaul, particularly the administration of Calcutta University which had 'fallen into the hands of a coterie of obscure native lawyers who regard educational questions from a political point of view',[32] and in 1902 he appointed a commission to draft reforms. As a result of its report, official control of all higher education was

[30] Curzon to Lord Hamilton, 4 June 1903, in C. H. Philips (ed.), *The Evolution of India and Pakistan, 1858–1947. Select Documents* (London, 1962), p. 74.

[31] Lord Ronaldshay, *The Life of Lord Curzon* (London, 1928), Vol. II, pp. 28–30 and 73–75.

[32] GI, Home Education, A34–42, Feb. 1904.

tightened and the governing bodies of Calcutta, Bombay, and Madras universities were reorganised, with a large proportion of Government-nominated members.[33]

Meanwhile Curzon had been busy with an even larger scheme: the readjustment of provincial boundaries in eastern India. This was a hoary problem with which the British had wrestled throughout most of the nineteenth century.[34] At one time the whole of northern India from the Assam Valley in the east to the river Sutlej in the west had been under a single administration in Calcutta, but by 1874 this Government's charge had been reduced to Bengal proper, Bihar, Chota Nagpur, and Orissa. It was generally agreed that even this area was too large for efficient administration, but the Government of India could not decide on a new division. The question was still being debated after Curzon's arrival, and when it came to his notice in 1902 he gave it his enthusiastic attention.

He agreed that territorial reorganisation was essential, and defined its basic objectives as the relief of the Government of Bengal and the enlargement of Assam to provide it with administrative responsibilities sufficient to attract a more able civil service.[35] In March, 1903, Sir Andrew Fraser, Curzon's protégé and Lieutenant-Governor of Bengal, proposed that Chittagong Division and Dacca and Mymensingh Districts of his province should be transferred to Assam, under which administration these areas could be given more attention, and the political infrastructures which because of Government neglect 'the educated section of their inhabitants' had succeeded in erecting, 'would be more easily reduced to their proper level of importance'. Curzon agreed that 'it would be an unqualified advantage to Bengal to lose these elements of weakness and dissension,'[36] and after a personal tour of the eastern districts in February, 1904, he decided that an even larger area should go to Assam.

[33] Ronaldshay, *op. cit.*, pp. 187–194.

[34] For a discussion of the nineteenth-century background, see the author's: 'The Partition of Bengal: A Problem in British Administration, 1830–1912,' *Indian History Congress, Proceedings of the Twenty-Third Session, Aligarh 1961*, pt. 2, pp. 13–24.

[35] For detailed discussion of the partition decision see: J. R. McLane, 'The Decision to Partition Bengal in 1905', *Indian Economic and Social History Review*, Vol. II, No. 3, July, 1965, pp. 221–237; Z. H. Zaidi, 'The Political Motive in the Partition of Bengal, 1905,' *Journal of the Pakistan Historical Society*, Vol. XII, pt. 2, Apr., 1964, pp. 113–149.

[36] Curzon, minute, 1 June 1903, GI, Home Public, A149–160, Dec. 1903.

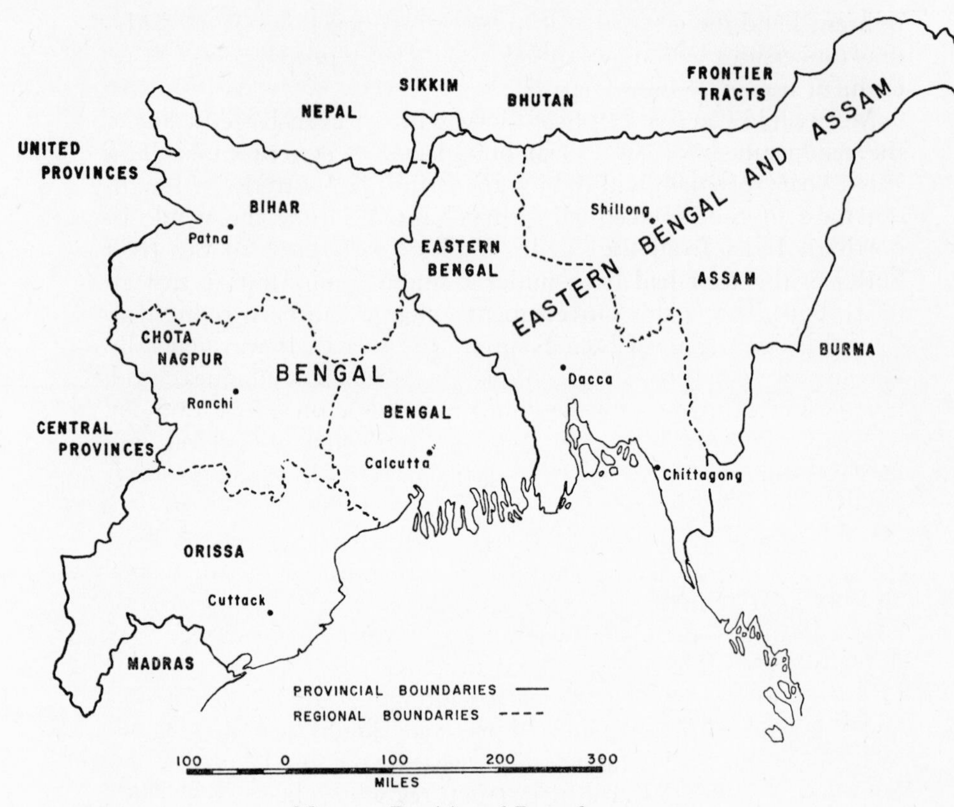

MAP 3. Partitioned Bengal, 1905–1912

Two provinces of almost equal size could be created by drawing a new boundary line through central Bengal. (see Map 3). This arrangement would achieve the two primary administrative objectives, and it would have the fringe benefit of weakening bhadralok political integration. By giving a majority to Muslims in the new eastern province, and to Biharis and Oriyas in the west, it was hoped 'to encourage the growth of local centres of opinion' and to destroy the ability of Bengali bhadralok political groups in Calcutta to influence mufussil opinion. In particular, it was hoped to cut short bhadralok nationalist attempts to find allies in other communities.[37]

[37] H. H. Risley, minute, 6 Dec. 1904, GI, Home Public, A155–167, Feb. 1905.

The partition of Bengal on 16 October 1905 was an unambiguous demonstration of the British Indian administration's antipathy to the political aspirations and cultural ideals of the bhadralok. It revealed a thorough indifference to the creative potential of this elite and an insensitivity to the critical ideological choice with which the group was confronted. How thoroughly the British misconstrued the social and political forces with which they were dealing in Bengal was revealed by their unpreparedness for the outburst which their measure provoked.

THE ANTI-PARTITION AGITATION

For bhadralok intellectuals the partition of Bengal and the agitation against it was a seminal experience that influenced their political thinking for forty years. It gave them a new pride in their country, and a pantheon of nationalist heroes and martyrs which could be invoked for inspiration or justification. It revealed to them the potentialities of radical political agitation, and it left them with an uneasy awareness of its dangers. It provoked an open clash between liberal secular and Hindu revivalist ideals, but it left that crucial conflict unresolved.

The course of the anti-partition agitation is fairly well known[38] and we need give only an outline. It had four overlapping but identifiable phases.

In the first of these, which opened in December, 1903, with the publication of the initial partition scheme, its leader was Surendranath Banerjea, the most distinguished of Bengal's National Congressmen and secretary of the province's main political organisation, the Indian Association, who had dramatised the opposition to Curzon's reconstruction of municipal government by leading 28 Indian members out of the Calcutta Corporation with an oath never to return until nonofficial control was restored. Against the partition scheme Banerjea used the same weapons he had employed in opposing Curzon's earlier measures—press articles, public meetings of protest, petitions, and deputations—and he had the same lack of success in deflecting the British from their purposes.

[38] See S. Sarkar, 'Trends in Bengal's Swadeshi Movement, 1903–1908', *Bengal Past and Present*, Vol. LXXXIV, 1965, pt. 1, pp. 10–37, and pt. 2, pp. 140–160; *Sedition Committee, 1918, Report* (Calcutta, 1918); and the extensive works of Haridas and Uma Mukherjee.

By July, 1905, it was clear that these methods had failed, and this realisation led to the second stage of the agitation in which verbal protests were subordinated to a campaign for the withdrawal of office-holders from Government institutions, the boycott of British manufacturers, the encouragement of *swadeshi* goods, and the foundation of 'national educational' institutions. The inspiration for this programme came from younger men who were not politicians, and although Banerjea and his lieutenants in the Indian Association endorsed the campaign, they showed such obvious reluctance in discarding their accustomed constitutional techniques that they lost the initiative to more radical politicians–Bipin Chandra Pal, Aswini Kumar Dutt, and Aurobindo Ghose.

In 1906, under this leadership the agitation entered its third and most impressive phase, in which large numbers of bhadralok men were given an active involvement in the movement through the organisation of volunteer brigades, *samitis*, trade unions, and *ākhrās* (gymnasiums). At the same time there was an outright attack on the old, constitutionalist school, their techniques and their liberal secular ideals. Their appeal to British reason and justice was derided as self-delusory, and their attachment to British institutions was stigmatised as anti-national. From the eloquent pens of Rabindranath Tagore, Bipin Chandra Pal, and Aurobindo Ghose came a call for cultural self-reliance: for a revival of indigenous institutions and the use of traditional Hindu symbols to galvanize Bengal to action.

These ideas and the continued intransigence of the British led into the final phase of the agitation in which violence was openly preached and clandestinely practiced. The two principal advocates of violence were Barin and Arobindo Ghose, whose pamphlets and newspapers in 1907 glorified revolution as a religious duty. They reminded their readers that Kali, the Goddess of Destruction, the Mother of Strength, was created by the Gods to destroy the Demons who had usurped their kingdom. Kali, the avenger whose many hands dripped with blood, was not a symbol of savagery but of selflessness, they taught. As Kali drove out the Demons so should the bhadralok, strengthened by the worship of Kali, drive out the British. This teaching evoked an enthusiastic response from young bhadralok, and there was no shortage of volunteers for the terrorist *samitis* which the Ghose brothers and their associates founded to organise political assassinations.

The most striking, and ultimately the most important, aspect of the anti-partition agitation was the combination in each phase of exciting with disturbing elements, for this was to leave bhadralok intellectuals with a curiously ambivalent attitude to what was unquestionably their greatest political experience in a generation.

Initially they had been exhilarated to discover that after years of rather academic political protests they finally had a cause with which they could identify the rank and file of their community.[39] The partition affected all the bhadralok, for it divided the two halves of their cultural world: Calcutta from the mufussil. While it succeeded in uniting the bhadralok in protest, however, it also revealed their unpopularity with other communities. Oriya, Bihari, and Eastern Bengal Muslim politicians welcomed the measure as their chance to escape from Bengali bhadralok domination, and the Assamese condemned it because it would force them into closer association with the Bengalis.

These dissenting voices could be explained away as the inevitable result of British policies of divide and rule; but the second and third phases of the agitation brought equally unwelcome developments for which rationalisations were more difficult to produce. Again these stages opened with stirring achievements: the evolution of new agitational modes and the creation of organisations to facilitate popular political participation. But first the Banerjea group and then the radicals who had displaced them found to their chagrin that they lacked the technical experience necessary to coordinate a variety of social, economic, and political activities, or to provide large numbers of followers with a constructive and sustained political role.

The volunteer brigades and *samitis* for a time found stimulating work in policing the boycott and promoting *swadeshi* products, but this activity in its turn provoked a hostile response from non-bhadralok—Muslims, Namasudras, and Marwaris—who had no desire to be involved. The manner in which the new bhadralok lead-

[39] The new interest in politics generated by the partition can be illustrated by a comparison of the circulation figures for 1904 and 1905 of some of the newspapers which opposed the measure (GI, Home Public, B200, June 1906):

	1904	1905
Amrita Bazar Patrika	2000	7500
Bengalee	3000	11000
Epiphany	1000	5000
Hitavadi	16000	20000
Sandhya	500	7000

ership was using Hindu symbols to identify their nationalism was particularly offensive to the Muslims, and when a few bhadralok zamindars and lawyers attempted to use their economic and social power to coerce their inferiors,[40] the Muslims organised resistance. The result was serious communal rioting in Calcutta and various parts of Eastern Bengal.

At the same time there were disquieting, if less serious, trends within bhadralok society itself. The criticism by Aurobindo, Bipin Chandra, Rabindranath and others of the old Congress group for their denationalised and exclusive political methods, which accompanied the radical extension of the agitation, was eagerly taken up by the Bengali-language press and transmuted into an attack on the behaviour of the bhadralok elite in general. Playing to the new audience of poor, semieducated bhadralok which the political excitement had brought them, the vernacular papers ridiculed the elite for their English affectations of speech, dress, and manners,[41] and accused them of monopolising professional appointments, of allying with the British bureaucracy to their own advantage, and of selfishly excluding the mass of their fellow bhadralok from participation in politics. The obvious popularity of these criticisms revealed to the elite the disturbing fact that there was now considerable class feeling within bhadralok society.

Between about 1880 and 1905 sections of the bhadralok appear to have been faced with serious economic difficulties. A marked rise in population in that period had been accompanied by increasingly frequent subinfeudation of landed rent holdings, as a result of which the return from a former major source of bhadralok income had been reduced to negligible proportions in many cases. At the same time there was growing pressure on that limited area of white-collar employment which the bhadralok considered respectable. Population growth was one reason for this, and another was competition from Muslims, who were now acquiring English-language education in small but significant numbers. Difficulties at home

[40] GI, Home Police, A140–148 and B112–114, May 1906; A. H. L. Fraser to Sir Earle Richards, 20 Feb. 1907, No. 2(e), Erle Richards Collection, India Office Library, MSS Eur. F 122.

[41] There were a number of popular Bengali satires on the westernised elité which the journalists could use as models. Two good examples which have recently been republished are Kaliprasanna Singha, *Hutom Pyanchar Naksha* (Calcutta, 1955); and Tekchand Thakur, *Alaler Gharer Dulal* (Calcutta, 1961).

were compounded with difficulties 'up-country'. Throughout the cities and towns of north India, which up until the 1880's or 1890's had provided employment opportunities for enterprising Bengal bhadralok, new indigenous educated groups were appearing to contest the available jobs, and to demand of the local Governments the exclusion of outsiders. By 1900, office doors were shut to many younger bhadralok. So, too, were the doors to the best colleges, and the inferior institutions to which they were forced to turn were unsatisfactory substitutes.[42] To all of these difficulties was added an unprecedented inflation in the cost of living in 1906 and 1907, accompanied by a shortage of credit on which the bhadralok normally relied to finance their education and their prestigious religious ceremonies.[43]

Economic deprivation, frustrated ambition, and injured pride made the lower-class bhadralok ready recruits for radical political action. The same factors made them jealous of their fellow bhadralok who had obtained the education and jobs they desired. This class feeling was then little more than an embarrassment for the elite, but it did reveal to them a volatile and potentially divisive element within their own community.

The organisation of the terrorist *samitis*—small, tightly disciplined, religiously inspired secret societies—can be understood, in part, as a reaction to the organisational failures and social disturbances of the third, popular phase of the agitation. The bravery the young terrorists displayed in their assassination bids and in their court trials was of great psychological importance to the bhadralok as a riposte to the hated British jibes about *bābu* verbosity and unmanliness, but the relative ease with which the British were able to suppress the revolutionary leadership was a pointed and unwelcome reminder of their power. The British could meet force with superior force, and the nakedly racist ideology of the terrorists gave them a sanction to do so. In 1907 and 1908 they

[42] *Census of India, 1911*, Vol. V, pt. 1, pp. 66 and 553–554; *ibid.*, 1921, Vol. V, pt. 1, p. 385; *Bengal District Administration Committee, 1913–1914, Report* (Calcutta, 1915), pp. 13–14, 19, and 176; J. C. Jack, *The Economic Life of a Bengal District, A Study* (London, 1916), pp. 89–95; B. B. Misra, *The Indian Middle Classes, Their Growth in Modern Times* (London, 1961), pp. 276–277.

[43] *Prices and Wages in India* (Calcutta), 24th issue 1907, p. 17, and 25th issue 1908, p. 12. (For this reference I am indebted to N. Gerald Barrier, University of Missouri.) *Census of India, 1911*, Vol. V, pt. 1, pp. 64–66; Jack, *op. cit.*, pp. 98 and 103–104.

imposed a strict censorship on the press; they extended the activities of their secret police, placing high schools, colleges, and voluntary associations under political surveillance; they resorted to imprisonment without trial, the deportation of political offenders, and the externment of political suspects. By the end of 1908, they had stifled the anti-partition agitation and along with it a great deal of healthy political activity.

The most celebrated casualty of the Bengal partition was the unity of the Indian National Congress. The disagreements over agitational methods in Bengal led to the division of the Congress into two parties–Moderates and Extremists; to a clash between these two parties at the December, 1907, Congress session at Surat; and to the exclusion of the Extremists from the organisation for a decade thereafter.[44] Our ability to identify Bengali figures among the leading protagonists in each party (most notably Surendranath Banerjea among the Moderates and Bipin Chandra Pal among the Extremists) and the apparent decisiveness of this schism should not mislead us into thinking that for the bhadralok, or even for their politicians and intellectuals, the anti-partition agitation was an ideologically decisive experience.

Certainly the partition imbued the bhadralok with a thorough distrust of British intentions and a hearty scepticism toward their expressions of goodwill. The first phase of the agitation also discredited the old Moderate style of protest and petition, but against this had to be weighed the unpleasant consequences of radical methods. The difficulties experienced by the elite bhadralok politicians in organising and controlling a mass agitation had been patent, as had their failure to communicate effectively with non-bhadralok groups. They had learned to their cost that radical agitation disturbed social stability and that the political use of religious symbolism had explosive consequences in a multi-religious society. They had also learned that a resort to force invited a general invasion by the British of the freedom of their political and social institutions. The anti-partition agitation undoubtedly left bhadralok intellectuals older and wiser, but it gave them no greater certainty in their ideological commitment.

[44] See P. Singh, 'The Indian National Congress–Surat Split', *Bengal Past and Present*, Vol. LXXXIV, pt. 2, No. 158, July-Dec., 1965, pp. 121–139; P. C. Ghosh, *The Development of the Indian National Congress, 1892–1909* (Calcutta, 1960).

For this reason the opportunity for the British to influence their thinking through institutional development—the chance that Curzon had rejected at the turn of the century—was not wholly lost; now, when confronted with evidence of gross political misjudgment, the British tried to recapture this opportunity.

MORLEY-MINTO REFORMS

Curzon had resigned the Viceroyalty in August, 1905. His successor, Lord Minto, although also a Conservative, disagreed with much that Curzon had done; in particular, he considered that his predecessor had been unwise in riding roughshod over Indian opposition. He saw that the trend to authoritarianism and centralisation had been carried so far that the Government of India had been burdened with an immense load of detailed administrative work which prevented it from taking a broad view of events. It had lost touch with Indian opinion, and, as a consequence, was dangerously isolated and top-heavy. Minto believed that there was an urgent need to reduce its vulnerability by descentralising power and opening new channels for the expression of Indian opinion.

He was fully supported in this view by John Morley, who became Secretary of State for India on the formation of a new British Liberal Government in January, 1906. Morley, an old partisan of Irish rights, was convinced that there had to be a fundamental change in the nature of British government in India. 'Cast-iron bureaucracy won't go on for ever, we may be quite sure of that', he remarked to Minto.[45] Morley understood the significance of the conflict of ideals with which the bhadralok and similar elites were faced, and he saw the danger of failing to satisfy the ambition of secular nationalists for development of their liberal institutions and extension of their political responsibilities. He proposed reforms of the Indian executive and legislative councils to provide new opportunities for this group. 'Moderates are always at a disadvantage', he observed. 'The same forces that begin the move, continue their propulsive power. The only question is whether by doing what we can in the Moderate direction, we can draw the teeth of the Extremists'.[46]

[45] Morley to Minto, 6 June 1906, in J. Morley, *Recollections* (London, 1921), Vol. II, p. 141.

[46] Morley to Minto, 11 Oct. 1906, *ibid.*, p. 153.

Morley placed particular importance upon the admission of Indians to the executive councils, for he realised that the best chance of overcoming the nationalists' distrust of the higher bureaucracy, which two decades of autocracy had engendered, was to give them a share in its work. As he expected, the proposal scandalised the I.C.S., but he insisted that to regain the confidence of the Moderates, the British had to give an earnest of their good faith by opening to them these jealously guarded doors. In August, 1907, he made two Indian appointments to his Council in London, and two years later, after a hard struggle with the officials, he placed a Bengal bhadralok, S. P. Sinha, in the Viceroy's Council as Law Member. The Governments of Bengal, Bombay, and Madras were instructed to follow suit with their executives.[47]

The nature of the legislative council reforms was worked out between Morley and Minto in a correspondence extending over four years, 1906 to 1909. The two men were agreed that the purposes should be to rally support for a Government that had become dangerously isolated, to associate nonofficials with an overtaxed administration, and to provide that administration with a means of feeling the pulse of public opinion, thereby enabling it to avoid another misjudgment like the partition of Bengal. They also agreed that while the elective principle should be introduced, the legislatures should not have power over the government. It was to be responsive, not responsible.

Where the two men disagreed was over the relative political importance of various Indian communities and the manner in which they should be represented in the councils. Morley maintained that the essential object of the reforms must be to satisfy the Western-educated groups, like the bhadralok elite, and to provide their leaders with opportunities for worthwhile political service. We must 'do our best to make English rulers friends with Indian leaders', he wrote to Minto, 'and at the same time . . . to train them in habits of political responsibility'.[48] As a good Whig, he also realised that the *form* of the constitutional concessions had an intrinsic impor-

[47] The Morley-Minto reforms have been the subject of three recent monographs, M. N. Das, *India under Morley and Minto* (London, 1964); S. R. Wasti, *Lord Minto and the Indian Nationalist Movement, 1905–1910* (Oxford, 1964); and S. A. Wolpert, *Morley and India, 1906–1910* (Berkeley, 1967).

[48] Morley to Minto, 2 Apr. 1909, quoted in J. Buchan, *Lord Minto. A Memoir* (London, 1924), p. 289.

tance for the secular nationalists, who wanted India's parliamentary development to follow the pattern set by Britain and the 'white' colonies. With this in mind Morley urged that the basis of representation should be territorial, not communal.

Minto dissented. He insisted that there were other communities equally as important as the westernised urban intelligentsia, and that the legislatures would be truly representative only if these were included. 'Personally my object has been in the proposed reforms to secure the representation of landed proprietors, and of those who have a stake in the country, and of communities', he explained.[49] Supported by his subordinates in the Government of India, he emphasised that the great landholders and the Muslims should be given special consideration as loyal conservatives on whom the British could rely. Morley was told that these groups would be swamped unless they were provided with separate communal representation, and he finally conceded the point, to the disgust of the nationalists who considered that communal representation was a calculated attempt to keep the Indian nation divided.

The legislative councils as reconstituted under the Indian Councils Act of 1909 had nonofficial majorities, with a large proportion of elected members returned from communal and sectional constituencies. In recognition of its political maturity, Bengal alone was given Representative Government (see Table 2). The councillors were now empowered to discuss 'any matter of general public interest' and to move resolutions on the budget.[50]

In 1907, Morley and Minto had appointed a Royal Commission to advise on decentralisation. Its report was presented in the following year, and as a result of its recommendations a slow process of reform was begun in the institutions of local government.[51] The Commission was severely critical of the concentration of power in the hands of the Government of India and it insisted on a devolution to the provinces, the larger of which should all have non-I.C.S. Governors assisted by executive councils.[52] Acting on its advice, Morley provided an executive council for Bengal in 1909.

[49] Minto to Governor of Madras, 15 June 1908, GI, Home Public, A116–146, Oct. 1908.

[50] PP, 1910 [Cd. 4987], Vol. LXVII, pp. 617–1101.

[51] See H. Tinker, *The Foundations of Local Self-Government in India, Pakistan and Burma* (London, 1954).

[52] PP, 1908 [Cd. 4360], Vol. XLIV, pp. 157–160.

TABLE 2

COMPOSITION OF BENGAL, AND EASTERN BENGAL AND ASSAM LEGISLATIVE COUNCILS UNDER INDIAN COUNCILS ACT, 1909[a]

Bengal	
Ex officio members:	
Lieutenant-governor	1
Executive councillors	2
Nominated members:	
Officials, maximum	17
Indian commerce	1
Planters	1
Experts	2
Others, minimum	3
Elected members:	
Corporation of Calcutta	1
Calcutta University	1
Municipalities	6
District boards	6
Landholders	5
Muhammadans	4
Bengal Chamber of Commerce	2
Calcutta Trades Association	1
Maximum Total	53

Eastern Bengal and Assam	
Ex officio member:	
Lieutenant-governor	1
Nominated members:	
Officials, maximum	17
Indian commerce	1
Experts	2
Others, minimum	2
Elected members:	
Chittagong Port Commission	1
Municipalities	3
District and local boards	5
Landholders	2
Muhammadans	4
Tea interest	2
Jute interest	1
Maximum Total	41

[a] PP, 1910, [Cd. 4987], vol. LXVII, pp. 883 and 1021.

REUNIFICATION OF BENGAL

Because of the trouble over the partition, Bengal occupied an inordinate amount of Morley's and Minto's time. Both men were aware of the depth of bhadralok feeling on the issue and they regretted that they had 'been committed to a somewhat unfortunate piece of legislation.'[53] In an attempt to smooth things over, the Viceroy forced the resignation of Curzon's appointee, the impulsive Lieutenant-Governor of Eastern Bengal and Assam, Bampfylde Fuller. This had Morley's wholehearted approval. 'Partition is a disagreeable pill', he wrote. 'Well, that is all the more reason why we should take any chance of gilding it. Fuller and his like seem to think that the best plan is to gild the pill with wormwood.'[54] The policy of appeasement was a failure, for the agitation grew in strength and violence. Minto finally resorted to imprisonment without trial and press censorship, which restored a semblance of order but was no permanent solution, as Morley realised. '. . . nobody will be more ready than you to agree that the forces with which we are contending are far too subtle, deep, and diversified, to be abated by making leading articles expensive', he remarked to Minto.[55] There were some who argued that peace would return to Bengal only with reunification, but neither Morley nor Minto was willing to grasp that nettle.

In October, 1910, Morley was succeeded as Secretary of State by another Liberal with Irish experience, Lord Crewe, and a month later a career diplomat, Lord Hardinge of Penshurst, took office as Viceroy. Both men fully agreed with the objects of their predecessors' reforms, and they were equally reluctant to meddle with the partition of Bengal. There was, however, another new figure in British public life, the recently crowned King George V, who was to play an unusual role in Indian affairs in the first year of his reign. As Prince of Wales he had visited India in 1905–1906 and had been convinced that the partition of Bengal was a mistake. He

[53] Minto to Morley, 20 Dec. 1905, quoted in Pardaman Singh, 'Lord Minto and the Partition Agitation', *Bengal Past and Present*, Vol. LXXXV, no. 160, July–Dec. 1966, p. 141.

[54] Morley to Minto, 3 May 1906, quoted in M. N. Das: 'Curzon's Successors and the Partition of Bengal: A Conflict in Conscience', *Journal of Indian History*, Vol. XXXIX, pt. 3, No. 117, Dec., 1961, p. 399.

[55] Morley to Minto, 3 Feb. 1910, in J. Morley, *Recollections* (London, 1921), Vol. II, p. 282.

now decided that he should return as Emperor to spur the loyalty of his Indian subjects, and he suggested to his Ministers that Bengal should be reunited as a grand gesture of Imperial goodwill.[56]

Hardinge and his Government initially opposed the suggestion, insisting that 'fireworks or any political concessions designed to produce an effect' were the last thing India needed after five years of 'something very like a revolution on a small scale'.[57] They agreed, however, that a 'boon' of some sort had to be given to mark the King's visit, and if it were not the reunification of Bengal, what was it to be? This question was unanswered for six months until finally in June, 1911, the Home Member, James Jenkins, with a *volte face*, made the dramatic proposal that Bengal should be reunited and the Imperial capital moved from troublesome Calcutta to Delhi. Hardinge was now willing to accept the idea for he had been convinced 'that a grave injustice has been done to the Bengalis,[58] seeing that they are in a minority in both provinces, and this injustice should certainly be rectified'.[59] The prospect of an escape from Calcutta, which had become increasingly unpopular with the officials because of its vociferous public opinion, both Indian and British, was sufficient to persuade the remainder of his Council that the scheme had merit, and Crewe gave his approval.

The details of the rearrangement were worked out in secret. Reunited Bengal (see Map 1) would be given a Governor-in-Council. Bihar and Orissa under a Lieutenant-Governor would form a separate province on one side, and Assam on the other would again have its own Chief Commissioner. These changes and the removal of the capital to Delhi, it was to be made clear, were to enable the Government of India to detach itself from the provinces, which might then gain a greater measure of autonomy and enjoy increasing nonofficial influence in their administration.[60]

King George announced the scheme to an incredulous audience at a spectacular durbar at Delhi on 12 December 1911. The date chosen for the reunification of Bengal was 1 April 1912, and Crewe

[56] F. A. Eustis II and Z. H. Zaidi, 'King, Viceroy and Cabinet: The Modification of the Partition of Bengal, 1911', *History*, Vol. XLIV, No. 166, June, 1964, pp. 171–173.

[57] Hardinge to Crewe, 22 Feb. 1911, quoted *ibid.*, p. 175.

[58] At this time the British customarily restricted the term 'Bengalis' to Bengali Hindus.

[59] Hardinge to Crewe, 13 July 1911, quoted Eustis and Zaidi, *op. cit.*, p. 179.

[60] PP, 1911 [Cd. 5979], Vol. LV, pp. 582–592.

was careful to select as the first Governor a man of liberal sympathies and wide experience. His choice was Lord Carmichael of Skirling, who had been Gladstone's successor as Liberal Member of Parliament for Midlothian and later a popular Governor of both Victoria and Madras. Crewe sent him to Bengal with a special charge to exercise 'fine tact' in an effort to convince his subjects, and his official subordinates, that a new era had opened.[61]

[61] Crewe to Carmichael, 15 Jan. 1912, *Carmichael*, pp. 150–152.

I

A MAN WITH A MISSION

THE GOVERNOR'S TASK

In the opening weeks of 1912 Bengal newspapers were busy with the time-honoured British Indian sport: picking the new Governor. Their editorial tips were delivered with the usual air of authority, but for once all were wrong. 'Lord Carmichael is the steed we did not fancy for the Governorship', remarked one paper. 'He had just won the Madras Cup, and it is very rare for such horses to run twice in one month'.[1] Carmichael had been appointed Governor of Madras in November, 1911, after three successful years in Victoria, Australia.[2] By his friendly informality and his liberal speeches he had achieved rapid popularity in his new post, and it was obvious that his premature transfer to Bengal was intended as a public demonstration of the British Government's determination to pursue a new policy there. He went with a mission: to appease the anger of this unsettled province. By his liberal influence on the administration he was to prove that the reunification betokened a change of heart, not merely a modification of institutions, and he was to seek a corresponding change of heart in Bengal politics. It was hoped in this way to reconcile the dissentious communities and put an end to terrorism.

The Secretary of State, Lord Crewe, wrote to Carmichael on 15 January 1912 outlining his task and suggesting possible courses

[1] *Indian Daily News*, quoted *Statesman*,* 24 Jan. 1912.
[2] For biographical details see DNB: and *Carmichael*.

of action.[3] The letter revealed a sophisticated and sympathetic understanding of Bengal politics. Crewe emphasised that the situation in Bengal had distinctive features which marked the province out from the rest of India and which made unusual demands on its Government for the exercise of political finesse. 'If I were going to Calcutta myself', he wrote, 'I should draw a rough sketch in my own mind of the three main classes of my future subjects, with a provisional outline of the reasonable way to treat each'. Crewe's 'three main classes' were the British nonofficials, the Muslims, and the Hindu bhadralok.

The first of these, the British nonofficials of whom there were 23,000 in Bengal,[4] were a rich and influential community. Through the Bengal Chamber of Commerce and private influence they had always been able to put strong pressure on the Government and, if checked, their displeasure found expression in the columns of the *Englishman*, the *Statesman*, *Capital*, and *Commerce*, Calcutta's four main British-owned newspapers. The community had a powerful lobby in Whitehall and at Westminster, and its opinion was normally sought by the officials on matters of importance. In 1912, it was smarting from the blow to its influence and pride which had been dealt by the transfer of the capital to Delhi. Its leaders had not been consulted about this move, and it confirmed them in their belief, born of the admission of Indians in greater numbers to the councils, that the Government was giving way 'before the attacks of a democracy of literati, who have a sense of nothing beyond their own importance'.[5] The Government of India, they feared, had put its foot on a slippery decline which might slide British rule, and with it British commerce, into the sea.

Crewe was confident that Carmichael would handle them tactfully. He wrote:

> The Calcutta English seem to be disposed, many of them, to take a more sensible view of the changes than they did at first; but there seems likely to remain a noisy and violent minority, represented by *The Englishman*, who will more probably expend their wrath on Hardinge, moreover, than on the new Governor. The community includes, I am sure, a number of honest, capable, and likeable people: but I am not less sure that they are spoilt children in

[3] *Carmichael*, pp. 150–152.
[4] *Census of India, 1911*, Vol. V, pt. 1, p. 217.
[5] *Englishman*,* 25 Dec. 1913.

> many respects, full of their historical and social importance, anti-Indian *au fond*, and keen to scent out 'disloyalty' in any independent expression of opinion, hidebound too in class prejudices. You will have to ride them with a light hand, as you are well competent to do—all the more as their mouths are sore for the time being.

The second of Crewe's 'classes', the Muslims, were also up in arms over the annulment of the partition, which they regarded as an unwarranted destruction of a great opportunity for a community that was in need of assistance. By all admissions the Bengal Muslims were a depressed group. Their old elite of zamindars, administrators, and soldiers, which had dominated most of Bengal in the Mughal period, had been almost totally destroyed by the changes in the political, legal, and land-revenue systems that had accompanied the establishment of British rule. The few landed families that had survived had maintained the community's traditions of Persian and Arabic learning, but they had shared none of the Hindu bhadralok's passion for English-language education. The mass of the Muslim community in Bengal were peasant converts from the lower Hindu castes, with no chance of competing for education; in consequence command of the government services, the learned professions, higher education, and even landholding had gone to the caste Hindus, virtually by default.[6]

Despite their economic depression, the Bengal Muslims had maintained their separate communal identity with remarkable vigour. The efforts of the upper class to preserve the study of Islamic history and literature was matched in the nineteenth century by work among the peasantry of revivalist *mollās*, who developed a vernacular religious literature in the distinct Eastern Bengal dialect, and founded puritan sects which gained widespread popular support by their militant attacks on rural injustices. Efforts to popularise the pilgrimage to Mecca provided a common ground for coopera-

[6] The 1911 Census gave the following figures (Vol. V, p. 1, p. 551):

	Proportions		
	Hindus	to	Muslims
Tenants	5		9
Landlords	7		3
Lawyers	9		1
Doctors	5		1
Teachers	7		2
Policemen	2		1
Civil servants	3.5		1

tion between the great zamindars and the *mollās*, the former supplying funds and the latter publicity and organisation.

Not until the last quarter of the nineteenth century was a section of Bengal's wealthy Muslim landholders finally persuaded by Syed Ahmed Khan and his Aligarh school to sponsor English-language education for Muslim youth, but by the turn of the century there was a small group of Bengal Muslims ready to compete with the bhadralok Hindus for access to the learned professions.[7] To these men and their zamindar patrons, the partition of Bengal seemed to offer an opportunity for the share in public affairs that they had previously been denied. Khwaja Salimulla, Nawab Bahadur of Dacca, the community's most influential political figure,[8] writing early in 1906 voiced their optimism:

> There are many good things in store for us . . . and the Mahomedans being the largest in number in the New Province, they will have the largest share. . . . This is the golden opportunity which God and His Prophet have offered us, but if we do not now profit ourselves by the opportunity, we may not get another chance. Now or never. Our destiny is in our hands. We must strike while the iron is hot.[9]

Their hopes were not disappointed. In justifying the partition, the British had reckoned it a virtue that the new province of Eastern Bengal and Assam would have a Muslim majority and that the eminence of the old Mughal capital, Dacca, would be restored.[10] Following this lead, the new provincial government openly favoured the community, preferring Muslims for appointment to the

[7] The best English-language sources for a picture of nineteenth-century Bengali Muslim society are: *Census of India, 1901*, Bengal volume; 'Faraidi Sect', *Encyclopedia of Islam* (London, 1927), Vol. III, pp. 57–59; M. A. Huque, *History and Problems of Moslem Education in Bengal* (Calcutta, 1917); J. C. Jack, *The Economic Life of a Bengal District. A Study* (London, 1916); Muin-ud-Din Ahmad Khan, *History of the Fara'idi Movement in Bengal, 1818–1906* (Karachi, 1965); B. T. McCully, *English Education and the Origins of Indian Nationalism* (New York, 1940); A. R. Mallick, *British Policy and the Muslims in Bengal, 1757–1858* (Dacca, 1961).

[8] For biographical details see DIB; and BLCP, 19 Jan. 1915, Vol. XLVII, pp. 5–6.

[9] K. Salimolla: 'The New Province—Its Future Possibilities', *Journal of the Moslem Institute*, Vol. I, No. 4, Apr.–June, 1906, pp. 410–411.

[10] H. H. Risley, minutes, 1 Sept. and 6 Dec. 1904, GI, Home Public, A155–167, Feb. 1905.

large number of new posts in the Provincial and Subordinate Services that were sanctioned in July, 1906, allotting special funds and personnel for Muslim education, preparing plans for a new university and High Court for Dacca, and installing the Nawab as their chief nonofficial adviser and their main agent for the distribution of patronage.[11] Dacca and Chittagong, the capital and port of the new province, boomed.[12] It was an Indian summer which came to a sudden and frosty end with the Delhi announcement in December, 1911. This cut the Muslims to the quick. The British, it seemed, had deserted them simply to pacify the Hindu extremists. Their resentment was tempered only by a determination to gain as many concessions as possible as indemnity for this British treachery.

Crewe advised Carmichael to take a firm line with them:

> As regards the Mohammedans, especially those of Eastern Bengal, I am glad that Hardinge agreed with me that we ought not to delay in going to Dacca and having it out with them on the spot. They are trying, as one would suppose was likely, to extract every sort of 'favourite's' treatment from Government on the strength of losing their vast numerical predominance. There is a great deal that they cannot have, and I am clear that the right road is to help them as a community by educational facilities and the like, to run at even weights with the Hindus, rather than to continue indefinitely the practice which has been found necessary at first, of giving them an advantage in the handicap. . . . I anticipate that there will be a good deal of talk and writing before the new machine begins to grind corn. But I feel confident that the total result will be an alleviation, not an exacerbation, of feeling in Bengal between Moslem and Hindu, and that the task of the police will thus be far easier.

Among Crewe's third 'class', the Hindu bhadralok, there was jubilation over the reunification of the province. The Moderate politicians, led by Surendranath Banerjea, claimed this as their victory. Many of their Extremist rivals, whom they had succeeded in ousting from the Congress at Surat in 1907, had been arrested and deported under the Government's severe antiterrorist measures in 1908, and those who retained their freedom had been forced either

[11] GI, Home Public, A29–31, July 1906; and Carmichael to Crewe, 21 Aug. 1912, *Carmichael*, pp. 168–169.

[12] In the decade 1901-1911 the population of Dacca rose by 21% and that of Chittagong by 30%. The increase for Greater Calcutta was only 11.9% and for Bengal as a whole only 8%. (*Census of India, 1911*, Vol. I, p. 31; Vol. V, pt. 1, pp. 37 and 152).

to leave politics or to operate secretly. The field was thus cleared for the Moderates who had continued a restrained agitation against the partition through the liberal Indian Association. In 1911 they had sent Bhupendranath Basu to press their case in England,[13] and their memorial to the Government of India on the subject of re-unification had provided much of the wording for Hardinge's despatch recommending the measure.[14] Banerjea and his men were well pleased with the fruits of their labours, and they led the bhadralok's rejoicing for the province regained.

Crewe, however, realised that this one measure, no matter how spectacular or welcome, was not sufficient to repair the breach between the bhadralok and the British, and he warned Carmichael against a hasty assumption that the current mood would last.

> You will find the Bengalis immensely civil, and effusive to a degree over the new province. I think it is clear that the party led by Surendra Nath Banerji has won the day, and that the orders are that the loss of the capital is not to be treated as a public grievance, in view of the benefits actually conferred. In conversation, therefore, one finds little but outpoured gratitude. But there are certainly some sulks in Calcutta itself, particularly as some leading people are owners of house property. Had one of our friends gone there who would be likely, however able he might be, to take too literally the underlined expressions of Bengali feeling, I should have looked forward with some nervousness to the future, not so much because I should have feared his becoming enthralled by the Bengalis, as because I should have dreaded the subsequent disillusionment and its possible results. But in your case I have no such fears, because I know you won't be tempted to begin by too much credulity, and then break off into a completely unsympathetic course.

COMMUNITIES AND COLLEAGUES

Armed with Crewe's good advice, Carmichael approached his new work with optimism. By disposition an amiable man, he believed that others would always respond to goodwill; and he saw no reason to think that, in this respect, human nature in India was any different from elsewhere.[15] He was encouraged in his optimism by the enthusiasm with which his appointment was greeted in the

[13] IA, General meeting proceedings, April 1911.

[14] IA, Annual Report 1911, appendix E, pp. 19–42, and PP, 1911, [Cd. 5979], Vol. LV, pp. 582–598.

[15] See his first speech in Bengal, 1 April 1912, *Carmichael*, p. 157; and Carmichael to Crewe, 14 May 1913, *ibid.*, pp. 181–182.

Bengal press,[16] and, upon arrival in Calcutta in April, 1912, he immediately set out to establish contact with leading members of the various communities.

In his efforts to win the friendship of the nonofficial Europeans he enjoyed the inestimable advantage of being a Scot, for both the commercial and planting communities were led by Scots. He made it clear that he was eager to learn all he could about the needs of Bengal industry, and when he left his desk at Government House to inspect the port facilities along the Hooghly and to examine the neglected canals in Eastern Bengal, the nonofficials were quick to contrast this with the reluctance of former I.C.S. Lieutenant-Governors to desert their files.[17]

Carmichael was a keen and knowledgeable agriculturalist, and on his first tours he was horrified by the state of rural Bengal. He believed that for any improvement to be effected the Government had to gain the cooperation of the great zamindars.[18] He was soon on intimate terms with their leader, Bijay Chand Mahtab, Maharajadhiraja of Burdwan, who, for his part, was merely renewing the position of gubernatorial confidant which he had maintained for the preceding nine years.[19]

Carmichael, however, would not be satisfied simply with courtiers. He was determined to understand all sections of Bengali society, including those who were regarded as his Government's opponents. He caused a stir by inviting the leading nationalists to Government House and by letting it be known that he would learn Bengali.[20] His desire to keep in touch with Indian opinion was illustrated by a letter he wrote on 18 May 1912 to Motilal Ghose, the veteran nationalist editor of a leading Calcutta English-language daily, the *Amrita Bazar Patrika*. Observing that he found the *Patrika's* editorial comments extremely helpful, Carmichael asked Motilal to assist him by drawing his attention to any matter which the journalist considered important. Although he was 'sincerely anxious to help any one who is trying to make Bengal a happier place for its people to live in', he knew that he would inevitably disappoint

[16] Selections from all major papers published in *Statesman*,* 23 and 24 Jan. 1912.

[17] *Capital*,* 12 Dec. 1912; and Carmichael to Crewe, 21 Aug. 1912, *Carmichael*, pp. 170–171.

[18] Carmichael to Crewe, *ibid.*, pp. 168–170.

[19] For biographical details see DIB; *Who's Who in India* (Poona, 1923); and *Who Was Who, 1941–1950* (London, 1951).

[20] Author's interview with Hemendra Prasad Ghose, Calcutta, 19 Nov. 1960.

many people, he said, and at times would be the object of public anger, despite his efforts. This, he wrote, was as it should be.

> . . . in the case of a Governor it is often I fancy only because he is blamed that he is able to get others whose advice he must often listen to even when sometimes he least trusts it to agree to try things worth trying. . . . I do not suppose that even if a Governor came here full of local knowledge instead of coming here as I do ignorant of even the language of my neighbours he could do a tenth part of what he would like to do.[21]

He could have chosen no better way of gaining bhadralok goodwill than by emphasising that he valued their opinions. His hint that he would not follow blindly after the officials was certain to be noted with favour, and his apology for his ignorance of Bengali was a masterly touch.

Carmichael's greatest initial problem was with the Muslims. He had to try to win their goodwill while at the same time making it clear that the Government felt itself under no obligation to recompense them for their lost province. Acting on Crewe's advice, he took the bull by the horns. Three days after his arrival in Calcutta, in reply to an address of welcome from the Muslim League, he made his position clear. 'I am not here to uphold the interests of one religion or one body of people', he said. 'I am here to do what I can for all, and no body will feel that more than the Mohammedans'.[22]

His task was made easier by the attitude of the Nawab of Dacca, the head of Eastern Bengal's oldest and largest Muslim zamindar family. This powerful leader was as determined as any of his followers that the Muslim community should gain all it could, but he was convinced that it would be a mistake to offend the Government by pressing too hard. This was consistent with a strategy of communal politics that he had evolved and applied successfully in the preceding decade. His strategy assumed that the Muslims, as an educationally and economically depressed community, could not hold their own with the Hindu bhadralok in the rough and tumble of electoral or agitational politics. It also assumed that the British were worried by the growing strength and increasingly aggressive tone of Hindu nationalism, and would welcome the clientage of the Muslim community, whose leaders (great zamindars, educational-

[21] Quoted in P. A. Dutt, *Memoirs of Motilal Ghose* (Calcutta, 1935), pp. 196–197.

[22] *Carmichael*, p. 159.

ists, and provincial officials) would serve as a counterpoise to the Congress politicians, and whose peasant mass might be kept immune from disturbing nationalist propaganda. The strategy was for the Muslim leaders to proclaim the loyalty of their community to the British raj and offer it in liege to the Imperial Government. In return, they would expect to be welcomed as courtiers at Government House–able to advise and receive advice from the Lieutenant-Governor and his officials–and in any constitutional or political resettlement they would expect their community to be given favoured treatment.[23]

The British were in need of support, especially in Bengal, and they willingly accepted the arrangement on the Nawab's terms. As a result, the Bengal Muslims gained many concessions in the decade up to 1911. In their discussion of the proposals for partition, the Members of the Government of India recognised the Dacca Nawab's service in countering nationalist influence in his community and expressed their confidence that the creation of the new province would assist his work.[24] As we have seen, the Government of Eastern Bengal and Assam gave him every encouragement in his efforts to advance Muslim interests. At the imperial level the British yielded to nationalist pressure for constitutional reforms, but the Muslims were given the preferential treatment they requested. The British rejected the Congress demand for parliamentary institutions, retaining the consultative councils composed of the representatives of interest groups and communities. The right of election was conceded, but the Muslims were provided with separate electorates. The right of Indians to serve on the highest executive councils of the Empire was also conceded, but the Muslims secured *de facto* recognition of their claim that these appointments should be communally apportioned.

For almost a decade the arrangement with the British worked well, but like all systems of patronage, this one depended upon the maintenance of a fine balance between the interests of patron and client. In this case the balance would be disturbed if the British considered that it was in their interest to make concessions to com-

[23] The Nawab publicly expounded his policy in 1906 when Congress agitation for constitutional reforms and Hindu bhadralok violence against the partition of Bengal had removed any need for reticence. See his statements at the time of the formation of the Muslim League, quoted in E. E. Lang: 'The All-India Moselm League', *Contemporary Review*, Vol. XCII, July–Dec., 1907, pp. 344–352.

[24] Risley, minute, 6 Dec. 1904, GI, Home Public, A155–167, Feb. 1905.

munities other than the Muslims, and by 1910 there were officials in Calcutta and London who were convinced that it was no longer politic to disregard Hindu bhadralok anger at policies in Bengal. The result was the reunification of the province, which profoundly shocked the Bengal Muslims. Many of their younger men were convinced that after this betrayal there could be no question of maintaining the old loyalist stance. Others, equally angry, were determined to make the British pay for their action,[25] but the Nawab of Dacca cautioned both groups against rash action. He was as perturbed as any of his followers, but he could see no viable alternative to a policy of dependence on the British. He agreed that the Muslims should be given reparations for their loss, but he emphasised that they had to maintain the right balance between their demands and their expressions of loyalty.

It was essential to the success of this scheme that they should at all times have leaders close enough to the Government to sense when the time was right to tip the balance one way or the other. Fortunately for his plans, the Nawab found Carmichael keen to receive him as a friend, and they were soon on intimate terms.[26] The Muslims had two other links with the Government in the persons of Nawab Khan Bahadur Syed Nawabaly Chaudhuri, a large zamindar from Mymensingh and a candidate for election to the new Bengal Legislative Council, who had a number of close contacts among the senior officials,[27] and Nawab Syed Shamsul Huda, a High Court lawyer and a member of a great landholding family in Tipperah, whom Carmichael appointed to his Executive Council.[28] Both men had formerly been members of the Eastern Bengal and Assam Legislative Council, where they had proved themselves adept exponents of the Dacca Nawab's strategy of balance.

Carmichael had got off to a good start. His initial contacts with the European nonofficials, the bhadralok, and the Muslims were encouraging. The success of his mission, however, would depend as much on the attitudes of his colleagues in the provincial Government as on the response from the Bengal communities. Unless they were men of liberal sympathies he could hope to achieve little. His

[25] E.g., see demands of Central National Mahomedan Association's Committee of Management, *Statesman*,* 23 Jan. 1912.

[26] Carmichael to Crewe, 25 Feb. 1915, *Carmichael*, p. 204; and BLCP, 19 Jan. 1915, Vol. XLVII, pp. 3–8.

[27] For biographical details see *Who Was Who, 1929–1940* (London, 1941).

[28] For biographical details see *Who's Who in India* (Poona, 1923); and *Who's Who, 1923* (London, 1923).

good fortune was remarkable, for although he had no say in their appointment his two I.C.S. Executive Councillors, Sir William Duke and Percy Lyon, were well disposed toward his plans.

Duke had officiated as Lieutenant-Governor of Bengal in the eight months preceding Carmichael's arrival, and his experience was invaluable in the difficult period of transition following the reunification. He was a reserved man, severe of countenance, and to the casual observer he appeared to have little time for the critics of Government, Indian or British. His intimate acquaintances, however, knew him as a man of scrupulous fairness and, what was less usual in a Civilian, of political imagination.[29] Lyon came to the Bengal Executive Council from Eastern Bengal and Assam, where he had been Chief Secretary during the partition period.[30] Where Duke was cautious and reserved, Lyon was outspoken. At this time he made no secret of his sympathy for the Eastern Bengal Muslims,[31] and later he was to scandalise the Government of India by speaking to bhadralok students of 'the inherent right of the Indian nation to govern itself'.[32]

THE LEGISLATIVE COUNCIL

The rapport which Carmichael had achieved with his colleagues and the leaders of the major communities would assist him greatly in his task of effecting a rapprochement between the Government and the people. He was under no illusion as to the difficulty of that task, but he pinned his hopes of success on the Legislative Council. All the main communities would be represented in this body, and there they would have an opportunity to thrash out their difficulties with the Government and with one another. Moreover, the Legislative Council might provide the bhadralok with a means of satisfying their political aspirations. Carmichael understood the significance for the bhadralok of parliamentary institutions and he was aware of their need for political 'elbow-room'.[33] He was determined to give them this in the Legislative Council. He would ensure that the new powers of the members were circumscribed in

[29] For biographical details see DNB; and Montagu, pp. 377–378.
[30] For biographical details see *Who's Who, 1923* (London, 1923); and *Statesman*,* 24 Mar. 1912.
[31] GB, Appointment, 4M–4(1–2), A30–31, Sept. 1917.
[32] *Amrita Bazar Patrika*, 19 Jan. 1916.
[33] Carmichael to Crewe, 14 May 1913, *Carmichael*, pp. 181–182.

no way. He would invite their opinions on all important matters and demonstrate by his subsequent actions that he valued the advice they gave. In return, he would ask for their cooperation in interpreting his policies to the people.[34]

In this there was no dissembling. Carmichael was a devoted admirer of the parliamentary system and was convinced that the Morley-Minto reforms had been a step in the right direction. He believed that for representative institutions to develop properly in India, the Government had to encourage the Council members to exercise their statutory powers of discussion and surveillance, and in this way associate them closely with its decisions.[35]

There were many technical problems to be dealt with before the new Council could meet. Electorates had to be formed that would satisfy the groups which had sent representatives to the two old Councils of Bengal and Eastern Bengal and Assam. In the light of the experience gained at the 1909 elections and subsequently in the conduct of legislative business, it also seemed advisable to amend the Council regulations and the rules of business.[36]

Under the statutory regulations of 1909 the Bengal Council had 53 members, of whom three (the Governor and his Executive Councillors) sat *ex officio* and 24 were nominated. The other 26 were elected.[37] In 1912, the Government decided to reduce the number of seats reserved for nomination, thus allowing for two additional elected members. One of these new seats was given to the nonofficial members of the Calcutta Corporation, and the other was to be filled at alternate elections by the local bodies of the Presidency and Burdwan Divisions, the two Divisions most strongly influenced by Calcutta (see Table 3). This was obviously an effort to increase bhadralok representation on the Council, and it was in keeping with the Government of India's declared policy of encouraging greater nonofficial influence in provincial administration.

A similar spirit of liberality was shown in redrafting the rules of business. This was particularly significant, for the work was done by the Bengal Secretariat under Duke's guidance, and, as Duke himself pointed out, the Government on this occasion had a free hand

[34] St. Andrew's Day Dinner speech, 30 Nov. 1912, *Statesman*,* 1 Dec. 1912.

[35] See his evidence before Parliamentary Joint Select Committee on Government of India Bill, PP, 1919 (203), Vol. IV, evidence, pp. 322–329.

[36] GB, Appointment, 18L–28, A1–11 of 1910; *ibid.*, 18L–5(K-W) of 1911, A1–11.

[37] PP. 1910, [Cd. 4987], Vol. LXVII, p. 883.

TABLE 3

COMPOSITION OF BENGAL LEGISLATIVE COUNCIL AND ELECTORATE UNDER REVISED REGULATIONS OF 1912

	Members[a]	Voters[b]
Ex officio:		
Governor	1	
Executive councillors	3	
Nominated:		
Officials, maximum	16	
Indian commerce	1	
European commerce in the mufussil	1	
Experts	2	
Others, minimum	2	
Elected:		
Corporation of Calcutta	2	
Calcutta University	1	
Bengal Chamber of Commerce	2	
Calcutta Trades Association	1	
Chittagong Port Commission	1	
Tea planters	1	
Municipalities	6(5)[c]	1193
District and local boards	5	1115
Landholders	4(5)[c]	635
Muhammadans	5	6346
Totals	54	9289

[a] PP, 1913 [Cd. 6714], vol. XLVII, p. 199.
[b] Figures for 1916 General Election. *Report of the Franchise Committee* (Calcutta, 1919), p. 38; and GB, Appointment, 18L–1(11–12), B272–273, Nov. 1917.
[c] At the second election in 1916 the Landholders were given an additional seat (for a total of five) at the expense of the Municipalities.

to frame the rules as it wished, without the usual necessity of submitting them for the approval of the Legislative Council. That no attempt was made in such circumstances to restrict the Council certainly suggests a measure of goodwill on the officials' part.[38]

THE RETURN OF THE MODERATES

One of the most significant features of the discussions over the new Council regulations was the participation in them of the

[38] GB, Legislative, A1–6, Jan. 1913.

Moderate nationalists. Early in 1912 the Indian Association had submitted a memorial outlining the changes it desired,[39] and in June Surendranath Banerjea and Bhupendranath Basu had gone to Darjeeling for talks with Carmichael on these proposals.[40] They had emphasised their dissatisfaction with an arrangement which provided the Muslims with separate communal electorates and yet restricted the Hindu bhadralok to the representation they could secure through the university and local-body seats. 'The members of the middle class as such, who form the backbone of Indian society have no votes', they had complained. They had asked for the formation of a general electorate, with a franchise based on income tax or local rate payment.[41]

Carmichael was not prepared to go as far as this, but he was willing to concede the Moderates' lesser demands—an increase in the elected membership of the Council and in Calcutta's representation —for he appreciated the importance of securing the Moderates' willing participation in the new Council. In 1909 both wings of the Congress in Bengal, Extremist and Moderate, had refused to enter the reformed legislatures as a protest against the British failure to reunify the province. This abstention had defeated in Bengal Morley's aim of bringing 'British rulers and Indian leaders' together, and it had prolonged the dangerous situation created by the absence of institutions to contain bhadralok political energies. Carmichael knew that he had to have the Moderates in his Council if he were to have any hope of checking terrorism and relieving racial and communal tension. Indeed, the survival of the liberal secular ideal among the bhadralok depended upon the Moderates entering the Council and playing a significant role in its affairs.

Surendranath Banerjea and the group which had heeded his injunction to boycott the 1909 councils were aware of the importance of their participation in the new legislature. As a simple matter of political expediency they could not afford to neglect the opportunity, which the reunification provided, of returning to the Council without a loss of face. Having been excluded for three years by their self-denying ordinance from all institutional politics, they had found it increasingly difficult to maintain their influence, and, more

[39] IA, Annual Report 1912, appendix E, pp. 19–24.
[40] *Statesman*,* 5 June 1912.
[41] IA, Annual Report 1912, appendix E, p. 23.

particularly, they had been hard-pressed to offer a worthwhile alternative to the Extremists' campaign of violence. Their style was constitutionalism, and it was high time they got back ino legislative politics to show that it had some value.

They were under constant attack from the vernacular press, which had maintained its readership among the lower-class bhadralok who had had no political experience prior to the anti-partition agitation and who were greatly attracted by racial and cultural extremism. Playing on these themes, many of the Bengali-language papers attacked British political forms and British institutions. These, they asserted, would distort Hindu society and, for that reason, their advocates—the Moderates—were to be regarded as national enemies. This criticism reached a peak as the Council elections approached. On 3 December 1912 *Nayak*, one of the most influential Bengali dailies, wrote:

> The right of voting is one of the serious evils which, in the guise of boons, English rule has introduced into this country. The Municipalities and District Boards and similar institutions have really nothing to do with the country and with society, either Hindu or Moslem. . . . Only men who have money and possess influence and can manipulate the voters get into these bodies, which again return members to the Legislative Council. . . . These Babus who are briskly canvassing for votes, whom do they represent? . . . These Babus, who are utterly without religion, may be likened to poison thrown out by the churning of Hindu society by the English, and it is for the English like another *Nilkantha* must grapple with them. Why, instead of doing that, do Englishmen allow this poison to scatter itself over the whole framework of Hindu society?[42]

The Moderates were disturbed by the effects of this anti-liberal press campaign[43] but, like Carmichael they pinned their hopes of restoring the situation on the new Council. If they could recapture bhadralok attention by their actions in the legislature and win widespread support with the measures they sponsored, then the community's faith in constitutional methods would surely be renewed.

[42] The allusion is to the God Siva, who drank the poison raised by the churning of the ocean by Gods and Demons, and thus saved the universe from its effects. The poison stuck in his throat, which became blue, and thereafter he was known as Nilkantha, the god with the blue throat.

[43] A. C. Mazumder to Pramathanath Banerjea, 13 May 1913, enclosure, IA MSS.

THE ELECTIONS

The elections for the new Bengal Legislative Council were held in December, 1912, and January, 1913.[44] This was the first time that Banerjea's group of Moderates had faced a Council electorate, and they framed their appeal to their constituents in terms of their ability to uphold constitutional principles and to discharge the grave responsibilities of legislators.[45] The result of the voting was a great disappointment to them, for they won only four of the 23 Indian elected seats. Banerjea himself was elected, along with Surendranath Roy, Devaprasad Sarvadhikary, and Abul Kasem.

The group's failure can be attributed to two main factors, both of great significance for the future of electoral politics in Bengal.

The first was the absence of a satisfactory organisation for the conduct of an election campaign. All the members of the Banerjea group belonged to the Indian Association, a liberal political club of Calcutta bhadralok professional men. It had a proud record of achievement from the pre-Morley-Minto period, where it had been remarkably successful in the politics of consultation and protest, but it could offer its members little assistance with the new tasks of electoral politics. There was, for instance, no machinery to ensure that only one Indian Association candidate contested each seat. Banerjea, although the doyen of the Association, was no formal party leader who could dictate to his followers. More serious was the absence of a campaign fund on which the candidates might draw, and the restriction of the Association's activities to Calcutta. Most of the constituencies were in the mufussil, where the Indian Association had no organisation and little direct influence.[46] It is significant that of the four members of the Banerjea group elected in 1912, one was returned for Calcutta University and two others for the Presidency Division municipalities.

In the strictly limited electorates of the Morley-Minto Council, this lack of organisation was not an insuperable obstacle, but if no

[44] For a more detailed analysis of the elections see the author's: 'The Vote and the Transfer of Power: a Study of the Bengal General Election, 1912–1913', *Journal of Asian Studies*, Vol. XXI, No. 2. Feb., 1962, pp. 163–181.

[45] See Abdul Rasul's election manifesto, GB, Appointment, 18L–3, B427–433, July 1914.

[46] Nominally there were branches of the Association in each District but all were moribund. Frequent suggestions at Committee meetings that they should be revived came to nothing.

attempts were made to rectify the situation, as indeed was the case, then it would have serious consequences when the franchise was extended. As we shall see, this was to be one of the main factors in the Moderates' downfall ten years later.

The second reason for the failure of the Banerjea group at the 1912 elections was their inability to speak the new 'language' of electoral politics. The grounds on which they rested their claim to election–their reputation as opponents of the partition and as agitators for constitutional advance; their experience in Congress politics and in local self-government–were not the grounds on which most voters made their choice. Although the electorate was select (there were in all only 9,000 voters[47]), the electors were primarily concerned with questions of their personal obligation to the candidates, or with the acquisition of local, communal, and personal advantages. Most candidates, for their part, regarded these as natural considerations, for they valued election to the Legislative Council, as to Municipalities and District Boards, chiefly as a means of raising their social standing and increasing their local influence. As the Banerjea group discovered to its chagrin in 1912, what mattered most at an election was not a candidate's political beliefs or experience of public affairs, but the length of his rent roll, his local prestige, his religion, caste, and family, his connections, his wealth, and his benefactions.

This can be illustrated by the story of the contest in the Rajshahi Division District and Local Boards electorate. Rajshahi Division comprised the whole of Northern Bengal, and the majority of its population was Muslim. The candidates for election were Jogesh Chandra Chaudhuri, M.A., Surendranath Banerjea's son-in-law, a member of the Indian Association and of the Pabna District Bar; Maharaja Girija Nath Ray Bahadur, a large zamindar in both Dinajpur and Rajshahi Districts, an influential member of the British Indian Association in Calcutta, and a former member of the Legislative Council of Eastern Bengal and Assam; Mahendra Ranjan Ray Choudhuri, Raja of Kakina, also a member of the Eastern Bengal and Assam Legislative Council and of the Eastern Bengal Landholders' Association, and a titleholder in Rangpur district; and Maulvi Hafizar Rahman Chaudhuri, a young man, the only Muslim candidate, who was a small landed proprietor from Bogra.

Jogesh Chandra Chaudhuri, hoping to win the favours of the

[47] *Report of the Franchise Committee* (Calcutta, 1919), p. 38.

Muslim voters, persuaded two Muslims to propose and second his nomination, but this did him no good. The Muslim community in this area had bitter memories of communal rioting during the boycott agitation six years before, and for this they blamed Chaudhuri's father-in-law, Surendranath Banerjea. Besides, Chaudhuri had chosen unwisely in selecting his seconder. This man, Maulvi Emaduddin Ahmed, proved to be the chief electoral agent of the Raja of Kakina, and he did his best to wreck Jogesh Chandra's chances. To this end he used a standard ploy of the period: he informed the voters that the Rajshahi District Magistrate was opposed to Jogesh Chandra's candidature and that his wrath would be felt by any who voted for him. The Raja was an invalid, but his 'following and his purse were long'. Reputedly, he spent Rs. 2,000 on 'inducements' to voters; he offered travelling expenses to many; and Emaduddin, on his behalf, provided those who came to vote in Rajshahi town with hospitality 'much above his own and their ordinary style of living'. It was the Raja, not Babu Jogesh Chandra, nor even Maulvi Hafizar Rahman, who caught the ear of the Muslims. He let it be known that he was willing to pay off the local Muhammadan Association's debt amounting to Rs. 1,500, and, better still, he received public support from the Nawab of Dacca. Where the Nawab went, many Bengali Muslims were accustomed to follow. The Raja was elected.[48]

In the light of this story it should come as no surprise to discover that 17 of the 26 Indian nonofficial members of the 1913 Bengal Legislative Council were landholders. In other respects, those who had succeeded in their bid for election had the same social qualifications as the men in the Banerjea group whom they had defeated. Apart from the Maharaja of Burdwan who was Khatri, the Hindus were all Brahmin or Kayastha by caste. Most of them were university-educated and resided in Calcutta or a mufussil town. Like the members of the Banerjea group, who apart from Banerjea himself were all lawyers, they were from the bhadralok elite, but they had the one decisive advantage of holding land.

The postscript to the general election was written in February, 1913, when the nonofficial members of the new Bengal Legislative Council proceeded to elect their two representatives on the Imperial Legislative Council. The result was something of a surprise. Of the 68 total votes, 39 were secured by the two nominees of the Banerjea

[48] *Bengalee*,* 29 Dec. 1912. GB, Appointment, 18L–4, B444–462, Oct. 1913.

group: Banerjea himself and Bhupendranath Basu. Both men would have been elected had the votes been distributed evenly as had been arranged. By some mischance Banerjea got 22, and Basu, who got only 17, was forced into third place behind the Maharaja of Nashipur, Ranajit Sinha, who had the backing of the European members and some of the large zamindars.[49]

The striking thing here was the reversal of the general election verdict against the Banerjea group. This points to an important conclusion, which helps to explain much of what happened at this and subsequent elections: there existed in Bengal at this time a number of distinct levels of politics, and, for a politician to be successful, he had to be capable of speaking in different idioms at these various levels. He had to talk the language of local influence and community to the electors, and the language of nationalism to his fellow legislative councillors. This explains the inconsistencies that one can observe in this period in the actions of politicians on different occasions. We find, for instance, that when the Raja of Kakina came down to Calcutta from Rajshahi in January, 1913, he changed, chameleon-like, from a mottled manipulator of local and communal interests to a true-blue nationalist. In the Legislative Council he followed Banerjea's lead. Here is the explanation of the discrepancy between the amount of influence that the Banerjea group could wield in the electorate and in the Council: although they were not fluent in the idiom of one level of politics, they were the masters of the language of another and were recognised as such.

This disjuncture between the various levels remained a feature of Bengal politics throughout the period of this study. With the extension of the electorate in 1919 and the resort by the Congress to mass politics in the early twenties, it was to become a crucial factor.

TO GRIND CORN

The first meeting of the Legislative Council of reunited Bengal was held on the morning of Saturday, 18 January 1913, in the former Imperial Council chamber at Government House. There was a good attendance of members and visitors to hear Carmichael's inaugural speech. Here was his opportunity to strike his desired note of liberalism and make his plea for cooperation. With a polite

[49] GP, Appointment, 18L–56, B1891–1906, Dec. 1913. *Englishman,** 28 Feb. and 5 Mar. 1913.

bow in the direction of bhadralok aspirations, he welcomed the councillors as fellow parliamentarians and expressed his pride at presiding over their deliberations. He continued:

> Our meeting today is a formal one, but we look forward to other meetings when we shall show that much as we differ among ourselves in some things—possibly in many things—we are all united in our determination to do what we can for Bengal, for India, and for the Empire.
>
> Bengal has been without a Council for nearly ten months. Some of you perhaps thought this unfortunate. You may have wished for legislation—some of you, I know, would have liked to ask questions and to move resolutions. But the delay was unavoidable. Now that there is a Council you will, I feel sure, make full and fair use of it, and I feel sure that those of us who have to answer questions or to give consideration to criticism will do so fully and fairly.[50]

Looking back on his first nine months in office, Carmichael must have felt pleased with the progress he had made and optimistic for the success of his mission. All communities had responded favourably to his obvious sincerity and goodwill, and the bhadralok seemed reassured that the promise of a new policy was not idle words. He had established friendly relations with the Muslim leaders and it seemed reasonable to hope that he might, with their help, placate the community. The warm welcome he had received at the St. Andrew's Day dinner, in Calcutta a recognised barometer of British opinion, set the seal upon his acceptance by the European nonofficials.[51] He had loyal and sympathetic I.C.S. subordinates, and undoubtedly he was satisfied with their preparatory work for the new legislature. Most important of all, the Moderate nationalists had decided to return to the council. Although they had not been given all that they had asked for in the revised Council regulations, they had assured Carmichael of their appreciation of his efforts to meet their demands,[52] and they had been particularly pleased when he chose S. P. Sinha and Nilratan Sarkar, both distinguished nationalists, to fill two of the seats reserved for nomination.[53] Banerjea, on whom in the last resort the success of Carmichael's mission might

[50] BLCP, Vol. XLV, p. 3.
[51] *Capital,** 5 Dec. 1912.
[52] NP, 23 Nov. 1912.
[53] NP, 25 Jan. 1913.

depend, was back in the Council, and he seemed cheerfully disposed to work within the new institution.

So far everything had gone according to plan, but Carmichael had yet to get 'the new machinery to grind corn'. As he had pointed out in his speech on 18 January, there had been a hiatus in institutional politics in Bengal, and with their resumption the real test would begin. 'Now that there is a Council you will, I feel sure, make full and fair use of it', he had said. Disappointment awaited him, for none of the communities would cooperate in working the Legislative Council as he wished.

BRITISH AND MUSLIM ANGER

The secondary effects of the bitterness of the Calcutta European nonofficials and the Muslims over the Delhi announcements were yet to be felt. As we remarked earlier, the British regarded the talk of a new policy as an admission of official weakness in the face of seditious Indian agitation, and they pointed to the Viceroy, Lord Hardinge, as the chief offender. From the first he had displayed an unconscionable tenderness for Indian opinion and a distaste for Calcutta European society. Obviously it was he who was responsible for moving the Government of India away from the salutary influence of the Bengal businessmen.[54] The British community, they said, must organise as a political force to combat the pernicious influence of Indians in the government of the Empire.[55] In 1912 the European Defence Association was reconstituted in Calcutta. It received large monetary contribution from British firms and, within three months, had enrolled 1,400 members.[56]

An attempt to assassinate the Viceroy on his state entry to Delhi in December, 1912, infuriated the British and brought immoderate demands for reprisals. Now, it was said, the Government must recognise where its foolish policy of concessions was leading.[57] Their anger was still running high when the new Bengal Legislative Council assembled. Carmichael's inaugural speech was immediately

[54] C. F. Andrews to Rabindranath Tagore, 18 Mar. [1913], Andrews MSS. Lord Hardinge, *My Indian Years, 1910–1916* (London, 1948), pp. 65–66 and 68.

[55] 'Hotspur': "Evolution of European Political Agitation in India", *Calcutta Review*, Vol. CXXXIV, April, 1912, p. 136. *Englishman*,* 6 Mar. 1913.

[56] *Capital*,* 12 Dec. 1912; *Commerce*,* 12 Mar. 1913.

[57] *Commerce*,* 1 Jan. 1913.

followed by a resolution, moved by Surendranath Banerjea, expressing the Council's horror at the assassination attempt. The sight of this 'arch seditionist' pledging his countrymen's support in the search for the culprit was too much for Norman McLeod, the spokesman of the European nonofficials.

> It is beyond the bounds of belief that the Delhi and similar outrages could take place unnoticed in the midst of a crowd, and yet no one has come forward to denounce the miscreant [he declaimed furiously]. We hear all round of the sins of the Police—a deserving but much-maligned body—but not a word of the sins of the people, and I have read and heard of sympathy unveiledly expressed for the most cold-blooded murders. As long as this attitude of mind exists, as long as the Indian populace display apathy, how can any one expect a reasonable man to admit the possibility of giving an equal voice to such people in the administration of this country—people who so little understand what their duties and responsibilities are as loyal citizens?[58]

This speech and its endorsement in the Calcutta European papers[59] provoked a sharp bhadralok reaction and added to the resentment between the bhadralok and the British.

As the Council proceeded to business, the European newspapers turned their attention to what they described as the intolerable nuisance of Bengali verbosity. 'Talk, endless, wearisome and often ignorant talk, is taking the place of action', complained the *Englishman* on 3 April, and on the following day it wrote: 'It is better to gag the Councils than to clog the executive'. This newspaper campaign was followed by a letter to the Government of Bengal, written by McLeod on behalf of the British nonofficial members of the Council, asking for some limit to be placed on question time. Acting on the advice of his officials, who were already feeling the strain of the long Council sessions, Carmichael reluctantly agreed to set a maximum to the number of questions for which an oral answer could be demanded.[60] The first retreat from his liberal position had been forced.

Among the Muslims there was growing dissatisfaction with the policy advocated by the community's leaders. A small group of younger professional men in Calcutta were insisting that the community must adopt a more aggressive stance if it were to improve

[58] BLCP, Vol. XLV, pp. 6–8.
[59] E.g., *Englishman*,* 20 Jan. 1913.
[60] GB, Legislative, A1–3, Aug. 1913.

its lot. The Nawab and his supporters managed for a time to prevent any public statement of this dissent, and in the Legislative Council the orthodox, loyalist approach was maintained for the first three months, but in the budget debate a new voice was heard. On 4 April 1913 Fazlul Huq, a young Muslim member from Dacca, brushed aside the polite conventions of his aristocratic elders, and in a powerful extempore speech warned the Government that continued failure to heed Muslim demands would lead to trouble. However much the Government might deny it, the Muslims were entitled to compensation for their past ill-treatment, he declared.

> To me it seems that Government has arrived at a parting of the ways, and has got to decide, once for all, its future policy regarding questions affecting the Muhammadan community. . . . in spite of their aversion to agitation, Muhammadans are drifting, owing to sheer force of circumstances, into the arena of political warfare. We feel that we have got to move with the times or else we are doomed. Let not the officials think that the feelings of the entire community can be soothed simply by the bestowal of titles and decorations on our leaders, or by providing for a transitory stay of the officials at Dacca with all the paraphernalia of Government. We require something more than a mere concession to our sentiments, something tangible which can be reasonably set off against our loss by the annulment of the Partition.[61]

Shamsul Huda was quickly on his feet to deny the truth of what he euphemistically described as this 'pessimistic view',[62] but the response which Huq's speech drew from various sections of the Muslim community suggested that there were many who thought as he did. The attention which he attracted throughout the province left no doubt that a new political reputation had been made.

Huq is an important figure for the political historian of this period, for he brought a new style to Muslim politics in Bengal.[63] Born of a family of Barisal lawyers, he followed the well-worn track to Calcutta for education, finishing on the benches of the elite Presidency College. In 1895, at the age of 22, he returned to Barisal with the degrees of Master of Arts and Bachelor of Law to teach in the local college; later he assisted his father with his legal practice. After five years Calcutta drew him back and he became an articled clerk

[61] BLCP, Vol. XLV, pp. 576–581.

[62] *Ibid.*, pp. 595–596.

[63] For biographical details see obituary notice, *The Times* (London),* 28 Apr. 1962; and *Indian Year Book and Who's Who, 1939–40* (Calcutta, 1940).

to the great High Court lawyer, Asutosh Mookerjee. The discussion over the partition found him keenly supporting the measure, and his first opportunity for political work came in 1906, when the Nawab of Dacca used him as a runner in his negotiations with Muslim leaders in other parts of northern India prior to the formation of the Muslim League. The Nawab had at his disposal a number of Government appointments in the new eastern province, and he was able to reward Huq with a place in the Provincial Executive Service. By 1908 he had become Assistant Registrar of Rural Cooperative Societies. At the time of reunification, however, he was aggrieved at his nonappointment as Registrar for the whole of Bengal, and he left the service in disgust. Again the Nawab came to his aid, ensuring his unopposed return for the Dacca Muslim seat in the Legislative Council.

Here was a potential Muslim leader of a new kind. Unlike the traditional communal leader, whose influence was locally based on landholding and who was usually a member of one of the great Muslim families, Huq had made his way by personal ability—for it was his ability which had won him the necessary patronage. His education and his experience in teaching, law, administration, and political organisation set him apart from the old leadership and, what was equally important, made him acceptable as a bhadralok. Here was a Muslim who (to adapt W. S. Gilbert) was the very model of a modern politician. It was important, too, that while retaining his contacts with his Eastern Bengal district he had established himself as a figure in Calcutta, for this enabled him to provide communal leadership on a new level.

Equally significant was the fact that his anger—personal and communal—was directed primarily at the Government. Although remaining a communalist, he would be willing on occasions to ally with other groups in attacks upon that Government, for he shared with other bhadralok aspirations quite foreign to the old Muslim leaders. In the years that followed, under the influence of pan-Islamism and a growing distrust of British intentions toward the Khilafat, men like Huq were willing to form an alliance with the Hindus that would have horrified their predecessors.

THE OPPOSITION OF THE MODERATES

The intransigence of the British nonofficials and the Muslims was a severe disappointment to the Government of Bengal's hopes for a reconciliation. Equally disturbing was the attitude of the bhadralok members. Although they obviously valued the Legislative Council as an institution and were ready to participate fully in its work, they were not willing to cooperate politically with the Governor. They had undergone an apparent metamorphosis in moving from their electorates to the Council chamber. In place of the motley and ill-assorted crew which the elections seemed to have produced, the Government found itself confronted on the Indian benches with a squad of determined nationalists.

The unity they displayed is to be explained by Surendranath Banerjea's ability as a parliamentary leader and the high regard in which he was held by his fellow councillors because of his unique contribution to the nationalist movement in Bengal.

Banerjea had had a colourful career.[64] Son of a westernised doctor, born in 1848 into Calcutta Brahmin society astir with the excitement of a religious reformation and a revival of learning, he had spent his school days among British and Anglo-Indian boys at Doveton College. Having taken a B.A. degree in English literature from Calcutta University, he had gone to London and in 1869 passed the I.C.S. examination, only one Indian ever having done so before. His elation was short-lived, for the India Office declared that he and another successful Indian candidate had falsified their ages. Their names were struck from the list. Banerjea challenged the decision in Queen's Bench, won his case, and returned to Bengal, unwelcome in a service which until then had been the exclusive preserve of the British. Three years later he was dismissed for a minor and what was almost certainly an accidental error in the return of a law case. He went to England again in an effort to have the decision reversed but was unsuccessful, and when he tried to make an alternative career at the Bar he was refused admission as a dismissed Government employee. Banerjea the official was finished; Suren Babu the nationalist was born. 'I felt that I had suffered because I was an Indian, a member of a community that lay disorganized, had no public opinion, and no voice in the counsels of their Government', he wrote later. 'The personal wrong done to me was an illustration of the helpless impotency of our people. Were others to suffer in the future as I had suffered in the past? They *must*, I thought to myself; unless we were capable as a community of redressing our wrongs and protecting our rights, personal and collective'.[65]

[64] For biographical details see DIB; and *Nation in Making*.
[65] *Nation in Making*, pp. 32–33.

Banerjea returned home, his heart set upon the political regeneration of India. With his material worries allayed by a Chair of English literature, provided at a Calcutta college by an Indian benefactor, he campaigned his cause through the columns of the *Bengalee*, an English-language newspaper for which he built an international renown in the half-century of his editorship. He founded as his political platform the Indian Association, a bhadralok organisation, which had only one influential rival (the landholders' British Indian Association) in Bengal in the following 40 years. At the end of the seventies he toured northern India, firing his audiences with his gospel of nationalism; in the eighties he established himself as one of the leading figures in Congress; in the nineties he visited England to seek support for Indian demands, and he took the lead of the radical elements in the Calcutta Corporation and the Bengal Legislative Council.

Then came his clash with Curzon. In 1899, he led the attack on the Calcutta Municipal Act, and throughout the following six years, as bhadralok anger at Curzon's measures mounted steadily, it was his voice that was raised in protest. He was a great orator and his public meetings at the Calcutta Town Hall attracted thousands. A well-built man in his early fifties, with strong features and striking white beard, he was a commanding figure. He had the emotional fire characteristic of his people, a command of English which few Englishmen could surpass, and an Augustan delivery. When Bengal was partitioned in 1905 his political star was at its zenith. From platform and press he thundered his condemnation, and the extraordinarily vociferous response which it evoked from the bhadralok surprised him little less than it did the British.

To his dismay he found that he could not control the agitation he had started, and by early 1907 things were so far out of hand that he joined the great zamindars and the Muslims in a delegation to ask for the Viceroy's intervention. 'It was simply marvellous', wrote Minto, 'with the troubles and anxieties of a few months ago still fresh in one's memory, to see the "King of Bengal" sitting on my sofa with his Mahommedan opponents, asking for my assistance to moderate the evil passions of the Bengali, and inveighing against the extravagances of Bepin Chandra Pal'.[66] Banerjea had caught a disease that has infected so many nationalist politicians since his day: he had become a moderate in spite of himself.

[66] Minto to Morley, 19 Mar. 1907, Lady Minto, *India, Minto and Morley, 1905–1910* (London, 1935), p. 109.

By 1912 he was no longer the unchallenged leader of the bhadralok, but he still had great influence. His steadfast refusal to enter the Calcutta Corporation and the legislative councils until the partition was revoked had been greatly admired, and his paper, the *Bengalee*, still shaped the opinions of many of the English-literate bhadralok. His claim to a large share in the triumph over the reunification of Bengal could scarcely be denied, and he was able to return to the Bengal Legislative Council in 1913 as a victor.

From the day that the new Council assembled it was obvious that he was to be the leader of the opposition. In this his age was an advantage, for most of his fellow-councillors were his juniors by ten to fifteen years. More important, perhaps, was his experience. His twenty-eight years as a member of the North Barrackpur municipality, the Calcutta Corporation, and the Bengal and Imperial Legislative Councils had made him a master of legislative manoeuvre and management. His ability as a debater was unmatched in the Council, and his judgment of when to remain silent could rarely be faulted. Outside the chamber, he worked with the industry of an able chief whip: holding informal consultations on coming business; persuading the indolent to attend and the waverers to support his line; compromising or threatening; always actively marshalling a united front for the nationalist cause.[67]

And what did the nationalist cause mean? What was Banerjea's line of action in the Council? Quite simply, it was opposition to the Government. Carmichael would make repeated appeals for cooperation; Banerjea would respond with qualified promises—but always the opposition continued, unremitting and, as far as the Government could see, unreasoning. The explanation lay partly in the nature of the powers of the Council and partly in the demands the bhadralok made on its politicians.

Under the constitution of 1909 the Indian members of the Council were placed in the classic position of an irresponsible colonial opposition, with powers of interpellation and censure, but with no responsibility for formulating or implementing policy. It had been one of Carmichael's early promises that he would try to increase opportunities for nonofficials to influence Government policy,[68] and he attempted to honour his promise by placing the broadest

[67] Author's interview with Hemendra Prasad Ghose, Calcutta, 19 Nov. 1960.

[68] *Statesman*,* 12 May 1912.

possible construction on the powers of the various standing and select committees of the Council, and by creating *ad hoc* bodies to advise on important questions. This encouraged the Moderates in their initial hopes that they might have sufficient power to refashion Government proposals so as to make them more acceptable to bhadralok opinion, and they took advantage of every opportunity to press their views. They had success on many limited issues; but it was soon apparent to them that they could achieve little, with the Government choosing the questions to be considered and retaining full responsibility for their implementation.[69] In this situation, the existence of a well-organised and effectively led party only aggravated the tensions in the Council and increased the frustration of the bhadralok members.

Equally important was the fact that politically their limited gains brought no reward. To whom could the councillors report their success in modifying a clause of a bill, or in persuading the Government to reexamine some aspect of policy? Certainly not to their constituents, for they understood nothing of such subtleties. They might respond if their representative could gain some concession for their locality or community—and the members were always busily engaged in securing such concessions—but they had no concern with high policy decisions. That was not the stuff of electoral politics.

Nor, for that matter, was it the stuff of nationalism. This was vital. To a majority of councillors the opinions of the electors counted for little, but the opinions of their fellow-members of the nationally conscious elite counted for a great deal. What they demanded was opposition to the Government. To oppose was the work of a nationalist, whether he was a member of the legislative council, a journalist, a public orator, or a terrorist. All must oppose, or cease to claim the title of nationalist. This was a legacy of the partition period. The British actions which had destroyed bhadralok trust had also dealt a deathblow to cooperation with the Government as a viable political style for any bhadralok politician. In the future a nationalist, to be worth his salt, had to gain an advantage over the Government. Thus the bhadralok members of the new Bengal Council, under Banerjea's direction, tried to embarrass the Government at every turn. In their speeches they accused it of disregarding Indian opinion and of injuring Indian in-

[69] *Bengalee*, 21 Sept. 1913.

terests. By their questions they drew attention to injustices and inequalities, and by moving resolutions and calling for divisions on legislative amendments they attempted to outvote the officials.

Confronted with this barrage, Carmichael's first reaction was to insist upon concessions. His officials were to accept whatever resolutions they could; enquiries into alleged grievances were to be instituted; extended time for consideration of controversial legislation was to be allowed; full information was to be given in reply to all questions, no matter how embarrassing; and outside the Council chamber, members were to be consulted on administrative matters affecting their districts.[70] He was willing to give this ground in the hope that the nationalists would meet him halfway. Again he was relying on a demonstration of goodwill to gain their cooperation.

But cooperate they could not, for that was tantamount to committing political suicide. If the Government was giving ground, they must push it harder, and experience was teaching them when and where to push. In particular, they developed an effective tactic of offering the Government more than it wanted, thereby putting it in the awkward position of having either to accept inconvenient proposals, almost always framed so as to increase opportunities for nonofficial interference in administration, or to appear churlish in rejecting magnanimous offers.

One example will illustrate this point. On 1 December 1913 Banerjea moved a resolution for the appointment of a Council committee to enquire into dacoity in Bengal and to recommend preventive measures. He recalled that the subject was one of frequent and adverse comment, and that the Government had asked for nonofficial cooperation in dealing with it. He offered this advisory committee as the Council's contribution, and he expressed his confidence that its findings would prove the Government wrong in imputing political motives to most of the dacoits then so numerous in the mufussil. Duke replied that dacoity was a matter for experts, that the Government was conducting extensive enquiries of its own and could see no likelihood of anything valuable being produced by the proposed committee. The Indian members of the Council would be more profitably engaged in using their influence in public life to combat terrorism. This reply left the Government open to a charge

[70] E.g., see BLCP, 2 Apr. 1913, Vol. XLV, p. 505; *ibid.*, 30 June 1913, Vol. XLV, p. 625; *Capital*,* 29 Jan. 1914; *Englishman*,* 6 Jan. 1914; and GB, Legislative, A1–2, Oct. 1913.

of insincerity in its professed desire for nonofficial assistance, and Banerjea was quick to see his opportunity. Although unconvinced by Duke's arguments, he said he would not press the issue. 'But let it go forth to the world, let it be reiterated, that we were, from this side of the house at any rate, anxious to help the Government, that we made a suggestion which we thought a good suggestion in the circumstances, and if that suggestion is not accepted the responsibility is no longer ours'.[71]

TERRORISM

This question of political violence was the greatest obstacle in the relations of the liberally motivated Governor and the Moderate nationalists. It posed a perplexing problem for the bhadralok members of the Council. They were constantly under pressure to define their position, but few, if any, were certain in their own minds as to what was their real attitude. While intellectually repelled by the resort to violence, they were emotionally sympathetic with those responsible. On the one hand, they feared that further constitutional development and the transfer of more power to Indians, which were their goals, would be retarded by terrorist outrages and the existence of revolutionary organisations.[72] Temperamentally many of them were averse to violence, and they were disturbed by the indiscipline in bhadralok society which it revealed. When groups of well-bred youths could roam the countryside committing dacoity with impunity, it seemed apparent that the fabric of the social order was endangered.[73] On the other hand, they felt a sneaking admiration for these boys, their own flesh and blood, who were willing to risk life and liberty in attacks upon the foreigners. As bhadralok and as opponents of the imperialists, the terrorists' credentials as members of the political elite were beyond question. They were patriots, no matter how indiscreet.

Thus it would have been an outrage to their personal and communal integrity for the bhadralok Council members to have joined in any Government-sponsored condemnation of the terrorists. Politically it would have been disastrous. Here again, they were caught in a cleft stick. There could be no shadow of doubt that, to the

[71] BLCP, Vol. XLV, pp. 797–804.
[72] Carmichael to Crewe, 25 Feb. 1915, *Carmichael*, p. 205.
[73] A. C. Mazumder to P. N. Banerjea, 13 May 1913, IA MSS.

majority of the bhadralok, the terrorists were heroic figures whose valour was removing the stigma of Bengali cowardice.[74] The community would not tolerate any public criticism of their actions. Yet the councillors had to find some means of disassociating themselves from these acts of violence if the Government were not to lose faith in their protestations of belief in peaceful and constitutional methods. They attempted to circumvent the problem by asserting, as on the occasion of Banerjea's resolution, that most of what the Government described as political crime was, in fact, common dacoity. Such sophistry satisfied no one. The British accused them of attempting to shield seditionists, and their fellow-bhadralok berated them for imputing such vulgar motives to patriots.

Another dimension was added to their problem by the fact that theirs was but one of the two groups competing for political influence in Bengal, and their way was only one of the two offering for the political elite. To declare openly for the terrorists was to let the contest go by default. Conversely, even to hint at disapproval of terrorism was to provide ammunition for their rivals who, it should be added, suffering from none of the limitations of Council membership, could talk as irresponsibly as they wished. These rivals were always ready to recall the early days of the anti-partition agitation, when men as eminent as Banerjea himself had encouraged youthful extremism. How old and cautious have our former leaders grown, they sneered. How low the fires of patriotism have burned.[75]

Crimes of violence were a major problem for the Government of Bengal, as well. In the seven years preceding 1913 there had been more than 1,100 cases of dacoity reported to the Bengal police, and of these only a handful had resulted in convictions.[76] It had been established beyond doubt that a small but significant proportion of these robberies were committed by revolutionary bands which had been effectively sealed off from their former elite patrons by the police actions of 1908, and were in search of funds to buy arms and sustain their activities. More spectacular were the periodic terrorist attacks upon civil and police officers. There had been a significant

[74] E.g., consider Rabindranath Tagore's attitude in 'The Call of Truth', *Towards Universal Man* (London, 1961), pp. 258–259. In considering the bhadralok's condonation of violence, account must be taken of the fact that it was non-bhadralok moneylenders who were the chief victims of political dacoities. (GI, Home Political, A138–139, Nov. 1913).

[75] E.g., *Amrita Bazar Patrika*, 29 Dec. 1915.

[76] BLCP, 13 Mar. 1913, Vol. XLV, p. 170.

lull in these attacks in 1912, but, following the unsuccessful attempt to assassinate Hardinge late in December of that year, the campaign had been resumed in all its horror.[77] If the Government were to retain the confidence of the public and its own officers, it had to put an end to this violence.

Carmichael, upon whose shoulders rested the responsibility for choosing a course of action, was convinced that a return to the authoritarian methods that had been tried in 1908 would do more harm than good. Unless the police received general assistance, there could be no hope of more convictions. Repression would make the terrorists martyrs and the objects of public sympathy. Carmichael was convinced that a lasting solution could be found only by marshalling bhadralok opinion against violent methods; this could best be done by demonstrating that the British were sincere in their desire for increasing Indian participation in government. The problem was basically political, he held, and a political solution had to be found. He pointed out that if the Government were to enforce an ordinance dealing with political crime over the head of the Legislative Council, the bhadralok would rightly regard the talk of reform and a new order as insincere. If any additional legislation were needed to deal with terrorism, it had to be passed by the Legislative Council, preferably with the concurrence of bhadralok members. His own political experience enabled him to appreciate the difficult position in which they were placed, and he understood the ambivalence of their attitude. He knew that personally and politically they would be reluctant to speak in public against the terrorists, but he realised the importance of encouraging them to commit themselves before the Government acted. If action were taken without this commitment, there could be little hope of later support.[78]

Carmichael's attitude toward the Moderates brought him into serious conflict with the Government of India, who rejected what the Home Member, Sir Reginald Craddock, described as this 'tame cat theory of treating seditionists'. In Craddock's opinion men like Banerjea should be told quite frankly that the Government regarded them as enemies and would treat them accordingly. He wrote of Banerjea:

[77] GI to Secretary of State, 26 Mar. 1914, GI, Home Political, Despatch No. 13, 1914.

[78] See his numerous letters to Crewe in 1913 and 1914, *Carmichael*, pp. 180 ff.

> I am convinced that his *dossier* would show the truth of every word said, that he is an arch-enemy of the Government without a spark of honesty in his composition. I do not for a moment believe that Lord Carmichael knows his past history or regards him as any more than an advanced politician. With the 'tame cat' policy a man of this kind gets a swollen head, and struts about hugging himself with pride at the thought that he is so clever and powerful that Government is afraid of him, and dare not assume any attitude except friendship and conciliation towards him. What if he is driven into the arms of the enemy? He will be less and not more dangerous than he is at present. These are the lines on which I would act in Bengal. There is no via media between futile conciliation and stern discountenancing of these mischievous pseudo-constitutionalists.[79]

The Government of India, deeply shocked by the attempt on Hardinge's life, was angered by Carmichael's apparent indifference to terrorism. They interpreted his reluctance to act without public support as a sign of weakness, and they were perturbed, in particular, at his failure to silence the Bengali press which, in their opinion, was spreading hot sedition. Craddock maintained that they should immediately take the matter out of Carmichael's hands by enforcing a repressive ordinance, but most of his colleagues disagreed on the ground that this would make nonsense of the policy of liberalisation and the devolution of power to the provinces. Some of them hinted that they were not in agreement with that policy, but they pointed out that it was Crewe's darling and that he would not countenance any attempt to push the provinces against their will.

The only course was to convince Crewe and the Bengal Government that a firmer line was needed. To this end a despatch was sent to Bengal emphasising the Government of India's concern and asking the provincial Government to outline its proposals for dealing with terrorism.[80] Craddock went to Calcutta to suggest to Carmichael and his officers what those proposals should be, but he returned in disgust to report that although the Bengal Government recognised the gravity of the matter, they were unwilling to apply strong measures. What was worse (and this was obviously beyond his comprehension), they could give no guarantee that their own policy of conciliation would work.[81]

Craddock was convinced that the Government of Bengal had

[79] Minute, 4 Jan. 1913, GI, Home Political, A9–13, May 1913.
[80] GI, *ibid.*
[81] GI, *ibid.*, A72–75, May 1913.

only a superficial understanding of the problem, and on 27 April 1913 he wrote a long minute to demonstrate its complexity. This document was a masterly social analysis, masterly but for one grave flaw: a lack of any appreciation of the bhadralok's desire for political self-expression. Because of his failure or refusal to recognise the strength of this desire, Craddock could explain terrorism only as a product of some evil inherent in Bengali society.

He attributed Bengal's administrative ills to the difficulties of communication in the delta, the weakness of the revenue agency under the Permanent Settlement, and the consequent paucity of British officers. He pointed to another result of the Permanent Settlement: the subinfeudation of landed tenures, with its product, the bhadralok. This class, Craddock said, had shown an extraordinary liking for English-language education, and as a result the professions in Bengal had become overcrowded. The disappointed and half-educated men that the system produced were easily swayed by the outpourings of a seditious press. The result, as he saw it, was a society in which evil had taken possession of men's minds. He wrote:

> It is a strange world, a topsy-turvy arrangement under which all the maleficent influences are hailed as deliverances, and all the benevolent influences are howled down in press and on platform as tyrannical and malevolent. . . . In no other country in the world than India, and in no other part of India except Bengal, could such an absolute inversion of right and wrong apparently find acceptance among people, who are more than ordinarily gifted with intellectual gifts. In Bengal there is apparently nobody to rally round the Government and no means of securing a rally . . . .[82]

From this can be seen the gulf which separated Craddock from Carmichael. Whereas the latter believed that terrorism resulted from the frustration of the bhadralok's legitimate political aspirations, the former could see it only as the evil product of a diseased society. Carmichael believed that the British had to change their ways;[83] Craddock said that Bengali society had to be refashioned, 'for if there are poisonous humours in the body politic which produce these growths, the mere application of caustic or the knife to the growths themselves can produce no permanent beneficial effect'.[84]

[82] *Ibid.*
[83] Carmichael to Crewe, 20 May 1914, *Carmichael*, p. 191.
[84] Minute, 27 Apr. 1913, GI, Home Political, A72–75, May 1913.

REGIMENTATION

Craddock warned his colleagues that the trouble in Bengal, if left unchecked, would spread rapidly to other provinces. The Government of India had to consider its wider responsibilities. 'Whatever value we may attach to provincial autonomy or decentralization', he wrote, 'we cannot overlook ourselves, or let local Governments overlook, the Imperial aspects of any weakness or defects in administration'.[85] This argument, although apparently straightforward, was based on an assumption of far-reaching consequences. What Craddock was saying in effect was that the problem of maintaining order in British India was to be solved by keeping the provinces regimented. For the sake of the whole company no individual should be allowed to step out of line. If there had to be movement, all should move in unison.

This was the principle that had governed Curzon's policies, but it had been discarded by the reformers in the period 1909 to 1912. Morley, for instance, recognised that although Bengal had only a Lieutenant-Governor, its administrative problems demanded that, unlike other Lieutenant-Governors' provinces, it should not be denied an Executive Council.[86] In the legislative reforms of 1909, Bengal's superior political maturity was acknowledged by the provision of Representative Government. No other province was given this. The 1911 arrangements took careful account of Bengal's special needs, and Crewe, in his letter to Carmichael of 15 January 1912, emphasised the importance of encouraging the separate development of the province. The new Legislative Council regulations of 1912 provided another opportunity to make special local adjustments, and it was one of Carmichael's basic tenets that Bengal was not to be treated like the rest of India.[87]

This provoked the clash with the Government of India, and, unfortunately for the bhadralok, the Government of India had the final say. Bengal was ready for an advance to Responsible Government by 1914, but, because of the Government of India's insistence that no province should be allowed to get out of step with the rest, it had to wait until 1921, with serious consequences for the liberal ideal in bhadralok politics.

[85] *Ibid.*

[86] Secretary of State to GI, 27 Nov. 1908, PP, 1908, [Cd. 4426], Vol. LXXVI, pt. 1, p. 52.

[87] GB, Political, A45–62, Mar. 1913.

CARMICHAEL'S DEFEAT

Most of the remedies for the situation in Bengal which Craddock advanced in his minute of 27 April 1913 were considered too drastic by Hardinge and the other Members of the Government of India. They did, however, accept his suggestion that there should be stricter control of appointments to teaching posts in Bengal, in order to keep 'seditionists' from poisoning the minds of the young. They also agreed to the appointment of a committee to investigate the subordinate administration of the province, for its report was certain to provide evidence to support their demands for firmer measures.[88]

For Carmichael, things were going badly. He was convinced that if he were to have any hope of success in his wider mission, he must be given the opportunity to move cautiously against the terrorists, carrying with him some degree of Moderate support. With the Government of India pressing ever harder for action, however, it was obvious that he had only a limited time to secure that support. He was disheartened by the lack of response from the Moderates. In personal conversations and in his speeches in the Legislative Council and on tour, he had appealed for their assistance.[89] He had succeeded in obtaining encouraging promises from a number of leading nationalists, but their resolve faltered when it came to translating private assurance into public action.[90] In the Legislative Council the bhadralok members continued their harassing methods, until the Government finally felt itself obliged to show less indulgence in providing information and in replying to attacks in conciliatory tones.[91] The lines in the Council were now drawn in just the way Carmichael had striven to avoid, with the officials and the European nonofficials on one side opposing the Indian nonofficials on the other.

In the British community at large, feeling was running high at the frequency of terrorist killings; and alarmist writing in the European press did nothing to ease the Governor's task of reaching a *modus vivendi.*[92] British nonofficials were growing impatient at his persistence in negotiating with the nationalists. 'Is it not time to

[88] GI, Home Political, A72–75, May 1913.

[89] E.g., see BLCP, 4 Apr. 1914, Vol. XLVI, pp. 681–682; and *Carmichael*, pp. 183–187.

[90] Carmichael to Crewe, 15 July 1914, *Carmichael*, p. 193.

[91] E.g., see BLCP, 2 Apr. 1914, Vol. XLVI, pp. 544–560.

[92] E.g., See *Capital** editorial, 'Crimes of Violence in India', 16 Apr. 1914.

discriminate between legitimate political aspiration and open or semi-veiled sedition, to ask straight out who is on our side and who is against us?' demanded the president of the European Defence Association, F. H. Stewart, at the 1913 St. Andrew's Day Dinner.[93]

The actions of the Government of India were also disturbing bhadralok opinion in just the way Carmichael had wished to avoid. Frustrated in most directions by the new policy of decentralisation, the Government of India had seized upon the University of Calcutta and the education service, over which it retained direct control, to teach the 'seditionists' and the Government of Bengal a lesson. In May, 1913, the Vice-Chancellor of the University of Calcutta, Asutosh Mookerjee, submitted the names of three lecturers for the Government of India's confirmation. The men—Abdul Rasul, Dr Abdulla-al-Mamun Suhrawardy, and K. P. Jayaswal—had already taken up their posts with the Government of Bengal's sanction, but the Government of India refused to confirm their appointment on the ground that they had been active in politics and could not be trusted to refrain from expressing anti-British sentiments.[94] Earlier it had issued orders aimed at tightening official control over schools and colleges,[95] and in June, 1913, in appointing a new Director of Public Instruction for Bengal it disregarded the claims of the Provincial Education Service and brought out a young man from England, in the hope that a new broom would sweep clean.[96]

These moves were seen by the bhadralok as an encroachment on their control of education. They smacked strongly of the Curzon era, and speakers at a Calcutta Town Hall protest meeting declared that the 'Spirit of Partition' was still rampant.[97] An even greater uproar was narrowly averted early in 1914 when the Government of India was persuaded by Carmichael and Crewe to drop a proposal to put an Englishman in Asutosh Mookerjee's place as Vice-Chancellor of the University.[98]

It was patent that in its educational decisions the Government of India had disregarded the wishes of the provincial Government.

[93] *Englishman*,* 1 Dec. 1913.
[94] *Ibid*., 23 June 1913. GI, Education, A1–11, June 1913.
[95] *Englishman*,* 4 July 1913.
[96] GI, Home Political, A72–75, May 1913; *Capital*,* 17 Apr. 1913.
[97] *Englishman*,* 29 July 1913.
[98] Carmichael to Crewe, 15 Jan. 1914, *Carmichael*, pp. 178–179; IA, General meeting proceedings, 13 Feb. 1914.

This confirmed the bhadralok politicians' suspicions that the policy of devolution of power was a sham, and they asked what price now for the other arm of the new order: liberalisation?[99] As early as June, 1912, Crewe had disclaimed the suggestion that there had been any intention at the time of reunification to establish provincial autonomy,[100] and this provoked the inevitable retort that he was trying to explain away an indiscreet promise.[101] By the beginning of 1914 it was an open secret that the Government of Bengal enjoyed little freedom of action, and the Bengal Moderates were losing faith in Carmichael's ability to keep his side of any bargain.

Carmichael was also having trouble with his own Government. From the first, many of his officers, including those most sympathetic to his liberal aims, had thought him overoptimistic in his hopes of a positive political response from the bhadralok leaders. Moreover, the officials' goodwill for the Moderates in the Legislative Council was sapped by their organised resistance under Banerjea's effective leadership to all proposals that impinged on the vested interests of landed property. When the first measures sponsored by the newly formed Calcutta Improvement Trust were publicised, they were roundly attacked in the bhadralok press, and the Indian nonofficial MLCs prepared amendments, shamelessly designed to benefit urban landlords, that would nullify the proposals' main objects.[102] A bill to prevent land alienation from the backward Santal tribals in West Bengal was equally roughly handled by the bhadralok members when it was circulated in draft.[103] This provoked sarcastic comments from the officials on the quality of the Moderates' professed liberalism, and it made them impatient with Carmichael's insistence that the Councillors were in a difficult position. Faced with the continued failure of his efforts to secure nonofficial approval of counterterrorist measures, with the unabated violence of terrorism, and with incessant complaints from Delhi, they began to urge the Governor to take stronger action.

[99] *Nayak*, 15 Jan. 1914.

[100] S. R. Mehrotra, 'The Politics Behind the Montagu Declaration of 1917', C. H. Philips (ed.), *Politics and Society in India* (London, 1963), p. 78.

[101] IA Annual Report, 1912.

[102] BIA Annual Report, 1911–12 and 1913–14; *Capital*,* 11 June 1914; *Bengalee*, 19 June 1914; *Calcutta Gazette*, 27 Jan. 1915, pt. 4, pp. 9–18; BLCP, 2 and 3 Mar. 1915, Vol. XLVII, pp. 35–82.

[103] GB, Legislative, 1–47, July 1918; *ibid.*, 1–34, Apr. 1919; BIA Annual Report, 1914–1915.

By the time Hardinge came to Calcutta at Christmas, 1913, he found Carmichael finally resigned to the necessity for action against the terrorists. The Governor insisted, however, that the administration use only the statutory powers it already possessed until such time as a bill extending those powers could be put through the Bengal Legislative Council with the approval of at least some of the Indian nonofficials.[104] He was supported in his stand by Crewe and the British Cabinet,[105] much to the annoyance of the Government of India who saw how little real hope existed of obtaining Indian support for such measures.[106]

Throughout the first half of 1914 Carmichael struggled vainly to prove them wrong. He failed to obtain the legislation he needed, and he repeatedly saw charges that his Government laid against suspected terrorists under the existing law dismissed by the Calcutta High Court, which at that time was a confirmed antagonist of the executive, distrusting police evidence on principle.[107]

The Government of India was almost at the end of its tether when it was suddenly presented with a chance to cut short Carmichael's 'shilly-shallying'. The outbreak of the European war in August, 1914, gave it the excuse it had been looking for to take the matter out of his hands. It informed Crewe that under the changed conditions of war exceptional measures could no longer be avoided.[108] In December, it assumed complete charge of the handling of conspiracy, and in March, 1915, it passed a Defence of India Act which gave it power to arrest and detain suspects without trial.[109]

'These are the lines on which I would act in Bengal', Reginald Craddock had written in January, 1913. 'There is no via media between futile conciliation and stern discountenancing of these mischievous pseudo-constitutionalists'. To Craddock's mind it was best to clear the ground of the complex uncertainties of politics that threatened to ensnare British officialdom in a subtle tangle of ill-

[104] GI, Home Political, A39–48, Nov. 1914.

[105] Carmichael to Crewe, 20 May 1914, *Carmichael*, pp. 191–192.

[106] GI, Home Political, A39–48, Nov. 1914; and Lord Hardinge, *My Indian Years, 1910–1916* (London, 1948), p. 96.

[107] Carmichael to Crewe, 25 Feb. 1915, *Carmichael*, p. 205; and GI, Home Political, A172, May 1916.

[108] GI, Home Political, A39–48, Nov. 1914.

[109] Carmichael to Crewe, 17 Dec. 1914, *Carmichael*, pp. 201–203; and Lord Hardinge, *op. cit.*, p. 116.

defined relationships. Bold, forthright action, he asserted, would make the Government's task easier by revealing who were its friends and who were its enemies. Carmichael believed that this view was totally mistaken. He valued the intricacies of politics and understood the importance of preserving subtle differences of opinion. He knew very well that the Moderates' professed attachment to constitutional methods was no pretence, and he appreciated the potential danger to the future of bhadralok politics of dismissing them as mischievous frauds. From the beginning his actions had been based on the conviction that a *via media* between 'futile conciliation and stern discountenancing' *had* to be found to save the liberal secular ideal in Bengal. He had clashed with the Government of India on this issue and had been defeated. With the passage of the Defence of India Act the Craddock line had triumphed, to the ultimate destruction of Carmichael's attempt to gain the cooperation of the bhadralok through the Legislative Council.

II

'TALL TALK AND LOW PERFORMANCES'

THE MODERATES IN TROUBLE

Among the bhadralok there was indignation at the Government of India's actions in the early months of 1915. In January it published the report of the Bengal District Administration Committee. This was the committee of enquiry established at Reginald Craddock's request in October, 1913, and its report was virtually an elaboration of his minute of 27 April 1913, concentrating attention upon the shortcomings of the provincial administrative structure and system of education, and the role of educated Hindus in 'seditious' activities. The report had been withheld for some months; when it did appear it roused the ire of the bhadralok, who regarded it as an offensive attack on their community.[1]

The passing of the Defence of India Act in March brought immediate protests from all sections of Bengali political society, Hindus and Muslims alike. The Government was accused of having taken advantage of the general state of uncertainty to restrict civil liberties. The manner in which the bill had been hustled through the Imperial Council, without reference to a select committee, was held to be evidence of the Government's disregard for the elected representatives of the people. When its provisions were first enforced, many of those imprisoned or placed under house arrest

[1] NP, Feb. 1915; and A. C. Mazumder's presidential address, IA, 14 May 1915, IA General meetings proceedings.

were bhadralok students, and there was an outcry against handing innocent youths over to the cruelties of the police.[2]

In his presidential address to the Indian Association on 14 May 1915, A. C. Mazumder declared that the Government had forfeited the trust of Bengalis. 'Co-operation is a word easily uttered and easily repeated, but not as easily acted upon', he said. 'Let both sides be frank and acknowledge that there is no sympathy and therefore no co-operation between the people and the Government. The co-operation can only come with trust and confidence which unhappily are very much wanting'.[3] It is significant that just over three years earlier Mazumder had been one of the signatories to the Moderate nationalists' declaration expressing 'our profound homage, our devoted loyalty and our heartfelt gratitude' at the 'happy Reunion of Bengal',[4] and that in May, 1913 he had urged upon his fellow members of the Indian Association executive the necessity of assisting the Government in its efforts to restore order. '. . . it seems to me that the public cannot be wholly exonerated from the charge that they have as yet done very little actively to help the administration', he had written. 'A well directed and sustained practical effort on our part may count for much and will at all events serve to justify our position with the government'.[5]

That the same man was now castigating the bureaucracy for its 'deplorable' attitude toward the public suggests how serious had been the Bengal Moderates' loss of confidence in this period. The optimism with which they had greeted the reunification as the signal of a new era had died, for their high hopes in entering the Legislative Council had not been realised. Their elected majority had proved to be of no real advantage, for they had no power over the executive, and their well-organised legislative party had found nothing better to do than to needle the Government. Frustrated by such a profitless occupation, they abused the officials for their unwillingness to take notice of nonofficial opinion.[6]

The continued activities of the terrorists had proved a severe embarrassment to the Moderates, whose evasion of Carmichael's

[2] IA Committee meeting proceedings, 19 and 23 Mar. 1915; and NP, Mar. 1915 ff.

[3] IA General meetings proceedings.

[4] *Bengalee*,* 16 Dec. 1911.

[5] A. C. Mazumder to P. N. Banerjea, 13 May 1913, IA MSS.

[6] E.g., see Byomkes Chakravarti's presidential address, Bengal Provincial Conference, Apr. 1914 (*Hindu Patriot*, 20 Apr. 1914).

requests for a repudiation of violent methods had further strained their relations with the Bengal Government. It had also hastened the direct intervention in provincial affairs of the Government of India, which obviously had none of Carmichael's sympathy for the Moderates' aspirations. The enactment of the Defence of India Act was the final demonstration of the Moderates' impotency, and, as if to complete their humiliation, the Government of India had directed that the nonofficial members of the legislative councils should show their support for the war effort by foregoing all discussion of controversial subjects.[7] Thus, at a time of rising bhadralok anger at British actions, the Moderate MLCs had to content themselves with loyal utterances and petty talk of local affairs.

When they had entered the new Legislative Council in 1913 it had been to the accompaniment of a chorus of jeers from the Extremists, who declared that the Moderates had been duped by the British into thinking that they were being given something worthwhile.[8] It now seemed that the Extremists had been right, and the Moderates were held up to ridicule in the bhadralok press. 'What a tempting and beautiful picture was drawn by the Congress leaders when the bonbon of the reformed Councils was dangled before the eyes of the people, and how sad and deplorable is the reality!' scoffed the *Amrita Bazar Patrika*.[9]

In an article on 'Lord Morley's "Reforms" ' in the Calcutta *Hindu Review* of April, 1914, Bipin Chandra Pal[10] had claimed that the expansion of the legislative councils was not what had been wanted. The 'new patriotism' which had manifested itself in the anti-partition agitation, he wrote, had sought 'a little more freedom of self-expression and self-reliant civic activities', but these it had not gained. The Reforms had 'rallied' the Moderates but they had unwittingly strengthened the hand of the 'revolutionary party'.

> For, the failure of every Resolution brought before the Councils by the popular leaders, and the rejection of every amendment proposed by them in any Bill under the consideration of the legislatures, inevitably strengthen the conviction of the impossibility of working out any reasonable reconciliation between popular rights

[7] BLCP, 13 Dec. 1915, Vol. XLVII, p. 494.

[8] E.g., see *Nayak*, 3 Dec. 1912 and 14 June 1913; and B. C. Pal: 'Indian "Council-Reforms" and Indian Culture', *Nationality and Empire. A Running Study of Some Current Indian Problems* (Calcutta, 1916), pp. 194–218.

[9] *Amrita Bazar Patrika*, 17 Apr. 1916.

[10] For biographical details see A. C. Gupta (ed.), *Studies in the Bengal Renaissance* (Calcutta, 1958).

and the British connection with this country. Lord Morley's 'Reforms' have, thus, only increased the difficulties of an already difficult situation.[11]

By early 1915 the Moderates were forced to admit that there was much truth in what Pal said. Their failure to achieve anything worthwhile in the Council because of their lack of power had further weakened their influence with the bhadralok, and, what was more serious, it had largely discredited their political style: constitutional nationalism.

As a debating point, they had always argued that the Extremists were foolish to criticise the Morley-Minto councils for what they were not, without considering what they might become. They had to be regarded merely as staging points on the road to self-government, the Moderates insisted.[12] This assertion, however, depended upon faith–faith in the British intention to give India self-government–and the Extremists maintained that this faith was groundless. They poined out that the British had never declared self-government to be the object of their policy in India, and they held that there was nothing in British actions to suggest that they would ever voluntarily give up power. The reformed Legislative Councils and the talk of liberalising provincial administration were simply sops to appease an angry people. The Craddocks, not the Carmichaels, were the real force in British Indian government, and the Defence of India Act was the true product of their work.[13]

The logical conclusion of this argument was, as Pal had said, 'the conviction of the impossibility of working out any reasonable reconciliation between popular rights and the British connection with this country', and that almost certainly meant violent revolution. To the Moderates this was a frightful conclusion.

They could see only one sure way of defeating that logic: to secure a clear declaration from the British that they intended India to be self-governing. This should be followed immediately by the transfer of some measure of real power to the Indian members of the legislative councils and a guarantee that more would be given at successive stages. The object was to restore that faith in the value of liberal, constitutional methods of political action which had been so badly shaken, first by the partition of Bengal, and later by the

[11] *Nationality and Empire*, *op. cit.*, pp. 222–223.

[12] E.g., see *Indian World*,* 19 Nov. 1913. (*Indian World* was edited by Prithwis Chandra Ray, a leading member of the Indian Association.)

[13] NP, Mar. 1915; and *Nationality and Empire*, *op. cit.*, passim.

Moderates' difficulties in the reformed councils. To achieve this object, there had to be a minimum of hesitation on the part of the British in making their declaration, and no display of reluctance in giving the powers demanded by the Moderates.

DEMANDS FOR CONSTITUTIONAL ADVANCE

This critical point in their thinking had been reached by the Moderate nationalists in Bengal by the middle of 1915. As we have seen, the actions of the Government of India in the months following the outbreak of the war had had a negative influence in forcing them to this conclusion. The declaration of war itself had had a more positive effect. In India, as elsewhere in the British Empire, August, 1914, sent a wave of excitement and hope through the educated classes. There was talk of a short and glorious campaign, to be followed by a readjustment of international relations, in the forefront of which would be a new partnership of the nations of the British Empire. A new conception of India caught the imagination of many Indian nationalists: a self-governing India taking its place as an equal beside the other British dominions in an Imperial federation.[14] Already, they declared, India's new status had been foreshadowed by the deployment of large numbers of Indian troops beside those of Great Britain and the white dominions on the European battlefields. 'Comrades in arms, it will be difficult to treat them as helots in politics', declaimed the *Bengalee* in September, 1914.[15]

Excited by this prospect, the Moderates set about preparing schemes for constitutional reform, typical of which was one published in July, 1915, by Surendranath Banerjea. It is worth studying in detail, for it contained the essence of important later proposals: S. P. Sinha's Indian National Congress presidential address of December, 1915; the memorial presented to the Viceroy in October, 1916, by 19 members of the Imperial Legislative Council; and the Congress-Muslim League scheme of December, 1916.

Banerjea assumed that a constitutional reconstruction was imminent, and he argued that the best way for the Indian leaders to draw attention to their demands was for Hindus and Muslims to agree to a common plan. 'The ideal is self-government within the

[14] E.g., see *ibid.*, pp. 140–161.
[15] *Bengalee*, 9 Sept. 1914.

Empire, and every part of the scheme must tend towards it', he wrote. The demands should be for the appointment of a higher proportion of Indians to the Civil Service, real autonomy for the provinces, and an Imperial Legislative Council with extended powers. The Government should be bound by council resolutions, and elected members should be in a two-thirds majority in all deliberative bodies, with effective representation for 'every district and every interest'. Most important of all, the legislative councils should have the power of the purse, for this, Banerjea held, was the key to real self-government.[16]

In this, as in the later schemes, the demand was for extension of the powers of the existing institutions; the Moderates understood that the root of their troubles in the councils was the limitations of Representative Government, and, from their reading of British constitutional history, they knew that an advance to Responsible Government offered a way out. Moreover, such an advance along a recognised line of constitutional development would afford them a clear victory and would justify their participation in the old councils. Accompanying their programmes of reform was an appeal to the British to make a declaration that India was to be given self-government—a declaration 'with regard to which there will be no evasion, no misunderstanding possible'. The words are S. P. Sinha's in his Congress presidential address of December, 1915, and he accompanied them with an article from the Moderates' creed: 'if the noble policy of Malcolm and Elphinstone, Canning and Ripon, Bright and Morley, is not steadily, consistently and unflinchingly adhered to, the moderate party amongst us will soon be depleted of all that is fine and noble in human character'.[17]

The Moderates had made their plea and it was important to them that the British should respond quickly and generously, for any hesitation, any hint of neglect for constitutional aspirations, would reinforce the growing impression that the Moderates had no influence. The British acted neither quickly nor generously. More than three years had elapsed from the declaration of war before the British Government announced its plans for India's future, and then only when its hand had been forced by Indian agitation and by nonofficial British action.

[16] *Ibid.*, 2 July 1915.

[17] *Congress Presidential Addresses, 1911–1934* (Madras, 1934), pp. 192 and 193.

At the outset the attention of the British and Indian Governments was fully occupied with the urgent problems of reorganising for war, and, although the excitement in India over the possibility of constitutional reforms did not pass unremarked, it was agreed that consideration of such questions should await the return of peace.[18] Even when hopes of a quick victory had receded, the Government of India was reluctant to make any move that might disturb political order in India and thereby jeopardise its contribution to the war effort.

For the first two years of the war its primary concern was the handling of conspiracy. Bengal occupied a large part of its time, for it was afraid that the terrorists there would receive direct aid from German agents, and it could not persuade Carmichael to apply the Defence of India Act as rigorously as it considered necessary.[19] Although the Governor's liberal policy was virtually wrecked, he refused to give in completely to Delhi; his last two years in office were devoted to a struggle to prevent the use of the extraordinary powers the executive had acquired to stifle healthy public life in his province.

To the Government of India's reiterated demands for extreme action, his customary reply was: 'we must wait patiently and not lose our heads'. He opposed suggestions for the deportation of political suspects. He insisted on the formation of committees to examine the evidence on which suspects were detained, and he proposed the inclusion of Indian nonofficials on these committees to gain public support. 'Till there is general confidence in the fairness of our enquiries, we shall not get on very far'. He stood firm against pressure from the Government of India and his own officials to use the Defence of India Act retroactively against men who had been involved in political crime as far back as 1908.[20] He insisted that members of the Legislative Council should be given full information in reply to their questions on the application of the Act,[21] and whenever he addressed the Council he explained the reasons for actions his Government had taken.[22]

[18] GI, Home Public, A128–131, Oct. 1914.
[19] GI, Home Political, A172, May 1916.
[20] Carmichael to Crewe, 25 Feb., 25 Mar., and 5 May 1915, *Carmichael*, pp. 205–8.
[21] E.g., see BLCP, 4 Sept. and 13 Dec. 1916, Vol. XLVIII, pp. 446–447, 454, 472–475, 478, and 532–561.
[22] E.g., see *ibid.*, 4 July 1916, Vol. XLVIII, pp. 370–371.

THE 1916 ELECTIONS

He had his reward for this persistence in trying to mitigate the severity of British wartime administration, in the decision of the Moderates to contest the June, 1916, Legislative Council elections. The Extremist press in Bengal ridiculed the idea of any further participation in the Morley-Minto legislatures,[23] and it is not unlikely that the Moderates would have repeated their 1909 boycott had Carmichael been less sympathetic.

In these elections nationalist politics played a more important role than in the 1912–1913 contests. In the ten local body constituencies, where bhadralok opinion was most clearly expressed, there was a decisive change. The five sitting members for the District and Local Boards seats were defeated by men who were younger and angrier, if we may judge from their subsequent behaviour in the Council. The Municipalities seats were won by angry old men, five veterans of the anti-partition campaign, all Indian Association lawyers: Kisori Mohan Chaudhuri, K. B. Dutt, Ambika Charan Mazumder, and two reelected members, Surendranath Roy and Mahendranath Ray. This suggests that a considerable change had occurred in the electorates since the Banerjea group's debacle in 1913, and a comparison of the political affiliations of the members of the old and new Councils points to the same conclusion. Of the sixteen elected Hindu members in 1913, ten belonged to no organisations outside their local regions, whereas in 1916 all but one Hindu member belonged to some province-wide association. While local influence was still important in securing votes—and the contests gave good evidence of this—a nationalist reputation or conviction now carried considerable weight at the polls.

What this evidence points to is the surprising but extremely important fact that between 1913 and 1916 in Bengal, Council politics had had an impact on the second 'level' of the political system. It is surprising because the Council had so obviously failed to satisfy any of the politicians; but it bears out our original point that in Bengal a representative legislature had an excellent chance of involving the bhadralok because of the group's rewarding experience with other liberal institutions, and because of their need (in Bipin Chandra's words) for 'self-reliant civic activities'. The nationalists' boycott of the first Council elections in 1909 had delayed a meaningful experience of representative politics, and had strengthened the

[23] *Amrita Bazar Patrika*, 17 Apr. 1916; and *Nayak*, 9 June 1916.

forces of localism and communalism in the electorates, but the Moderates' work in the Council from 1913 had (as they had hoped) drawn attention and provoked comment. It was indicative of the institution's enhanced importance that it should have been the object of repeated criticism from eminent Extremists such as B. C. Pal and Motilal Ghose, and from the vernacular press. Ironically, these widely read critics must have played an important part in making Council politics a subject of interest among the electors.

There was a great opportunity here for the British and, at the same time, a grave potential danger. In Bengal, the Legislative Council was no longer the exclusive concern of the active political elite, and this meant that the question of its reform had assumed a new significance. If the British were prepared to carry through a bold and arresting reform of the institution to satisfy the politicians' desire for power, they obviously had a chance to restore control of the political system to the Moderates or to draw the Extremists back into constitutional politics. That it was not too late to do this was indicated by the Moderates' participation in the 1916 elections, particularly the participation of the young, uncommitted men. Conversely, if the British failed to meet the clearly articulated demands of the politicians, thereby leaving the anger of the upper 'level' unchecked, there was now a serious likelihood of that anger running through the second 'level' or beyond, with possible revolutionary effects.

That the anger of the politicians was real was demonstrated in the Legislative Council as soon as it assembled. The first act of the new members was to reject Surendranath Banerjea as their representative on the Imperial Legislative Council.[24] This was a serious blow for him, for, faced with a new regulation which prevented members from sitting in both a provincial council and the Imperial Council,[25] he had not contested a seat for the Bengal legislature, relying upon his return to the centre. His defeat was an obvious gesture of impatience with the restrained, decorous methods of protest for which he stood, and it was an ominous sign for the British.

Having given this warning, the councillors set out to demonstrate that, unlike the old representatives, they respected public opinion more than any directive from the Government of India. Taking their cue from the vernacular press, they probed every case

[24] *Calcutta Gazette*, 19 July 1916; and *Nation in Making*, p. 300.
[25] PP, 1914, [Cd. 7370], Vol. LXIII, p. 69.

of house search, internment, and deportation under the Defence of India Act, alleging illegality or injustice wherever they sensed a weakness.[26] They attacked the police without restraint. In the budget debate early in 1917, one member after another criticised its work and demanded a reduction in expenditure on the force. 'We are not very proud of our Police', declared Mazumder, 'and I do not realize the justification of such lavish expenditure on their account unless some definite scheme is arrived at to make them more efficient and useful to the public'.[27] There were repeated complaints that the Government was denying the Indian nonofficial members information, disregarding their suggestions, and using the official bloc to vote down their resolutions. 'I have now been four years in Council and know that going against official opposition is like dashing one's head against a stone wall', complained Fazlul Huq.[28] Speaking at the end of the budget debate on 14 March 1917, one of the new men, Akhil Chandra Datta, who represented the Chittagong Division District and Local Boards, told the Government that its obstructive attitude had cut the ground from under the feet of the Council supporters. 'Will not the impression go forth from one end of the country to the other that our much vaunted reformed Council is not, for all practical purposes, a whit better than that of pre-reform days?' he asked. 'My Lord, as the proceedings of the Council went on these two days from resolution to resolution, the feeling that oppressed me most was that we non-official members sit here only to play the part of the chorus in a Greek tragedy'.[29]

A WARNING DISREGARDED

The political discontent in Bengal and its open expression in the provincial Council and press was a constant irritation to the Government of India whose primary concern was still to maintain peace and quiet for the duration of the war. Law and order throughout India, it reiterated, was menaced by this undisciplined province. Craddock was adamant that the solution lay in the reform of the provincial administrative structure and education system, and the provision of new economic opportunities for the bhadralok,

[26] E.g., see BLCP, 4 Sept. and 13 Dec. 1916, Vol. XLVIII, pp. 446–478 and 532–561.
[27] *Ibid.*, 13 Mar. 1917, Vol. XLIX, p. 158.
[28] *Ibid.*, 7 Aug. 1916, Vol. XLVIII, p. 435.
[29] *Ibid.*, Vol. XLIX, p. 237.

together with a more aggressive use of police powers.[30] In an effort to get the Government of Bengal's endorsement of this programme, the Government of India requested it in April, 1916, to outline the remedial measures it thought necessary, having regard to the Bengal District Administration Committee's recommendations.[31]

The reply received from the provincial Chief Secretary was satisfactory, but with it came a provocative and unwelcome note of dissent from the Senior Member of the Executive Council, Percy Lyon. In this note Lyon hammered home the point that Carmichael had been trying to make for four years: that the British must recognise and accommodate the bhadralok's political aspirations. Certainly Bengal was out of step with the rest of India, as the Government of India complained, but the moral was not to try to bludgeon it back into line, for that was to invite political disorder. The British had to face the fact that, because of its superior political development, Bengal must now become the pacemaker for the rest of India. The moment was critical, Lyon said. There could be no delay.

> I am profoundly convinced that the authors of this letter have failed to diagnose correctly the root-cause of our present trouble in Bengal—which is political in its nature. In considering the various influences which have given it a violent and explosive character, they have overlooked entirely the spirit of nationalism which inspires it, and they have consequently restricted themselves to schemes for the improvement of the administration and of our system of education, while omitting all reference to the urgent need for an advance towards self-government, without which such schemes will fail to remove the distrust with which Government and all its measures are regarded. This feeling of nationality is at the basis of the propaganda of the revolutionaries whom we are actually fighting: it is the 'idea' which is being spread to them in most of the schools and colleges of Bengal. . . . Sir Satyendra Prasanna Sinha made it the burden of his presidential address at the last National Congress: it is the constant theme of every leading speaker and writer in Bengal; and, under the stimulus that has been given by the World War to the spirit of patriotism in all civilized countries, the vast majority of the educated classes and almost every student who thinks of public questions at all are deeply affected by it. Moreover these classes can no longer be regarded as an isolated and insignificant minority of the population. They are already learning to identify themselves with the masses,

[30] GI, Home Political, A225–232, Aug. 1917.
[31] *Ibid.*, A172, May 1916.

> and are spreading their own distrust of British rule amongst them, and they will ultimately carry the people with them in their demands that nationalist views should be introduced into the government of the country.

The revolutionaries, however deplorable their methods, had the same 'aspirations to political freedom' as 'moderate and loyal Bengalis', Lyon continued, and no true Briton could fail to sympathise with these aspirations. To give them their just recognition and to remove the distrust with which British rule was regarded, there had to be an effective advance to self-government at the end of the war.

> It appears to me that a frank declaration of the ultimate goal and aim of our policy in governing India is the first step we have to take. I believe that this goal should be proclaimed to be such self-government within the Empire as will enable India to take her place as one of the self-governing nations which constitute that Empire. . . . The war has given us an opportunity of adopting a broad and constructive policy of reforms with these objects in view. If we fail to obtain them, our proposals will lead inevitably to coercion followed by an administrative collapse, and it may then be too late to guide the political evolution of the country along any safe and peaceful course.[32]

What Lyon was demanding was not simply reforms but a revolution in British thinking about India. He was asking his colleagues in the I.C.S. to discard their romantic and outmoded notion that they could hold India 'steady' by the authoritarian discouragement of the *déraciné* westernised elites and the paternalistic protection of the rural masses. He was inviting them to acknowledge the superior capacity of the bhadralok, to admit the legitimacy of nationalism, and to transform the political role of the Indian bureaucracy.

His plea fell on deaf ears. As he himself pointed out, he was merely restating in this note what the Moderate nationalists had been saying over and over again in the preceding twelve months. The Government of India had refused to acknowledge their appeals,[33] and once more it preserved a stony silence. In its opinion Lyon would have been better occupied in applying himself to the neglected task of restoring law and order in his province instead of trying to teach the Government of India its business.

The endorsement of Lyon's sentiments by Carmichael confirmed

[32] *Ibid.*, A225–232, Aug. 1917.
[33] See S. R. Mehrotra, *op. cit.*, p. 87.

Craddock and his school in their opinion that these two senior members of the Government of Bengal were fundamentally unreliable.[34] Earlier in 1916 the Government of India had even considered asking for their resignations because of what it regarded as their attempts to obstruct the proper handling of terrorism, and it was only in consideration of the fact that both were due to retire within a year that they had been left in office.[35] Craddock had already given his verdict on Carmichael's administration:

> Lord Carmichael's conciliatory policy and his efforts to meet the politicians at every turn has brought him some personal popularity but it has not had the smallest effect on anarchy. His affability to the extremist politicians and journalists may have secured some surface quiet, but it has not made the work of Government smoother. Under that policy anarchy has continued to grow and it was only when he was assisted by war legislation and able to take stern measures, that he secured a lull.[36]

Carmichael, a sad and disappointed man, gave his own verdict on his achievement. Writing on 2 September 1916 to his wife, who had returned to England because of illness, he said:

> I feel horribly sad today, though it is a lovely, lovely day. . . . ever since you went away I have been working very hard–it mayn't come to much, but I can, at any rate, claim I have worked really hard, and have never gone to bed without feeling dead tired, and it isn't always easy to get even a few minutes to do what one wants. I tell Gourlay [his secretary] it's like Grotius's epitaph '*Vitam perdidi operose nihil agendo*', but old Gourlay won't hear of the nothing and talks of casting bread on waters, etc. But all the same, India is for everyone a throwing away of work.[37]

THE NEW MEN

The departure of the two Liberals from the Bengal Government early in 1917 gave the Government of India its opportunity to inject some 'backbone' into the provincial administration. Lyon's place was taken by Sir Henry Wheeler, who had capped a brilliant secretariat career with service under Craddock as Home Secretary

[34] GI, Home Political, A225–232, Aug. 1917.
[35] *Ibid.*, A172, May 1916.
[36] Minute, 21 Feb. 1916, *ibid.*, A225–232, Aug. 1917.
[37] *Carmichael*, pp. 213–214.

to the Government of India from 1912.[38] The new Governor was the Earl of Ronaldshay, a 40-year-old Conservative member of Parliament who had travelled extensively in Asia and written a number of books on his experiences. He had served in India for a short period in 1900 as Curzon's aide-de-camp, and had returned in 1912 as a member of the Lothian Commission on the public services.[39]

These appointments perturbed the Bengal nationalists who feared a return to the reactionary policies of the partition period. They regarded a Curzonite and a Delhi secretariat man as unwelcome replacements for Liberals like Carmichael and Lyon, and Ronaldshay's arrival in Calcutta on 21 March 1917 was greeted with protests from the newspapers and political associations.[40] Ronaldshay recognised the need to mollify this hostility, and he took care in his first speeches to emphasise that he was approaching his new duties free from rigid preconceptions.[41]

Despite this denial, he did have well-formed ideas of the way in which he should act. He believed that the tasks facing his administration were twofold, the first being to advance the material welfare of the Bengali populace. He wrote:

> Previous acquaintance of the problems of rural India had taught me that the average Briton has a genius for assuming the role appropriately termed in India that of *ma-bap* (mother-father), when dealing with backward peoples, and I had little difficulty in deciding that the key-note of my policy so far as the great mass of the population were concerned, must be encouragement and support of the members of the numerous Public Services from the Indian Civil downwards. . . .

The second task was to deal with the Bengali intelligentsia with its predilection for terrorism. This he saw as a problem 'of far greater complexity as it was concerned with the psychology of a people–a people moreover whose history, traditions, modes of thought, philosophies and religions–whose whole outlook on life in short, differed profoundly from that of the West'. Ronaldshay saw terrorism as the product of a reaction against European institutions and values. He believed that it was inspired by a deep-seated fear

[38] For biographical details see *Who Was Who, 1941–1950* (London, 1951).
[39] For biographical details see obituary notice, *Proceedings of the British Academy, 1961* (London, 1961); and *Essayez*.
[40] *Nation in Making*, pp. 340–341; *Essayez*, p. 67; and NP, 30 Sept. 1916.
[41] *Essayez*, p. 68.

that in embracing an alien culture 'India was immolating her own soul'.[42]

There is a marked and significant contrast between his views and those Carmichael had expressed as he approached the same problems four years before. Carmichael had written: 'I conclude that we should do well if we assumed less often than we do that the Indian mind is entirely different from the European mind, and expected the Indian more often to be swayed by the same motives which actuate Englishmen'.[43] From this assumption he argued that a rational approach to Indians, an appeal to their innate liberalism and goodwill, would have beneficial results. Ronaldshay, working from a different assumption, argued differently. He held that it was pointless to reason with the terrorists because of the psychological gulf separating them from Englishmen. In the interests of orderly government, their anarchical activities could not be tolerated. The executive had a clear duty to stamp them out.

The executive's duty, as Ronaldshay saw it, was equally clear in another field, and to the same pragmatic end of orderly government. The administration and the legitimate political institutions should be developed along tested and well-understood lines, for this would guarantee the Government a stable and responsible body of Indian support. Ronaldshay had always believed that the logical outcome of the 1909 reforms was the development of a parliamentary system in India.[44] He was therefore amazed to discover when he arrived in Bengal that the Government of India still denied that this was the direction which constitutional advance should take. In a despatch to the Secretary of State a few months earlier it had written: 'We have no wish to develop the Councils as quasi-Parliaments'.[45]

SNAIL'S PACE

Events in India and Great Britain in 1916 had finally forced the Government of India to give serious consideration to the question of constitutional reforms. To the insistent demands of the Indian nationalists had been added the comments of an influential group of British public men, students of Imperial affairs, who had

[42] *Ibid.*, pp. 68–69 and 76. Cf. Lord Ronaldshay, *The Heart of Aryavarta: a Study of the Psychology of Indian Unrest* (London, 1925).

[43] Carmichael to Crewe, 14 May 1913, *Carmichael*, pp. 181–182.

[44] *Essayez*, pp. 81–83.

[45] Quoted *ibid.*, p. 82. Cf. Mehrotra, *op. cit.*, p. 86.

reached the conclusion that India had to be given some measure of self-government to qualify it for admission to the Imperial federation they advocated. This group, the Round Table as it called itself, was led by Lionel Curtis, a former administrator and politician in the Transvaal. It numbered among its members men who were well placed to influence the thinking of the British Cabinet, and others, such as the retired Sir William Duke, whose long Indian experience lent authority to the schemes of reform which they drafted.

The Government of India resented what it regarded as the interference of these men in Indian affairs,[46] but it also realised that unless it took some action itself it was in danger of losing the initiative to them. If this happened some 'reckless' scheme might be foisted upon it. Hardinge had already sketched out a plan of limited reforms. Lord Chelmsford, who succeeded him as Viceroy in April, 1916, was convinced that the British should define the aim of their rule in India, and he pressed his Government to agree to a declaration of policy. The Members conceded that some such gesture would be a fitting reward for India's loyal contribution to the British war effort.[47]

The deliberations went on throughout 1916, as the Government of India slowly and cautiously considered every possible aspect of a policy statement, without any apparent realisation that time was fast running out. As Lyon vainly tried to tell them in September, there was an urgent need for a bold and arresting declaration to save the situation in politically advanced regions like Bengal. The purpose of that declaration was to demonstrate the British desire to further Indian constitutional advance, to prove that they valued the loyal aspirations of the Moderate nationalists and were prepared to heed their requests, and to discount the assertion that concessions would only be made in the face of violent agitation. None of this would be achieved if the British hesitated too long, for by then Indian demands would have become extreme and any subsequent British action would appear to have been forced.

When Lyon wrote his minute of dissent in September there may have been just time enough to act. By the beginning of the new year it was too late, for in the closing months of 1916 the Extremists had been taken back into the National Congress, which had formed

[46] Secretary, Home Department, GI, to Chief Secretary, GB, 5 Mar. 1917, GB, Appointment, 18L–10(1–80), A93–172, May 1917.
[47] Mehrotra, *op. cit.*, pp. 82–85.

an alliance with the Muslim League with the purpose of extracting constitutional concessions from the British.

By December, 1916, the question of Indian reforms was already under discussion between the Government of India and the Secretary of State, but throughout they had obstinately refused to give any public indication of the direction in which they were moving.[48] And they were travelling at a snail's pace. It took them another eight months before they made their announcement. On 20 August 1917, Edwin Montagu, who had been appointed Secretary of State for India in the preceding month, rose in the House of Commons to state that

> The policy of His Majesty's Government, with which the Government of India are in complete accord, is that of increasing association of Indians in every branch of the administration, and the gradual development of self-governing institutions, with a view to the progressive realisation of responsible government in India as an integral part of the British Empire. They have decided that substantial steps in this direction should be taken as soon as possible . . . .[49]

BHADRALOK DISTRUST

The British had made their bold, arresting declaration, but for Bengal, at least, it had come a full year too late. The bhadralok politicians, frustrated by the limitations of the Morley-Minto councils and angered by the years of delay in securing as much as an acknowledgment of their demands for reforms, were no longer to be satisfied by a nicely phrased statement of British intentions. As early as June, 1917, a contributor to the *Modern Review* had written:

> . . . history is strewn with the graves of pious promises issuing in reactionary deeds. Ever since the foundation of British rule in India there has been a continued shower of utterances breathing sympathy with the final goal of Indian aspirations, but actually so little has been done that these utterances are now regarded merely as a convenient cloak, under which the task of preparing for freedom the subject races of India may continue to be the white man's pleasant burden for evermore.

[48] *Ibid.*, pp. 85–87.

[49] Parliamentary Debates, Great Britain, House of Commons, Fifth Series, Vol. XCVII, col. 1695–1696.

The same scepticism characterised Bengal press comment on Montagu's declaration in August. Attention was concentrated on the reservation contained in the second paragraph of his statement that progress toward self-government 'can only be achieved by successive stages' and that the British 'must be judges of the time and measure of each advance'. It was generally agreed that this qualification could be made the excuse for years of delay. Unless some definite time limit were fixed, there could be no certainty of the British ever fulfilling their promise. Similarly, although most papers were pleased that Montagu had accompanied the declaration with an announcement that he was personally coming to examine the situation in India, they feared that the Europeans, official and nonofficial, would dominate his thinking throughout his visit.[50] Even Surendranath Banerjea's vernacular paper, the *Bangali*, could summon only enough enthusiasm to remark: 'But we must rest content, as half a loaf is better than no loaf'.[51]

In Bengal the British had failed to restore faith in their good intentions. The bhadralok now watched with suspicion the developments that flowed from the August declaration, genuinely fearing that the 'pious promise would issue in reactionary deeds'. They expected the British to procrastinate and hedge before they gave anything. They predicted that the I.C.S. would contrive to build barriers into any scheme of reforms to protect its autocratic powers and that concessions would be made to reactionary groups, such as the European business community and the Muslims, to buttress British rule in India.[52] Nothing that happened during the three and a half years it took the British to frame a new constitution and get it working served to dispel these initial fears. To illustrate this point we shall examine the attitudes toward the reform proposals of the official and nonofficial Europeans in Bengal, and in the following chapter we shall consider the Bengal Muslims' position.

THE BENGAL OFFICIALS

In his memoirs, Ronaldshay recalled that Montagu's declaration 'caused considerable fluttering in the official dovecots in Simla and in those of the capitals of the Provinces. His further announce-

[50] NP, 1 Sept. 1917.
[51] *Bangali*, 22 Aug. 1917.
[52] Montagu, pp. 66–67; and NP, Sept.–Dec. 1917.

ment that he proposed coming to India *in propria persona* to gather material for the construction of the constitutional edifice of which he had visions, added to the fluttering a chorus of squawks'.[53] The I.C.S. distrusted Montagu, for he had notoriously radical ideas on Indian politics and administration, and was severely critical of the bureaucratic methods by which the country was governed. In the House of Commons, just a week before he entered the Cabinet as Secretary of State, he had attacked the Government of India as 'too wooden, too iron, too inelastic, too antediluvian'.[54] That such a man should now have responsibility for a major reconstruction of the Indian constitution was profoundly disturbing to the I.C.S.

In these circumstances it was some reassurance to the Bengal Civilians that they had Ronaldshay as Governor, for he fully recognised the difficulties and dangers that lay ahead in the period of readjustment, and he emphasised his determination to maintain a firm, conservative Government in his province to provide the bedrock on which experimental structures could be built with greater safety.

He already had Wheeler, an acknowledged strong man, as his second-in-command, and he appointed a former Chief Secretary, J. G. Cumming, to take special charge of the administration of the Defence of India Act. Shortly after his arrival he had made S. P. Sinha a Member of his Executive Council,[55] but when Sinha went to England in 1918, Ronaldshay appointed the leader of the Bengal great zamindars, the Maharajadhiraja of Burdwan, to fill his place. This brought a protest from Montagu, who wanted another nationalist politician included in the Bengal Government; but Ronaldshay refused to give way, arguing that he would have enough to do with politicians when the proposed reforms were implemented, while Burdwan would bring with him the support of Bengali conservatives.[56]

Cumming retired in 1920, and his portfolios of Justice and Jails were given to Sir Abdur Rahim, a Bengali Muslim judge of the Madras High Court who had served with Ronaldshay on the Lothian Commission.[57] A few months later the Executive Council was

[53] *Essayez*, p. 82.

[54] 12 July 1917, Parliamentary Debates, Great Britain, House of Commons, Fifth Series, Vol. XCV, col. 2205.

[55] For biographical details see DNB.

[56] *Essayez*, p. 133.

[57] For biographical details see *Who's Who in India, Burma and Ceylon, 1938* (Poona, 1938).

enlarged to four members, and the Chief Secretary, J. H. Kerr, a man of great vitality, was included as Finance Member. Thus throughout this period of uncertainty, Ronaldshay was able to provide himself with conservative subordinates of outstanding ability and experience who were a match for any of the Bengali nationalists with whom his Government had to deal.

For the Bengal officials, the Governor's conservatism was one element of security in an insecure situation. Another was the Viceroy's evident concern that the nationalists should not monopolise Montagu's attention while he was in India. In a private letter to Ronaldshay on 27 September 1917, Chelmsford wrote:

> It is all-important that the interests of every class, including those of the European and commercial communities, those of the landed aristocracy and those of people professing moderate and conservative opinions, as well as of people holding advanced opinions, should be represented before the Secretary of State and myself.
>
> If you find that any important classes or interests which ought to be moving in the matter are not alive to the position, I would suggest that you should point out to them the desirability of their taking steps to secure that their views receive proper consideration.[58]

This was music to the ears of the officials, and they busied themselves with the task of sorting out the right people for Montagu to meet. The names of 54 conservatives and moderates were suggested as a 'Rough list of persons who might be asked to see the Secretary of State'. We must see that the conservative men do not hold back', wrote the Governor's Secretary, W. R. Gourlay, emphatically.[59]

Montagu came to India in November, 1917, and for five months toured the subcontinent with Chelmsford. As a result of their enquiries, the two men presented a joint report to Parliament in July, 1918. It recommended a greater devolution of power by the Home Government to the Government of India, and by the Government of India to the provinces. It insisted that Indianisation of the services should proceed more rapidly. It suggested the enlargement of the legislatures, an extension of the franchise, and the transfer in the provinces of responsibility for some functions of government to Ministers responsible to the legislative councils.[60]

These proposals brought protests from the I.C.S. officers in Ben-

[58] GB, Appointment, 6R–1(17), B441–455, Mar. 1919.
[59] Gourlay to J. H. Kerr, 3 Oct. 1917, *ibid.*
[60] *Report on Indian Constitutional Reforms* (Calcutta, 1918).

gal, as in other parts of India. J. H. Kerr, Chief Secretary to the Bengal Government, wrote:

> Official opinion is, on the whole, frankly dubious as to the working of the scheme, and the most experienced administrators in this Presidency regard it with serious misgivings, even as a temporary measure during a transitional period. . . . there is a widespread feeling that the line of advance proposed in the Report is attended with even graver difficulties than are in fact admitted and that these may cause a serious breakdown. Whatever the intentions of the framers of the Report . . . it is apprehended that the scheme is bound, in practice, to lead, at any rate in the first instance, to the establishment of an oligarchy, the smooth working of which in conjunction with an official element of different traditions is at least problematical.[61]

This was the Bengal Civilians' greatest fear: that an immediate advance toward Responsible Government would mean the consolidation of power in the hands of the small group of bhadralok nationalist politicians, whose intentions they distrusted. What, they asked, would become of the I.C.S. tradition of protecting the weak and uplifting the impoverished if the members of the service had to obey the dictates of high-caste politicians? Closer to home, what security would an English officer have if his career were subject to Indian political control? In the higher branches of the administration they saw the danger of a disastrous collapse if politics were allowed to influence vital departments like police and justice.[62]

Montagu and Chelmsford had invited criticism of their proposals, and the Bengal Government made the most of the opportunity. It also began preparing its submissions for the two committees that were to tour India at the end of 1918 to consider schemes for a new franchise, and for the division of functions between the Government of India and the provincial Governments, and between the two branches proposed for the new provincial Governments.

The Bengal Civilians decided that their major effort should be directed toward securing a large extension of the franchise in the province, for this seemed to be the only possible means of preventing, or even mitigating the effects of, the monopolisation of power

[61] Kerr to Secretary, Home Department, GI, 15 Oct. 1918, *Government of India's Despatch of March 5th, 1919, and connected papers* (Calcutta, 1919), p. 194.

[62] *Ibid.*, pp. 194–213; and GB, Appointment, 6R–19(1–51), A8–58, Dec. 1918.

by the 'bhadralok oligarchy'. A broad electorate would ultimately enable the mass of the people to exert their rightful control over the administration of the transferred powers. The alternative, as far as the officials could see, was to acquiesce in the perpetuation of corrupt and self-indulgent bhadralok politics. 'I am aware that there are numerous objections to this proposal [for an extended electorate]', wrote the District Magistrate of Tipperah, D. H. Wares, 'but they will have to be faced ultimately, and the sooner this is done, the better it will be for the country'.[63] Wares' superiors in the provincial government were of the same opinion, and they accepted this as the guideline in formulating their reform proposals.

The practical limitation to the extension of the franchise was the machinery available to prepare electoral registers and poll votes. Inevitably most of this burden would have to be borne by the district and subdivisional officers as an addition to their normal duties. Previously they had had to handle no more than a few hundred voters at each election, but now the electors would be numbered in thousands and the majority would be illiterate. The officers would be unable to turn for guidance to the experience of their fellow administrators in other colonial territories, for this was the first time in the history of the British Colonial Empire that an attempt had been made to form a mass electorate.

The Government of Bengal refused to be discouraged by these formidable obstacles, and, to the dismay of the Government of India, it proposed an increase in the number of voters from the nine thousand registered to elect the old councils, to an estimated one and a half million.[64] The bulk of these would be in rural areas, where the main franchise qualification would be the annual payment of a minimum of one rupee in cess. The provincial government explained that, unless the qualification were kept as low as this, even well-to-do cultivators would be excluded and Hindu voters would greatly outnumber the Muslims, in spite of the general numerical superiority of the latter.

> The importance of this consideration will be somewhat qualified if separate Muhammadan electorates are created [wrote the Government committee on electorates], but even so, it is necessary to

[63] Wares to Chief Secretary, GB, 10 May 1918, GB, Appointment, 18L–6 (1–83), A1–83, Oct. 1918.

[64] GB, Appointment, 6R–34(1–2), A1–2, Aug. 1919. This proved to be a considerable overestimate. (See Simon Commission, Vol. VIII, p. 130.)

> have a fairly numerous electorate in order to prevent corruption and also in order to give a wide body of Muhammadans a political education which will enable them to hold their own when communal representation is abolished.[65]

The Montagu-Chelmsford report had recommended that the Muslims be given separate electorates only where they had a minority of voters, but the provincial government insisted that the Bengal Muslims be given communal representation throughout the province to safeguard them against the domination of Hindu landlords and moneylenders. The Hindu backward classes should be provided for by nomination. In an attempt to lessen the influence of the bhadralok stronghold, Calcutta, which the Government regarded as 'tending to swamp all else' in the political life of the province, it proposed to give the city only three general seats (two Hindu and one Muslim) and to prevent carpet-bagging by insisting upon a residential qualification for candidates.[66]

The Franchise Committee accepted the Government of Bengal's recommendations for a wide franchise and for separate communal electorates for the Muslims throughout the province. It yielded to bhadralok pressure, however, and opposed the suggested residential qualification for candidates. It also recommended eight seats for Calcutta and an additional five seats for the neighbouring areas of the Presidency Division. The Government of Bengal prepared figures to show that if this were done the city would be 'absurdly over-represented',[67] but its protest was ignored and it had to make the best of a bad job by organising the Calcutta Hindu constituencies in such a way as to ensure that minority groups, such as the Marwaris, secured representation.[68]

The reports of the Franchise and Subjects Committees were published in February, 1919, and in the same month a Cabinet committee was appointed to prepare the Government of India Bill for its introduction to Parliament on 29 May. It was then submitted to a Joint Select Committee, which spent three months examining witnesses and drafting amendments. The bill had its third reading in both Houses in December, 1919, and received the royal assent on the 23rd of that month.

[65] 5 June 1918, GB, Appointment, 6R–25 (1–59), A94–152, Dec. 1918.
[66] PP, 1919 [Cmd. 141], Vol. XVI, pp. 614–616; and GB, *ibid.*
[67] GB, Appointment, 6R–34(1–2), A1–2, Aug. 1919.
[68] *Ibid.*, 6R–75(1–142), A232–373, June 1920.

There was only one task left before the new constitution could be inaugurated: rules had to be framed for the reformed councils. This was the officials' last chance to protect their powers. The Bengal Government took its stand on the proposition that the British parliamentary model should not be applied to Bengal without modification, so that a large area of government might be left free from political interference. For this reason, it had favoured an Executive Council with a majority of European members, and it now rejected the Joint Select Committee's recommendation that a British parliamentarian should be brought out to preside over the Legislative Council.[69] It also opposed Montagu's suggestion for the appointment of Council Secretaries to fulfil the functions of British Parliamentary Under-Secretaries in assisting members of the Government with their departmental duties and representing them in the legislature. 'We strongly objected to it', explained the Chief Secretary, H. L. Stephenson, 'on the ground that there was no analogy between the conditions of Parliament at home and the Legislative Council here'.[70] Obviously what the officials found unpalatable was the thought of a politician being pitchforked into their tidy bureaucracy. 'I think there will be endless confusion', grumbled Wheeler, 'if the Council Secretary came, in any way as a cog in the Secretariat machine'.[71]

On looking back over this narrative of the part played in the reforms discussions by the Bengal officials, it will be seen that there was nothing that might have served to restore bhadralok faith in the beneficence of British intentions. The civilians were concerned throughout to safeguard their powers, just as the bhadralok press had predicted they would be, and they had made no attempt to conceal their animus for the bhadralok. This had led them to advocate separate communal electorates for the Muslims, a restricted representation for Calcutta, and a greatly extended franchise which, they hoped, would undercut the bhadralok nationalists by confronting them with the dilemma of having to appeal in parliamentary terms to an electorate that did not understand those terms. They obviously had no desire to see a parliamentary system developed in India, and could be expected to oppose a further transfer of power to Indians. They, at least, had fully justified the bhadralok's suspicions.

[69] *Ibid.*, 6R–2(1–8), A3–10, Apr. 1920.
[70] Minute, 29 Aug. 1920, *ibid.*, 6R–36(1), A1025B.
[71] Minute, 12 Aug. 1920, *ibid.*

THE EUROPEAN NONOFFICIALS

So, too, had the European nonofficials. As a small community with large vested interests in Indian commerce, they were greatly alarmed by the initial proposals for the establishment of parliamentary institutions in India. Up to this time they had relied upon their personal contacts with senior members of the I.C.S., with Governors and Viceroys, and with civil servants and politicians in London to maintain their considerable privileges. Knowing that real power lay with the Home Government and with the officials in India, and confident of their ability to influence their decisions, the British nonofficials had been able to disregard the legislative councils or, at best, to treat them with an air of amused tolerance. Service as a European representative in a legislative council had been regarded as an irksome distraction from the important business of money-making, and twelve months as a member was generally considered to be all that a man could be asked to devote to such unprofitable work.[72] That the Indian nationalists resented this cavalier attitude and regarded the community's privileged access to the Government as evidence of racial discrimination did not trouble the Europeans, for they were secure in the knowledge that the Indians could do nothing about it.

This security depended upon the maintenance of the existing arrangement, with the officials holding real power and according their nonofficial compatriots a preferential hearing. This explains why the British nonofficial community had been so perturbed by the reunification of Bengal and the transfer of the Imperial capital to Delhi in 1912. These moves were a response to Indian pressure, and, worse still, they had been kept secret with the express purpose of preventing the European nonofficials from exercising their normal influence on the decision.[73] The *Statesman*, in a revealing leading article, had described this as a violation of India's 'Constitution'. 'In the interests of commerce it is essential that the English public should know that India is not wholly subject to the caprices of a one-eyed bureaucracy', it wrote, 'that public opinion here insists on being consulted, and that the recent irregular and irresponsible proceedings have been vigorously challenged'.[74]

[72] In the period 1913–1920 the two Bengal Chamber of Commerce seats in the Bengal Legislative Council had eleven occupants.

[73] Lord Hardinge, *My Indian Years, 1910–1916* (London, 1948), pp. 38–50.

[74] *Statesman*,* 2 Feb. 1912.

Montagu's declaration in August, 1917, was even more alarming. Again it was a response to Indian demands, and this time the whole system seemed to be in danger. If parliamentary institutions were established, with a government responsible to a representative body, the old methods of confidential access and influence would have to give way to 'sordid' political negotiations.

Worse still, power would be transferred from British officials to the very Indians who were most antagonistic to the privileges of European commerce. A Calcutta businessman, commenting on Lionel Curtis' reform proposals earlier in 1917, had voiced his community's fears:

> You propose to destroy a Government in which British Commerce trusts, and to put in its place one in which British Commerce cannot trust.
>
> If you destroy the present Government you must put something in its place which will ensure that our Interests are safeguarded as at present, and that we are not placed at the mercy of Bengali Zemindars and Lawyers, and I am satisfied that you are attempting an impossibility.[75]

How could this disaster of bhadralok domination be averted now that Montagu had made his 'rash promise' of concessions? The European community saw two possible means. First, they would impress upon British opinion at home the dangers of establishing a parliamentary system in India. Second, they would frame a scheme of limited reforms which would stop short of a transfer of power from the provincial and Imperial Governments.

Their newspapers immediately launched a campaign to demonstrate how the interests of the British Empire in India and of the great mass of Indians would suffer if the misguided schemes of British radicals were accepted. In an article in the *Calcutta Review* of October, 1917, entitled 'The Evacuation of Asia', 'Brit' wrote:

> It is, of course, popular government that our British progressive proffers. But I am afraid it is something rather different that the educated, moneyed, landed Indian wants—it is not government '*by* the people' he wants; it is government *of* the people, *by* the educated, moneyed and landed classes *for*—themselves! It is a House of Lords he wants, but not a House of Commons; it is oligarchy, hierarchy, plutocracy he aims at, and not democracy. He is in a

[75] L. Curtis, *Papers Relating to the Application of the Principle of Dyarchy to the Government of India* (London, 1920), p. 161.

> hurry for autonomy, but his progress in democracy will be slower than ever. Zemindar and mandarin–it is only a difference of a letter, and (looking easterly for an illustration) it is mandarin-rule he wants.[76]

When Montagu and Chelmsford came to Calcutta at the beginning of December, the three European organisations–the Bengal Chamber of Commerce, the Calcutta Trades Association, and the European Association–put forward similar proposals for limited reforms. They emphasised that in their opinion the time was not ripe for constitutional changes of any kind, but that if the Government were determined to press ahead it must avoid 'experiments on a large scale that might mean large disaster'. Reforms should be limited to the development of local self-government, the extension of the legislatures as advisory councils, and provincial and local decentralisation. It was stressed that British nonofficial representation in the legislative councils should be maintained and that any suggestion of establishing responsible government at that stage was absurd.

> The European Association desires to state, definitely and deliberately, its opinion that a grant of anything approaching self-government to India at the present time would be utterly disastrous to the real interests of the country and a grave injustice to her peoples. It would place the many of the lower castes under the heel of the few of the higher castes, and could only impair the British tradition in India, that tie between the British and Indian peoples to which the lower castes look for their ultimate emancipation, and by which alone the future advancement of India can best be secured.[77]

In his interviews with the associations' representatives, Montagu urged that the British nonofficials should in future take part in politics and 'rest their claim to protection on the vindication of their case to the Indian people rather than for ever on the Government of India'.[78] This did nothing to reassure the community. Nor did the prominence given in the joint report to the need for a less exclusive racial spirit among the British in India.[79] It was adding insult to injury, the Calcutta European press asserted angrily, to conclude the document with an appeal to the Europeans for a sympathetic

[76] *Calcutta Review*, new series, No. 290, Oct. 1917, pp. 367–368.
[77] PP, 1918, [Cd. 9178], Vol. XVIII, pp. 495–498 and 508–509.
[78] Montagu, p. 80.
[79] *Report on Indian Constitutional Reforms* (Calcutta, 1918), pp. 218–219.

acceptance of Indian aspirations so that the proposed reforms might be a success. 'Statesmen who make a rash promise without consulting public opinion have no right to call upon the whole world to co-operate cordially in extricating them out of the thicket into which they have jumped', growled the *Statesman*.[80]

Montagu and Chelmsford were accused of riding roughshod over the British community in an effort to win the applause of a small group of self-interested Indians. It was asserted that their proposed reforms would leave the vital interests of British commerce unprotected and ruin the I.C.S. by placing it at the mercy of corrupt politicians.[81] The *Englishman* demanded that the report of the Rowlatt Committee, which had just concluded enquiries into the extent of seditious conspiracy in India, be widely distributed in England, for it 'is a necessary antidote to the easy nonchalance and frequent irresponsibility of the Chelmsford-Montagu proposals; it serves the purpose of a sign of warning upon a dangerous road'.[82]

On 2 October 1918 the Bengal Chamber of Commerce met to pass judgment on the joint report. Its president, W. A. Ironside, voiced the indignation of his community:

> Never before in the history of this Chamber have its members assembled together at a more momentous occasion, seldom perhaps in the history of the world has any community in similar circumstances, small in numbers yet vast in interests, been asked to face a future which presents to all sane, steady-thinking men of our community such far-reaching possibilities for evil to the country and its people.[83]

Despite their anger, the British nonofficials now realised that a reconstruction was coming, and that they had to concern themselves with the form it would take and with evolving new methods of action by which they could maintain their political influence. With this realisation came the opportunity for more moderate voices to gain a hearing. By the last quarter of 1918, the European journals were willing to devote space to articles deploring the earlier alarmism and calling for a positive effort to work with moderate Indians to make the reforms a success.[84] Similarly, there was a note-

[80] *Statesman*, 12 July 1918.
[81] *Ibid.*, 16 July 1918, *Englishman*, 8 and 9 July 1918.
[82] *Englishman*, 25 Sept. 1918; and *ibid.*, 6 Aug. 1918.
[83] GB, Appointment, 6R–18(1–10), A10–19, Mar. 1919.
[84] E.g., *Calcutta Review*, new series, No. 294, Oct. 1918, pp. 439–446; and *Capital*, 14 Feb. 1919.

worthy change of spirit in the European representations before the Franchise and Subjects Committees, although again there was a demand for safeguards: weighted representation for the community in the legislative councils, and the retention of powers of law and order in the hands of British Governors.[85]

At the annual meeting of the European Association in March, 1919, the president, P. L. Buckland, called for a new attitude of respect for the legislative councils. He observed that the reforms would give them increased power, in view of which the British nonofficials would have to take them more seriously than in the past. In particular, they would have to find representatives who were willing to devote their full attention to their legislative duties, and he suggested establishing a fund to pay their salaries.[86]

Under the reforms act passed at the end of the year, the Europeans were given a large representation (almost a sixth of all elected seats) in the provincial Legislative Council, and in the Imperial Legislative Assembly and Council of State.[87] Although they protested that this was inadequate and grumbled at having been 'more or less ignored' in the reforms discussions, they saw clearly enough that their political future now depended upon the ability of their representatives to form alliances with Indian groups in the legislatures and thus maintain the community's advantages.

Speaking in the Bengal Legislative Council on 3 February 1920 to a motion expressing the members' gratitude at the passage of the Government of India Act, R. M. Watson-Smyth, a representative of the Bengal Chamber of Commerce, said that the time had come 'for the British mercantile community to put their cards on the table'. Although they still thought 'that the time was not ripe for the introduction into India of a form of government on western democratic lines', and although they had not been given a fair hearing when the Government of India Bill was being discussed, he said, they were now willing to work the reforms 'without recrimination and with no illwill'.

> . . . to the moderates I say stretch out your hand and we will take it. Ask for our co-operation and you shall have it and you and

[85] GB, Appointment, 6R–18(1–10), A10–19, Mar. 1919; and *Evidence taken before the Reforms Committee (Franchise)* (Calcutta, 1919), Vol. II, pp. 426–427.

[86] *Bengalee*, 15 Mar. 1919.

[87] PP, 1920, [Cmd. 812], Vol. XXXV.

> we will then tackle this problem of reforms and turn the Bill into something for which thanks are really due—something to the great benefit of the people and to the lasting good of this mighty Empire of India which is both yours and ours.[88]

The bhadralok members could surely be excused the display of disgust with which they greeted this 'magnanimous' offer of co-operation.[89] The European nonofficials had changed their tune only when the pressure of circumstances and considerations of their own self-interest had forced them to do so. It could scarcely be credited that they had any genuine sympathy for bhadralok aspirations after having attacked the group so bitterly.

Throughout the reforms debate the European nonofficials had hit the bhadralok at their most sensitive points. They had denied Indian equality with their own race and declared India unfit for parliamentary institutions—'the time was not ripe for the introduction into India of a form of government on western democratic lines'. They had denounced the bhadralok's professed desire for constitutional advance as a subterfuge to gain selfish power—'it is not government "*by* the people" he wants; it is government *of* the people, *by* the educated, moneyed and landed classes *for*—themselves!' They had explicitly stated that the bhadralok could not be trusted to uphold justice between communities if India were granted self-government. 'It would place the many of the lower castes under the heel of the few of the higher castes, and could only impair the British tradition in India'. And all the time they had been using their fund of backstair influence and their vituperative press to restrict the degree of change so that their own privileged position might be maintained.

The effect of such opposition on the bhadralok's trust in the promises of the Imperial Government is too obvious to need elaboration. How could they believe that the British really intended to do for India what they had done for the white empire when the British nonofficial community in Calcutta was talking so arrogantly of Indian inferiority and when it was given such a disproportionate share of the legislative representation? How could they believe that liberal, constitutional methods of political action would be sufficient to secure real power from the British when this influential group was obviously prepared to use any device to maintain its

[88] BLCP, Vol. LII, pp. 63–64.
[89] *Ibid.*, pp. 64 and 66.

position in India? The British had been asked to give proof that they meant what they said, and this is what they had produced. 'Tall talk and low performances may be amongst the many and varied privileges of Englishmen', remarked Fazlul Huq bitterly, 'but do they seriously realize what the verdict of history is likely to be on the achievements of their own countrymen in India?'[90]

[90] Presidential address, All-India Muslim League session, Delhi, 30 Dec. 1918. Azizul Huq collection.

III

THE VOTE OR VIOLENCE

THE LUCKNOW PACT

When putting forward his constitutional reform scheme in July, 1915, Surendranath Banerjea had emphasised the advantage of Hindus and Muslims making a united demand. At the time he was writing, there seemed a reasonable chance of some agreement between the leaders of the two communities in Bengal.

The anger of the Bengal Muslims with the Government at the reunification of the province had been reinforced at the end of 1914 by their concern over Turkey's alliance with Germany in the war against England. Indian Muslims accepted the Sultan of Turkey, the Khalifa, as the leader of all Islam, and the fact that he was now at war with Great Britain imposed a severe strain on their loyalty to the British raj, especially as Pan-Islamic sentiment was then unusually strong.

In January, 1915, Khwaja Salimulla, Nawab of Dacca, the most intransigent of Bengal's old-guard Muslims, died, and many of those involved in the succession struggle that followed[1] were younger bhadralok Muslims like Fazlul Huq who spoke the same political language as the Hindu nationalists. In the twelve months following Salimulla's death, these men gained control of the Bengal Presidency Muslim League, with Fazlul Huq as Secretary.[2] Responding to the appeals from the Bengal Congressmen for a Hindu-Muslim alliance to secure constitutional concessions, they now offered their com-

[1] Carmichael to Crewe, 25 Feb. 1915, *Carmichael*, p. 204.
[2] GB, Political, lists of office-bearers of recognised associations, 1915–1916.

munity a new political strategy. The best future for the Bengal Muslims, as they saw it, lay in a nationalist alliance with the Hindu bhadralok against the common enemy, the British. The aim was to wrest power from the British; this power was then to be divided according to a prearranged scheme which would give the Muslims their fair share.

On this basis Fazlul Huq and his men entered into a series of negotiations with Congressmen and Muslim Leaguers from other provinces which produced a reform scheme jointly adopted by the Indian National Congress and the All-India Muslim League at Lucknow in December, 1916. The Lucknow Pact, as this was called, was based on a memorial presented to the Viceroy in October, 1916, by nineteen nonofficial members of the Imperial Legislative Council, calling for Representative Government and Dominion Status for India. To secure Muslim support, clauses were added at Lucknow providing separate electorates for the Muslims and giving Legislative Councillors the right to veto legislation affecting their own community. In addition, the proportion of seats the Muslims should have in each of the provincial councils was detailed, and in five of the seven provinces they were accorded considerable overrepresentation on the principle that the minority community should have weightage. On the same principle, the Hindus were to be overrepresented in the councils of the two Muslim majority provinces, the Punjab and Bengal.[3]

The Lucknow Pact was a remarkable diplomatic victory for the Muslim League and it was hailed as such by the Muslim press, except in Bengal where the concessions on Hindu representation in the local Legislative Council were denounced as a betrayal of the community's interests. By population the Bengal Muslims were entitled to 52.6 percent of the Council seats, but the Lucknow Pact would give them only 40 percent.[4] There was great anger at those who had agreed to such disadvantageous terms. The bhadralok Muslim

[3] Simon Commission, Vol. IV, pp. 138–140.

[4] How badly the Bengal Muslims had fared compared with Muslims in other provinces can be judged from the following figures (*ibid.*, p. 139):

(1) Province	(2) Muslim Percentage of Population	(3) Muslim Percentage of Total Legislative Seats	(4) Percentage (3) of (2)
Bengal	52.6	40.0	76.0
Bihar and Orissa	10.5	25.0	238.0
Bombay	20.4	33.3	163.0

Leaguers were accused of selling out the Muslim community to the Hindus, and there was a reaction against collaboration. 'Those who apprehend that the Moslems will suffer political death if they do not unite with the Hindus are greatly mistaken', declaimed a Calcutta Urdu daily, *Resalat*. 'We have already stood alone 1300 years. What is wanted is that we should firmly abide by our religious laws and not become fainthearted'.[5]

It was on this issue that debate among the Bengal Muslim politicians turned in 1917. The supporters of the Congress-League Pact insisted that the first aim of all Indians should be to force the British to yield power, while its opponents maintained that the protection of communal interests was the paramount duty of Muslim leaders. Montagu's declaration in August, bringing as it did the need for action, only added to the acrimony of the dispute.

THE REJECTION OF THE PACT

It was settled quite suddenly, however, by communal rioting in Bihar late in the following month. When the Muslims of Shahabad District attempted to perform their traditional cow sacrifice on the Baqr-Id, they were attacked by Hindus. The nature and extent of the rioting that followed—more fierce and prolonged than any that had occurred previously in British times—suggested a premeditated attempt on the part of the local Hindus to put an end to cow sacrifice in the District.[6]

This had serious repercussions on communal relations in neighbouring areas of northern India. In Bengal, where excitement was already running high at the prospect of constitutional reforms, Muslim politicians hurled the accusation of treachery at their Hindu opposites. Here, they declaimed, was an example of the use to which the Hindus would put any power they could wring from the British. This was a foretaste of Hindu raj.[7] All thoughts of collaboration were drowned in a wave of communal bitterness, and the old religious animosity of the two communities was swept to the surface.

Central Provinces	4.3	15.0	349.0
Madras	6.5	15.0	231.0
Punjab	54.8	50.0	91.0
United Provinces	14.0	50.0	214.0

[5] *Resalat*, 17 Apr. 1917.

[6] Simon Commission, Vol. IV, pp. 97–98.

[7] NP, Oct. 1917.

'In the West religion and politics can be separated but in the East never', declared the *Sadaqat*.[8]

In this atmosphere of recrimination, the Bengal Muslims set about drawing up their submissions on constitutional reform for Montagu and Chelmsford. There had already been a number of defections from the ranks of the provincial Muslim League of those who repudiated the Lucknow Pact. Some of the defectors joined the Central National Mahommedan Association,[9] a Calcutta organisation of long standing that had formerly concerned itself primarily with Muslim education, and others formed a new body, the Indian Moslem Association.[10] Both drew up memorials rejecting the Lucknow Pact and demanding a more generous legislative representation for the Bengal Muslims. The spirit of their submissions was characterised by the concluding sentence of the Central National Mahommedan Association's address: 'For England now to place the Indian Moslems, without proper, definite, and ample safeguards, under the heels of a hostile non-Moslem majority, would, your humble memoralists venture respectfully to submit, be a cruel act of breach of faith and violation of trust'.[11]

In the provincial Muslim League the supporters of the pact were now unchallenged, but they were uncomfortably aware of the unpopularity of the pact's provisions for Bengal and the consequent danger for them of being left out on a limb. They attempted to save themselves by advocating a modification of the scheme to give the Bengal Muslims 50 percent of the Council seats,[12] and, with the assistance of some United Provinces members of the League, they started a new Urdu daily in Calcutta to support the scheme in this modified form.[13]

Thus when Montagu and Chelmsford came to Calcutta in December, 1917, the three Muslim associations were united in their opposition to the representation provisions of the Lucknow Pact and all were demanding more generous treatment for their community.

Montagu had little sympathy with this demand. He believed that constitutional protection for minorities, particularly for large

[8] *Sadaqat*, 22 Nov. 1917.
[9] *Octennial Report of the Central National Mahommedan Association, 1917–1924* (Calcutta, 1925), pp. 5–6.
[10] *Mohammadi*, 2 Nov. 1917; and *Tirmizee*, 25 Nov. 1917.
[11] PP, 1918, [Cd. 9178], Vol. XVIII, pp. 498–499.
[12] NP, Nov. 1917.
[13] *Sadaqat*, 24 Nov. 1917.

minorities like the Muslims, encouraged their separatist tendencies, and at the same time discouraged them from making the effort to stand on their own feet in politics. He was eager to do away with communal electorates, but reluctantly discarded this idea when he realised the strain that such a reversal of British policy would impose on Muslim loyalty.[14] In the joint report published in July, 1918, he did make it clear, however, that he disapproved of communal representation in principle, and emphasised that he would not agree to its extension, or even to its maintenance in any province where the Muslims formed a majority of the voters.[15]

The Bengal Muslim leaders were aghast at the implications of this for their community. If the British accepted the provisions of the Lucknow Pact as a fair basis for the distribution of seats in the new legislative councils, the Bengal Muslims would not be given a representation proportionate to their over-all numerical majority, and yet, if Montagu had his way, that majority would be made the excuse for depriving them of their separate electorates. There were vehement protests from the political associations.[16]

FAILURE AND VIOLENCE

The Bengal Muslims were indeed in a serious position. At this crisis in Indian constitutional development, with the future of their community hanging in the balance, they were faced with the failure of both courses of political action they had pursued in the preceding decade.

The first of these, which had been evolved in the period of the partition agitation and the Morley-Minto reforms, was the Dacca Nawab's method of dependence upon the British Imperial rulers. This had survived the shock of 1911 only because Carmichael had been willing to include the Nawab and his men in his entourage, and to enable them as courtiers to secure some patronage for their community.[17] Despite this, they no longer had its united backing,

[14] Montagu, pp. 68, 100, and 115.

[15] *Report on Indian Constitutional Reforms* (Calcutta, 1918), pp. 147–149.

[16] E.g., see Honorary Secretary, Central National Mahommedan Association, to Chief Secretary, GB, 12 Sept. 1918, GI, Home Public (Reforms), Deposit 15, July 1919.

[17] E.g., Shamsul Huda's insistence that the proportion of Muslims in government service be raised resulted in the issue of a circular to subordinate offices instructing that no qualified Muslim candidate should be rejected in favour of a better qualified Hindu until one-third of all posts in Bengal were held by Muslims. (GB, Appointment, 4M–4(1–2), A30–31, Sept. 1917.)

and after Nawab Salimulla's death in January, 1915, the Government felt that there was no Muslim leader on whom it could fully rely for an expression of the community's views.[18] The old rapport was destroyed. A year later Carmichael and Lyon left the Bengal Government, and their successors were less willing to show favouritism to the Muslims.[19] Shamsul Huda's term on the Executive Council expired in June, 1917, and his seat was given to the Hindu bhadralok lawyer, S. P. Sinha, the immediate past-president of the Indian National Congress. The Bengal Muslims had lost their spokesmen at court.

The timing could not have been worse, for in August, 1917, Montagu made his declaration on Indian self-government. The destruction of the consultative system and its replacement with a parliamentary structure, which the old-guard Muslim politicians had always feared, seemed imminent; and at this moment when it was most important for them to be able to influence British decisions, they had lost their channels of confidential access to the Government. The disastrous consequences of this seemed to be foreshadowed in the opposition of the Montagu-Chelmsford report to the provision of separate communal electorates in Muslim majority areas.

The other method of political action which had been tried and found wanting by July, 1918, was collaboration with the Hindu bhadralok, as advocated by Fazlul Huq and his nationalist Muslims. Their confidence that a Hindu-Muslim alliance would force the British to yield power was shown by subsequent events to have been fully justified. This, however, had proved a doubtful blessing, for in negotiating the Lucknow Pact the Bengal Muslim politicians had failed to secure a sufficiently large slice of the new powers to satisfy their own community, and the resultant unacceptable settlement had been adopted by Montagu and Chelmsford as the basis for their reconstruction of the legislatures. Thus an arrangement that was originally intended to safeguard the Bengal Muslims had, by July, 1918, come to be regarded by that community as the gravest threat to their position in the impending constitutional resettlement.

Faced with this alarming failure of their efforts, the politicians were at a loss for constructive suggestions. Throughout July and

[18] Carmichael to Crewe, 25 Feb. 1915, *Carmichael*, p. 204; and Ronaldshay to Chelmsford, 9 Oct. 1918, GI, Home Public, Deposit 36, Apr. 1919.

[19] See GB, Appointment, 4M–4(1–2), A30–31, Sept. 1917.

August, 1918, they talked despairingly of the 'political extinction' of their community. They accused the British and the Hindu bhadralok of a desire to cripple its strength, and they accused one another of treachery.[20]

There could have been no worse moment for such a display of weakness, for the Muslim community in Bengal needed the reassurance of firm leadership. Among its educated members, the unwelcome tone of the Montagu-Chelmsford report and the increasingly extreme demands of the Hindu nationalists were the cause of grave anxiety. To the orthodox Muslims, the defeats suffered by Turkey and the widely credited rumours that Britain intended to depose the Khalifa were the cause of deep concern,[21] while the mass of the community was suffering from the effects of a bad harvest, heavy flooding due to an early monsoon, and extraordinarily high prices for cotton goods. Added to all this were the ravages of the great influenza epidemic, which had struck Bengal in July, 1918.[22]

With this general unrest and a demoralised leadership, the community was an easy prey for extremist agitators, and a group of such men were on hand to take advantage of the opportunity. Their leaders were three non-Bengalis—a Punjabi, Habib Shah; a Madrasi, Kalami; and a Bihari, Fazlur Rahman—whose chief influence was among the Urdu-speaking immigrant community of Calcutta: the Muslim traders, manufacturers, and lower-class factory labourers.[23]

Throughout 1918 these men had been looking for a chance to stir up trouble and they saw September as their best opportunity, for in that month the Muslim Baqr-Id would coincide with the Hindu Durga Puja. Such a concurrence of religious festivals always brought the likelihood of communal disorder and, with bitter memories of the previous year's rioting in Bihar still fresh in Muslim minds, the situation on this occasion promised to be unusually explosive.

The Muslim press was busy whipping up discontent. The Bihar riots were frequently mentioned, with heavy underscoring of the moral: 'The Moslems should be on their guard in time this year'.[24] Hoarders were blamed for the prohibitive price of cotton goods, and the finger of accusation was pointed at the Marwaris.

[20] NP, July–Aug. 1918.
[21] *Ibid.*
[22] *Census of India, 1921*, Vol. V, pt. 1, pp. 30–31; and BLCP, Vol. L, *passim.*
[23] *Essayez*, pp. 112–113.
[24] *Mohammadi*, 6 Sept. 1918.

This money-lending Jain community, which came from the Rajputana states, had established itself in force in Calcutta in the preceding decade.[25] In trade its members worked in closely knit family groups, and, with their flair for a good speculation combined with a large measure of unscrupulous dealing, they had quickly secured an important position in Bengal commerce. Communally exclusive and religiously ultraorthodox, they kept aloof from both the Muslims and Hindus in Bengal, which did nothing to dispel the jealousy and mistrust which their rapid success had engendered. They offended the Muslims, in particular, by their deep aversion to cow slaughter, and it was an unfortunate accident of geography that threw together large numbers of both communities in the overcrowded lanes around Burra Bazar in central Calcutta. By August, 1918, the Marwaris of this area were aware of the hostility surrounding them, and, fearing looting of their warehouses should rioting break out in September, they imported up-country guards. This was noted with disfavour in the Bengali press.[26]

The situation was perfect for the Muslim agitators. All they had to do was to strike the spark that would ignite this tinder. Habib Shah was the incendiary. At the beginning of August, in his Urdu paper, *Naqqash*, he took exception to a paragraph published a few days earlier in the *Indian Daily News*, on the ground that it contained an offensive reference to the prophet Muhammad. This created a furor. The other Muslim papers joined the *Naqqash* in its attack, and on 4 August the Bengal Presidency Muslim League called upon the Government to institute proceedings against the editor of the *Indian Daily News*. At a public meeting six days later there was wild talk of a holy war against the infidel, and it was decided to call an all-India gathering of Muslims in Calcutta for 8 and 9 September to consider the religious and political future of the community. 'At this moment, Moslems are being attacked from all sides,' wrote the *Naqqash*. 'They say that their feelings are hurt by everybody. But the mere expression of such a sentiment will not stop the mouths of the enemies of Islam. Practical steps should be taken. They should act on the motto, iron must be hammered by iron'.[27]

[25] *Census of India, 1921*, Vol. V, pt. 1, pp. 132–133; and Vol. VI, pt. 1, p. 32.
[26] NP, July–Aug. 1918.
[27] *Naqqash*, 15 Aug. 1918.

Moderate Muslim politicians were becoming alarmed by the trend of events, but they were reluctant to denounce the agitators publicly lest this endanger their personal popularity and in some way favour their rivals. They became a little more resolute when they found themselves excluded by the extremists from the reception committee formed after the meeting of 10 August to organise the following month's demonstration; but even then they would risk nothing more than a confidential appeal to the Government to prohibit the rally.

The Government of Bengal was slow to recognise the gravity of the situation. It handled the affair of the *Indian Daily News* ineptly and provided much ammunition for the Muslim press before the Government of India intervened to persuade the *Daily News* editor to publish an apology. Ronaldshay was absent from Calcutta, and not until his return at the end of August did his Government consider the matter of the all-India rally. Twelve Muslim leaders were then called to discuss the question with the Executive Council. The representatives of the reception committee denied any intention of fomenting trouble, but their moderate opponents accused them of deceit and favoured cancelling the gathering. At Ronaldshay's request, the reception committee met that evening to reconsider its decision, but it used the occasion as an excuse to heap abuse on the heads of the moderates for what it described as their collusion with the Government.

In the meantime, there had been much inflammatory writing in the Muslim press, and a number of religious leaders had arrived in Calcutta from other parts of northern India. On 4 September the Government banned the gathering, ordered the visitors to leave Bengal, and stopped the publication of *Naqqash* and a number of other Muslim papers. The reception committee, in defiance of the order, went ahead with its arrangements.

Most of the moderates were now thoroughly frightened, and some went so far as to request police protection. An exception was Fazlul Huq. For ten days from 26 August he had been absent in Bombay attending the special sessions of the Congress and the Muslim League called to consider the Montagu-Chelmsford report, and on his return he had been confined to bed with a fever. As soon as he recovered, he made an effort to ensure that the Government's order would be obeyed. Speaking to a meeting of the reception committee on the evening of 7 September, he persuaded all but three of its members to abandon the rally. The three were Habib Shah, Kalami, and Fazlur Rahman.

On the following day a crowd of five or six thousand Muslims assembled at the site of the rally, but they dispersed when they were told that the Government had granted another interview to the reception committee for the next afternoon. On the morning of the 9th a large mob gathered around the Nakhoda Mosque in Burra Bazar and, shortly after midday, began moving toward Government House. Huq asked for police permission to talk to the crowd, but this was refused. The march was stopped by armed constables and the men were forced to return to the mosque, where they milled angrily in the surrounding lanes. Fearing damage to their property, some of the Marwaris ordered their *dārwāns* to clear the footpaths in front of their gateways. Blows were exchanged, and, when a shot was fired from one of the Marwari houses, rioting broke out. The police charged with *lāthis* but were bombarded with bricks. They then opened fire, killing and wounding a number in the crowd. Looting and arson had already begun in many parts of the city, with the Marwaris as the chief victims. It took three days and the bayonets of a regiment of British troops to restore order.[28]

THE LESSONS OF VIOLENCE

Looking back over a half century disfigured with the scars of communal rioting in Calcutta, the pattern of these events seems too familiar to excite comment, but in 1918 it was novel and alarming. For men of property in general, and for the Marwaris in particular, it raised a vision of the disastrous possibilities of a breakdown of law and order in the face of a malcontent or fanatical rabble. They were uncomfortably aware that in some way the stability of Indian society had been shaken in the war years. The small delegation of businessmen—Bengali Hindus, Marwaris, and Muslims—which Byomkes Chakravarti, a prominent Congressman, led to the Writers' Building on 17 September to thank the Government for the suppressing the riots,[29] was expressive of a concern for what was to come as much as of relief for what was past.

The political implications of the riots were equally disturbing.

[28] This account of the riots and the events leading up to them is based on *Essayez*, pp. 108–116; and *Report of the Non-Official Commission on the Calcutta Disturbances (1918)* (Calcutta, 1919), pp. 4–29.

[29] *Bangali*, and *Nayak*, 18 Sept. 1918.

It was the first time since the unsettled days of the partition more than a decade before that mob violence had been used in Bengal as a political weapon. Certainly the political aims of the agitators were not clearly defined, but this does not alter the fact that in its organisation the 1918 rioting differed in kind from the normal communal disorder. Habib Shah and his fellows were engaged in a political contest in which they used violence and the threat of violence against their opponents. The organisations through which they worked were political, and they played upon political as well as communal grievances.

Their success showed that there was now latent mass discontent which could be exploited for personal or communal advantage by unscrupulous politicians. This gave a new significance to the numerical strength of the Muslim community, and forced the basic fact of its majority on the attention of the British, the Hindu bhadralok, and the Bengal Muslim politicians—courtiers and collaborators alike—all of whom had been acting as though they had forgotten that majority.

There were other lessons to be learnt from the riot. In the first place, it had shown the Muslim politicians that a resort to violence could provide a means of expressing their anger and frustration when other forms of political action had failed. Moreover, it was apparent that the mere threat of violence could force the British and the Hindu bhadralok to pay more serious attention to Muslim demands. Violence had been proved an effective mode of political action, and the techniques for promoting it had been well noted. Future Muslim agitators appreciated all too well the response which could be evoked with the watchcry 'Islam in danger', and they valued the agency of the *mollās* in sounding the alarm. They understood the importance of the mosque as a rallying point, of the migrant groups of the bustee areas as a source for rioters, of the Marwaris as an alien and unpopular object of violence, and of the vernacular press as a medium for incitement.

Obviously, violence in Calcutta was a sword the Muslims might use against their communal opponents, but it was a double-edged sword. As this riot had shown, the instigators of an outbreak could never be certain that they would be able to control the disorderly elements they had set loose, and when the rabble got out of hand no one was free from danger, certainly no one of property. The size of the city; the overcrowding of its older areas, with their jumbled maze of narrow lanes and alley-ways; the mixed racial and religious composition of its population; its drifting and unstable migrant section; its large criminal class; its spectacular inequalities of wealth and opportunity; its influential yellow press—all of these factors contributed to the exceptional difficulty of maintaining order in Calcutta or of arresting disorder once it had begun. And this problem of law and order was a matter of concern for politicians as well as police. After the September, 1918, riot no Bengali political leader could ever again disregard the possibility that extreme action on his part might provoke mass violence in Calcutta, with possibly disastrous consequences. This consideration, as we shall see, loomed large in the minds of the bhadralok leaders as they searched for new methods of political action in the following two years.

The Government of Bengal was shaken by what had happened in September, 1918. Clearly it had misjudged the situation. Its initial hesitation, and its later reliance upon police and troops to the exclusion of assistance from Muslim leaders, almost certainly cost lives. Its actions were censured by both the Government of India and a nonofficial commission of enquiry,[30] and Ronaldshay, writing his memoirs thirty years later, still felt the need for a lengthy apologia.[31] Some good came of the affair. Apart from a reorganisation of armed police in Calcutta in an attempt to obviate the use of troops, there was a realisation among the officials that new forces were at work in Bengal society and that the politics of the post-war years promised to be very different from those of the past.[32]

A NEW COURSE

The events of August and September left many reputations tarnished. The willingness of most of the Muslim politicians to subordinate public duty to considerations of personal advantage and security, their preoccupation with petty intrigue and factionalism, had been plain for all to see.

Fazlul Huq had come through the affair better than most, but he was in disfavour with the bulk of his community because of his persistent support of the Lucknow Pact. His election to preside at the December, 1918, session of the All-India Muslim League won

[30] *Essayez*, p. 116; and *Report of the Non-Official Commission on the Calcutta Disturbances (1918)* (Calcutta, 1919), p. 29.

[31] *Essayez*, pp. 108–116.

[32] GB, Police, 2C(4–6), B15–19, Dec. 1918.

him few friends in Bengal, and his characterisation, in his presidential address on that occasion, of talk of Hindu raj as a 'gross libel'[33] was particularly unwelcome in the atmosphere of communal acrimony following the Calcutta riots. Huq had tarred himself with the brush of collaboration, and it was a long time before this was forgiven. 'He has a strong desire to gain a reputation among all communities,' wrote the *Moslem Hitaishi* contemptuously in October, 1919. 'So he keeps himself in the good graces of a certain section of Moslems and is ready, without the least hesitation, to sacrifice Moslem communal interests in order to win fame and position among the Hindus'.[34]

What the Bengal Muslims were looking for late in 1918 was not a leader who would compromise, but one who would put communalism before all else in the battle about to be fought over Muslim legislative representation. The man who supplied the need was Nawab Khan Bahadur Syed Nawabaly Chaudhuri, the Eastern Bengal representative in the Imperial Legislative Council. He had much to recommend him. A Bengali and a great landholder, he stood apart from the Urdu-speaking group in Calcutta who had been chiefly responsible for the recent troubles. At that time he had spoken out strongly against the encouragement of violence[35] and yet had retained the appearance, at least, of noninvolvement in the various intrigues.

More important, at no stage in his career had he had dealings with the nationalists. He was a communalist first and last. When the nonofficial members of the Imperial Legislative Council drew up their memorial on reforms in 1916, he had refused to sign on the ground that Muslim interests were not explicitly protected.[36] He had resigned the presidency of the provincial Muslim League in 1917 because of the terms of the Lucknow Pact, and in December had argued the case for his community in a personal interview with Montagu and Chelmsford.[37]

His main work lay before him. In August, 1918, he was elected president of the Central National Mahommedan Association and immediately set about preparing submissions for the Franchise and Functions Committees. The latter he regarded as supplying an op-

[33] Azizul Huq collection.
[34] *Moslem Hitaishi*, 31 Oct. 1919.
[35] *Essayez*, p. 111.
[36] *Mohammadi*, 20 Oct. 1916.
[37] GB, Appointment, 6R–1(17), B441–455, Mar. 1919.

portunity for a public protest against the 'serfdom' imposed upon the Muslims by the Hindu bhadralok. It would be suicidal for the Muslim to agree to any scheme for the progressive realisation of self-government, the committee was told, for there was 'no common sentiment of nationality between the Moslem and the Bengalee'.[38]

The evidence for the Franchise Committee was of more practical importance, for the distribution of legislative seats was still an open question. The Government of Bengal, preparing its recommendations, had come to the conclusion that no satisfactory franchise qualification could be devised which would give the Bengal Muslims a majority of voters and that, this being so, they were entitled to separate electorates. It accepted the Congress-League scheme as 'a convenient solution' of the problem of apportioning seats between the two communities and recommended a Legislative Council for Bengal of 112 members. Fifty-nine of these should be elected from territorial constituencies, with the Muslims providing 27 and the Hindus 32.[39] The Central National Mahommedan Association strongly opposed this suggestion. The Lucknow Pact was acceptable for the rest of India, it asserted, but for Bengal it was unfair to the Muslims. Their population entitled them to at least 50 percent of the Council seats.[40]

The Franchise Committee did not agree. It accepted the Government of Bengal's argument for communal electorates and its apportionment of 45 percent of the territorial seats to the Muslims.[41]

Chaudhuri had not appeared as a witness before either of the committees, but he had not been idle. As an old comrade of the Dacca Nawab, he knew the value of personal intercession at the highest level, and he had been active in Delhi talking with members of the Government of India. He had insisted that the Muslim League did not truly represent the Muslim community in Bengal and that the application of the Congress-League scheme to the province would be regarded by his community as a betrayal similar to that of the reunification of 1912.

He had spoken persuasively. 'I have been much impressed by the

[38] *Ibid.*, 6R–18 (1–10), A10–19, Mar. 1919.
[39] *Ibid.*, 6R–25(1–59), A94–152, Dec. 1918.
[40] *Evidence taken before the Reforms Committee (Franchise)* (Calcutta, 1919), Vol. II, p. 393.
[41] *Report of the Franchise Committee*, (Calcutta, 1919), pp. 9–10 and 52.

arguments which have since been addressed to the Government of India by Saiyid Nawab Ali Chaudhuri', wrote Sir William Vincent, the Home Member, in opposing the Franchise Committee's proposals.[42] Vincent spoke for his colleagues. They had all been impressed by Chaudhuri's plea, and they insisted that the Bengal Muslims be given 44 seats instead of the 34 recommended by the Southborough Committee.[43] The question was referred back to the Government of Bengal, with the request that it prepare a scheme to increase Muslim representation, but it stood by its earlier recommendation that 45 percent of the territorial seats was sufficient.[44]

Chaudhuri would not give up without a fight. Throughout the remainder of 1919, by personal interviews and letters he kept up his pressure on the members of the provincial and Indian Governments.[45] Through the Central National Mahommedan Association he organised Muslim conferences in various parts of the province, at which resolutions were passed disavowing the right of the Muslim League to speak for Bengal and urging the British to honour their pledges to the Muslim community.[46] Forwarding a final note to the Government of Bengal on 10 January 1920, he warned of the consequences of a failure to satisfy Muslim demands:

> Any decision to adhere to the recommendation of the Southborough [Franchise] Committee would leave the moderate element among the Muhammadans practically without any influence or following in the reformed Council and in the country. Disappointed in securing what they justly regard, and what was also confirmed by the very mature and considerate decision of the Government of India as the proper ratio of representation, the Mussalmans, if they do not maintain a spirit of aloofness, will certainly look with disfavour and rankling discontent on a constitution in which, in spite of their numerical superiority, they shall be in a decided political minority. Should the state of things be left as they are, it does not require much imagination to conceive their eventual capture by the extremists to wreck the constitution.[47]

42 *Fifth Despatch on Indian Constitutional Reforms (Franchises)* (Calcutta, 1919), p. 388.

43 *Ibid.*, p. 373.

44 GB, Appointment, 6R–34(1–2), A1–2, Aug. 1919.

45 GI, Reforms Office, Bundle 1920 Jan.–May B(2), B244–245, Jan. 1920; and GB, Appointment, 6R–8(1–3), A166–168B, Feb. 1920.

46 *Octennial Report of the Central National Mahommedan Association, 1917–1924* (Calcutta, 1925), pp. 35–37.

47 GB, Appointment, 6R–8(1–3), A166–168B, Feb. 1920.

The British disregarded this admonition. Although the total number of members in the new Bengal Legislative Council was raised to 139, with 85 territorial seats, the Muslim percentage was kept at 45. They were to have only 39 seats to the Hindus' 46 (see Table 4). Chaudhuri was disappointed, but he recognised that there had been worthwhile gains. 'The treatment accorded to the Mussalmans

TABLE 4

Composition of Bengal Legislative Council and Electorate under Government of India Act, 1919

	Members[a]	Voters[b]
Ex officio:		
Executive councillors	4	
Nominated:		
Indian Christians and depressed classes	2	
Labour	2	
Others	18	
Elected:		
Non-Muhammadan urban	11	67,291
Non-Muhammadan rural	35	473,898
Muhammadan urban	6	15,745
Muhammadan rural	33	449,382
European	5	4,006
Anglo-Indian	2	2,901
Landholders	5	737
Calcutta University	1	6,144
European trade and commerce	11	826
Indian trade and commerce	4	488
Totals	139	1,021,418

[a] PP, 1920 [Cmd. 812], vol. XXXV, pp. 295–299.
[b] Figures for 1920 General Election. (PP, 1921 [Cmd. 1261], vol. XXVI, pp. 10–13).

by the British government has not been quite satisfactory indeed', he wrote, 'but it has at any rate saved us from being swamped by more powerful interests'.[48] Separate communal electorates, which had seemed in jeopardy in Bengal following Montagu's strictures in 1918, had been preserved, and the Muslims had secured five seats more than a rigid adherence to the Lucknow Pact would have given

[48] *Views on Present Political Situation in India* (Calcutta, 1920), p. 12.

them. This meant a gross reduction of ten in the voting power of the Hindus.

Chaudhuri's note of 10 January 1920, as we remarked, contributed nothing to these gains, but that must not mislead us into overlooking the significance of the argument used therein. Chaudhuri did not approach the Government as a courtier, with a humble petition for concessions in recognition of his community's loyalty. Nor did he take a stand with the bhadralok nationalists in demanding India's just constitutional deserts. Instead, he drew the Government's attention to the fact that the Muslims had a 'numerical superiority' in Bengal, and he demanded the constitutional recognition of that majority. As a sanction, he added the comment that a failure to satisfy this demand would endanger political order.

Chaudhuri had recognised the crucial fact that in the new system numbers would count. The small consultative council of the past was about to be replaced by a large quasi-parliament, controlling some departments of government and responsible to a mass electorate. In place of the 28 members of the old Legislative Council elected by 9,000 educated and propertied voters, there were now to be 113 elected members with a total enfranchised population of more than a million, of whom the majority would be peasants.[49] In mass politics numbers could count in two ways. As September, 1918, had shown, they could be made to count in a crude, negative fashion by provoking mob violence; or they could be made to count more positively through electoral organisation. The vote or violence were the implied alternatives in Chaudhuri's note of 10 January 1920. The vote and violence were to remain for Bengal Muslim politicians the main alternative instruments of power for the next three decades.

THE HINDU BHADRALOK'S FEARS

For those who valued friendly intercourse and political cooperation between Hindus and Muslims, the years of the constitutional reforms debate in Bengal—1915 to 1920—had given little cause for pleasure. Surendranath Banerjea's hopes of July, 1915, for a united campaign against the British looked sad when compared

[49] PP, 1920, [Cmd. 812], Vol. XXXV, pp. 295–299; GB, Appointment, 6R–25(1–59), A94–152, Dec. 1918; and Statutory Commission, Vol. VIII, p. 130.

with the acerbity which characterised communal utterances in 1919 and 1920. The object of Banerjea and his fellow Moderates had been to restore the bhadralok's confidence in the efficacy of liberal, constitutional methods of political action. The whole trend of Muslim politics in Bengal from 1917 had been in the opposite direction. The Muslim community had rejected Fazlul Huq and the other men of compromise who had subscribed to the Lucknow Pact, and had taken as its leader an unblushing communalist who regarded the nationalists, Muslim or Hindu, as the enemies of Indian Islam. When thwarted in their demands for a larger share of constitutional concessions, the Muslims had resorted to violence in Calcutta, and from that time onward had placed an increasingly aggressive emphasis on their numerical majority.

Nothing could have been better calculated to alarm the Hindu bhadralok, and their fears were sharpened by their distrust of the British. How could the bhadralok be sure that the British would not encourage this new spirit of Muslim hostility, or themselves use the Muslim population figures for some nefarious purpose? The British officials obviously had no time for the bhadralok leaders, Hindu or Muslim, while they always seemed ready to spare a friendly moment for Chaudhuri and his kind. For the Hindu bhadralok it was a bad sign that certain provisions of both the Lucknow Pact and the Montagu-Chelmsford report had been disregarded by the Government in order to strengthen the position of the Bengal Muslims. This was no encouragement to the bhadralok's faith in the value of liberal constitutionalism.

IV

THE INTERREGNUM

YEARS OF UNCERTAINTY

In making their demands for reforms in 1915, the Bengal Moderates were not motivated simply by a desire to further the constitutional ideal—they were also concerned to save themselves. Their political influence had been seriously weakened by their difficulties in the Morley-Minto councils and by the general trend of Government policy in 1914 and early 1915. Hard-pressed by the Extremists, they pinned their hopes of repairing their position upon a satisfactory British response to their demands. If the British immediately made the desired declaration regarding self-government, the Moderates would be able to point to this as proof of their ability to influence the Government. If reforms were implemented along the lines proposed by the Moderates, they would be able to assert a proprietary title to the new constitution—to speak with assurance of the reforms as 'their reforms'.

As we have seen, the declaration was not made with despatch, nor was the new constitution—with its built-in safeguards for the officials, the European nonofficials and the Muslims—what the Moderates had wanted. The very length of the reforms discussions worked against them and, indeed, against the security of the bhadralok as a whole. The consequence was the inordinate extension of the period of flux and uncertainty in politics. Instead of being a brief transitional stage between one political order and another, the interregnum was so long as to become almost a new order in itself.

In this lengthy interlude the balance of political relationships was upset: new relationships developed, owing their form primarily to the existing state of uncertainty and not to the future order, as would have been the case had the period of reconstruction been brief. That swift and direct progress from one system to the next, which would have kept intact the structure of the old political society and enabled the Moderates to rule a straight line from their first intentions to their final achievement, was replaced by five years of confused movement and countermovement in which the clarity of original intentions was blurred. In this chapter we shall trace the development of bhadralok politics through these five uncertain years, 1916 to 1920.

RETURN OF THE EXTREMISTS

For the nationalists, as for their opponents, the prospect of reforms brought the need for reappraisal and action. The future of political India was in the making. One had either to take part or stand back and be content to see others shape the nation's destiny. If one did stand back, one had to accept the fact that those who had a hand in the construction would almost certainly attempt to secure for themselves a favoured position.

The Extremists had been content to remain outside the Morley-Minto councils and pepper the participants with the grapeshot of their criticism. Their studied refusal to become involved constituted their political style, and it had served them well while that political order lasted. But the constitutional reconstruction brought it to an end. All groups had now to search for a new strategy which would give them a position in the new order. In doing this they were faced with difficulties, for they had to look in three directions at once: to their own immediate past; to the reforms that were being evolved; and to their position in the political system of the future.

In all three ways the Extremists had the greatest problem. Looking to the past, they had in some way to maintain a semblance of consistency. Certainly in the excitement accompanying the first news of reforms there was an opportunity to discard their old style of nonparticipation, but there was then the danger that they would be unrecognizable in their new colours. In particular, they might be identified with the Moderates, which could be disastrous for their political future. To avoid this, they had to give convincing reasons for their reengagement in constitutional politics.

To demonstrate that they had not become camp followers of the Moderates and in order to remain true to their past, the Bengal Extremists aimed their constitutional demands high. They insisted, and there is no reason to doubt their sincerity in this, that the British would give nothing worthwhile unless they were pushed hard. Under the pretence of reform they would attempt to buttress their rule in India by making concessions to reactionary groups such as the Muslims, the Moderates, and their own commercial community, and the nation at large would be left to suffer at the hands of these strengthened vested interests. It was the Extremists' self-imposed duty to ensure that the Indian people were not sold out to the foreigner by a handful of selfish opportunists. *Nayak* of 11 July 1917 warned its readers to beware of the nefarious activities of 'Surendra Nath and his followers'.

> What we want, however, is to place the handful of educated Babus in the background and to uplift the inarticulate masses whose interests are never cared for by our so-called leaders. These latter give displays of oratory in the halls of the Indian Association and the British Indian Association with the object, not of ameliorating the miseries of the people at large, but to advance their own self-interests.

Where the Extremists were weak, the Moderates were strong: their consistency in advocating reforms could not be questioned. But they had other problems. Knowing full well that whatever reform scheme they advanced would be whittled away by the British, they had, as a matter of tactics, to demand more than they expected to receive and declare this to be an 'irreducible minimum'. There was then the risk that unreal expectations would be aroused, in view of which the final achievement would appear disappointing.

The Moderates had to succeed and succeed gloriously. Similarly, they had to prevent rival groups from stealing a share of the credit for whatever was achieved, and yet they were obliged to encourage those groups to associate themselves with their reform proposals in an effort to convince the British that these were 'national' demands. This was what prompted them to readmit the Extremists to the Congress of 1916 and to enter upon the series of negotiations with the Muslims which produced the Lucknow Pact. It is significant that the Moderates were at pains to stress that they were still in control of the reform movement, having merely enlisted the Extremists and the Muslim Leaguers as recruits. Commenting on the 1916 Congress session, Surendranath Banerjea wrote in the *Ben-*

galee: 'All are now gathered together under the banner of self-government, which they are resolved to achieve by and through the aid of all constitutional means at their disposal. The constitutional party derives added strength by this union'.[1]

The Moderates had to face a challenge from another quarter: from new men who were entering politics. As at the time of the anti-partition campaign ten years before, so now in the activity of the constitutional reconstruction there were opportunities for newcomers to break into politics in Bengal. With the old political order in dissolution, the sources of influence and power on which its leaders had depended—their reputation as anti-partition agitators; their control of local bodies, public organisations, and political associations; their membership in the legislative councils—were, for a time at least, of reduced importance. It became possible for a man to cut a figure simply by adopting a striking attitude toward the reforms, provided of course that he had social standing.

The outstanding example was the rapid rise to prominence in 1917 of Chitta Ranjan Das.[2] Socially Das was everything a bhadralok should be. His family were Brahmos (originally Baidyas) from Dacca District. His father and uncle were Calcutta High Court lawyers and he had been educated at Presidency College, where he had been an active member of the Students' Association in the exciting days following Surendranath Banerjea's dismissal from the I.C.S. After graduation he had been sent to England by his family as a candidate for the I.C.S. but, having failed, he had turned to the bar. As in so many similar cases, his father was impoverished by the financial effort required to send him to England and, for ten years after his return to the overcrowded legal profession of Calcutta, Chitta Ranjan was unable to build up a practice large enough to repair the family fortunes.

All was changed by his part in the political trials of 1907–1908. His successful defence of Aurobindo Ghose, Bipin Chandra Pal, and other leading nationalists brought him fame and riches. In a few years he had become the city's leading barrister, enjoying the luxury of frequent trips to Europe during the legal vacation, and renowned in Calcutta society for his hospitality and his Bengali poetry.

[1] *Bengalee*, 5 Jan. 1917.

[2] For biographical details see P. C. Ray, *Life and Times of C. R. Das* (London, 1927); and H. N. Das Gupta, *Deshbandhu Chittaranjan Das* (Delhi, 1960).

He took no direct part in politics until the talk of constitutional reforms caught his interest. In the discussions at the influential Calcutta Bar Library he emerged as a leader of radical opinion[3] and, as a result, was asked to preside at the Bengal Provincial Conference held in April, 1917, in his home suburb of Bhowanipur. It was ironical, but indicative of the problems faced by the established leadership, that it was Surendranath Banerjea who formally proposed that Das should take the chair.[4] His speech was a huge success, winning the acclaim of the Bengali press as a turning point in provincial politics: 'the message of a new life for Bengalis, a call to patriotic service, an appeal for the development of education in the interests of the national welfare'.[5]

Das has established an immediate claim to be included in the first rank of Bengali politicians. When, three months later, a Town Hall meeting nominated a deputation of six to carry its protest to the Government against the internment of Annie Besant, the English radical who had assumed the lead of the Madras nationalists, Das was one of those named. The composition of this deputation is interesting, for with the exception of Bipin Chandra Pal who was then absent from Bengal, it included all the chief contenders for provincial leadership: the two old rivals of political journalism, Surendranath Banerjea of the *Bengalee* and Motilal Ghose of the *Amrita Bazar Patrika*; Sir Rashbehari Ghose, one of the great figures of the National Education movement; and a trio of younger men, all lawyers, Byomkes Chakravarti, Fazlul Huq, and C. R. Das.[6]

The rivalry among these men was soon revealed. On 29 August the B.P.C.C. (Bengal Provincial Congress Committee) met to choose a president for the all-India Congress session to be held in Calcutta in December. With Banerjea's backing, a Moderate landholder, P. C. Mitter, proposed an Oudh *taluqdar*, the Raja of Mahmudabad, but Byomkes Chakravarti nominated Mrs Besant and this was seconded by C. R. Das. Mahmudabad was chosen by 34 votes to 30. The Congress Reception Committee met the following evening to ratify this decision, and both parties attempted to pack the meeting with their supporters. It was immediately apparent to Banerjea that his group was hopelessly outnumbered, and, after a brief angry exchange over the accuracy of the minutes of the

[3] Montagu, pp. 66–67.
[4] Das Gupta, *op. cit.*, p. 30.
[5] *Dainik Basumati*, 23 Apr. 1917.
[6] *Nation in Making*, pp. 241–245.

previous night's meeting, he and his supporters left the hall to shouts of 'Get out'. The chairman, Baikunthanath Sen, went with them, but this did not deter those who remained from proceeding to the election of Mrs Besant as Congress president.[7] The dispute was resolved two months later when a compromise was patched up through outside intervention;[8] but in the meantime the old rift in the Bengal Congress had been opened wide.

The local press attributed this new hostility between Moderates and Extremists to Montagu's 20 August declaration, which had reinforced the determination of both parties to gain control of the forthcoming All-India Congress Session where the reforms would be debated.[9] Banerjea, who felt his position threatened, urged his opponents not to create trouble.

> If India is to obtain her political emancipation, it must be by the cultivation of a spirit of discipline, by veneration for great leaders, through the strict observance of constitutional usages, and the avoidance of all rowdyism. Any departure from these principles would supply the enemies of Indian aspirations with a powerful weapon for denouncing their claims to self-government.[10]

No one would accept this advice. Already the chief protagonists for political power in Bengal were declaring their positions on reforms, and Banerjea alone stood squarely behind the Lucknow Pact, with its restrained demand for Representative Government at the centre and for greater Government accountability to the legislatures in the provinces. Fazlul Huq, caught in the cleft stick of communalism and nationalism, hesitated between the Congress-League scheme modified to give increased representation to the Bengal Muslims, and a proposal for an Indian federation with provincial Cabinet Government.[11] C. R. Das,[12] Motilal Ghose,[13] and Byomkes Chakravarti[14] all demanded full Responsible Government in the provinces. Their stand won the loudest applause, for it was clear and unqualified. Unlike Banerjea, they had nothing to lose

[7] *Amrita Bazar Patrika,** 30 and 31 Aug. 1917; and P. Dutt, *Memoirs of Motilal Ghose* (Calcutta, 1935), pp. 262–263.

[8] *Amrita Bazar Patrika*, 6 Oct. 1917.

[9] E.g., see *Dainik Bharat Mitra*, 6 Sept. 1917.

[10] *Bengalee*, 4 Sept. 1917.

[11] Montagu, p. 92.

[12] *Ibid.*, p. 91.

[13] *Ibid.*, p. 84.

[14] GB, Appointment, 6R–1(17), B441–455, Mar. 1919; and PP, 1918, [Cd. 9178], Vol. XVIII, pp. 512–513.

if they failed to secure their demands, and indeed their almost certain failure was to their advantage, for the prevailing mood was one of distrust of British intentions. '. . . nobody believes that we are in earnest', a British newspaper correspondent in Calcutta told Montagu; 'nobody believes that we will do anything'.[15]

THE CAPTURE OF CONGRESS

It was obvious that the Moderates were losing the initiative to the Extremists, but they retained one major advantage: they had control of the Indian Association and, through it, of the Provincial Congress Committee. It was a testimony to the power Banerjea had once wielded in Bengal nationalist politics that the Indian Association had the local Congress organisation in its pocket. It enjoyed the right to nominate the majority of the members of the Provincial Congress Committee and to fill casual vacancies; it was customarily asked by District reception committees to suggest presidents for the annual Provincial Conferences; and it could send as many delegates as it wished to the all-India Congress sessions.[16] In 1914 there had even been a resolution passed at the Provincial Conference recommending that the Provincial Congress Committee become a subcommittee of the Indian Association.[17] Certainly there was little for a separate Provincial Congress Committee to do. The few District Associations which existed were inactive and, apart from the agenda for the Provincial Conference, all matters of importance were decided at the Indian Association.

The Besant-Mahmudabad election dispute, however, had shown how valuable control of the Provincial Congress Committee could be at a time of crisis. On that occasion the Extremists obviously commanded the larger following, but, had Mahmudabad's election not required ratification by the Reception Committee, they would have been helpless.

Their lack of an organisation through which to work was indeed a serious problem. Earlier in 1917 they had enthusiastically taken up Annie Besant's idea of a Home Rule League, and under Byomkes Chakravarti's control it had provided a useful platform.[18] The locus of power, however, remained in the established political or-

[15] Montagu, p. 66.
[16] IA, Committee meeting proceedings.
[17] IA, Annual Report, 1914.
[18] *Nayak*, 15 and 23 June 1917. For biographical details concerning Byomkes Chakravarti see obituary notice, *Statesman*,* 22 June 1929.

ganisations, and after the election dispute it was apparent to the Extremists that they had to gain control of these organisations.

Their first answer was an attempt to capture the Indian Association executive. Looking ahead to the election of office-bearers at the annual general meeting to be held on 31 January 1918, they put forward the names of 79 men for admission to the Association; however, Banerjea and his supporters replied by nominating 62 new members of their own, and at a committee meeting on 16 January these 62 were accepted while the others were rejected.[19]

Despite this reverse, the Extremists went ahead with their plan. The Indian Association hall was packed for the annual general meeting, with every notable Bengali nationalist present for this trial of strength. Fighting on his home ground, Banerjea was invincible. His nominee for president was Baikunthanath Sen, while C. R. Das put forward Byomkes Chakravarti. Sen received 86 votes to Chakravarti's 23. The tale was the same right down the line. Das and Chakravarti both failed in their bids for the five positions of vice-president, and Fazlul Huq was outvoted in his effort to enter the committee. Banerjea, with a final gesture of magnanimity, personally nominated Das and Chakravarti for the committee, and they then had to face the humiliation of gaining the bare minimum of votes necessary to secure their election.[20]

The victory was Banerjea's, but it was to be his last; for the Extremists had found a new source of support which would shortly give them control of the Provincial Congress and leave the Moderates stranded in a devitalised Indian Association. This new source of power was the mufussil towns. Immediately after the clash over the Congress presidency at the end of August, 1917, the Extremist press had questioned the legitimacy of a Provincial Congress Committee on which the districts were unrepresented, and in September a group of influential men from the mufussil were brought for a meeting in Calcutta 'to settle the matter of the Reception Committee dispute'. Predictably, they complained of the capital's domination of provincial politics, and at their invitation C. R. Das toured the mufussil towns in October and November, addressing meetings and organising committees to send delegates to a proposed All Bengal Political Conference.[21]

[19] IA, Committee meeting proceedings, 4 and 16 Jan. 1918.
[20] IA, General meeting proceedings, 31 Jan. 1918.
[21] *Amrita Bazar Patrika*,* 17 Sept., 1, 11, 15 and 18 Oct., and 30 Nov. 1917.

This conference was called for the beginning of December to coincide with a meeting of the B.P.C.C., and it was attended by more than 100 rural delegates. The Moderates, who did not want to be associated with this obvious attempt to undermine the influence of the Indian Association, made the serious mistake of absenting themselves from both the conference and the B.P.C.C. meeting. Taking advantage of this, the Extremists nominated a slate of delegates to the A.I.C.C. (All-India Congress Committee) which excluded all of the opposing party.[22]

The following month brought the Moderates' triumph at the Indian Association annual general meeting, but the Extremists immediately countered with a call for an extraordinary general meeting of the B.P.C.C. to discuss its unrepresentative composition. The Moderates, who still held the executive positions on the committee, refused to convene a meeting on a day when the mufussil members could attend, so the Extremists proceeded with one of their own. On 16 February, with Chakravarti in the chair, Das proposed that the Indian Association membership of the committee should be reduced and that the District Committees should be accorded direct representation. The meeting approved his recommendation, and resolved that the new rule should take force on the following day.[23]

The Moderates could do nothing to reverse these legally dubious proceedings, for the Extremists now had an extremely active popular backing in Calcutta and the mufussil, which gave them the ability to dominate any political meeting outside the Indian Association. Their command of the B.P.C.C. also gave them a platform from which to publicise their doctrine of no compromise, and on 6 June they issued a circular in its name calling for general opposition to the Montagu-Chelmsford proposals should these fall short of their demand for full Responsible Government in the provinces.[24]

The Moderates' position was desperate. The reform proposals, on which they had staked their future, were about to be published and, at this juncture, they had lost control of Congress to a group which was sworn to reject any moderate scheme. Their only possible course of action—and it was tantamount to an admission of defeat—was to form a new political organisation through which they could fight for the reforms. Early in June the National Liberal League

[22] *Ibid.*, 3 and 5 Dec. 1917.
[23] *Ibid.*, 9, 11 and 18 Feb. 1918.
[24] *Bengalee*, 6 June 1918.

was founded in Calcutta for this purpose, with Surendranath Banerjea as its first president.[25]

The Extremists poured scorn on this new development. After this, they asked, who could doubt that the Moderates were prepared to pick up any crumb that fell from the British table?[26] No hope was left of the Montagu-Chelmsford report being considered on its merits in Bengal. It was published on 8 July, to receive the plaudits of the Moderates and to be rejected out of hand by the Extremists.[27] Both parties went to defend their position at a special session of the Provincial Conference on 14 July, but the Moderates got no hearing, and a series of resolutions were passed condemning the Montagu-Chelmsford scheme.[28]

The Extremists' argument was straightforward. They said that the proposed reforms were hedged about with so many provisions to protect the bureaucracy, British commerce, and 'loyal' Indian groups that the nationalists would be merely consenting to their own ensnarement should they accept them. The British would listen to no reasoned protest; hence the only hope of gaining anything worthwhile was to force their hand by rejecting the whole scheme. 'The British Government have not proposed to introduce the reforms of their own accord', observed the *Millat* on 24 July. 'You asked for them and they have opened the door a little in response to your knocking. So the more you agitate for them the larger number of concessions will you get'.

ROWLATT ACT AND AMRITSAR

The Moderates were in worse trouble than ever. They, too, were dissatisfied with what was proposed, but they were afraid that nationalist opposition would play into the hands of the 'diehards', the ultraconservatives in Britain, enabling them to block all reforms. A difficult situation was made impossible for them by the publication of the Sedition Committee's report at the end of July, 1918. This committee had been set up under the chairmanship of Justice S. A. T. Rowlatt by the Government of India in December,

[25] National Liberal League, Annual Report, 1918–1919.

[26] E.g., see *Amrita Bazar Patrika*, 19 June 1918.

[27] *Bengalee*, 9 July 1918; IA, Committee meeting proceedings, 12 July 1918; *Dainik Bharat Mitra*, 12 July 1918; and *Dainik Basumati*, 13 July 1918.

[28] IA, Committee meeting proceedings, 12 July 1918; and *Bengali*, 16 July 1918.

1917, to report on the extent of revolutionary conspiracy in India and to suggest remedial measures. It recommended that the Government arm itself with permanent legislation to enable it, whenever it felt the need, to take extraordinary powers to deal summarily with seditious offenders.[29] This brought a storm of protest from all political groups in India. The Moderates pointed out reproachfully that nothing could be better calculated to lend colour to the Extremists' assertion that within the Jekyll of the reforms lurked the old Hyde of repression.[30]

A special session of Congress had been called for 29 August at Bombay to consider the Montagu-Chelmsford report but the Moderates decided not to attend, knowing that they would be in a hopeless minority. Instead, they would hold an all-India conference of their own to support the reforms.[31] This met on 1 November, also in Bombay. The separate meetings emphasised the division between the two parties. The Indian Association appealed to the Congress to open negotiations for a reconciliation, but the only reply was a curt note from the local secretary informing it that its representation on the B.P.C.C. had been reduced from 40 to 15.[32]

When the Franchise and Subjects Committees were formed at the end of 1918, the leading Moderates were asked to serve as members; their compliance was proclaimed by the Extremists to be a further proof of their readiness to lackey for the British.[33] In January, 1919, Montagu appointed S. P. Sinha as Under-Secretary of State for India, with a seat in the House of Lords. This gesture of goodwill was well received in India, but again the effect was ruined. A fortnight later the Government of India introduced a bill to the Imperial Legislative Council to implement the Rowlatt Committee's recommendations, and it was forced through against the vote of every Indian nonofficial member. The Moderates were appalled by this slap in the face to Indian opinion. '. . . there will be agitation, intense, bitter, widespread, accentuated by deep discontent', lamented Banerjea. 'Is this a prospect which the Government contemplates with unconcern?'[34]

[29] *Sedition Committee, 1918, Report* (Calcutta, 1918).

[30] NP, Aug. 1918.

[31] IA, Committee meeting proceedings, 10 Aug. 1918; *Statesman*, 16 Aug. 1918; and *Nation in Making*, pp. 305–310.

[32] IA, Committee meeting proceedings, 30 Dec. 1918 and 1 Feb. 1919.

[33] NP, Dec. 1918.

[34] *Bengalee*, 4 Feb. 1919.

The A.I.C.C. called for *hartāls* in protest against the Acts, and, as a result, there was rioting in a number of north Indian cities in the first and second weeks of April. In Amritsar in the Punjab five Europeans were murdered by a mob on the 10th, and the city was placed under military rule. On the 13th a prohibited meeting held in a walled square, the Jallianwala Bagh, was fired on without warning by British troops and there were heavy casualties. Two days later martial law was proclaimed in Amritsar and neighbouring cities, under which floggings and other humiliations were imposed upon the Indians as reprisals for the loss of British lives.

With the news of this brutality, a wave of anger swept over the country. '. . . what has happened can never be forgotten or forgiven', wrote C. F. Andrews with emotion to his friend, Rabindranath Tagore. 'I find that every Indian I meet is saying "Take away your d—d Reforms: we dont want them & we wont have them. Answer us this, are we to be treated as serfs, with no human rights at all?" '[35]

As Andrews was writing, the Government of India Bill was being prepared in London for its introduction to Parliament. At long last the Moderates were to have their constitutional reforms, but there was to be no triumph. Instead of the jubilation they had expected, there was anger and distrust. They were abused, not acclaimed, for their efforts. They had lost control of Congress and there seemed no hope of their dominating the new political order.

THE EXTREMISTS' DILEMMA

On 23 December 1919 the royal assent was given to the Government of India Bill. For the Extremist party, in undisputed command of Congress since the Moderates' withdrawal sixteen months before, this posed a serious problem. Should they persist in their opposition to the Montagu-Chelmsford reforms or should they now accept them as a *fait accompli* and use their power to dominate the new institutions? Certainly their reputation in the preceding two years had been built upon their steadfast rejection of all British reform proposals and their condemnation of those Indians who were prepared to cooperate with the British, but they could contend, with some degree of truth, that this had been a strategem designed to force the British to yield more power. That game was

[35] 1 May [1919], Andrews MSS.

played out (so the argument ran), and the only result of a continued refusal to participate in constitutional politics would be the loss of the field to 'a tribe of timid, little-souled people who will think of themselves first and of their country last or not at all'.[36] Even under the Morley-Minto constitution, the Extremists had had qualms about leaving the legislative councils to the Moderates,[37] and the danger seemed greater now that some of the functions of the provincial governments were to be transferred to Indian Ministers.

On the other hand, the Extremists asked, was there any reason to believe that participation in the new councils would be more profitable than it had been in the old? No matter what concessions had been made to Indian demands, the British bureaucracy was still in command, and (the Extremists held) the Amritsar tragedy of April, 1919, had shown that it was as reactionary as ever. 'If the fountain remains as it is', wrote Motilal Ghose, 'the addition of a few more conduits will not make the water any more drinkable than it was'.[38] What was needed was a change of heart, and this, the Extremists maintained, had not happened. The racial arrogance that had characterised British Indian policy in the past had been in evidence throughout the reforms discussions. Even the basic assumption upon which the Montagu-Chelmsford scheme rested: that Indians had yet to learn the art of self-government; and its corollary: that they should be given constitutional protection against their ignorance, were considered offensive.[39]

To accept the reforms, even under protest, would be to acquiesce in this judgment of Indian inferiority, and this would injure the growth of national self-confidence. Many of the Extremists believed that it was self-confidence, above all else, that India needed. As a subject people, Indians had lost faith in their ability to act independently. For nearly two centuries they had been taught to distrust their own judgment and to accept without demur the decrees of a paternalistic foreign regime. To save their soul they had to repudiate the right of others to think and act for them. It was on this point that Swami Vivekananda, the influential Bengali Hindu revivalist, had laid stress during his famous lecture tour of India

[36] *Amrita Bazar Patrika*, 2 July 1920.

[37] E.g., see B. C. Pal: *Nationality and Empire* (Calcutta, 1916), pp. 217–218.

[38] *Amrita Bazar Patrika*, 1 Dec. 1919.

[39] *Dainik Bharat Mitra*, 12 July 1918; *Dainik Basumati*, 13 July 1918; and *Amrita Bazar Patrika*, 17 Aug. 1918.

in 1897,[40] and it was a principle that had been elaborated by the advocates of 'national institutions' during the partition agitation. It was the underlying reason for the Extremists' rejection of the Morley-Minto reforms. They believed that merely to accept institutions provided by the British and work them as the British instructed would do nothing to advance India's self-reliance, for this was just a new form of the old dependence. To prove their independence, to themselves as much as to the British, Indians had to reject what was proffered.[41]

The question was, what then? In the Morley-Minto period some individuals in Bengal had avoided this problem by turning away from politics—to religion, like Aurobindo Ghose, or back to literature, like Rabindranath Tagore—and for the Extremist party as a whole no satisfactory answer had been found. The years between 1909 and 1916, the years of negative opposition, had been full of frustration. Again in 1920 they had the chance to reject a British constitution and again they had to ask, what then? This time more depended upon their answer, for now they had political power, with its opportunities and responsibilities. In 1909 they had been outside the Congress, but in 1920 they had control of the organisation and commanded a large following. If they did not participate in the new councils, they had to formulate a satisfactory programme of action of their own.

It was a measure of their uncertainty when faced with this difficult decision that they vacillated for a year before finally rejecting the Montagu-Chelmsford constitution. The December, 1919, Congress at Amritsar resolved to work the reforms, but this decision was reversed by a narrow majority at a special session in Calcutta nine months later, and the plenary meeting at Nagpur in December, 1920, voted overwhelmingly for withdrawal of all cooperation with the British.

Between Amritsar and Calcutta, Calcutta and Nagpur, there were some remarkable changes of mind, none more striking than those of the Bengalis. At Amritsar the Bengal contingent, led by Chitta Ranjan Das, Byomkes Chakravarti, and Bipin Chandra Pal, voted against the reforms. At Calcutta they voted for them. At Nagpur

[40] Swami Vivekananda: *From Colombo to Almora* (Madras, 1904).

[41] B. C. Pal, *Swadeshi and Swaraj: the Rise of New Patriotism* (Calcutta, 1954), pp. 4 and 188; Aurobindo Ghose, *Speeches*, 2nd ed. (Calcutta, 1948), pp. 83–84, 88–89, 148, and 151–152; and Rabindranath Tagore, *Towards Universal Man* (London, 1961), pp. 49–66 and 101–128.

they were all for noncooperation. To understand why they wavered, it is necessary to understand their attitude to the person and policy of M. K. Gandhi. It was Gandhi who commanded the majorities at Amritsar and Calcutta, where the Bengal nationalists voted with the minority, and it was to Gandhi that they capitulated at Nagpur.

GANDHI

Mohandas Karamchand Gandhi, a Gujerati lawyer who had won a great reputation in South Africa with his work for Indian rights, had emerged in the first rank of nationalist leaders after a spectacular success in leading a protest movement against the indigo planters of Bihar in 1918. At his instigation the *hartāls* of April 1919 had been organised in protest against the Rowlatt Acts. The nationwide response to his appeal was testimony to his extraordinary influence, but the resulting violence had shocked him deeply. He was convinced that without greater self-discipline India could not challenge the British, and for this reason he urged the Congress to accept the Montagu-Chelmsford constitution. To those, like the Bengalis, who argued that the 1919 Congress session at Amritsar should reiterate the earlier uncompromising resolutions on the reforms, he replied that this would be irresponsible if Congress had nothing constructive to offer in their place.[42]

Two incidents in January, 1920, forced him to think again: the hero's welcome accorded on his arrival in Britain to General Reginald Dyer, the officer responsible for the Amritsar tragedy; and the rejection by the British Government of Indian Muslim protests over the Turkish peace terms. Gandhi was convinced that after these demonstrations of British disregard for their feelings it would be degrading for Indians to maintain their contact with British imperialism. He therefore set out to formulate a programme of noncooperation which Congress could offer to the nation in place of the reforms.[43]

First, support for the institutions of British Indian government—offices, councils, courts, colleges, and schools—should be withdrawn and Congressmen should devote themselves to the construc-

[42] NP, Dec. 1919–Jan. 1920.

[43] The development of Gandhi's thought in this period can be followed through his articles in *Young India, 1919–1922* (Madras, 1922).

tion of national institutions in their place: 'a government of one's own within the dead shell of the foreign government'.[44] Resistance, nonviolent and symbolic, might be offered to individual acts of British oppression, but the really important work was in national reconstruction.

For the nation as for the individual, Gandhi taught, salvation could be gained only by internal reformation. Society had to be rid of its evils, especially those of dissension and human exploitation. As a first step he called for a reconciliation between religious communities, and he took up the Khilafat issue as a means of cementing Hindu-Muslim unity. He also demanded that caste barriers be broken down and that the untouchables be accepted into the body of Hinduism. Congressmen of all castes should work with the Harijans (the 'Children of God', as Gandhi called them) to help them rise from their degradation.

Similarly, there had to be an end to economic oppression. Gandhi was adamant that self-government for India would be a travesty if the mass of the people were not freed from the exploitation of capitalists, landholders, and moneylenders. The nationalist movement had to be the people's movement, to benefit the mass of the people. 'I don't want Swaraj at the cost of the depressed classes or of any other classes for that matter', he wrote.[45] He therefore insisted that Congress demonstrate its concern for the welfare of the Indian poor by adopting a programme of economic rehabilitation. Congressmen should leave their urban professions and go into the villages to start cottage industries. The local manufacture of cotton cloth should be revived. The spinning wheel should become the symbol of India's new life and the wearing of *khādi* a gesture of the nation's rejection of imperialism.

OPPOSITION FROM BENGAL

Apart from having a rare ability to sway great masses of people, Gandhi was an astute politician, and throughout the first half of 1920 he was gathering around him an influential group of personal adherents on whose support he could rely when he put his programme of noncooperation before Congress.[46] Despite this, there remained powerful sections who were opposed to the adoption of

[44] Andrews to Rathindranath Tagore, 6 Sept. [1920], Andrews MSS.

[45] Gandhi to Andrews, 23 Nov. 1920, quoted in *Andrews*, pp. 156–157.

[46] J. Nehru, *Toward Freedom. The Autobiography* (New York, 1941), pp. 51–53.

the scheme and who were determined not to acquiesce in his domination of the nationalist movement. Foremost among these were the Bengali leaders.

An obvious reason for their opposition, and the one most often cited, was that they saw Gandhi as a rival. C. R. Das certainly aspired to national leadership, and his frequent appearances on public platforms outside Bengal in the preceding two years had already won him a national reputation. Byomkes Chakravarti and Bipin Chandra Pal may have had similar ambitions.

Personal rivalry aside, there was reason for the Bengal nationalist leaders to be apprehensive, for Gandhi made it clear that there would be no room for dissenters in any political organisation he commanded. '... so long as you choose to keep me as your leader', he told a meeting of Muslims early in 1920, 'you must accept my conditions, you must accept dictatorship and the discipline of martial law'.[47] This was something new to Indian nationalism. Formerly the great Congress leaders—Naoroji, Mehta, Banerjea, Lajpat Rai, Gokhale, Tilak, Besant—had derived their power from one province, and they had worked in alliance with leaders from other provinces on the understanding that there would be a minimum of mutual interference in regional activities. Gandhi relied far less on the support of any one area, and his ambition was to subordinate regional differences to his national plan.

This the Bengal leaders were not in the least inclined to accept. Bengalis had enjoyed power in the nationalist movement for too long to be willing to abdicate on request. Nor were they willing to have an outsider dictate the form and content of their provincial politics. To Gandhi's demands for a strong central authority under his control, they replied that personal dictatorship in the nationalist movement and a rigidly uniform policy would stunt national development. 'Blind reverence for Gandhiji's leadership', wrote Bipin Chandra, 'would kill people's freedom of thought and would paralyse by the deadweight of unreasoning reverence their individual conscience'.[48]

In doctrine the Bengal Extremists appeared to have much in common with Gandhi, for the need to encourage Indian self-confidence through the development of self-reliant activities on which he placed so much emphasis was, as we have seen, one of their basic tenets. Gandhi, however, gave a radically different ethical justification for

[47] *Ibid.*, p. 53.

[48] B. C. Pal to Motilal Nehru, n.d., quoted in A. C. Gupta, *Studies in the Bengal Renaissance* (Calcutta, 1958), p. 577.

his doctrine, and from this ethic he derived a plan of political action which was unacceptable to most Bengal bhadralok politicians. Coming from a Gujerati trading caste, he had been strongly influenced by the quietist doctrines of Vaisnavism and Jainism, and determined to apply the principle of *ahimsa* (nonviolence) to politics, he had developed a technique of passive resistance to which he gave the name *satyāgraha*.[49] What he proposed was the application to nationalist politics of a method of protest that was familiar in the Gujerati society in which he grew up: self-abasement and self-denial to force an individual who had given personal offence to realise the injury that had been inflicted and to see the error of his ways.[50]

To many Bengal bhadralok, particularly to that large section for whom the writings of Bankim Chandra Chatterjee, Vivekananda, and Aurobindo Ghose were gospel, this seemed an absurd doctrine. What India needed was self-assertion, not self-abasement, of which it had had centuries. 'What we want is strength, so believe in yourselves', Vivekananda had exhorted his countrymen in 1897. 'What we want is muscles of iron and nerves of steel. We have wept long enough. No more weeping, but stand on your feet and be men'.[51] Strength would not come through love and self-denial alone—indeed, that had been India's great mistake in the medieval period—it would come only through struggle. Gandhi, with his manipulation of popular Vaisnava symbolism and imagery, could no doubt win a great following, but in the opinion of many bhadralok intellectuals, the mass emotionalism he inspired was no contribution to national strength. Bipin Chandra Pal explained:

> I am not blind to the possibilities of good in the great hold that Mahatmaji has got on the populace; but there is the other side; and in the earlier stages of democracy these personal influences, when they are due to the inspirations of mediaeval religious sentiments, are simply fatal to its future. This does not remove the inherited slave-mentality which is the root of all our degradations and miseries.[52]

There was another, more pragmatic, reason why Gandhi's insistence on *satyāgraha* was unwelcome to the Bengal leaders. At least

[49] This was a coinage of Gandhi's from: *satya* = truth; and *āgraha* = firmness.

[50] See S. H. Rudolph, 'The New Courage. An Essay on Gandhi's Psychology', *World Politics*, Vol. XVI, No. 1, Oct., 1963, pp. 98–117.

[51] Vivekananda, *op. cit.*, p. 116.

[52] B. C. Pal to Motilal Nehru, n.d., quoted Gupta, *op. cit.*

initially, they could see in his programme no prospect of a satisfactory engagement with the British. Passive resistance no doubt had its value as a last resort for suppressed majority communities, but the bhadralok were a dominant minority with a position to maintain, and their politicians demanded a form of action which enabled them to exert themselves against their adversaries, the British, and at the same time reinforce their social and political ascendancy. These requirements were met by terrorism and legislative politics, both of which provided opportunities to hit at the British and yet involved relatively few people. It was in these activities that the bhadralok politicians had experience.

Gandhi was demanding that they jettison this experience. He was also demanding from them action instead of words in the rejection of British institutions. The nation could never be creative, he claimed, until the alien debris that overlay Indian society was cleared away. Indians must disengage themselves from the foreign system at every level, from the civil service, the legislative council, and the university down to the district courts and local bodies. They must regain their cultural integrity by a thorough readoption of Indian forms.

On the surface there was nothing novel for Bengal in this. Attacks on 'Anglicisation' and appeals for a return to the 'strength and simplicity of true Bengali life' had been heard frequently from political platforms throughout the province in the preceding fifteen years, and they were recurrent themes in vernacular papers like *Nayak*; but formerly the orators and writers were all bhadralok, often the most westernised elite politicians and journalists, men who valued the European elements in their culture too highly to consider acting on their own advice. They were no more inclined now than they had been at the beginning of the century to make the difficult and costly decision against imported institutions, with which they were as closely involved as ever. Gandhi, on the other hand, had demonstrated in his own political career that he meant what he said, and his personal life was an example of renunciation which he was now insisting that all nationalists should follow. A return to simplicity of living to gain freedom from the tyranny of material possessions; the renunciation of all nonessentials; a total commitment to the struggle against foreign domination—these were Gandhi's demands.

To the bhadralok intellectuals this was philistinism. They were passionately proud of the richness of their culture and were unconvinced that they should strip their life bare in this way. Charles Freer Andrews, who had gained from his work with Rabindranath Tagore at Santiniketan a deep sympathy for bhadralok values,[53] described their reaction. Writing to Tagore in January, 1921, of the joys of painting, he remarked:

> Here are things which Mahatma Gandhi finds it difficult to understand, and he would suspend them all, while we get Swaraj—but not I, not I! I could *never* give up these! . . . No, there is some fundamental difference there: & perhaps it runs through the whole of Bengal as compared with Gujerat. Here, in Bengal, Mahatmaji is saying 'Let every student take up spinning & weaving, & drop everything else'. But the Bengali students say 'We will take up spinning & weaving, but we shall *not* drop everything else'. —There again, is the difference![54]

Tagore himself spoke from the heart of the bhadralok when he demanded rhetorically of Gandhi: 'The mind, surely, is not of less account than a length of cotton thread spun on the wheel!' In a series of public addresses in Calcutta in August, 1921, on his return from an extended trip abroad, he protested against Gandhi's anti-intellectualism and narrowness of view. He spoke for a bhadralok generation which had had ten years to reflect upon its first experience of radical agitation when he said: let us not obscure our vision of the wider world with the dust raised by political passion. Let us seek universal truth, for 'India's awakening is a part of the awakening of the world'.[55] Earlier he had written: 'Our present struggle to alienate our heart and mind from the West is an attempt at spiritual suicide'.[56] His attack brought Gandhi to Calcutta, but discussions between the two men revealed (in the words of a contemporary) 'a difference of temperament so wide that it was extremely difficult to arrive at a common intellectual understanding'.[57]

These differences of culture and temperament certainly stood as barriers between Gandhi and the bhadralok nationalists, but there

[53] For biographical details see B. Chaturvedi and M. Sykes, *Charles Freer Andrews. A Narrative* (London, 1949).

[54] 31 Jan. [1921], Andrews MSS. Cf. Andrews to Tagore, 26 Jan. 1921, quoted *Andrews*, p. 176; and Tagore to Andrews, 5 Mar. 1921, R. N. Tagore, *Letters to a Friend* (London, 1928), pp. 131–133.

[55] 'The Call of Truth', 29 Aug. 1921, Tagore, *Towards Universal Man*, pp. 267 and 270–273.

[56] Tagore to Andrews, 13 Mar. 1921, Tagore, *Letters to a Friend*, p. 136.

[57] Quoted in Tagore, *Towards Universal Man*, p. 377.

were other, less unimpeachable, reasons for their reluctance to follow his lead. This had been brought home to Andrews on a visit to Calcutta in September, 1920, when he met a friend, Promothanath Chaudhuri, 'bitter beyond words & crying out against his countrymen for their folly in following any one who is an Ascetic, as though wisdom must necessarily come from fasting & starving & hunger-striking'.

> But though my intellect went with Promotho Babu & I could never follow Mr Gandhi in his extravagances [Andrews recalled later] I could not help contrasting the other side: for there was Promotho Babu . . . and others in the Camac Street Club with every single luxury of a London Club-life around them,—playing bridge & taking their strong glasses of whiskey & brandy. Say what one would to justify it, they were parasites, living on immense fees taken from others. And if one had to choose, was not their judgment,—their *moral* judgment,—far more warped by luxury & luxurious living than Mr Gandhi's by starvation.[58]

There was more than politics and poetry to the good life the bhadralok elite was defending.

THE BURDEN OF POLITICAL MEMORIES

The Bengal Congressmen's memory of the anti-partition agitation was another difficulty with which Gandhi had to contend in his effort to win Bengal for noncooperation. 1905 was uppermost in bhadralok minds as they faced the decisions of 1920. 'I find our countrymen are furiously excited about Non-co-operation', remarked Tagore in September. 'It will grow into something like our Swadeshi movement in Bengal'.[59] 'In Bengal we have passed through the stage of non-co-operation', wrote Surendranath Banerjea a month later. 'We practiced it in the days of the *swadeshi* movement and the anti-partition agitation. We were non-co-operators before the rest of India thought of it'.[60] As this suggests, there was a certain satisfaction in the thought that the rest of India was now following a path which Bengal had trodden fifteen years before, but there was also an element of pique at the temerity of an outsider like Gandhi in bringing forward as his own inventions and under

[58] Andrews to Tagore, 5 Oct. [1920], Andrews MSS.
[59] Tagore to Andrews, 18 Sept. 1920, Tagore, *Letters to a Friend*, p. 95.
[60] *Bengalee*, 26 Oct. 1920.

labels of his own choosing, the old methods of boycott, *swadeshi*, and national education.

Nor were the bhadralok leaders at all certain that they wished to retrace their steps. The campaigns of the partition period had been exhilarating, but in retrospect the risks that had been taken seemed very grave. For a cause as dear to bhadralok hearts as the unity of Bengal those risks had been worth while, but were they similarly justified for 'a political chimera'[61] such as Gandhi's *swarāj*? Admittedly the anti-partition agitation had achieved its ultimate object, and in bhadralok lore it was reckoned a great victory; but there were many private doubts as to the efficacy of the political methods that had been used.[62] The effects of British retaliation had been serious. Public life in Bengal in the years following 1908 had suffered severely from the suppression of *samitis*, the imprisonment and deportation of political suspects, and the extended activities of the C.I.D. Bengal had pushed out its chin once and been punched hard. It was still suffering from the after effects, and it was naturally reluctant to invite another blow.

What carried even greater weight in the thinking of the bhadralok leaders was the social repercussions of the anti-partition campaign. In trying new methods of direct action in 1906 and 1907 in an effort to involve more people in their agitation against the British, the politicians had stirred up a hornets' nest of regional, communal, and class dissension. For thirty years the Bengal nationalists had maintained as their ideal the ultimate involvement of the 'masses' in the nationalist movement, but previously there had been no occasion for them to seek mass support, nor had they shown any particular concern at the lack of such an opportunity. As A. J. P. Taylor wrote of early nineteenth-century nationalism under the Hapsburg monarchy: 'The masses were evoked as a shadowy presence off-stage, reinforcements that were not expected to appear'.[63] The anti-partition agitation, however, brought a few of them onstage, and the resulting commotion left a deep impression on bhadralok thinking. Although the group's leaders did not totally

[61] An expression used in a manifesto opposing noncooperation published by five leading Bengal Extremists. (*Servant,** 29 Sept. 1920).

[62] E.g., see Surendranath Roy, 26 July 1915, BLCP, Vol. XLVII, pp. 437–438; P. N. Bose, *Swaraj: Cultural and Political* (Calcutta, 1929), pp. 157–159; and Tagore, *Towards Universal Man*, pp. 258–259.

[63] A. J. P. Taylor, *The Hapsburg Monarchy, 1809–1918. A History of the Austrian Empire and Austria-Hungary* (London, 1948), p. 30.

discard the ideal of mass participation in nationalism, they were convinced that an incautious appeal for wider support might endanger the bhadralok's political, and even social, dominance. This conviction reinforced their preference for the elitist and socially secure forms of political action, such as legislative politics and terrorism, to which they were accustomed.

When seen against this background, their reluctance to support the noncooperation movement in 1920 can be readily understood. It was bad enough that Gandhi should insist upon their discarding 'safe' political methods in favour of direct action, but it was adding insult to injury for him to emphasise that it was the exclusive character of those old methods to which he objected. His aim was to take politics to the masses and, by involving them in the nationalist movement, give them political education. He wanted to lead a people's movement. All of which was anathema to most of the bhadralok politicians, who had no taste for popular politics.

Their aversion aside, there were real difficulties in the way of their leading a mass movement. The great bulk of the peasantry, who comprised 75 percent of Bengal's population, were Muslims, and the bhadralok had little in common with the low-caste Hindus who made up the rest. As we have already observed, the manual labourer in Bengal was traditionally separated from his superiors by a wide social gap, and this had been maintained by the exclusive education system established under the British. The peasantry shared nothing of the bhadralok culture, and their values were neither understood nor appreciated by the English-speaking zamindars and urban professional men who were engaged in politics. In Bengal, as in most other parts of twentieth-century Asia and Africa, there was a great problem of communication between the small westernised intelligentsia, eager to build a nation free from European imperialism, and the rural populace, traditionalist and illiterate.

In an editorial published on the eve of the special Congress session in Calcutta in September, 1920, the *Bangali* declared: 'We Bengalis are opposed to non-co-operation. For a period of 10 years, from 1906 to 1916, we played that game. And we are not prepared to take back what we rejected on deliberation then. Even Gandhi had admitted that to act up to this resolution would mean rebellion and revolution, and we are not ready to proceed to such a course'.[64]

[64] *Bangali*, 11 Sept. 1920. This paper was the Bengali-language counterpart of Surendranath Banerjea's *Bengalee*.

The *Bangali* was generally regarded as a voice of the Moderate party, but on this occasion its concern at the effects of mass agitation was shared by a wide range of Bengal nationalists, Extremists as well as Moderates.[65] They were apprehensive that mass agitation would lead to violence, and that violence against the foreigner might quickly change to violence against the socially privileged. The bhadralok elite were afraid of the social consequences of a disturbance of the established political order.[66]

They were afraid because they had much to lose. This elite held much of Bengal's land and a significant share of its wealth. Their domination of all levels of the education system gave them almost exclusive access to the learned professions and government service. They controlled the press. They played a leading part in all forms of civic and village affairs. Politics was their business. They gave Bengal its literature, music, and art. They were its cultural and social leaders. In city and countryside they were indeed the 'respectable people'. All of this they stood to lose from any social upheaval. 'Scratch a Hindu and you will find him a conservative', remarked Surendranath Banerjea.[67] Certainly Banerjea's Hindus, the bhadralok elite, were conservative, and well might they be so.

It must be recognised that their fear was largely a fear of the unknown. They did not understand the 'masses', and they felt no confidence in their ability to lead or even control them should the existing order of political and social relationships be shaken. Their fear was blind, but it was not unreasonable. A leap into the political unknown could well be a leap into revolution and anarchy. In a society like that of India of the early twentieth century, in which there was no system of communication extending vertically through

[65] E.g., compare the following extract from *Nayak*, 9 Sept. 1920: 'Should Gandhi's motion be carried, a revolution would break out in the country and there would be hostility between the rulers and the ruled. It is said that this will be a non-violent and bloodless war. Nevertheless, we must confess that this bloodless and non-violent revolution will surely terminate in bloodshed. Indeed, non-co-operation is another name for rebellion. So we are determined to protest against it at all costs. Let us tell Gandhi that the goal is yet far off.'

[66] In his letters in this period C. F. Andrews frequently contrasted the eagerness of the peasantry to join in mass agitation, with the reluctance of the bhadralok. (E.g., see Andrews to Rathindranath Tagore, 6 Sept. [1920]; Andrews to Rabindranath Tagore, 5 and 15 Oct. [1920]; and Andrews to W. W. Pearson, 12 Nov. [1920], Andrews MSS.

[67] *Nation in Making*, p. 397.

the community; in which there were few universally accepted social values; in which there was no general knowledge of the functions of the state; in which there were great economic inequalities; and in which there were huge new urban centres where traditional restraints had been weakened by the rapid influx of a heterogeneous migrant labour force, the line between order and disorder was thin. It was a perilous undertaking to rock the ship of state, even if it were officered by unwanted foreigners.

CHALLENGE FROM BELOW

The events of the years immediately preceding 1920 had given the bhadralok politicians little reason for confidence. The war of 1914–1918 had had a profoundly unsettling effect on Bengal society, and this social unrest was aggravated in the immediate post-war years by economic difficulties. A succession of natural disasters in 1918 and 1919, including the great influenza epidemic, led to an extraordinarily sharp rise in the prices of foodstuffs and cotton goods,[68] and early in 1920 a severe slump brought to an end a five-year boom in Calcutta trade and industry.[69] Already there had been serious labour trouble in Bombay;[70] there were disturbing rumours of peasant unrest in the United Provinces and Bihar;[71] and strikes among the industrial workers of Howrah and Hooghly-side were becoming distressingly frequent.[72]

Events in Russia in 1917 had left the bhadralok elite extremely sensitive to any potential threat to property from labour. Indeed, their reaction to the Russian revolution had laid bare their basic social conservatism. They had welcomed the success in March of Kerensky and his Provisional Government in deposing the Czar, as an exemplar for India's political emancipation;[73] but their delight had turned to dismay with the violent attack on the propertied classes that followed the Bolshevik revolution in November. They were afraid that a similar disaster might befall India.[74]

The Calcutta Muslim riot of September, 1918, had shown how

[68] BLCP, 3 Feb. 1920, Vol. LII, p. 104, and 10 Feb. 1921, Vol. I, pt. 2, p. 195.
[69] *Census of India*, 1921, Vol. V, pt. 1, p. 34.
[70] *Bangali*, 29 Jan. 1919.
[71] NP, 1920, *passim.*
[72] BLCP, 23 Nov. 1921, Vol. V, pp. 182–183.
[73] E.g., see *Modern Review*, Apr. 1917; and *Dainik Bharat Mitra*, 25 Apr. 1917.
[74] NP, 1918, *passim.*

much inflammable social material was now available in Bengal for political incendiaries, and the concern of the Hindu bhadralok at this development had been manifest in the support accorded by their newspapers to the Government in its use of force to suppress the disorders.[75] This incident had also underlined the fact—a distressing fact for the Hindu bhadralok—that in Bengal it was Muslim rather than Hindu politicians who could best make use of a mass appeal. Although the Muslim leaders had to overcome the same problems of class distinction and, to a lesser degree, differences of culture, sect, and caste, they could speak directly to their coreligionists, in a way the Hindu bhadralok politicians could never do, in the name of Islam. There was a fraternity among Muslims such as was unknown to Hindus in Bengal. The best ground for an appeal was of course religious—Islam in danger—(again cool comfort to the Hindus), and in the post-war years the perfect issue was at hand in the Khilafat movement.

Late in 1919 Khilafat committees had been established in various parts of Bengal 'to circulate news on the Moslem world',[76] and the official peace celebrations in December had provided their organisers with an opportunity to incite communal feeling against the British. 'So far as we are associated with the "Victory", it means defeat for Moslems', declaimed the Bengali-language daily *Mohammadi* angrily. 'The bier of Moslem nationality is being carried out —are we to rejoice thereat?'[77] With the return to Calcutta in January, 1920, of Abul Kalam Azad, a young Urdu-speaking Muslim journalist who had been interned for four years at Ranchi, the movement took a radical turn. Azad and his followers went among the Muslim workers in the mill towns of West Bengal spreading propaganda about the British attitude to the Khilafat. When moderate appeals failed to stir up general anger, resort was had to provocative rumours. It was whispered that the Government had ordered prayers to be said on Sunday instead of Friday, and had proscribed the Koran.[78]

The dangerous possibilities of such an exploitation of ignorance and religious fanaticism were evident to the Hindu bhadralok leaders, and when Ghandi urged them to support the Khilafat

[75] NP, 21 Sept. 1918.
[76] *Mohammadi*, 7 Nov. 1919.
[77] *Ibid.*, 5 Dec. 1919.
[78] Simon Commission, Vol. VIII, pp. 98–99; and *Essayez*, p. 138.

movement in order to cement Hindu-Muslim unity, they angrily protested against his encouragement of such a campaign. Andrews reflected their mood when he wrote: 'The truth is that the "Khilafat" appeals to the very worst side of Islam—that religious arrogance, which is every whit as bad as racial arrogance'.[79] The Bengal Congressmen found it objectionable that Gandhi should insist upon coupling a communal issue of this kind with noncooperation and according to men like Azad a place of prominence in his movement. It strengthened their conviction that his campaign was fraught with danger.

More remarkable than this Hindu opposition was the antipathy toward Azad's campaign displayed by Bengali Muslim politicians. One group, among whom the most outspoken was Nawabaly Chaudhuri, took objection to Azad's stand alongside Gandhi as an apostle of intercommunal amity,[80] which was ironical in view of the Hindu alarm at the appeal to religious sentiment. Others, including many of the bhadralok Muslim League politicians, made no secret of the fact that they regarded Azad and the Urdu-speaking Calcutta group that supported him as outsiders.[81] Although unwilling to join in his campaign among the industrial labourers, they were not blind to the potential advantages of securing some form of mass support, and they were experimenting with organisations that might win them a following among the Muslim peasantry. As early as December, 1917, Fazlul Huq and a group of fellow lawyers and journalists had formed the Calcutta Agricultural Association,[82] and at the beginning of 1920 another body, the Bengal Joatdars and Raiyats' Association, was founded, with office-bearers drawn from Calcutta and the towns of Eastern Bengal.[83] The talk of constitutional reform, in particular the possibility of an extended franchise, had awakened an interest in politics among sections of the

[79] Andrews to Rabindranath Tagore, 9 Aug. [1920], Andrews MSS. Cf. B. C. Pal to Motilal Nehru, n.d., quoted in Gupta, *op. cit.*, pp. 576–577.

[80] See Syed Nawab Ali Chowdhry, *Views on Present Political Situation in India* (Calcutta, 1920), p. 12.

[81] Ill-feeling between the Urdu- and Bengali-speaking communities, which had flared up on various occasions in the past, had recently been aggravated by accusations in the Urdu press that the Bengali Muslims were so parochial that they had lost touch with their coreligionists elsewhere. (See NP, Nov.–Dec. 1919.)

[82] *Moslem Hitaishi*, 21 Dec. 1917.

[83] GI, Reforms Office, Bundle 1920–1, June–Dec. Dep (3), Deposit 34, June 1920.

Bengal peasantry,[84] and it was in the hope of taking advantage of this new awareness that these organisations were formed. They achieved nothing of immediate importance, but they were the precursors of the peasant organisations formed by Muslim politicians in the mid-twenties, which later provided a backing for Fazlul Huq's Krishak Praja Party in the Legislative Council.

These were disturbing developments for the Hindu bhadralok. It was bad enough that the peasantry should be taking an interest in politics, but it was far worse that it should be the Muslim leaders who had the opportunity to keep in touch with at least the larger were at a serious disadvantage. Unlike the Muslim professional men who had the opportunity to keep in touch with at least the larger cultivators through their District communal associations, they had no regular institutional contact with the peasants. Moreover, as a rentier and landholding class, their interests and those of their tenantry were too obviously opposed for them to stand forward as champions of the peasant interest. However hurtful it was to their nationalist pride, they had to face the fact that they were regarded by the lower orders as interested spokesmen for the upper 'exploiting' castes.

In the decade preceding 1920 there had been a remarkable development in the organisation, among the lower castes in Bengal, of caste associations, which had given them a new sense of self-reliance.[85] During the reforms discussions they had rejected all suggestions that high-caste men were qualified to speak on their behalf. Writing to the Government of Bengal in December, 1918, to convey the opinion of a series of caste meetings held in the preceding months, Mukanda Behari Mallick, president of the Bengal Namasudra Association,[86] emphasised that his community was opposed to the Montagu-Chelmsford proposals because their imple-

[84] GB, Political, 8A–10(1), B65, Nov. 1917; and *Nayak*, 17 Feb. 1920.

[85] *Census of India, 1911*, Vol. V, pt. 1, p. 483; and *1921*, Vol. V, pt. 1, pp. 346–347.

[86] The Namasudras, with a population of 2,500,000, were the largest agricultural caste in Bengal. They had had the assistance of British missionaries in the establishment of schools, hospitals, and dispensaries, and in the formation of district unions in Eastern Bengal where they were most numerous. A few of their castemen had secured sufficient education to enter the professions, and in 1912 they had established the Bengal Namasudra Association with its headquarters in Calcutta; but their attempts to interest the caste in politics had been unsuccessful until the talk of constitutional reforms aroused peasant interest. (GB, Political, 8A–10,(1), B65, Nov. 1917.)

mentation would mean increased power for high-caste men. His people, he said, were alarmed at the apparent readiness of the British to give way before 'a vociferous and small band of organised castes pretending to represent the interests of the masses'. Is the past loyalty of the Namasudras, he asked 'now to be rewarded by asking them to seek the redress of their grievances at the hands of an unsympathetic oligarchy of a few limited castes specially of Brahmins, Kayasthas and Baidyas?'[87]

Such talk was extremely embarrassing for the bhadralok nationalists, and while they could save face by explaining away meetings of protest against self-government as machinations of the British,[88] they could not dismiss lightly the democratic ideas that were abroad among the lower castes. '. . . we have now realised what we are, and how great is our strength', a Namasudra journal, *Pataka*, declaimed.

> A caste with a population of 25 lacs cannot remain asleep for ever. We had been put to sleep by the blind Hindu kings who ruled over Hindu society. Today we have woken up from that slumber through the grace of the mighty British, who believe in the equality of men and not in caste.[89]

This rhetoric had its logical outcome in a Namasudra demand in 1920 for the reservation for their caste of one-third of all the non-Muhammadan seats in the Bengal Legislative Council.[90]

Such unwonted assertiveness from the lower castes, particularly their interest in gaining legislative representation, raised for the Hindu bhadralok the old, thorny problem of reconciling liberal institutions with high-caste dominance. It seemed as though they would soon be forced to face the issue they had avoided for so long. *Nayak* commented bitterly:

> The hatred between Brahmans and non-Brahmans in Madras–the spirit of enmity in Bengal among many of the Namasudras against the higher castes–underlying all this is not there the instigation of strangers–of conquerors? Unless our society is revolutionized and the social bonds relaxed, business cannot flourish and money cannot be earned easily. That is why steps are being taken to

[87] Mallick to Governor's Secretary, 31 Dec. 1918, GB, Appointment, 6R–36(18), B376–625, Apr. 1919.

[88] E.g., *Bengalee* and *Amrita Bazar Patrika*, 7 Nov. 1917.

[89] Quoted in N. K. Bose, 'Some Aspects of Caste in Bengal', in Milton Singer (ed.), *Traditional India: Structure and Change* (Philadelphia, 1959), p. 200.

[90] GI, Reforms Office, Bundle 1920 Aug. A(6), A54–119, Aug. 1920.

> demolish the barriers between the different castes. When we get the Montagu Reforms, the spirit of strife and quarrel and enmity among us will be aggravated and a terrible social revolution brought about![91]

For the bhadralok, the obvious line of defence against this threatened attack from below was to oppose any radical extension of the franchise or the provision of special legislative representation for the lower classes, and every bhadralok witness before the constitutional enquiry committees of 1918 and 1919 took this line. They insisted that a restricted franchise based on a property qualification should be maintained 'in order to secure competent voters and manageable electorates'. The towns that were the bhadralok strongholds, particularly Calcutta where the high castes formed 50 percent of the Hindu population, should be given considerable weightage, 'because men of political capacity and public spirit and intelligence were to be mainly found in the towns. If the towns were not given separate seats, the town candidates would be overwhelmed'.[92] For a similar reason they argued that no residential qualification should be required for candidates.[93] They rejected on principle the demand for separate communal electorates and opposed every concession suggested for the Muslims.[94] 'They on no account should be allowed to have the balance of power in their hands', said Shib Shekhareswar Ray, a member of the Bengal Legislative Council. 'Such a state of affairs would not only spell disaster to the cause of good Government in the country, but would seriously jeopardise the interests of non-Muhammadans'.[95] Nor should the Hindu lower castes be given special representation, as Surendranath Banerjea explained to the Joint Select Committee.

> There is a tendency in some quarters to make a fanciful line of cleavage between the masses and the educated community. The educated community are the natural protectors of the masses, and I desire to emphasise that fact . . . . We are the natural protectors of the masses, and have always been so, because they are our people—the bone of our bone and the flesh of our flesh . . . .[96]

[91] *Nayak*, 22 Aug. 1919.
[92] *Evidence Taken Before the Reforms Committee (Franchise)* (Calcutta, 1919), Vol. II, pp. 383 and 390.
[93] *Nation in Making*, pp. 318–319.
[94] PP, 1919 (203), Vol. IV, evidence, pp. 70–71.
[95] BLCP, 1 Dec. 1921, Vol. V, p. 531.
[96] PP, 1919 (203), Vol. IV, evidence, p. 68.

NATIONALIST AND SOCIAL RADICALISM

All that has been said about the attitudes of the bhadralok politicians toward the masses points a lesson of general application: that nationalist radicalism is not to be equated with social radicalism. It would seem a statement of the obvious to observe that the desire of colonial nationalists to rid their country of imperial domination is not, of necessity, accompanied by a desire to reconstruct the internal social order; yet the failure to grasp this point, or at best to state it explicitly, has been a frequent source of misunderstanding of the different forms nationalism may take in colonial countries.

The confusion that prevails over the reasons for the Bengali reaction to Gandhi's noncooperation proposals provides a striking illustration of this. Following the lead given by various participants,[97] commentators have applied the term 'Right Wing' to the Moderates and others who favoured council entry, and 'Left Wing' to the Extremists and terrorists.[98] By the logic of their metaphor they are then convinced that Gandhi's nonviolent noncooperation movement must have been of the 'Centre', and it is with perplexity that they discover that while the Bengal nationalists favoured both council entry and terrorism (the 'Right' and the 'Left'), they were most reluctant to accept noncooperation (the 'Centre').

It is evident that these writers have been led astray in their interpretation by their failure to distinguish between nationalist and social radicalism. The terms 'Right and Left Wing' have socio-economic connotations acquired from their European usage. If these terms are to have any meaning in the Bengal context (and their value is doubtful), both council entry and terrorism must be regarded as 'Right Wing', for they were esteemed by the bhadralok politicians as elite activities, and noncooperation as 'Left Wing', for it was regarded as socially hazardous.

Gandhi himself was aware of the importance of this distinction between nationalist and social radicalism. 'In fighting the Govern-

[97] E.g., *Indian Struggle*, pp. 39–40, 46, and 55; N. C. Banerji, p. 210; and *Reports on the Working of the Reformed Constitution, 1927* (Calcutta, 1928), p. 178.

[98] E.g., V. A. Smith et al., *The Oxford History of India* (London, 3rd ed., 1958), pp. 783 and 790; J. Coatman, *India, The Road to Self-Government* (London, 1941), pp. 39, 82, 97, and 101; R. C. Majumdar, H. C. Raychaudhuri, and K. K. Datta, *An Advanced History of India* (London, 1946), p. 955; and R. C. Majumdar, *History of the Freedom Movement in India* (Calcutta, 1963), Vol. II, p. 161.

ment the motives of co-workers can be mixed', he explained. 'In fighting the devil of untouchability I have absolutely select company'.[99] Here in a nutshell is the explanation of the Bengal Congressmen's reaction. Gandhi was not simply offering a fight against the Government. He was also calling for an attack on the devils in Indian society, and the socially conservative bhadralok politicians were convinced that these devils should be left well alone lest all hell be let loose.

LOWER-CLASS BHADRALOK

The trend of our argument has presented us with a logical problem: if, as we have asserted, the Bengal Congressmen were so implacably opposed to Gandhi and his programme of noncooperation, why did they capitulate to him at Nagpur in December, 1920? The answer basically is that he undercut them by capturing the support of a section of their own community: the lower-class bhadralok.

This group, as we saw, were brought into politics for the first time during the anti-partition campaign, when men like Bipin Chandra Pal, Aswini Kumar Dutt, and Aurobindo Ghose had taken advantage of the lower-class bhadralok's jealousy of the elite and their resentment at their exclusion from active politics, to snatch the initiative from Surendranath Banerjea's party. These radicals brought the lower-class bhadralok onto the streets and fundamentally altered the character of the agitation, but they did not have the experience or techniques to control large numbers of followers, nor was it in their power to provide them with a permanent political role. With the withdrawal of the Extremists from Congress and the collapse of the anti-partition agitation under British repression in 1908, the lower-class bhadralok were again condemned to the political wilderness.

It was eight years before there was another direct appeal to them, and again it came from the Extremists. Attempting in 1916 and 1917 to reassert themselves in Congress and to wrest control of the provincial political organisations from the Moderates, the Extremists raised the old cry of exclusivist politics. The way was prepared for them by the vernacular press which had maintained in the interim a constant attack on the Moderates on this ground. These papers

[99] Gandhi to Andrews, 23 Nov. [1920], quoted in *Andrews*, p. 157.

had developed stereotyped lines of criticism, with a terminology which is highly misleading if taken out of context. When, for instance, they spoke of the '*bābus*' they referred to those objects of righteous scorn, the bhadralok elite. 'The people' or 'the mass' were their approving readers, the lower-class bhadralok. Their criticism was usually levelled at the '*bābus*' ' selfish disregard for 'the people', their 'Anglicisation' and divorce from 'true Bengali Hindu society', and their concern with British institutions, titles, and honours. Two passages will suffice as illustration.

> This is the Congress of the Babus. These irreligious, luxury-loving beggars are the creation of English education. The country and society have nothing to do with them. The mass do not know them, neither do they care for the mass. By virtue of their begging through the Congress they secure high posts, start subsidised papers and try to win fame and respect in the country.
>
> *Dainik Chandrika*, 30 December 1914

> . . . whatever our Babus do, they do for the furtherance of their own self-interest and not for the benefit of the people at large. The Congress and conferences and what not keep these agitators perpetually before the public eye and bring them something for their pockets also. And that is all that our 'patriots' care for.
>
> *Basumati*, 17 April 1915

Against this background we can understand the applause with which Chitta Ranjan Das' maiden political speech—his presidential address to the Bengal Provincial Conference in April, 1917—was greeted by the old Extremist politicians and the vernacular press. Whether or not it was his intention (and there is reason to doubt that he meant his words to be interpreted so narrowly), his speech was seen as an attack on '*bābu*' politics and as a direct appeal to the lower-class bhadralok against the Moderates.[100] If we compare his language with that current in the vernacular press, we can appreciate why this construction was put on his words.

> . . . we have become largely and unnecessarily Anglicised in our education, culture and social practices. The mere mention of 'politics' conjures up before our eyes the vision of English political institutions; and we feel tempted to fall down before and worship the precise form which politics has assumed under the peculiar conditions of English history. . . . Only we neglect the one thing essential. We never look to our country, never think of Bengal or the Bengalees, of our past national history, or our present material

[100] NP, Apr.–May 1917.

> condition. Hence our political agitation is unreal and unsubstantial –divorced from all intimate touch with the soul of our people . . . . We boast of being educated: but how many are we? What room do we occupy in the country? What is our relation to the vast masses of our countrymen? Do they think our thoughts or speak our speech? I am bound to confess that our countrymen have little faith in us.[101]

This speech established Das' reputation, and it was the keynote for a vigorous and successful Extremist effort to mobilise lower-class bhadralok support in Calcutta and the mufussil towns. In the battles of late 1917 and 1918 between the Moderates and Extremists for command of the local Congress machinery, the latter's ability on almost every occasion to produce a numerous and noisy backing to outvote and outshout their rivals proved the decisive factor.

There was danger, however, in what the Extremists were doing. The nature of their appeal to the lower-class bhadralok, especially the terms they were using, gave them a false appearance of social radicalism that might expose them to a charge of hypocrisy should there arise a demand for radical action. In fact, the Extremist politicians were as much a part of '*Bābudom*' (as *Nayak* described elite society)[102] as were the Moderates, and should there be an attack on that society they were almost bound to turn in its defence–which is what happened when Gandhi appeared on the scene. Here was a man who spoke of 'the mass' and 'the people' without any mental reservations, who attacked Anglicisation root and branch, and who would sever all ties with British institutions. He offended the bhadralok politicians, Extremist as well as Moderate, and they turned against him; but in doing so they lost the support of their own lower-class who saw in this yet another example of '*bābu*' betrayal. *Nayak* spoke for them:

> The Babus openly advocate democracy to obtain cheap notoriety, while they secretly associate with Government, with a view to securing titles and high posts carrying fat salaries. When their object is accomplished they identify themselves with Government. This is the reason why one who is an Extremist today becomes a Moderate tomorrow. Mr Gandhi's non-co-operation movement strikes at the root of this turncoat policy, and this is why the Babus are opposed to it.[103]

[101] C. R. Das: *About Bengal* (Calcutta, 1917), pp. 4–5.
[102] *Nayak*, 8 Aug. 1916.
[103] *Ibid.*, 24 Dec. 1920.

With their excitement running high at their new share in politics, the lower-class bhadralok were in no mood to tolerate diffidence. If the '*bābus*' lacked the courage to lead them against the British, then they would find leaders who did not. At first they were doubtful that Gandhi was the man for the task, for the one thing that was clear among his otherwise perplexing political utterances was his unwavering opposition to any violent conflict with the British. However, by the middle of 1920, as he clarified his ideas and they were given better publicity in Bengal, the lower-class bhadralok grasped the fact that he was offering a fundamental challenge to British authority and that his agitation would provide unprecedented opportunities for political involvement. Enthusiastically they declared for noncooperation, and the cautions from the elite politicians about the dangers to bhadralok dominance of mass politics went unheeded. 'No one is listening', wrote Andrews: 'all is clamour and noise & strife'.[104]

THE POLITICIANS' SURRENDER

The Bengal Congressmen were now faced with a painful choice. Should they stand by their principles at the risk of committing political suicide, and possibly being displaced by radical and irresponsible men? Or should they give way before Gandhi's popularity in the hope that ultimately they might be able to exercise some restraint on the agitation in Bengal? Fazlul Huq, presiding at the 1920 Provincial Conference in April, had given a pertinent word of advice: 'Leaders of the people must always have the courage to face the people and if they find that they can no longer lead, they must either give up their politics or be prepared to be led'.[105] As the year passed and Gandhi's following grew, many of the Bengal politicians decided that they would have to consent to be led. 'The whole country is with Mr Gandhi, but the politicians are holding back. Yet one by one they are obliged to declare themselves,' reported Andrews early in September.[106]

By that stage Gandhi, a master of political tactics, had manoeuvred his opponents into a corner. In April and May he had arranged for the Central Khilafat Committee and the A.I.C.C. to discuss

[104] Andrews to Rabindranath Tagore, 3 Aug. 1920, Andrews MSS.
[105] 3 Apr. 1920 at Midnapore, Azizul Huq collection.
[106] Andrews to Rathindranath Tagore, 6 Sept. [1920], Andrews MSS.

noncooperation, and it was announced that a special session of Congress would be held in September to decide for or against his scheme. In the meantime, he went ahead with his own preparations and on 1 August began personal noncooperation. This forced the provincial Congress committees to reach some decision, and, with the knowledge that direct opposition to Gandhi would bring down upon them public wrath, they could do no more than search for some form of compromise. The Bengal committee decided for noncooperation in principle, but urged that the legislative councils should be boycotted from within.[107] All the leading Bengal Extremists were candidates for the first elections for the new legislatures to be held at the end of the year, but the uncertainty as to the policy which Congress would adopt was a handicap to them in their canvassing. Worse still, their advocacy of council entry, even if the purpose were to obstruct from within, put them perilously close to the Moderates.

They went to the September Congress in this awkward, compromised situation, while Gandhi, well aware of his strength, went full of confidence. The main debate on noncooperation took place in the Subjects Committee. For three days the Bengalis struggled vainly to swing the majority against Gandhi, who was obdurate in his insistence that Congress give immediate support to every item of his programme. When his resolution came before the full session on the 8th, Bipin Chandra Pal moved an amendment to accept the principle but delay the implementation of noncooperation. His concern, he explained, was to avoid a failure on a national scale such as had occurred in Bengal during the *swadeshi* campaign of the partition period. In the voting on the following day, Pal's amendment was rejected and Gandhi's resolution carried by a large majority, against the votes of all but a handful of the Bengal delegates.[108]

What were Gandhi's opponents to do now? Should they withdraw from the Congress and go ahead with their preparations for the elections? Should they remain in the Congress in the hope that they could reverse the decision at the annual session in December? Or should they forget their qualms and accept noncooperation? They were in a quandary, but they could not hesitate for long for they were under pressure from the Gandhians to declare themselves. After a week of agonised debate, the main group in the

[107] NP, Aug. 1920.
[108] *Servant*, 15 Sept. 1920; and Jayakar, Vol. I, pp. 390–397.

Bengal Congress, under the leadership of C. R. Das and Byomkes Chakravarti, decided to adopt the second course: they would bow to the majority decision for the present but would work for its reversal at the end of the year. This meant, however, that they would be unable to contest the elections, and on 15 September they issued a manifesto withdrawing their candidature.[109]

In the twelve weeks that remained before Congress met again at Nagpur, there was much confused activity among Bengal Congressmen and Khilafatists. Abul Kalam Azad's party was busy discouraging Muslim voters from going to the polls,[110] while Das, Chakravarti, and B. C. Pal travelled extensively in Eastern Bengal in an attempt to rally their dispersed supporters.[111] The popular excitement over Gandhi's activities which had been mounting steadily through the year had reached such a pitch that it had engulfed many who earlier had been sceptical. Andrews was one of them. 'It is good to be alive in these days', he wrote delightedly on 1 November, 'even if one has not the heaven, which Wordsworth speaks of, of being young'.[112] In this atmosphere there was no place for equivocation, and the cry 'For or against?' became insistent. 'Are you a whole-hogger? If so you are a non-cooperator. Do you contend that some of the items in the programme are calculated to do more harm to the people than to the bureaucracy? Well, damn you, you are no non-cooperator but a renegade.'[113]

This mood augured ill for the success of the revisionist party at Nagpur, but it was determined not to let the issue go by default and it was as active as its opponents in organising supporters for the trip to the Central Provinces. The result was an extraordinary migration. '. . . whilst many of the prominent politicians were present, the Bengal contingent included hundreds of ex-detenus and the intelligentsia, which dominated earlier Congresses, seems to have been swamped in a mass of semi-educated persons swept up from all parts of India', reported the Government of India.[114]

Within the Bengal delegation there were a number of groups warring for ascendency, and feeling between them was so embittered that the two meetings held on 26 and 27 December to elect

109 *Servant*, 15 Sept. 1920.
110 GI, Reforms Office, Bundle 1921 Jan.–Mar. B(5), B34–99, Mar. 1921.
111 *Amrita Bazar Patrika*, 9 Nov. 1920.
112 Andrews to Rabindranath Tagore, 1 Nov. [1920], Andrews MSS.
113 *Amrita Bazar Patrika*, 24 Nov. 1920.
114 GI, Home Political, Deposit 3 (Confidential) and K-W, July 1921.

the province's representatives on the Subjects Committee ended in free-for-all fights. Order was restored only when Gandhi intervened in person.[115]

C. R. Das had come to Nagpur determined to offer stout resistance to noncooperation, but it was now clear that he could not even carry the whole Bengal contingent with him if he opposed Gandhi. Although his position was difficult, he still had room for manoeuvre, for of all the contenders for nationalist leadership in Bengal in the preceding two years he had been the most equivocal in his attitude to Gandhi's programme. At the Bengal Provincial Conference in April, 1919, for instance, he had proposed the implementation of *satyāgraha* in Bengal, and when he failed to gain support for this resolution he had threatened 'to leave the Conference and go to the masses'.[116] It was significant that he had not made good his threat and had therefore been available in the following year to speak for Bengal against Gandhi, but gestures of this kind undoubtedly made easier the somersault he now turned at Nagpur. Having secured Gandhi's private assurance that he would be left free to pursue his own political propaganda, he made the dramatic announcement that he would move the main resolution in support of noncooperation.[117]

With this bold change of front Das turned defeat into victory. Provided he could carry his own group with him—and his personal influence was sufficient to enable him to do this—he now had a chance to unite the whole Bengal contingent under his leadership. He had stolen his opponents' platform and, by securing Gandhi's endorsement, had climbed a step above them. They remained merely provincial politicians, while he had reasserted himself as a national figure. Most important of all, he could return to Bengal with a reunited battalion at his back and a job of work in hand. Even had he been successful in persuading the Congress in favour of council entry, he would have been unable to provide action for his party, for the first elections were over and the Moderates ensconced in the legislatures for a three-year term. With noncooperation he had a task for his eager followers, and a popular task at that.

[115] *Bengalee*, 30 Dec. 1920 and 1 Jan. 1921; and N. C. Banerji, p. 146.
[116] GI, Home Political, B494–497, May 1919. (For this reference I am indebted to Hugh Owen, University of Western Australia.)
[117] P. C. Ray, *Life and Times of C. R. Das* (London, 1927), p. 159.

V

THE MODERATES' FAILURE

THE COUNCIL AND THE POLITICIANS

'I wish I could get the damned bureaucracy to realise this, but we are literally sitting on an earthquake', Edwin Montagu noted in his diary on 1 December 1917.[1] Montagu was exasperated at the inability of the British Indian officials with whom he was working on the reforms to see that a lengthy delay in their implementation could have revolutionary effects. What the I.C.S. described as cautious progress seemed to him dangerous hesitancy, which prolonged the uncertain period in which there were no satisfactory institutions to give direction to politics. It had been evident from the response to his 20 August declaration that the legislative councils were of sufficient importance for the Indian nationalists to consider their reconstruction a critical issue, and Montagu saw that the British would be losing a golden opportunity if, by their dilatoriness, they encouraged the development of an agitation that distracted attention from these institutions.

As we have seen, he failed to impress the officials with his sense of urgency, and there was a gap of three and a half years between his parliamentary statement and the inauguration of the new constitution, during which time the agitation he had hoped to forestall had been organised. The British had missed their opportunity, but, for Bengal at least, the remarkable thing was by how narrow a margin. Despite the intense frustration in Bengal resulting from years of British stalling, the constitutional reform negotiations

[1] Montagu, p. 77.

had captured and held the attention of all political groups, and even the Extremists had resisted the counterattraction of the noncooperation movement until the very last months before the new constitution was implemented.

In fact, the Bengal Legislative Council, for all its shortcomings and the abuse heaped upon it as a consequence, had become the focal point of Bengal politics in the period between 1913 and 1920. This Gandhi discovered when he attempted, like some Pied Piper, to lead the Bengal Extremists away to a joyous land. They could hear the promise in his tune but were reluctant to leave the familiar political haunts of their people. They followed Gandhi, but with many a regretful backward glance at what they were leaving to their political and social rivals.

The situation in Bengal at the beginning of 1921 was not unlike that of 1913. Again there was a new constitution and renewed hope of a stabilised political order. Again the Government and one section of politicians were eager to work the reforms to achieve this stability and to build for themselves a commanding position in the new system. Again there was a group outside the Council determined to prevent this.

There were, however, significant differences. The promise of future self-government had now been made by the British; and under the constitution of 1919, as a first installment of responsibility, the Council had been given greatly extended powers, including control over the administration of a number of departments of the provincial Government under a system called 'dyarchy'.[2] These advances encouraged the Government and the Moderates to hope that the work of the new Council would be free from the frustrating limitations that had done so much to discredit the Morley-Minto legislatures.

Against this had to be placed the greater strength of the opposition outside the Council. There was no comparison between the small disorganised group of Extremists, dispirited by police persecution, which had made a series of haphazard verbal attacks on the members of the old councils, and the noncooperators, full of shining zeal for a great cause, and united in a campaign of destruction under

[2] Under this system there were 'reserved subjects' (such as finance, police, gaols, and justice) over which the Governor and Executive Council retained control, with no direct responsibility to the Legislative Council; and there were 'transferred subjects' (such as local self-government, public health, education, public works, and agriculture) which were the charge of the Governor and Ministers, who were responsible to the legislature.

an acknowledged national leader whose charisma enabled him to appeal even to the mass of the peasantry at times of crisis.

It is the purpose of this chapter to trace the efforts made by the Government and the various groups of participating politicians to get the new institutions of legislation and government working satisfactorily in the period 1921 to 1923, against the background of this hostile nationalist agitation. The story of the noncooperation movement, which will appear here only incidentally, will be told in full in the following chapter as a prelude to the Swarajists' triumph at the 1923 elections and their domination of the second Montagu-Chelmsford Council.

THE GOVERNOR AND HIS MINISTERS

Surveying the political prospect in January, 1921, Tej Bahadur Sapru, Law Member of the Government of India and a leading Moderate politician, wrote:

> I believe that one of the most important determining factors in the situation will be the character of the relationship which is established between the Government and the Legislative Assembly and the Council of State, and in the provinces, the manner in which the Ministers work and are allowed to work. If at the end of the forthcoming legislative session the country finds that the new Councils have given a good account of themselves, and have exercised a more decisive influence than their predecessors, there is, I feel, every chance of a corresponding change in public sentiment towards the Government making itself manifest.[3]

The importance of this observation is that it was made, just as the reformed constitution was inaugurated, by one who was intimately in touch with the two parties most vitally concerned with the new institutions: the Government and the Moderates. It gives an insight into the attitude with which they approached their task. The assumptions underlying Sapru's comment are significant. He believed that if the Government and the Moderate nationalists concentrated their attention upon the reformed legislatures, if they evolved a relationship that allowed the Indian Ministers and MLCs a demonstrable influence in the government of the country, and enabled them to implement measures that would secure wide public approval, they could effect a shift of opinion in political society at

[3] Minute, 25 Jan. 1921, GI, Home Political, Deposit 3 (Confidential) and K-W, July 1921.

large in favour of constitutional methods and cooperation with the British. Presumably he hoped that this 'change in public sentiment' would result in the collapse of noncooperation and the reunification of the National Congress to work in the reformed legislatures after the second general election in 1923.

Sapru had put his finger on one spot on the blueprint of the reconstructed system and said: this is the vital point. Make this part work satisfactorily and the system as a whole will be a success. By implication he was saying that the other parts of the system were of less importance. The Government need give less attention to other institutions than to the legislature. Its handling of nationalist agitation, violent or nonviolent, outside the legislature was not of equal importance to its relations with the nationalists inside. The work of the Moderates in the Council was more important than their work in other public or political bodies. Their victory at the next elections would be secured by their achievement in the Council chamber and not primarily by their activities in their constituencies. Although we must not dismiss the possibility that Sapru was wrong, it is incontestable that his attitude was shared by most Government members and Moderate politicians. As we follow the story of the reformed Council in Bengal from 1921 to 1923, we shall see that they acted on these assumptions.

The most important initial event for all participants in the new institutions was the Governor's selection of Ministers, for the men he chose would form the link between the Government and the Legislative Council, and the principles by which he made his choice would determine the character of the relationship established.

Lord Ronaldshay, who was entering his last year as Governor of Bengal, realised how unsettling the extended period of political reconstruction had been, and he considered it essential to get the reformed institutions working with whatever material was to hand in order to offer a centre of political interest to rival noncooperation. At all events, the Government must not appear to be discomfited by Congress opposition. Addressing the final meeting of the old Bengal Legislative Council on 1 September 1920, he calmly told 'those who think the reforms are not worth having' to stand aside if they wished. They would soon realise their mistake, he said, and those who thought they could wreck the reform scheme would be shown to have 'an altogether exaggerated idea of their own importance'.[4]

[4] BLCP, Vol. LII, p. 948.

While dismissing the noncooperators with such nonchalance in public, Ronaldshay was careful to keep open his private lines of communication with them, for he recognised that they commanded wide public support, and, if possible, he wished to persuade them to participate in the new Council. They rejected his overtures,[5] and he then turned to the Moderates with the intention that they should serve as a counterpoise.[6] There could be no question of their refusing to participate in the formation of the new Government, for they were committed to the Montagu-Chelmsford constitution, having fought for the reforms for five years and finally having withdrawn from Congress to support them. The British, for their part, realised that such devotion to the constitutional ideal should not go unrewarded and that their obligation to the Moderates could best be discharged by appointing their leaders as provincial Ministers.

With this as his criterion, Ronaldshay had a straightforward task. 'I had no difficulty', he recorded, 'in selecting as my chief Minister, my old critic, Babu Surendranath Banerjea'.[7] He was also willing to accept for the second ministerial post Banerjea's nominee, Pravas Chandra Mitter, Secretary of the National Liberal League, who had earned the Government's gratitude by braving public obloquy to serve on the Rowlatt Committee.[8] To maintain a communal balance among his Ministers as he had done in his Executive Council with Sir Abdur Rahim's appointment in 1920, Ronaldshay chose Nawabaly Chaudhuri for the remaining position. Chaudhuri was an East Bengali, which the Government considered an advantage, and he had recently published a forthright attack on noncooperation.[9]

For the Ministers, their appointment was both a goal attained and an opportunity for further achievement. Chaudhuri's aspirations were communal. He had fought hard to secure advantages for the Bengal Muslims in the reformed constitution, and then to persuade them that they could further their communal interests by entering the new institutions. As the Nawab of Dacca had done ten years before, he argued that the Government held power independently of the two great Indian communities and that it could be

[5] *Essayez*, p. 135.

[6] Chief Secretary, GB, to GI, 19 Feb. 1921, GI, Home Political, Deposit 3 (Confidential) and K-W, July 1921.

[7] *Essayez*, p. 136.

[8] For biographical details see *Nation in Making*, pp. 337–340.

[9] In a pamphlet: *Views on Present Political Situation in India* (Calcutta, 1920). On Chaudhuri's appointment see *Nation in Making*, p. 338.

influenced to use that power to the Muslims' advantage.[10] His ministerial appointment gave him the opportunity of exerting this influence personally. He saw himself in a position similar to that which Nawab Khwaja Salimulla had occupied under Carmichael's administration: able to talk privily with the executive and, at the same time, gain information that would assist his community in determining its course of action. In the new order he would have an additional role: that of political broker. By trading the votes of his communal bloc in the Legislative Council, he would be able to secure direct concessions for his community from his fellow Ministers and Executive Councillors.

If the vision that Banerjea and Mitter had of their task was not as clear as Chaudhuri's, it was also not as limited. As lifelong campaigners for constitutional advance, they felt a sense of personal achievement in the new powers that had been secured in 1919, and they took up their portfolios happy in the knowledge that at last they could turn from agitation to construction. By a positive achievement they might prove to the British, on the one hand, that Indians could govern themselves, and to the noncooperators, on the other, that the Moderates had been justified in supporting the reforms.[11]

For Surendranath Banerjea in particular January, 1921, was a milestone. He was a tired old man of 72 who had travelled a long way and taken many hard knocks from the Government, and lately from a younger generation of Indian nationalists. Now it all seemed worth while. He was to be the first Indian 'chief minister' of Bengal, with a protégé as one of his colleagues, and a knighthood to boot. It was a great triumph for a man who had been dismissed ignominiously from the I.C.S. and who had spent most of his days at daggers drawn with the alien rulers of his country.

He was of good heart as he approached his new work. Revealing himself a true son of bhadralok Bengal, he asked for the portfolios of Education and Local Self-Government but was told that secretariat arrangements would not permit of this combination. He then chose Local Self-Government with Public Health, for his ambition was to introduce a bill to amend Curzon's Calcutta Municipal Act, in opposing which he had staged his famous walkout from the Corporation in 1899. The reforming act was to be his *magnum opus*: the

[10] *Views on Present Political Situation in India* (Calcutta, 1920), pp. 34–35.
[11] *Nation in Making*, pp. 312–313.

proof that the day had come when, by constructive constitutional endeavour, Indians could rectify the wrongs from which they had suffered for so long.[12]

COMPOSITION OF THE COUNCIL

The 1920 elections had apparently given Banerjea what he needed: a Council composed largely of Moderates. It was his good fortune that the noncooperators had abstained from the contest, for they were extraordinarily popular. As it was, they had shown their strength by putting up five low-class candidates in the Chittagong and Noakhali electorates, having them returned by large majorities, and then holding this up as proof of the disrepute of the reformed Council.[13] If this cynical demonstration were disregarded, as also the success of the Khilafatists in dissuading many Muslim urban voters from going to the polls,[14] the election results could be considered favourable to the Moderates. Of the 56 elected Hindu seats in the new Council (see Table 4), 27 were filled by members of the Indian Association and Moderate Party, and another 16 by British Indian Association members.

It seemed reasonably certain that the Ministers would command a majority, but there was a group among the new members who talked of obstruction within the Council. No one could offer more than a guess as to its potential strength. As the Chief Secretary to the Government of Bengal explained to Delhi on 3 February 1921: 'There are no clearly defined political parties, and individuals are swayed considerably by their own personal predilections and opportunities'.[15]

If the political complexion of the Council left room for speculation, its social composition certainly did not. Despite the extension of the franchise, there was a reassuring similarity between the successful Hindu candidates at this election and those who had sat in the Morley-Minto councils. High-caste men again took most of the seats, with zamindars and lawyers predominant. Almost two-thirds of the Hindu members were university-educated, and ap-

[12] See his speech introducing the Bill to Legislative Council, BLCP, 22 Nov. 1921, Vol. V, pp. 131–132.

[13] *Noakhali Sammilani*, 2 May 1921; and GI, Reforms, Bundle Jan.–Mar. 1921 B(5), B34–99, Mar. 1921.

[14] GI, Reforms, *ibid.*

[15] *Ibid.*

proximately the same proportion had had experience in local government. It appeared, moreover, that local influence—from landholding, caste, family, connection, wealth, or personality—was still a decisive factor in election contests. It was significant that the one Hindu candidate who had campaigned on a platform of land reforms in an attempt to win the votes of the newly enfranchised cultivators had been well trounced by the local Maharaja.[16]

The contests for the Muslim seats revealed many of the features characteristic of Muslim elections in Bengal throughout the preceding decade: a bewildering number of candidates,[17] and in west Bengal the manipulation of the electoral regulations by influential Calcutta families, with the well-educated and experienced Suhrawardys proving most adept. In eastern and northern Bengal, however, there was a significant development. Of the 19 Muslims elected from rural constituencies in these areas, ten came from cultivating families and stood as representatives of 'the agricultural interest'.[18] It was a straw in the wind.

Addressing a meeting of Indians in London in 1909, Surendranath Banerjea had said: 'Next to the approbation of his own conscience, the highest reward to which a public man aspires is the applause of his fellow-countrymen'.[19] There was no applause for Banerjea and his Moderate followers in 1921. For once the local Hindu and Muslim press was united, and its sympathy was wholly with the non-cooperators. It poured its scorn on the 'charade' of the elections, and greeted the formation of the new Government of Bengal with howls of derision. Here, it said, was proof of the hollowness of British protestations of a new respect for Indian opinion. The appointment of a reactionary communalist like Nawabaly Chaudhuri and a discredited time-server like P. C. Mitter could only be intended as an affront to political Bengal. As for Banerjea, with his comfortable billet and his knighthood, the best that could be done was to bid him a sad farewell from the nationalist camp. 'Surrender Not Banerjea' of partition fame was now 'Sir Surrender'.

'The Lost Leader'

I am sending you, Mr. Editor, a copy of the poem, a no more ap-

[16] BLCP, 11 Feb. 1921, Vol. I, No. 2, p. 237.

[17] One hundred thirty-two candidates contested the 39 seats. (PP, 1921, [Cmd. 1261], Vol. XXVI, pp. 25–26).

[18] GI, Reforms, Bundle Jan.–Mar. 1921 B(5), B34–99, Mar. 1921.

[19] S. N. Banerjea, *The Trumpet Voice of India* (Madras, 1910), p. 43.

propriate greeting than which, I believe, could be addressed to the erstwhile leader of Bengal.

'Just for a handful of silver he left us,
Just for a riband to stick in his coat—'.[20]

The effect of this attack on the Ministers—and this was true for all the Moderates—was to force them on to the defensive from the beginning. When all their energies were required for the problems of initiating the reforms, they were obliged to devote time and effort to the profitless business of self-justification. And this cross they had to bear for the duration of their term of office.

FINANCIAL DIFFICULTIES

On 11 January 1921 Ronaldshay convened the first meeting of his new Government. To the dismay of the Ministers, the Finance Member, J. H. Kerr, presented a draft budget showing an estimated deficit of more than two crores of rupees. He revealed that the provincial finances were in a parlous condition.

This was partly the result of the war, which had reduced the flow of British capital to India, had caused enormous inflation, and had left the Government of India with a heavy deficit. In the same period the provincial governments had been instructed to suspend all major development schemes, and the salaries of civil servants had been fixed. Thus with the return of peace there was the need for extra expenditure to make up this leeway; however, in the immediate post-war years there was a succession of poor harvests and finally a trade slump, which hit Bengal particularly hard because of the importance the export of jute, tea, and coal had assumed in its economy.

Even before the war, the Bengal Government had found it increasingly difficult to meet growing demands upon the provincial revenues because the Permanent Settlement denied to the public purse any share in the increment in land values. For this reason Bengal had come to rely far more than any other province upon income tax and customs duties. In 1920, however, the Meston Committee, formed to consider the financial changes that should accompany the introduction of the reformed constitution, recommended that these sources of revenue be given to the Government of India and that the provinces be left solely with land revenue. In

[20] *Amrita Bazar Patrika,** 30 Dec. 1920.

considering the contribution each province should make to meet the Imperial deficit, it took account of the relatively low yield of the land revenue in Bengal; for this reason it set the initial contribution of the province at only 6.5 percent of the deficit. It insisted, however, that there was a great scope for expansion in the Bengal revenues, and it imposed a sliding scale to raise Bengal's contribution to 19 percent in seven years.[21] The Government of Bengal objected strongly to these recommendations and in view of its protest, the Joint Select Committee suggested that the provinces should retain the benefit of any increment in income tax. This proposal was accepted by the Government of India, but the concession proved of little real advantage because of the trade recession.[22]

When confronted with this dismal prospect, the Ministers immediately talked of resigning for they could see all too clearly the alternatives facing them: either to impose new taxation, a sure way of provoking the wrath of the propertied classes, or to retrench. This would mean abandoning development schemes on which they had pinned their hopes of gaining credit for their administration of the transferred departments, and it would also mean that the number of jobs available for distribution as patronage would be reduced. In either case, the success of the reforms seemed to be in jeopardy.

Exercising all his natural geniality, Kerr persuaded the Ministers to take a less pessimistic view of the situation. He explained that the province had a credit balance of nearly three crores, the result of the freezing of provincial funds during the war, and that this could be used to tide the Government over the first year. In the meantime, he suggested that every effort should be made to persuade the Government of India and the Secretary of State to modify the Meston award.[23]

The Ministers accepted his proposal. They agreed to enlist non-official support for the Government's representations and to sponsor a resolution in the Legislative Council. They had no difficulty in securing backing for this from their fellow MLCs, for there was general anger at the way in which Bengal had been treated in the financial settlement; and when Surendranath Roy resolved on 9 February that the attention of the Government of India be drawn

[21] PP, 1920, [Cmd. 724], Vol. XIV, pp. 120–121.

[22] PP, 1920, [Cmd. 974], Vol. XXXV, pp. 111–115; *ibid.*, 1923 [Cmd. 2361], Vol. X, pp. 332–333; and BLCP, 21 Nov. 1921, Vol. V, pp. 3–9.

[23] *Essayez*, p. 136.

to the Joint Select Committee's recommendation that Bengal receive special consideration, there was not one dissenting voice in the chamber.[24]

THE MINISTERS AND THE COUNCIL

The Ministers had not reckoned with the demands that were then made for economy in government. At first there were one or two suggestions for a general reduction in the number of public employees, but such proposals were anathema to the bhadralok, and the members rejected them out of hand.[25] There was not the same tenderness, however, for the high officials, and there was a spate of resolutions to reduce the number of Executive Councillors and Ministers, and to cut the latters' salaries.[26] These resolutions had the support of the press.

The most distressing feature for the Ministers was the difficulty they experienced in organising an opposition in the Council to the resolutions. They found that their success in securing their portfolios was resented by many of their senior colleagues. The Suhrawardys, for example, considered that one of their family should have been appointed instead of Chaudhuri,[27] and Surendranath Roy, who for twenty years had been Banerjea's right-hand man in the Indian Association and the old legislature, was angered by the latter's nomination of Mitter as Education Minister.[28] As a sop Roy was offered the position of Deputy-President of the Council. He accepted this but refused to take any salary, emphasising that he, for one, recognised the need for economy.[29]

It was evident that the old informal contacts between councillors, which had sufficed for the conduct of nonofficial business in the

[24] BLCP, Vol. I, No. 2, pp. 142–152.

[25] '. . . we have come up with motions against the best interests of the country, against the educated community, against pleaders and against the Subordinate Judges and Munsifs. What is this? It is worse than anarchy'. (J. C. Ghose, member for Calcutta University, BLCP, 16 Mar. 1921, Vol. I, No. 5, p. 175).

[26] BLCP, 7, 9, 10, and 11 Feb. 1921, Vol. I, No. 2, pp. 66–88, 153–172, and 211–272.

[27] *Nation in Making*, p. 339.

[28] Information supplied by Biren Roy, M.P., Surendranath Roy's nephew, in interview with the author, Calcutta, 10 Mar. 1962. Cf. *Nation in Making*, p. 340.

[29] BLCP, Vol. I, No. 2, pp. 48–49.

Morley-Minto legislature, were unsatisfactory in the reformed Council with its enlarged membership and extended powers.

The trouble, as the Government observed later, lay partly in the unreal expectations of the ordinary MLC: 'Each individual member except for a few experienced hands is out to run Bengal in his own way and to interfere in every detail of the executive or judicial administration and in particular of the "nation-building departments" '.[30] Added difficulties were the existence of an extremist group of 25 to 30 Hindu members, whose sympathies lay with the noncooperators and who were determined to obstruct the Government, and the reluctance of the great majority of the Muslims to cooperate wholeheartedly with the Hindus.[31] But the crucial problem was the absence of organisation among the main body of Hindu Moderates—in *Capital's* words 'a rabble of freelances whose personal and parochial jealousies are a bar to concerted action'.[32]

The Ministers' experience in the old councils and local bodies, where their personal influence had been sufficient to give them control, had not prepared them for this situation, and at first they were at a loss for an answer. Banerjea, suggesting to his colleagues that the appointment of Council Secretaries might 'help to evolve order out of chaos and form a strong party organisation for Government', underlined this ineptitude. He wrote:

> My information is that parties are being formed today to be broken up the next day. Babu Surendra Nath Ray has, I understand, been deposed from the leadership of a party which he said he claimed as his own. Babu Radha Charan Pal tried to step into his shoes. Mr D. C. Ghose tried to throw oil upon the troubled waters. Everything seems to be in a fluid condition . . . .[33]

The attempt to cut their salaries, coming as it did before they had had time to find their feet, sapped the Ministers' confidence and gave them an uncomfortable feeling of isolation from the Council. As a result, they turned for support to the British officials, whom they implored to take up cudgels for them. The attack on the Ministers, Banerjea explained, was 'an extremist move inspired by a section of the extremist Press'. He hoped that the officials would be instructed to vote against the motions and that the Members of

[30] PP, 1924–5, [Cmd. 2361], Vol. X, p. 341.
[31] *Ibid*., pp. 342 and 351.
[32] *Capital*,* 17 Mar. 1921.
[33] Minute, 26 Mar. 1921, GB, Appointment, 6R–36(1), A1025B, May 1921.

the Executive Council would speak on the Ministers' behalf, for this would 'show the solidarity that exists between the two wings of the Government, official and popular'.[34] The Executive Councillors accepted his argument, and the heavy artillery was rolled out to shoot down the resolutions when they were put to the Council on 10 and 11 February.[35]

Ronaldshay, however, disliked using the official bloc in this way. He insisted that support for the Ministers should be organised in the Council itself, and he encouraged Satish Ranjan Das, Standing-Council to the Government, to act as a ministerial whip.[36] Das accepted the task and set about arranging conferences of members to discuss forthcoming business,[37] but he had great difficulty in overcoming the suspicion with which he was regarded by many MLCs as a 'Government man'. There was still a widely held conviction that the proper duty of a Council member was to agitate against the Government, and, with the noncooperators winning acclaim for their open defiance of the administration outside the Council, it seemed essential to keep attacking inside if all initiative was not to be lost.

The extremist group encouraged this thinking, and from the beginning were on the alert for an issue on which they could unite the nonofficials to defeat the Government. The voting on the budget seemed a likely opportunity, and they chose the police grant for a trial of strength. On 17 March, before a packed Chamber, Wasimuddin Ahmed, Muslim member for Pabna, moved that the demand for this department be reduced. He was offering the Government an opportunity, he said, to demonstrate its respect for the opinions of the MLCs and thus refute the noncooperators' assertion that the reformed Council was a puppet show. The abolition of some of the senior ranks in the police force would be a popular move and, at the same time, it would effect a worthwhile saving of funds. The Extremists had chosen their ground well, for even the old hands would join in an attack on the police. Sir Henry Wheeler, Senior Member of the Executive Council, was infuriated by this unconcealed attempt to embarrass the Government. 'This is, if I may say

[34] Minute, 1 Feb. 1921, GB, Appointment, 18L–5(1–5), A180–4, July 1921.
[35] BLCP, Vol. I, No. 2, pp. 211–271.
[36] One must be careful to distinguish between Satish Ranjan Das and his more famous cousin, Chitta Ranjan Das. For biographical details on the former see *The Indian Year Book, 1928* (Bombay, 1928).
[37] BLCP, Vol. I, No. 5, p. 173.

so, one of the most irresponsible resolutions which I have heard moved in this Council, and again, if I may say so, I have seldom heard a series of more irresponsible speeches', he declared angrily. His words were wasted. The motion was carried by 51 votes to 42.[38]

Ronaldshay regarded this resolution as an offence against the spirit of the constitution, and he considered himself justified in exercising his statutory right to restore the grant. He realised, however, that such action would discredit the Moderates and give the noncooperators another handle with which to beat the Council. So he decided, against the advice of Wheeler and Kerr, to try to manipulate the Council proceedings and have the grant revoted. He drafted a series of questions for Satish Das to put to the Government and the replies that Wheeler should give. Das was to ask what would be the effect of the Council's reduction of the police grant, and Wheeler was to reply that it would necessitate a decrease in the strength of the force. In response to a supplementary question he was to emphasise that it 'would obviously be improper' for the Government to provide extraordinary funds to maintain the existing police establishment even long enough to give the Council time to reconsider its action. It was arranged that C. W. Rhodes, a Bengal Chamber of Commerce representative, should then move for an adjournment to discuss the grave situation revealed by these replies.[39]

The matter came before the Council on 1 April and all went according to plan. The Government had been active in the preceding ten days enlisting support among the MLCs, and the adjournment debate was characterised by a more conciliatory tone.[40] This gave the Governor the excuse he wanted to avoid certifying the police demand; before the middle of the month he had persuaded the Council Standing Committee on Police to recommend a supplementary grant, which was carried through the Council on 21 April.[41]

'On the whole I think that we may congratulate ourselves upon having got round a rather awkward corner satisfactorily', wrote Ronaldshay to Montagu a week later.[42] He had avoided a direct clash between the Government and the Council, which at that early stage would have endangered the working of the institution, and he

[38] BLCP, 17 Mar. 1921, Vol. I, No. 5, pp. 196–206.

[39] *Essayez*, pp. 140–142; and BLCP, 1 Apr. 1921, Vol. I, No. 6, p. 32.

[40] BLCP, *ibid.*, pp. 125–148.

[41] *Ibid.*, Vol. II, p. 81.

[42] *Essayez*, p. 143.

had, he hoped, enabled the Moderates to retreat without losing face. He was unduly sanguine. In fact, his device was so transparent that it was treated with derision by the noncooperationist press. 'Are we to call this trickery by the name of co-operation?' asked *Nayak*. 'Do you mean to achieve the salvation of the country through these means? If that be so, we must frankly say that non-co-operation is a thousand times better than this servile form of co-operation'. 'Shamelessness, thy name is "Council membership" ', declaimed *Swatantra*.[43] Scorn was heaped upon the Ministers for their apparent inability either to influence the reserved side of the Government or to control the Council. '. . . as cockroaches are to birds our "Reform" Ministers are to the English and Dominion Ministers', sneered the *Amrita Bazar Patrika*.[44] In *Nayak's* opinion Banerjea was 'now nothing but a black edition of Sir Henry Wheeler', and *Liberty* spoke of the Ministers as 'mercenary partisans'.[45]

THE TESTING TIME

Writing to Tej Bahadur Sapru from London on 1 June 1921, Evan Cotton, a member of the India Office Advisory Committee, ventured the opinion that the reformed institutions would shortly face their severest trial. 'I do feel that while the reforms have been attended with remarkable success, the danger point has not yet been passed. Mid year will see the testing time: when Ministers have matured their plans and the question of providing funds becomes insistent. Finance has always been present to my mind as the great difficulty in the way. I should be sorry therefore if the public attention were in any way distracted'.[46]

The Ministers also realised that although the conclusion of the Budget session gave them a breathing space, they could not afford to remain idle. They had to consolidate their position in the Council if they were not again to be forced into a humiliating dependence on the officials. Banerjea therefore set about organising a legislative party, with Satish Das as his chief whip, and an MLCs' club—the Constitutional Club—as a rallying point. The Extremists refused to participate. Nawabaly Chaudhuri was willing to lend the support of his Muslim followers but made it clear that they remained, first

[43] *Nayak* and *Swatantra*, 23 Apr. 1921.
[44] *Amrita Bazar Patrika*, 10 Mar. 1921.
[45] *Nayak*, 22 Mar. 1921, and *Liberty*, 16 Apr. 1921.
[46] Sapru papers.

and foremost, a communal bloc. The European and Anglo-Indian nonofficials pledged their allegiance to the Ministers, and the balance of the Hindu members, 30 or so in number, expressed their willingness to cooperate with Banerjea and Mitter although they were reluctant to extend this to Chaudhuri.[47] They were also chary of becoming involved in a formal party organisation, for this suggested a public commitment to the Government, and that was no way to advance a political career in the prevailing atmosphere of hostility. Consequently, the Constitutional Club was no great success, and in the Council the Ministers could be assured of support only for less controversial questions concerning the transferred departments.[48]

The noncooperators also regarded midyear as a testing-time, and their determination was to distract public attention from the Legislative Council. In the early months of 1921 they had been stirring up labour trouble; they achieved their greatest success in April and May when they persuaded a large group of Assam tea labourers to leave the gardens for their homes in Bihar and the United Provinces. The majority of these coolies became stranded at Chandpur, a steamer station on the river Padma in Eastern Bengal, and they suffered severe hardship before arrangements were made for their forward transport. There was general anger at the Government's handling of the situation, and the noncooperators secured much publicity for their work among the distressed.[49]

The Moderates came badly out of the affair. For the two months, May and June, when it dominated the news headlines, the Council was not in session and the issue was fought out between the officials and the noncooperators. The latter were quick to draw attention to the Moderates' absence and to point the moral that they were no longer of significance.

When the Council met again in July they were faced with the awkward choice of either joining in the popular attack on the Government and thereby enhancing the noncooperators' victory, or echoing the Government's strictures on the noncooperators and being written off by their countrymen as lackeys of imperialism. They vacillated between the two, criticising first one side and then the other,[50] with the result that they got the worst of both worlds.

[47] PP, 1924–5, [Cmd. 2361], Vol. X, p. 343; and Simon Commission, Vol. VIII, pp. 151–152.

[48] B. P. Singh Roy, *Parliamentary Government in India* (Calcutta, 1943), pp. 87–101.

[49] See below, pp. 214–219.

[50] BLCP, 8 and 11 July 1921, Vol. III, pp. 383–427 and 452–485.

Each party dismissed them as the tools of the other,[51] and they were even upbraided by the Calcutta European press which until this time had commended them for their support of the reforms.[52]

Elated by this success, the noncooperators pressed home their advantage. They kept the agitation in Eastern Bengal alive through strikes on the railways, and in Calcutta they organised a series of demonstrations and *hartāls*. In October, the Congress leader in Chittagong, J. M. Sen Gupta, and a number of his followers were arrested and brought to Calcutta for trial. Nothing could have been more embarrassing for the Moderates than the sight of their rivals, bedecked with martyr's garlands, being cheered triumphantly to gaol–and well the noncooperators knew it. These are the fruits of the reforms, they said, the products of a mixed brown and white bureaucracy: a costlier administration, an unending prospect of new taxation and, worst of all, repression.[53] 'There are only two parties in India just now and not more', declared the *Dainik Basumati*. 'One is the nationalist party and the other the traitors'.[54]

The disorders continued, and after serious violence in Calcutta in November, 1921, the provincial Government applied the Indian Criminal Law Amendment Act and the Prevention of Seditious Meetings Act, under which wide-scale arrests were made in the second week in December. Now the Moderates were in serious trouble. The enforcement of this repressive legislation offended their nationalist sentiment, but how could they voice their anger without appearing to be merely spokesmen for the noncooperators? When on 19 December a Calcutta MLC, Surendranath Mallick, moved for an adjournment to discuss the matter, Wheeler had no hesitation in accusing him and his supporters of irresponsibility. R. M. Watson-Smyth, a Bengal Chamber of Commerce representative, was even more outspoken. 'Government has now taken action and its authority has been challenged, and the time has come when we must declare ourselves on one side or the other', he said. 'We have come to the parting of the ways . . . . Hatred, unfortunately, is at the bottom of a great deal of this movement against the Government. Racial hatred, the blind hatred of the East for the West'. This brought angry denials from the Indian nonofficials, and the Maharaja of Burdwan, rising late in the debate, felt the need for a

[51] GB, Political, 12–C–72(1), A27, July 1921; and NP, July 1921, *passim.*
[52] *Englishman*, 3 June 1921.
[53] *Amrita Bazar Patrika*, 30 Oct. 1921.
[54] *Dainik Basumati*, 5 Nov. 1921.

rallying speech. He was confident, he said, that the spirit in the country was not as bad as it was represented and that many responsible men approved of the action that had been taken. 'I, for myself, wish to state clearly that what has been done by the Government of Bengal has had my fullest support'. A voice: 'What about the Ministers?'[55]

This interjection touched a sore point. It was significant that none of the Ministers had taken part in the debate. They held their peace, for of all the Moderates they were in the most wretched position. Repressive legislation was no more agreeable to them than to their fellow nationalists, but in the light of the information about the riots that was available to them as members of the Government, they saw the question in a different perspective. With the whole of political Bengal up in arms at the Government's action, however, it would have been foolish for them to speak out as Burdwan had done; yet they could not join in the attacks without being disloyal to Ronaldshay and the Executive Council. They were not constitutionally responsible for the actions of the reserved half of the Government, but in the popular view they were implicated in what had been done.

Their position was made especially difficult by the prevailing practice in the Government of Bengal of joint consultation between Executive Councillors and Ministers on all important questions of policy. This system had been initiated by Ronaldshay, with the best of intentions and the full approval of the Ministers, to assist in the creation of a spirit of mutual confidence within his Government. The responsibility for a decision lay solely with one or other half of the Government, but by encouraging free discussion between both sides Ronaldshay hoped to build a team spirit. He considered it vital to keep the reformed institutions working, and joint consultation, although it offended against the strict division of functions, seemed to assist in doing that. Ronaldshay was pleased with the result. 'The relations between the two halves of my Government have been excellent', he told Montagu in April, 1921, 'and I have invariably discussed matters of importance round a table at which Members of the Executive Council and Ministers sat. Sweet reasonableness has been the outstanding feature of all such discussions'.[56]

Initially, the Ministers were well pleased with an arrangement

[55] BLCP, 19 Dec. 1921, Vol. VI, pp. 1–53.
[56] 28 Apr. 1921, *Essayez*, p. 143.

which brought all administrative issues within their cognisance, but it was soon public knowledge that they participated in the discussion of reserved subjects, and when unpopular decisions were taken they were considered blameworthy. Their only loophole was the fact that no vote was taken at the joint meetings, the final decision on reserved subjects resting with the Governor and Executive Council. In 1922, however, even this loophole was closed by Ronaldshay's successor, the Earl of Lytton.

ANOTHER MAN WITH A MISSION

Lord Lytton came to Bengal in March, 1922, fresh from the India Office where, as Under-Secretary for two years, he had been inspired by Montagu's enthusiasm for the reforms.[57] In taking up the governorship he had a strong sense of mission. 'At that time I felt that the moment was critical in the history of India, and that it was all-important to get the Reforms started on the right lines', he wrote in his memoirs. 'I believed that I might render valuable service in this capacity, and the call seemed to me one which I could not refuse'. He felt that he was making a great sacrifice in interrupting at the age of 45 a distinguished political career that could be expected to give him a position in the Cabinet at an early date. His intention was to return to England as soon as he had accomplished his task.[58]

Although he had no experience of India, he had a clear vision of what that task involved: the preparation of Bengal for a further transfer of power by the development of the parliamentary system, and the provision of opportunities for Indians to influence all decisions of Government.[59]

With the first end—the development of the parliamentary system—in view, he brought Evan Cotton out from England to succeed the ailing Shamsul Huda as President of the Bengal Legislative Council. Cotton came of a family that had served the Company and Crown of India for more than 150 years.[60] Following in the footsteps of his father, Sir Henry, one of that small group of I.C.S. officers who had supported Congress in its early days, he had given

[57] For biographical details see DNB.

[58] *Pundits and Elephants*, pp. 8 and 9–10.

[59] *Ibid.*, pp. 21–23.

[60] For biographical details see *Who's Who, 1926* (London, 1926); and C. H. Philips' introduction to Evan Cotton, *East Indiamen* (London, 1949).

up a successful career at the Calcutta Bar in 1906 to work in England for Indian constitutional reforms. He had lived off interest from investments and devoted his time to lobbying on behalf of the Indian National Congress. As a member of the India Office Advisory Committee he had assisted Montagu with the work involved in implementing the new constitution, and from 1920 he had been Honorary Secretary of the Indian Reforms Committee, 'a British Organisation in support of the Moderate Party in India'.[61] Eager as he was to return to India, and holding opinions similar to Lytton's own, he seemed the very man to assist the new Governor in his liberal undertaking.

In pursuing his second aim—the provision of opportunities for Indians to influence administrative decisions—Lytton was following a line marked out by Montagu. 'I am quite sure now, that we have got to go in for Indianization', Montagu had written in July, 1921. 'We have got to realize that self-government does not merely mean political reform, but the substitution of an indigenous administration for a foreign administration'.[62] This spirit of Indianization was what Lytton intended to promote, and he would give evidence of his intention by taking his Indian Ministers into his full confidence. He would conduct his Government as a unit, treating both Executive Councillors and Ministers as members of a single Cabinet. Henceforth there would be joint decision as well as joint discussion on all matters of substance.[63] And determined that his intention should be publicised, he informed the members of the Legislative Council of his decision in his reply to their address of welcome on 31 March 1922.[64]

The comparison with Carmichael is remarkable. Here again was a British Liberal with a sense of mission, coming full of goodwill and determined to press ahead faster than a strict interpretation of the constitution would allow because of his conviction that Bengal was ready for a further transfer of power. Unfortunately, there were the same heartbreaking disappointments in store for him and, like Carmichael, he was to leave Bengal a disillusioned man.[65]

His troubles began even before he reached Calcutta. On embark-

[61] Quoted from the Committee's letterhead (Sapru papers).

[62] Montagu to Lord Reading, 21 July 1921, Reading, Vol. II, p. 209.

[63] *Pundits and Elephants*, p. 9; and GB, Appointment, 18L–14(1–3), A1–3, Sept. 1927.

[64] BLCP, Vol. VII, No. 5, p. 442.

[65] See *Pundits and Elephants*, p. 9.

ing for India at Marseilles he learnt that Montagu had been forced to resign from the India Office following a dispute with the Cabinet. Lytton was unhappy at the prospect of working with his successor, Lord Peel.[66] As a further blow to his optimism, he found that his initial efforts to win public support in Bengal were regarded with suspicion. Replying to an address of welcome from the British Indian Association, for instance, he described the reformed constitution as a bridge over which India might walk to the promised land of self-government.[67] This provoked what to Lytton seemed a churlish retort from the *Amrita Bazar Patrika* under the heading 'Bridge or trap?': 'The mirage of a bridge is thrown over the river. And the majority of our countrymen fear that they will be drowned in trying to cross it. A few have made the attempt and are sinking in their full view'.[68]

When Lytton turned his attention to the details of administration, he was appalled by the state of the provincial finances. As expected, the deficit for 1921–22 had exceeded two crores, thereby depleting the provincial balances. The Government of India had remitted the provincial contribution for the year but it had refused to reconsider the Meston award, and continued complaints from Bengal had provoked a sharp reprimand from the Viceroy in December, 1921.[69] The prospect of reducing expenditure on the transferred departments, so vital to the success of the reforms; of imposing new taxation; and of conducting a running fight with the Government of India over the Meston award was almost too much for Lytton, and for some months he talked despondently of resignation.[70]

He was also distressed by the antipathy toward his policy of Indianization displayed by British I.C.S. officers, inside and outside his Government; by the end of his first year in Bengal he had reached the conclusion that further constitutional advance would have to await the growth of a new spirit among the officials.[71] The implementation of the Montagu-Chelmsford reforms had been accompanied by numerous resignations from the services, especially of senior I.C.S. officers,[72] and with a growing problem of recruit-

66 *Ibid.*, p. 20.
67 30 Mar. 1922, BIA, Publications, Vol. XIII.
68 *Amrita Bazar Patrika*, 1 Apr. 1922.
69 In address to Bengal Mahajan Sabha, 14 Dec. 1921 (Sapru papers).
70 Reading, Vol. II, p. 210.
71 *Pundits and Elephants*, pp. 33–34.
72 Simon Commission, Vol. I, p. 267.

ment in England, grievances over salaries, and resentment at the attacks made by Congress politicians, morale in the services was particularly low in 1922.[73] From the officials' viewpoint, nothing could have been more untimely than the new Governor's publicised determination to give Indians increased say in Government policy.

From the members of the Bengal Executive Council, who had previously kept their grumbles to themselves, Lytton's policy provoked open objections. They complained that 'the "decisions of joint meetings" have substantially influenced the "orders of the Executive Council" in a way that they were not intended to do',[74] and they protested the amount of their working time that was wasted 'in the present state of fusion between politics and administration'.[75] Their disagreements with Lytton came to a head over a suggestion from the Government of India to reduce the size of the provincial Executive Council. They thought this a reasonable proposal, but they were angered when Lytton suggested that it would be a friendly gesture to submit the matter to the Legislative Council for consideration. 'I consider it a very dangerous practice to allow the Legislative Council to have a finger in the pie with regard to appointments by the Crown, and I would strongly deprecate that procedure,' wrote Burdwan as Senior Member of the Executive Council. The two British members were of the same opinion, and Lytton had to drop the idea.[76]

His Ministers fully approved of his policies, but after a time even they were forced to admit that their difficulties had been increased. The practice of joint decision left them wide open to attack in the legislature and, at the same time, they were subjected to increasing pressure from the Executive Councillors to give public support to measures they had approved in private.[77]

The refusal by the members of the Legislative Council to recognise the distinction between reserved and transferred subjects greatly annoyed Lytton, and when dissolving the first reformed Council in August, 1923, he told them that this had been their chief shortcoming. 'There is no very marked difference of attitude towards that portion of the Executive which is responsible and that

[73] See Montagu to Reading, 27 Apr. 1921, Reading, Vol. II, p. 206.
[74] GB, Appointment, 6R–38(1–2), A5–6, July 1925.
[75] *Ibid.*, 18L–88(1–2), A24–25, Sept. 1922.
[76] *Ibid.*, 8R–1(10–11), A47–48, Oct. 1923.
[77] E.g., *ibid.*, 6R–43(4–150) of 1921, A234–380, May 1922.

which is still irresponsible', he said. 'Both are indiscriminately classified as the Bureaucracy and regarded as a fair target for invective'.[78] His complaint was unreasonable in view of his own determination to disregard dyarchy and, by the time he left Bengal in 1927, he had realised that the error was his own. He wrote in his memoirs: 'The only result . . . was to identify the Ministers with a Government that was disliked, and to weaken instead of strengthening their position'.[79]

UNIVERSITY OF CALCUTTA

Lytton's difficulties with the Executive and Legislative Councils were his most serious, but they received less public attention than a dispute in which he was involved with the University of Calcutta. This affair was significant for it arose from a clash between the Montagu-Chelmsford Government and legislature–new institutions exercising new powers–and the Vice-Chancellor and Senate of the University–old institutions trying to consolidate their powers.

The dispute revolved around the commanding figure of Sir Asutosh Mookerjee, one of the most outstanding and controversial personalities in bhadralok society.[80] Mookerjee's life had been ruled by two loves: the High Court and the University. His devotion to the former had been rewarded with a judgeship, and to the latter, with the position of Vice-Chancellor. He had been given this appointment first in 1906 after his unsuccessful but outstanding campaign against Curzon's Universities Act, and he served for an unprecedented term of eight years, during which time he was instrumental in widening the university's range of activities, particularly in the field of postgraduate teaching.

Autocratic by nature, he made many enemies. When, after his replacement as Vice-Chancellor in 1914, he continued to use his influence to control the development of the postgraduate departments, a party was organised in the Senate to oppose him. It was unsuccessful in preventing his having all postgraduate teaching con-

[78] BLCP, 21 Aug. 1923, Vol. XIII, p. 477; cf. *Pundits and Elephants*, p. 38.
[79] *Pundits and Elephants*, p. 180.
[80] For biographical details see DIB; B. C. Pal, *Character Sketches* (Calcutta, 1957); and N. K. Sinha, *Asutosh Mookerjee. A Biographical Study* (Calcutta, 1966).

solidated under the university's control, and this development received the approval of the Calcutta University Commission which reported in 1919.[81]

The Commission also recommended that jurisdiction over the university be transferred from the Government of India to the Government of Bengal. This was effected in March, 1921, with the Governor of Bengal replacing the Viceroy as Chancellor, and the provincial Minister of Education assuming responsibility for university affairs.

At the same time Mookerjee was invited by Ronaldshay to serve again as Vice-Chancellor. This perturbed his opponents, and in search of a course of action they conceived the idea of attacking his administration through the Legislative Council, which now had authority over the university. They were able to enlist allies among the Eastern Bengal members who feared that Mookerjee's expansionist policies would drain finance from the new University of Dacca, which had also been transferred to the control of the Government of Bengal.[82] In August, 1921, Rishindranath Sarkar, a High Court lawyer and member for Bankura West, moved for an enquiry into the financial administration of the university, alleging grave irregularities in the expenditure on the postgraduate departments. After a heated debate lasting two days in which charges of personal malice were made, the motion was carried by a narrow margin.[83]

This brought a vigorous counterattack from Mookerjee and his supporters. At meetings of the university Senate and in articles in the *Calcutta Review*,[84] which had just been taken over by the university, they accused the Legislative Council and the Government of partiality toward Dacca University and a desire to ruin the old centre of learning. The Education Minister, P. C. Mitter, was angered by what he considered unjust criticism and, introducing the education budget in the Council on 1 March 1922, he described the financial administration of the university as 'deplorable'. In his opinion, its deficit of nearly five lakhs was due to 'thoughtless expansion' of postgraduate studies.[85]

[81] *Hundred Years of the University of Calcutta* (Calcutta, 1957), p. 193.
[82] BLCP, 17 Mar. 1921, Vol. I, No. 5, pp. 214–243.
[83] *Ibid.*, 29 and 30 Aug. 1921, Vol. IV, pp. 138–175.
[84] E.g., *Calcutta Review*, 3rd series, Vol. I, pp. 124–128 and 177–178; Vol. II, pp. 112–115.
[85] BLCP, Vol. VII, No. 3, p. 118.

Mookerjee took this as a personal affront and let it be known that he had no intention of agreeing to the Government's interference in university affairs. He was supported by the Senate which entered into an acrimonious correspondence with the Education Department on the subject of university finance. A crisis was reached in August, 1922, when the Government offered the university monetary assistance on condition that there be no further expansion of its activities until it was solvent once more. This was too much for Mookerjee. 'There is a sinister, perfidious campaign against this University', he told the Senate. 'Take it from me that as long as there is one drop of blood in me, I will not participate in the humiliation of this University. . . . We shall not be a part of the Secretariat of the Government'.[86]

The Government's reply was to frame two bills, one for the creation of a board to take control of secondary education from the university, the other for the reform of the university itself. Lytton, who took very seriously his *ex officio* position as Chancellor, told Mookerjee of his personal interest in the legislation and asked for his support, but the Vice-Chancellor replied that he could not acquiesce in what appeared to be an effort to destroy the university's independence. There followed a lengthy correspondence and a number of interviews between the two men, with neither willing to give an inch; finally, in March, 1923, Mookerjee, whose two-year term of office was almost up, received a letter from Lytton which warned that he and Mitter would not consider the Vice-Chancellor for reappointment unless his opposition ceased.[87]

In taking this action Lytton had made a mistake. He could reasonably expect to have the support of Mookerjee's powerful enemies in an attack upon him personally, but in threatening the independence of the office of Vice-Chancellor he was bound to arouse the hostility of the bhadralok as a group. They were jealous of their control of the University of Calcutta, for it was the cornerstone of their monopoly of higher education. The Vice-Chancellorship was considered one of the most important and respected public offices in Bengal, and the bhadralok would not countenance an attack upon its powers by an English Governor.

[86] 8 Dec. 1922, quoted, *Hundred Years of the University of Calcutta, op. cit.*, pp. 288–289.

[87] Lytton to Mookerjee, 24 Mar. 1923, *ibid.*, pp. 294–296.

Mookerjee realised that Lytton had blundered, and he penned a thumping rejoinder:

> I am not surprised that neither you nor your Minister can tolerate me. You assert that you want us to be men. You have one before you, who can speak and act fearlessly according to his convictions, and you are not able to stand the sight of him. It may not be impossible for you to secure the services of a subservient Vice-Chancellor, prepared always to carry out the mandates of your Government, and to act as a spy on the Senate. He may enjoy the confidence of your Government but he will not certainly enjoy the confidence of the Senate and the public of Bengal. We shall watch with interest the performances of a Vice-Chancellor of this type, creating a new tradition for the office. I send you without hesitation the only answer which an honourable man can send, an answer which you and your advisers expect and desire: I decline the insulting offer you have made to me.[88]

Not to be thrown off balance by this broadside, Lytton offered the Vice-Chancellorship to one of Mookerjee's most distinguished enemies, Bhupendranath Basu. Mookerjee then read the Governor's letter and his own to the university Senate, and the uproar that followed the publication of the two letters in the press was extremely embarrassing for the Government. Lytton and Mitter were held to have come badly out of the affair,[89] and its effect was to contribute to the discredit of all connected with the reformed Government and Council in the opinion of the bhadralok at large.

CORPORATION OF CALCUTTA

While Mitter was in trouble with the university, Banerjea was struggling with problems of local self-government. In his first months in office he had offended his departmental officials and added to the number of his political enemies by appointing relations and friends to positions at his disposal in local bodies.[90] This was a minor issue, however, compared with the storm that blew up over the reform of the Calcutta Corporation.

[88] Mookerjee to Lytton, 26 Mar. 1923, quoted *ibid.*, pp. 298–300.

[89] NP, 14 Apr. 1923.

[90] Simon Commission, Vol. VIII, p. 190; J. G. Drummond, *The Working of the Bengal Legislative Council under the Government of India Act, 1919* (Cambridge University Ph.D. thesis, 1938–39), p. 327; *Hitavadi*, 15 Apr. 1921; *Amrita Bazar Patrika*, 24 Nov. 1921.

The legislation to effect this reform had been in preparation for some years before Banerjea took up his portfolio, but he immediately set to work to mould the secretariat's product into a shape conformable to his nationalist ideals. He was particularly concerned to reduce to a minimum communal and other special representation on the Corporation.[91] The bill he introduced to the Legislative Council on 22 November 1921 provided 13 reserved seats in general electorates for the Muslims and 12 seats in commercial electorates for the Europeans. Banerjea explained that he had avoided separate communal electorates because they were a hindrance to 'the upbuilding of a united Indian nationality'. 'In their own interests, I would ask the representatives of the Muhammadan community to discourage the system', he said.[92]

There was no debate at this stage, but 20 Muslims and one low-caste Hindu member voted against the motion as a protest against Banerjea's neglect of the principle of representation of minorities through separate electorates.[93] When a week later he moved for the circulation of the bill he brought down the wrath of the minorities upon his head. Muslims, Marwaris, and Europeans all demanded recognition of the principle of separate communal electorates. The Muslims were particularly incensed, accusing the Hindus of a plot to destroy the political existence of their community. 'It is a pity that in the first year of the Reforms the Muhammadans have been compelled to feel what *swaraj* in India will be', declaimed Syed Nasim Ali. Exercising great tact, Banerjea assured his opponents that the question of communal representation would be reconsidered if the public so demanded, and he persuaded them to agree to the motion without a division.[94]

The ensuing public discussion of the bill was characterised by a narrow sectional spirit, with each community striving to increase its representation at the expense of others.[95] For the first time in Bengal there was an expression of overt Hindu communalism, and Muslim anger was aggravated by a campaign against cow killing led by a member of the Corporation, Amulya Dhone Addy. Addy was also an MLC, and his inclusion on the select committee to con-

[91] GB, Legislative, 1–74, Dec. 1923.
[92] BLCP, 22 Nov. 1921, Vol. V, pp. 125 and 127–128.
[93] *Ibid.*, pp. 133–134.
[94] *Ibid.*, 29–30 Nov. and 1 Dec. 1921, Vol. V, pp. 409–456, 458–495, and 513–542.
[95] GB, Legislative, 1–74, Dec. 1923.

sider the bill brought the charge from the Muslims that Banerjea was packing it with opponents of communal electorates.[96]

The committee's report was not presented until February, 1923, and in the interim communal relations had deteriorated. The alliance between the Congress and the Khilafat party, which had given Hindus and Muslims a common ground, had been strained by Gandhi's sudden decision in February, 1922, to end civil disobedience. With his imprisonment in the following month one restraint upon Hindu communalism was removed, and fears of Hindu raj were revived in Muslim minds. The collapse of the Khilafat movement at the end of the year, following the overthrow of the Khalifa in Turkey, added to the general tension. In Bengal there was trouble between Hindus and Muslims over appointments to Government jobs.[97] The Hindu majority in the select committee on the Municipal Bill refused to consider the provision of communal electorates and, at the same time, accepted a proposal of Addy's to give the Corporation power to restrict the slaughter of cattle in the city.[98]

For the Muslims this was the last straw, and when the Council again took the bill into consideration in February, 1923, they marshalled all their forces against it. The activities of the bhadralok Hindu communalists had also upset the low-caste Hindus and the Europeans, and their representatives decided to support the campaign for communal electorates. The Government was divided on the question, with Sir Abdur Rahim and Nawabaly Chaudhuri insisting upon the officials being allowed a free vote. Finally, a small group of Hindu bhadralok MLCs announced that in the interests of communal harmony they, too, would support the Muslims' claim for separate electorates.[99]

Defeat stared Banerjea in the face. To save what he could of the principle he held so dear, he accepted a compromise suggested by a European member: the Muslims would have separate communal electorates for the first nine years, after which they would have only reserved seats in general electorates.[100]

This was regarded by the great majority of the Hindu bhadralok as an outright victory for the Muslims, and Banerjea was reviled as

[96] BLCP, 3 July 1922, Vol. VIII, pp. 87–108.
[97] E.g., see *ibid.*, 25 Aug. 1922, Vol. IX, pp. 159–170.
[98] GB, Legislative, 1–74, Dec. 1923.
[99] PP, 1924–5, [Cmd. 2361], Vol. X, pp. 346–347.
[100] BLCP, 19 Feb. 1923, Vol. XI, No. ii, p. 236.

a traitor to his own principles. Even the Indian Association and his old newspaper, the *Bengalee*, condemned him.[101] It was a tragedy that his last and greatest work should have been marred by those communal antagonisms with which he had struggled throughout his political life. His service as a Minister, which was to have set the seal upon a great career, had brought him disappointment and unpopularity.[102]

The dissension aroused by the Municipal Act was not simply Banerjea's private tragedy. It was also evidence that the lines separating the communal groups in the Legislative Council were now drawn hard and fast. The suspicion which prevailed between the three main sections–Hindus, Muslims, and Europeans–hindered the smooth working of the institution and poisoned the main stream of public life. Communalism had even divided the Government against itself. The compromise on Muslim representation, to which many of the Hindu MLCs had assented, was bitterly resented by the Hindu bhadralok as a whole, with the effect once again of discrediting the reformed Council and Government.

A REVELATION OF WEAKNESS

The despondency that filled the hearts of the members of the first Montagu-Chelmsford legislatures as they approached their last year's work is reflected in a letter Sapru received in June, 1922, from Sir Devaprasad Sarvadhikary, a Bengal representative in the Indian Legislative Assembly. Sarvadhikary wrote:

> You must have realised that moderates–real moderates–are having a bad time of it and will have worse. They are no favourites of the Government & the officials, nor of the people. Any protest against Government & official action mark them down as 'not different from Extremists'. They are disorganised among themselves and mutual jealousy is not the least of the weaknesses of some'.[103]

One man in Bengal who was determined not to give way to this despondency was Satish Das, now provincial Advocate General. In the latter half of 1922 he made another effort to rally support for the Government in the Legislative Council, and outside the Council

[101] IA Committee meeting proceedings, 3 Mar. 1923; and *Bengalee*, 23 Feb. 1923.

[102] See *Nation in Making*, pp. 348–349.

[103] 30 June 1922, Sapru papers.

he organised a Constitutional Party to work for the reforms. He had surprising success in enlisting among his followers a group of ex-terrorists, men who had been interned during the war and who now assured him that they had seen the error of their old ways. His work was commended by Lytton who gave it his full support, until he was informed by his police officers in mid-1923 that the Constitutional Party was a cover for a terrorist conspiracy. The conspirators had shrewdly reasoned that nowhere could they be safer than in an organisation headed by the Advocate-General. To his mortification, Das discovered that far from influencing others as he had intended, it was he who was being used.[104]

His fate was shared in lesser degree by his fellow MLCs. By 1923 they, too, were being used. They had been so thoroughly discredited in the public estimation, they were so divided among themselves, and their morale was so low that they had no resources with which to resist the pressures put upon them by the noncooperators, who had a large popular following. Most of the members saw no prospect of reelection to the new Council at the end of the year unless they made their peace with the noncooperators, and many concluded that their best course was to put themselves at the disposal of their local Congress leader. As a result, there was a sizeable and growing section of the Legislative Council acting under orders from the noncooperators: asking questions and moving resolutions at their behest; speaking and voting as they instructed.[105]

This display of pusillanimity gained the Councillors nothing. By selling their souls they further injured their public reputation and destroyed the Government's confidence. The humiliating position to which they were reduced is illustrated by the actions of Khan Bahadur Rahamatjan Chaudhuri, Muslim representative for Faridpur North, in connection with the Council enquiry into the Charmanair affair in July 1923.

Charmanair, a village near Shibchar in the Faridpur District of Eastern Bengal, was the scene of a struggle between a gang of dacoits and a police party in the early hours of the morning of 17 May 1923. Only three of the gang were captured, and before they could be taken away, the police were unexpectedly set upon by the villagers, severely beaten, and tied up. They were not released until further police arrived later in the day. Initial attempts to discover

[104] *Pundits and Elephants*, pp. 57–58.
[105] GB, Political, 12C–126 of 1922, B506–10, Jan. 1923.

why the villagers had behaved in this extraordinary fashion were frustrated by the fact that many had gone into hiding; for that reason a sudden descent upon the village was made by 48 constables and twelve officers on 5 June.

In the house to house search that followed there may have been brutality, and there was certainly rough handling of both men and women, with frequent intrusions into *pardā* quarters of Muslim homes. This was regarded by the village men as an outrage upon the modesty of their womenfolk, and a few days later the local Congressmen took up the matter. They sent telegrams to the Provincial Congress Committee and the Calcutta press, alleging murder, rape, and torture by the police. This caused a great stir. The District Magistrate, G. P. Hogg, conducted a personal enquiry at Charmanair, which convinced him that the allegations were grossly exaggerated; however, in spite of the publication of his findings, the charges against the police found wide credence.

On 4 July there was an adjournment debate in the Legislative Council on the affair and, writing a few days later to his Divisional Commissioner, Hogg commented on the part played by the local Muslim member:

> Before Khan Bahadur Rahamatjan Choudhuri, M.L.C. went down to Calcutta for the last Council meeting, he came to see me. I took advantage of the opportunity to give him a few details about Char Manair, and in particular told him the real facts surrounding the principal allegations. My idea, of course, was that he might be able to correct any false rumours that might reach him.
>
> This morning the Khan Bahadur called on me and I casually remarked that he had spoken in the Char Manair debate. He asked to be 'excused', and told me that two Mahommedans, one giving the name of Lal Meah, from some village in Shibchar P[olice]. S[tation]. had called on him in Calcutta and told him he would get no votes in the next election unless he said something. Some Shibchar students, now in Calcutta, also came to him (on a separate occasion), and gave him the same intimation. Mr J. N. Maitra, M.L.C. also asked him to say something.
>
> The Khan Bahadur's words included the following,—which I jotted down on a slip as they were made:—
>
> 'I know I have committed an offence against you,—but it was only for fear of not getting votes and nothing else.
>
> I was not only requested to say something,—but *threatened* that I could expect no votes next election.
>
> Only for fear of this, I said something, but moderately'.

> As a matter of fact, his speech was very moderate. It is pathetic, more than anything else, to reflect that he had not the nerve to make any use of the information which was in his possession, particularly as he was convinced of the falsity of the charges.

Lytton's comment when he read this report was: 'A most lamentable revelation of weakness!'[106]

A FAILURE AND A SUCCESS

In the general election held four months later the Khan Bahadur received no reward for his action. Instead, he was resoundingly defeated by a stalwart noncooperator.[107] Most of his fellow councillors fared as badly and, looking for an excuse, they naturally blamed the reformed constitution. P. C. Mitter was voicing their general opinion when he complained in June, 1924: '. . . our party tried to work dyarchy loyally, but dyarchy killed our party'.[108] Whether or not the form of the constitution was a vital factor, the Moderates were justified in believing that membership of the Council had discredited them. They had been unable to demonstrate a measure of control over the Government which would have enabled them to return to the electors with the boast that they were masters of the situation, and, in discharging their responsibility as legislators to assist the Ministers in carrying on the administration, they had injured their reputations as nationalists. The articulate section of political society in Bengal still demanded of its nationalist politicians agitation against the Government, and the Moderates' efforts in the Council on this score had paled into insignificance alongside the spectacular displays of the noncooperators.

For the Ministers the record of the first reformed Council was no more satisfactory than it was for the ordinary members. Looking back from the end of 1923, their original hope of vindicating their acceptance of the reforms by an outstanding administrative achievement and thereby establishing their party in a commanding position seemed rather absurd. At every turn they had met obstacles. Their developmental programmes had been stunted by the shortage of funds, and their legislation had been twisted out of shape by sectional pressures. They had been unable to control the Council with their old methods, and their efforts to develop a satisfactory

[106] GB, Police, P4A–5, B3–18, Oct. 1923 (East Pakistan Record Office).
[107] PP, 1924, [Cmd. 2154], Vol. XVIII, p. 528.
[108] PP, 1924–5, [Cmd. 2362], Vol. X, p. 632.

organisation had failed. They left office with the knowledge that their work had contributed to communal enmity and that they were held in contempt by many of their compatriots.

Sapru's hope of 1921 that at the end of the first session 'the country' would find that the new councils had 'given a good account of themselves' had obviously been disappointed. But the question arises, need this necessarily have meant electoral defeat for the Moderates? What was 'the country' of which Sapru spoke; what was the section of political society with which the Moderates were discredited by their actions in the Council? Simply, it was the urban educated groups and that small section of the rural bhadralok who subscribed to city newspapers. These were the people who were heard in politics, but the important fact was that under the 1919 constitution they were not the only people who voted, and the majority of those who did had no concern with what happened in the Legislative Council in Calcutta. A District Officer writing from Chittagong as late as 1929 emphasised that the main concerns of electors were to secure local and personal advantages or to satisfy importunate canvassers.

> The more highly educated, of course, have a better idea of the potentialities of the Council and of their votes, but even with them the determining factor is personal friendship; they are not sufficiently interested in politics other than local to follow the debates in the Council and to appreciate the attitude adopted by their member.[109]

Seen in this light, the Moderates' defeat at the 1923 elections appears less the result of their ineffectual performance in the Council than of their failure to realise that there were two levels in the politics of the reformed order: the upper level of the more sophisticated bhadralok and the lower level of the new mass electorate. By concentrating their attention on the Legislative Council, they had disregarded this lower level and ensured their own downfall. A few men like Satish Das had seen the danger of neglecting the constituencies and had urged their fellow MLCs to get to work outside the Council,[110] but their admonitions had been disregarded; most members shared Rahamatjan Chaudhuri's belief that an occasional demonstration in the legislature would satisfy their electors.[111]

[109] GB, Appointment, 1E–22(1–13), A5–17, May 1930.
[110] E.g., Das' letter to the *Englishman*, 12 Feb. 1921.
[111] See Reading to Montagu, July 1921, Reading, Vol. II, p. 202; and B. P. Singh Roy, *Parliamentary Government in India* (Calcutta, 1943), pp. 70–71.

All this points to a lack of understanding among the Moderate nationalists of the complexity of the task of working within the reformed institutions. It was not simply a question of making a good showing in the Council or reaching a satisfactory *modus vivendi* with the British as Sapru had suggested. To win elections, nationalist politicians required not only zeal and a good record but organisation and discipline, inside and outside the legislature. They needed money for local publicity and canvassing. They needed a leader who could appeal to the wider electorate; and they needed to respect the symbols and terms of the new mass politics.

The politicians were not alone, however, in their failure to comprehend the extent of their task. Lord Lytton had also revealed a lack of understanding, most notably in his clash with the university. This incident had underlined the continuing importance of institutions other than the Legislative Council. The frustrations and disappointments Lytton had encountered in his first two years in Bengal had left him disillusioned. It seemed that neither the officials nor the legislative councillors appreciated his crusading spirit, and his idealistic design had been spoilt by the hard facts of Bengali political life. By the time he dissolved the Legislative Council in August, 1923, his faith was so badly shaken that he was prepared to assent to the officials' proposition that the institution was useful merely as a consultative body. 'Looked at from the point of view of the Government', he said, 'the existence of a responsible element has been of the utmost value, as it has provided us with the means of testing the acceptability of our measures.[112]

The British officials had also had their difficulties with an unrealistic Governor, inexperienced Ministers, and a recalcitrant Legislative Council, but these had not been unexpected. More important for them was the fact that the stockade Ronaldshay had helped them throw up around the bureaucracy had held against the assaults of the politicians. Although the Moderates had proved to be a disappointingly irresolute set, they had provided the human raw material necessary to work under the constitution, and the officials were proud of having kept the reformed institutions functioning throughout the period.

Indeed, this was a significant achievement. Despite the stresses and strains of internal dissension and the severe battering to which it had been subjected by the noncooperators, the Legislative Council

[112] BLCP, 21 Aug. 1923, Vol. XIII, p. 478.

had survived to shield the Government from the hazards of rule by ordinance, and, equally important, to provide the nationalist movement with an alternative to mass agitation. As we shall see, this was an alternative which C. R. Das and his Swaraj Party in Bengal were glad to accept after the collapse of noncooperation in 1922. The Government had been right to emphasise the importance of keeping the reforms working, and the decision of the leading section of Congress to contest the 1923 elections was its reward.

VI

HE WHO RIDES A TIGER

Surveying the results of the general election for the second reformed Council, the *Statesman* of 1 December 1923 wrote: 'Bengal has declared itself Swarajist. In every kind of Bengali constituency the Swarajists have triumphed. Even the Muhammadan electorate, which was considered to be a safe asset for Government, has been rent asunder'.

How did the noncooperators gain sufficient strength to inflict such a humiliating defeat upon the Moderates? Here we shall offer an answer to that question, and to another which is related: why, after abjuring council entry in 1920, did C. R. Das form the Swaraj Party to contest the 1923 elections?

UNCERTAINTY

Das returned from the Nagpur Congress in January, 1921, to be greeted in Calcutta with excitement and enthusiasm. To symbolise his conversion to noncooperation he gave up his law practice, donated his property and possessions to the nation, and donned *khādi*. These gestures of self-sacrifice, so markedly in contrast to the behaviour of the newly appointed Moderate Ministers,[1] fired

[1] They were busy with the festivities connected with the visit to Calcutta of H.R.H. the Duke of Connaught and were guests at a Government House garden party on 1 February (*Essayez*, pp. 138–139). As the noncooperationist press frequently noted, they also enjoyed the Rs. 64,000 salary which accompanied their new office. (e.g., *Liberty*, 13 Mar. 1921.)

the popular imagination. Das' followers gave him the title of *Deshbandhu*, 'friend of the country', and the vernacular press acclaimed him as worthy of the honour.

Despite their apparent self-assurance, Das and his immediate colleagues faced the new year with considerable uncertainty. It had been a bold move to turn away from the secure and well-trodden paths of Council politics to the unfamiliar jungle of direct action with its demand for a new style. The Bengal leaders had now grasped the concept of mass support for the nationalist movement and they were aware of popular discontents, social and economic; but they were unsure of how to communicate with the masses or how to make political capital from their grievances. Das had no prepared plan of action, for his *volte face* at Nagpur had surprised him almost as much as it had surprised his opponents. There were many ideas but no agreement among the other members of the provincial Congress hierarchy.

The Montagu-Chelmsford Council had been elected and a Government formed, with the leaders of the Moderate party participating. For the noncooperators there was an element of menace in these new institutions, for their potential was unknown. They might prove to be a source of power and influence for their members, and the British would undoubtedly try to use them in some way against the noncooperation movement. C. R. Das and his men had the uncomfortable feeling that possibly they had thrown away a chance.

The leaders of the other sections of political society were equally uncertain. The Moderates were ill at ease in the enlarged legislature, 'rather like a set of children anxiously learning a new drill' as an I.C.S. officer described them,[2] and the Calcutta European community was talking hysterically of the danger of a second Mutiny.[3] The Government of Bengal was also alarmed, now that noncooperation had been accepted by the local Congress leaders. It lacked confidence in the ability of the Moderates, a 'timid and lethargic' group, to counter the movement; and it insisted that the Government of India should take immediate action to destroy its central organisation.[4]

[2] C. H. Bompas to J. G. Drummond [1921], quoted J. G. Drummond, *The Working of the Bengal Legislative Council under the Government of India Act, 1919* (Cambridge University Ph.D. thesis, 1938–39), p. 109.

[3] Andrews to Rabindranath Tagore, 21 Dec. [1920], Andrews MSS.

[4] Chief Secretary, GB, to GI, 19 Feb. 1921, GI, Home Political, Deposit 3 (Confidential) and K–W, July 1921.

The Government of India was reluctant to accept this counsel. It knew that even Gandhi was unsure of himself in the new medium of mass politics, and it thought it best to wait and watch the nature of the relationship that developed between the Congress leaders and the people. The events of the preceding twelve months had destroyed its confidence in its ability to gauge changes of attitude 'in the vast under-world of India' and it feared that hasty action against the noncooperators might precipitate a revolution. It had no desire to put an end to the general state of uncertainty by martyring the nationalists.[5]

PUBLICITY AND REORGANISATION

It was left to the noncooperators to make the first move. C. R. Das knew that the most direct and certain way to influence bhadralok opinion was through the Bengali and English-language press, and he made it his primary objective to secure its firm backing. He established a Congress News Service to supply the papers with information about noncooperation,[6] and he made preparations for the publication of a Bengali paper of his own.[7] The success of his press campaign can be judged from the following report from P. H. Waddell, District Magistrate of Bakarganj, dated 9 June 1921: 'The people in the town read nothing but violent journals like the *Amrita Bazar Patrika* and the *Servant*. Even the *Bengalee* is avoided as being moderate, and anyone who asks for it is looked upon with suspicion. These violent journals publish nothing in favour of Government, so that the public never learn the true facts'.[8]

At Nagpur Gandhi had insisted that Congress should be reorganised with stronger executive committees to direct its national and provincial affairs, and with active branches extending to the villages.[9] C. R. Das undertook this reorganisation in Bengal. It was to his advantage that his lieutenants came from a generation which had had little experience of the old Indian political associations and therefore had no fixed idea of the 'proper form' of political organisation. They had followed his example in giving up their employment, and he was thus able to use them full time in his new organisation.

[5] GI, Home Political, *ibid.*
[6] GB, Police, P-4A-5, B3-18, Oct. 1923.
[7] *Banglar Katha* which brought out its first edition on 30 Sept. 1921.
[8] GB, Political, 12S-4(1-43), A11-53, Oct. 1921.
[9] *Young India, 1919-1922* (Madras, 1922), pp. 833-839 and 842-845.

He established an office in Calcutta to direct noncooperation and he divided the city into four districts, with district commanders to supervise canvassing for funds and propaganda for the spinning campaign. He encouraged his followers in the mufussil to form district committees,[10] or, where they already existed, to organise the local bhadralok youth and with its backing oust the older office-bearers. The Superintendent of Police, Pabna, described the methods used in his district: Kumud Nath Sarkar 'soon infused a spirit of defiance among the so-called volunteers towards the authority of the Government and in no time he found himself raised to the rank of President of the local Congress Committee with two principal assistants in Pravash and Naresh Chandra Lahiri. . . . The whole committee was at this time re-organised—the elderly members of the same apparently making room for the younger ones'.[11]

C. R. Das personally visited the main mufussil towns, accompanied whenever possible by local men who had won a reputation in Calcutta. He talked to leading members of the professions, urging them to give up their jobs and support the new district organisations. He held frequent outdoor meetings which attracted large crowds eager to see the great *Deshbandhu*. With impassioned speeches[12] and symbolic donations for the Swaraj Fund, these gatherings were an exciting change from the monotonous routine of mufussil life.[13] The novelty of an active Congress organisation at the district level also captured public interest, and gave the rural bhadralok, in particular, a new feeling of involvement in the nationalist movement.

The Congress leaders tried to persuade the Muslims to unite their Khilafat committees with the new District Congress committees but they refused, insisting that the two organisations existed for different purposes.[14] They had resented the Bengali Hindus' refusal in the previous year to support their movement; although they were willing to work with the noncooperators, they were determined to leave themselves room for manoeuvre by keeping their organisation

[10] GI, Home Political, Deposit 63, June 1921.

[11] GB, Political, 12C–126 of 1922, B506–510, Jan. 1923.

[12] A District Officer reported that one Congressman, Sarat Kumar Ghose, 'a visionary fanatic', was such an impelling speaker that 'Even I.B. Inspectors have been moved to tears when taking down his speeches'. (P. H. Waddell to T. Emerson, 5 June 1921, GB, Political, 12S–13, B300–352, Sept. 1921.)

[13] H. N. Das Gupta, *Deshbandhu Chittaranjan Das* (Delhi, 1960), pp. 60–61; and N. C. Banerji, pp. 55–108.

[14] GI, Home Political, Deposit 63, June 1921.

intact. At this time they were also consolidating their position by infiltrating the executives of the local Muslim *ānjumāns*, whereas the Congressmen were concentrating all their energies upon their party reconstruction. This left the Moderates in command of the established bhadralok bodies: the Landholders', Ratepayers', Peoples', and District Associations.[15] Although for the time being these lost their influence, they were later to provide a base from which the Moderates could reassert themselves in local affairs.

THE BOYCOTTS

Gandhi had given another lead to the noncooperators with his call for the triple boycott: of councils, courts, and schools. Once Das had overcome his doubts about the first item, he had no hesitation in accepting the other two. In implementing this programme he would be required to address himself only to the bhadralok.

His own self-sacrifice was a powerful example; Subhas Chandra Bose was speaking for scores of Bengalis of his generation when he wrote in February, 1921: 'If C. R. Das at his age can give up everything and face the uncertainties of life—I am sure a young man like myself, who has no wordly cares to trouble him, is much more capable of doing so'.[16] In the early months of 1921 the students and lawyers of Bengal responded magnificently to the Congress call to join noncooperation. Strikes involving five colleges in Calcutta were followed by similar demonstrations in all but three districts of the Province, and more than 10 percent of the students in Government schools and colleges were withdrawn. There were numerous resignations among the teaching staff.[17] In some districts all lawyers suspended practice, and the work of the courts was severely handicapped everywhere except in Calcutta where the legal profession was strangely unresponsive.[18]

The recruits were organised into volunteer brigades, quasimilitary formations which had first been used in the anti-partition agitation. Where their organisation was efficient, they were com-

[15] GB, Political, lists of office-bearers of recognised associations, revised annually.

[16] Subhas Chandra Bose to Sarat Chandra Bose, 16 Feb. 1921, *An Indian Pilgrim or the Autobiography of Subhas Chandra Bose, 1897–1920* (Calcutta, 1948), p. 129.

[17] Simon Commission, Vol. VIII, p. 99.

[18] GB, Judicial, J. 6C–118(1–30), A130–159, Nov. 1921; and BLCP, 21 Nov. 1921, Vol. V, p. 54.

manded by a district captain and four vice-captains supported by two subordinate officers in each *thana*, and with a regular budget and funds.[19] Eleven hundred volunteers were enrolled in Calcutta in February, 1921, and by May there were 19 regular corps in various parts of the province.[20] The volunteers were put to work spreading propaganda, collecting donations, boycotting Government officials and cooperators, running arbitration courts and national schools to replace the British institutions, and assisting in village reconstruction.

It was a spectacular achievement which had the Government thoroughly frightened,[21] but it could not be sustained. The planning of the national schools and arbitration courts had been inadequate, and one by one they collapsed. Spinning, learning Hindi, and labouring among the villagers, activities by which Gandhi set great store, had no attraction for sophisticated bhadralok youths, and there was growing dissatisfaction among them at the lack of opportunity for more heroic means of demonstrating their patriotism.[22] After the first flush of enthusiasm had gone, the students and lawyers had second thoughts about the wisdom of deserting the Government institutions so important to their group; by midyear, most were back in their schoolrooms and courthouses.[23]

In this first phase, the noncooperation movement was strongest in the towns of Eastern Bengal where the Hindu leaders had found themselves equipped with a mass following by the pro-Khilafat *mollās*. The Hindu bhadralok were ill at ease in this unaccustomed situation but, in search of a course of action, they were able to draw upon experience gained in the partition period. At that time, influential Hindus (landholders and professional men) in Eastern Bengal had used their social position to impose sanctions upon the opponents of *swadeshi*. The victims had been denied the use of facilities such as shops and wharves under the control of a local magnate and, frequently, they had been treated as outcasts, losing the services of the washerman, the priest, and the barber.[24]

[19] BLCP, 19 Dec. 1921, Vol. VI, p. 39.
[20] Simon Commission, Vol. VIII, p. 100.
[21] GI, Home Political, 170, 1921.
[22] Andrews to Rabindranath Tagore, 13 Mar. [1921], Andrews MSS.
[23] Simon Commission, Vol. VIII, p. 99.
[24] GI, Home Police, A140–148, and B112–114, May 1906. The 1911 census report noted the growth of the power and influence of the local zamindar in Bengal and observed that he was taking over many of the functions of the caste *panchāyets* (councils). (*Census of India, 1911*, Vol. V, pt. 1, p. 488.)

With a much larger following, the noncooperators in 1921 were able to extend these activities. Reluctant contributors to the Swaraj Fund were intimidated,[25] and even Government officials were boycotted. In a number of towns the volunteer brigades picketed the markets, refusing access to Government servants and supporters and selling tickets to others, the money going into party funds. The noncooperators gained such a hold on some areas that the local British officers were forced either to arrange for their daily requirements to be brought in from neighbouring districts or to suffer the indignity of going in person to the market.[26]

The disadvantage of social boycotts and picketing was that they inconvenienced so many innocent parties. The barber and the priest, for instance, suffered as much as those who were denied their services; the shopkeepers were out of pocket because of the interruption in trade; and the general public, no matter how fervently nationalistic, were bound to resent having to pay a tribute to the Congress party whenever they used the market. Consequently there was support for the Government when it organised countermeasures.[27]

In some places the noncooperators' activities also aggravated existing social animosities. For example, in Faridpur District there was a long-standing rivalry between the two main peasant communities, the Muslims and the Namasudras. In 1921 the Namasudras opposed noncooperation, and when the Muslims excluded them from one of the main markets because of their refusal to forego foreign merchandise, they established their own shops. The old market suffered as a result, and feeling between the communities was embittered. From this time onward there were frequent riots between the two groups, until punitive police were stationed in the district in the late 1920's in an attempt to restore order.[28]

In Midnapore District of West Bengal the noncooperators scored a remarkable success by taking advantage of a faction fight. In January, 1921, the first elections were held in the district for Union Boards, new local bodies provided by the Bengal Village Self-Government Act of 1919. The electors were uncertain as to what they were voting for, but they had a vague idea that they were

[25] GI, Home Political, Deposit 1, Sept. 1921.

[26] GB, Political, 12S–13, B300–352, Sept. 1921.

[27] *Ibid.* Gandhi was opposed to the political use of social boycott for this reason. (See *Young India, 1919–1922, op. cit.*, pp. 299–302.)

[28] GB, Police, P.5R–2(4–12), B95–103, Mar. 1926.

electing representatives to arbitrate village disputes and thus save lawyers' and court fees. They were dismayed when they discovered that they had in fact assisted in the formation of new bodies empowered to levy taxes. They were convinced that the bhadralok would use these to swindle them.[29]

A local noncooperator, Birendra Nath Sasmal,[30] saw his opportunity. He organised meetings at which he warned the people that the Act opened the way for crushing taxation and other oppressions by the Government. Oppose now or forever be taxed, he said.

To win the all-important support of the educated classes he utilised a factional rivalry. In the Contai subdivision, to which he belonged, the bhadralok were divided into two groups: the locals, and people from outside districts who had established themselves in practice in the Contai courts or in other professions. The Legislative Council and Union Board elections had been fought out between candidates from these two groups and the 'immigrants' had triumphed. Sasmal, who was a member of the dominant Mahishya caste,[31] now took the leadership of the locals and carried them with him in his attack on the Union Boards.

The people were persuaded to refuse to pay taxes under the Village Self-Government Act and the members of the Boards were 'encouraged' to reconsider the wisdom of their operating the Act. By late June, the Contai bazaar and the walls along the village roads carried inflammatory posters threatening the members with violence. Resignations soon followed, and those who held out had

[29] S. N. Ray, Joint Magistrate, Midnapore, 1 Nov. 1921: 'I went into the Contai bazaar. I soon had a crowd round me vigorously showing their disapprobation of Union Boards. They had not had good crops for years, they could hardly afford to pay for their food and clothing in the present state of the market and now they were asked to pay more taxes. They could not possibly countenance a sevenfold increase of taxes. It was all very well to say that it rested with them to decide whether they should raise taxes or not, but the "Babus" were going to raise it all the same'. (GB, Local Self-Government Department, Local-Self-Government (Local Boards) Branch, L2U–5(1–7), A36–49, July 1922.)

[30] For biographical details see N. C. Banerji, pp. 204–205; *Nation in Making*, p. 358; and *Subhas Chandra*, pp. 68–69 and 91 ff.

[31] The Mahishyas were an agricultural caste of good status and were most numerous in Midnapore District. Many Mahishyas had entered the professions and they had no difficulty in gaining acceptance as bhadralok, for in proportion to its total Hindu population Midnapore had fewer high-caste Hindus than any other Bengal district.

social and religious boycotts applied to them. Some were even prevented from securing labour to reap their paddy.

Having brought the operation of the Act to a standstill in Contai, Sasmal turned his attention to other parts of the Midnapore District, with similar success. By November the Government was forced to admit that it would be better to withdraw the Act than to fight Congress on such shaky ground.[32]

All these activities brought fame to the noncooperators. Never before had British authority been challenged so openly and with such impunity, and the insolence with which C. R. Das and his party treated Englishmen delighted their compatriots. However, there were evident disadvantages about the methods they had used. The boycott of courts and colleges had demanded too great a sacrifice of the bhadralok, and its corollary, the organisation of arbitration boards and national schools, required of the Congress leaders a genius for construction which they did not possess. '. . . the difficulty does not lie in breaking,—any fool can do that!' remarked C. F. Andrews to Rabindranath Tagore, 'it lies in rebuilding, and only poets can do that! And today we have far too few poets,—& far too many fanatics! . . . Now the whole movement is reaching that constructive stage & men like C. R. Das are not able to do the building'.[33] Social boycotts and picketing had unwelcome side effects, and even where the noncooperators worked with the grain, as in Sasmal's case, and not against it, one section of society was left as an enemy of the noncooperation movement.

LABOUR AGITATION

One course of action which avoided all these pitfalls was the provocation of labour disturbances. The industrial workers in Bengal were Muslims and low-caste Hindus, and most were migrants from neighbouring provinces. Strikes would therefore involve few bhadralok, and no matter what their outcome, they were not likely to disturb the politically active strata of Bengali society. The conditions for industrial labour were poor. During the war, wages had not kept pace with the inflationary rise in prices. In the same period there had been a rapid expansion of industry, but this had

[32] GB, Local Self-Government Dept., Local Self-Government (Local Boards) Branch, L2U–5(1–7), A36–49, July 1922.

[33] [30] Jan. [1921], Andrews MSS.

been arrested suddenly by the post-war trade recession.[34] The workers had real grievances, but they needed leaders and an organisation to give expression to them. These the noncooperators were willing to supply.

Starting in the industrial complex around Calcutta where the ground had been prepared by the Khilafat agitators, and then moving into the mining areas of West Bengal, they formed trade unions and encouraged the workers to press for the amelioration of their conditions.[35] As a result, there were dozens of strikes throughout the province in the early months of 1921.[36] The main victims were British firms who were the largest employers of industrial labour in Bengal, and they naturally turned for assistance to their compatriots, the officials. The effect was to implicate the Government. This enhanced the noncooperators' success, for they could claim that they were striking at both pillars of British imperialism: trade and rule.

They realised that nothing was better calculated to alarm the Government, especially at a time of political crisis, than stoppages in the transport and communications services. They found that they could cripple Calcutta by bringing the tramway workers out on strike, but this had the disadvantage of inconveniencing too many bhadralok.[37] More satisfactory were stoppages affecting the railway and steamship services.

The great advantage of this trade union work for the noncooperators was that it enabled them to stand forward as leaders of a mass movement. In one place, at least, they had broken through the barriers to communication and they now had some justification for their symbolic use of the concept of 'the masses'. *Banglar Katha*, C. R. Das' new Bengali-language weekly, made the point in one of its early numbers in October 1921:

> No one is able to stop this world-wide awakening of the masses, for this is not a meaningless controversy, but the effort of a self-forgetful race to know itself. . . . The people are starving, Government is penniless to give them food and clothing, and we have no

[34] *Census of India, 1921*, Vol. V, pt. 1, p. 34.

[35] GB, Police, P5R–7(1–2), A39–40, June 1921; and Andrews to Rabindranath Tagore, 22 Mar. [1921], Andrews MSS.

[36] There were 108 strikes in Bengal between January and October, 1921. (BLCP, 23 Nov. 1921, Vol. V, pp. 182–183.)

[37] A tram strike always brought loud protests from the Calcutta press (See e.g., NP, 12 and 26 Nov. 1921.)

> voice in the matter of our trade and commerce. This is the root-cause of the present labour problem. Bengal has slept for ages. She must be roused from her sleep. This is our resolve.[38]

There were risks in what the noncooperators were doing. They had not the organisation or experience to ensure that the labour unrest they were fomenting stopped short of violence. For the same reasons, they were unable to protect the workers against the hardships that accompanied the strikes, and, as their primary objectives were political, they too often neglected the real interests of labour.

Gandhi was aware of these dangers, and he had warned his fellow Congressmen against exploiting workers' grievances. 'I don't deny that such strikes can serve political ends', he wrote on 16 February 1921. 'But they do not fall within the plan of non-violent Non-co-operation'.[39] C. F. Andrews was also perturbed by the effects of the agitation. He had always taken a keen interest in Indian labour, in India and other British colonies,[40] and convinced in 1921 that the workers were suffering unduly, he intervened to protect them. He explained to Rabindranath Tagore early in May: 'I had to finish all these strikes on the Railways which have caused untold miseries and have been entirely due to the ferment of the non-cooperation movement & are one of its bad effects'.[41] The more he saw of the situation in Bengal, the more he was convinced that the bhadralok politicians were using the masses instead of working for them. Speaking in Calcutta at the end of May, he called upon 'the educated leaders' to take stock: 'It will not be enough to excite the poor in their distress into a meaningless strike. That may add more to their misery. I speak sadly because I have been dealing with strike after strike during the last few months, which have brought very little but misery and starvation to the poor'.[42]

THE CHANDPUR AFFAIR

He made this appeal during the Chandpur affair, an incident which we must study in detail for it was here that the Bengal non-cooperators scored their most spectacular success against the Government by an unabashed exploitation of labour grievances.

[38] *Banglar Katha*, 21 Oct. 1921.

[39] *Young India, 1919–1922, op. cit.*, pp. 736–739.

[40] He had made a number of trips to various parts of Africa and to Fiji, on behalf of the Congress, to study Indian labour conditions. (See *Andrews*.)

[41] 10 May [1921], Andrews MSS.

[42] Quoted *Bengalee*, 31 May 1921.

In the first half of April, 1921, a group of Congressmen from Calcutta moved into the tea garden areas of Assam and started an agitation for higher wages among the tea coolies,[43] who were suffering severe hardship because of a slump in the industry.[44] Toward the end of the month there were strikes on many of the gardens, and, because the planters refused to meet their demands, the coolies accepted the noncooperators' offer to arrange transport for their return to their homes in Bihar and the United Provinces. In the following three weeks six to seven thousand workers, including the entire labour force of some gardens, left Assam and trekked more than 100 miles to Chandpur, a steamer station on the river Padma in Eastern Bengal (see Map 2), only to find that the Congressmen had failed to keep their promise to provide transport for the onward journey.

Faced with a growing crowd of half-starved and exhausted coolies[45] among whom disease might quickly spread, the Divisional Commissioner, K. C. De, authorised their shipment at the Government's expense to Goalundo, whence they could be moved by rail to their homes. This offended the tea planters who sent representatives posthaste to appeal to the Government of Bengal, then in summer residence at Darjeeling, not to assist in the removal of their labour force. The Government accepted their plea and censured De for his action. No more free passages were to be granted.

The exodus from Assam continued, and by the middle of May there were 3,000 coolies and their families stranded at Chandpur. Cholera was reported among them, and on 19 May De came up from his headquarters at Chittagong to review the situation. That evening a large mob of desperate coolies attempted to rush a steamer that was preparing to sail for Goalundo, and a number narrowly escaped drowning. De decided that if order were to be maintained and the spread of disease checked, the coolies would have to be shifted from the railway station, where they were camped in insanitary conditions, to a football field outside the town. They refused to move. A troop of Gurkha armed police was therefore

[43] Except for those incidents which have been separately footnoted, the account of the Chandpur affair is based on the following sources: GI, Home Political, Deposit 51, June 1921; *ibid.*, Deposit 63, June 1921; *ibid.*, Deposit 46, June 1921; GB, Political, 12C–70(1–2), A24–25, July 1921; *ibid.*, 12C–72(1), A27, July 1921; *ibid.*, 12S–13, B300–352, Sept. 1921; *ibid.*, 12S–4 (1–43), A11–53, Oct. 1921; and BLCP, 8 and 11 July 1921, Vol. III, pp. 3, 383–427, and 452–485.

[44] *Capital,** 6 Jan. and 26 May 1921.

[45] Andrews, report in *Bengalee,** 22 May 1921.

brought to Chandpur from Dacca, and on the night of the 20th the coolies were chased out of the station yard. A number were injured in the scuffle and in the ensuing stampede to the football field.

The following day Andrews arrived on his way to the tea gardens. When he discovered how serious matters had become at Chandpur, he decided to go to Darjeeling in an attempt to persuade the Government to revoke its order prohibiting the repatriation of the coolies. He was met with a cold refusal, and returned to Calcutta convinced that the Government was listening only to the tea planters.[46]

In the meantime, the 'Gurkha outrage' at Chandpur had captured the press headlines. Wildly distorted accounts were printed, with frequent comparisons being made with the Jallianwala Bagh tragedy of 1919.

> At Chandpur, the blood of inoffensive and unarmed Indian labourers was shed in consequence of the incompetence of short-sighted officials; and starving labourers, both male and female, were prevented from leaving the spot and met with an untimely death. But this dark cloud has a silver lining. It has united the educated community and the poverty-stricken labourers in a bond of sympathy and fellow-feeling.[47]

With public anger running high, the noncooperators saw their opportunity. If they could keep the coolies at Chandpur and fix the blame for their sufferings firmly upon the Government, they would have the British in a very nasty spot. They were fortunate that the noncooperation movement in the Chittagong Division was exceptionally strong. Its leader was J. M. Sen Gupta, a Calcutta High Court lawyer who had given up his practice in March, 1921, and returned to Chittagong to stir up labour trouble.[48] As president of the Railway Employees Union he was able to call for an immediate strike on the Assam Bengal Railway in protest against the Gurkha outrage. On 24 May all train services in Assam and the Chittagong Division were stopped. This cut the link between the tea gardens and Chandpur, and left almost 1,000 coolies stranded along the line. Four days later the steamship crews struck, thereby closing the coolies' only other route out of Chandpur.

[46] Andrews, speech in Calcutta, 29 May 1921, quoted *Bengalee*, 4 June 1921.
[47] *Dainik Basumati*, 27 May 1921.
[48] For biographical details see N. C. Banerji, pp. 149 ff.; *Subhas Chandra*, p. 68; and Drummond, *op. cit.*, pp. 153–154.

Andrews, who was compaigning in Calcutta for funds to repatriate the coolies, was horrified by this callous disregard for their suffering, but his appeals to the noncooperators went unheeded. 'A few thousand coolies might be sacrificed if India's 320,000,000 could obtain *Swarajya*', he was told at a meeting of Congress leaders on 29 May.[49]

On the same day the District Magistrate of Faridpur, G. P. Hogg, writing from Goalundo, advised his Government to take a stand against the noncooperators. The aim of the strike, he said, was to force the Government to repatriate the coolies at its own expense. He admitted that if that were not done the coolies would suffer, but he could see no way of avoiding this without giving in to Congress.

> The consequences of surrender at this stage are obvious. The noncooperators would claim a great victory. They have a wide-spread organisation which has been looking after the different contingents of coolies at every stage of their journey, and, to put it briefly, they would claim that they have, in a sense, replaced the Govt. That is to say, they would have imposed their will on the Govt. and on the public, and would be, with regard to this particular matter, a sort of 'de facto' government.[50]

Sir Henry Wheeler arrived from Darjeeling on 30 May and he accepted Hogg's estimate of the situation. The Government would stand firm on its decision not to provide the coolies' fares.

He was followed into Eastern Bengal by C. R. Das and a large group of Calcutta Congressmen who went from town to town organising *hartāls* in an effort further to dislocate the administration. Andrews was already back from Calcutta, attempting unsuccessfully to persuade the steamer and railway employees to return to work. He was obstructed by both the noncooperators and Wheeler, who resented the criticism he had levelled at the Government after his Darjeeling visit. With the assistance of Pakenham Walsh, the Anglican Bishop of Assam, and Satish Das, he opened a public subscription to assist the coolies, and by 7 June he had obtained the guarantee of sufficient funds to send off the first group from Chandpur. The only route open was the railway line via Mymensingh to Bahadurabad 250 miles north on the Jamuna River. The noncooperators immediately started a new strike among the steamer crews

[49] C. F. Andrews, 'Letters on Non-co-operation', *The Indian Problem*, 2nd ed. (Madras, 1923), p. 98.

[50] G. P. Hogg to J. Donald, 29 May 1921, GB, Political, 12S–13, B300–352, Sept. 1921.

at the rail head and once more blocked the coolies' exit. A day or so later, however, a private steamer was found to make the journey from Chandpur to Goalundo, and by the middle of the month all the coolies were on their way home.

For C. R. Das and his party the affair had gone admirably. The Government had played into their hands by attempting to maintain its prestige at the coolies' expense. It had published two long communiqués to give its version of events, but Bengal was in no mood to accept official accounts, and the noncooperationist press could write as it wished. The Congressmen were praised for their heroic opposition to the Government, for their self-sacrificing relief work among the sick and dying at Chandpur, and even for providing the final transport for the coolies.[51] The affair could not have been better timed for the noncooperators, for it distracted public attention from the drift of lawyers and students back to their old occupations.

C. R. Das was brimming with confidence. He announced that the railway and steamer strikes would continue and he proudly asserted that their purpose was 'national', not economic.[52] This infuriated Andrews who considered it offensive that the bhadralok leaders should talk so glibly of defending national honour and the people's rights. 'Honour is very cheap when another person has to maintain it!' he remarked bitterly.[53] Speaking at a meeting in Calcutta on 16 June, he appealed for a more responsible labour policy.[54] A few days later he wrote to Gandhi and asked him to use his influence with the provincial Congressmen:

> East Bengal is on the very border line of violence . . . it is highly emotional, quick tempered, hot and passionate. These strikes in such inflammable material are like straw to a fire, and I have been

[51] This episode has a piquancy reminiscent of the account in *The Ugly American* of the delivery of rice to Sarkhan (W. J. Lederer and E. Burdick, *The Ugly American* (London, 1960), pp. 34–37). Hogg to Donald, 10 June 1921: 'The position thus was that while Mr S. R. Das paid for the tickets, according to my information, the non-co-operators were allowed to retain practical control of the transport. And at Goalundo there were loud cries of "Chittaranjan Das ki jai", etc., while Mr S. R. Das' share in the transaction was completely ignored'. (GB, Political, 12S–4(1–43), A11–53, Oct. 1921.)

[52] Press statement, 16 June 1921, quoted, GI, Home Political, Deposit 64, June 1921.

[53] Andrews to Rabindranath Tagore, 23 Feb. [1922], Andrews MSS.

[54] GI, Home Political, Deposit 1, Sept. 1921.

greatly anxious about an explosion. What I felt was that only *you* could really preach *ahimsa*. I have done my very best and they have given me such treasures of love. Time after time the passion has died down as I have spoken about you. They do really understand that in my presence no word even of violence must be uttered. But when I am not at their meetings or leave after speaking I have constantly heard that the old passion flames up.

The terms offered by both steamship and railway companies are honourable terms. But . . . there is a strike mania. At a meeting I held about Chandpur (in Calcutta) the whole meeting was against me except three or four, who were such co-operators as Krishna Kumar Mitter and one or two Marwaris.[55]

Gandhi came to Bengal in August, but he was too late to prevent the violence in the eastern districts that Andrews had feared.[56]

AN ATTACK FROM WITHIN

In the meantime, however, C. R. Das' leadership of the provincial Congress had been challenged. Ever since Nagpur there had been a group within the B.P.C.C. that had followed Das with reluctance, suspecting that he was not a convinced disciple of Gandhi. The group was confirmed in its suspicions by his encouragement of labour disturbances, and when in June he openly admitted that he was using the strikes in Eastern Bengal for political gain, the group's leader, Jitendralal Banerjea, resigned from the B.P.C.C. in protest.[57]

The rebels were supported by the Calcutta Marwaris who were devoted followers of the Mahatma. As employers, they were opposed to the strikes. Up to this time they had been the main contributors to the Swaraj Fund, but they now accused Das of misappropriation of the money and withheld their contributions.[58]

In mid-July the Gandhians made a bid to oust their opponents from the provincial Congress executive, but they failed.[59] Counter-attacking, Das filled every office with his supporters. He also established a series of central boards to give him tighter control over the

[55] 21 June 1921, quoted *Andrews*, pp. 173–174.

[56] BLCP, 6 Sept. 1921, Vol. IV, pp. 565–566.

[57] GI, Home Political, Deposit 46, June 1921; *Subhas Chandra*, pp. 4–5; Jitendralal Banerjea, letter to the *Servant*, quoted *Statesman*, 8 June 1921.

[58] Andrews to Gandhi, 21 June 1921, quoted *Andrews*, p. 174; and GI, Home Political, Deposit 46, June 1921.

[59] *Englishman*, 15 July 1921.

party's activities.[60] As director of publicity he appointed a new recruit, 24-year-old Subhas Chandra Bose, who had just resigned from the I.C.S. and returned from Cambridge University to join noncooperation.[61]

Throughout the following three months there was a vigorous debate in the Bengal press between the Gandhians and the C. R. Das group. The *Servant* was the main spokesman for the former. It demanded the subordination of the provincial Congress to the national leadership.[62] In the papers that supported Das there were frequent attacks on Gandhi and the Marwaris, and there was a marked spirit of provincial exclusiveness. *Nayak* was in the van as usual:

> . . . many young Bengalis and adults still cherish the painful memories of the treatment which Burra Bazar people and Hindustanis accorded to Bengalis during the partition agitation;[63] and to add to all this, whatever Mahatma Gandhi is doing, is but an imitation of what Bengal once did. He has shown no sympathy for what happened in East Bengal and Chittagong. Consequently, the Hindus and Musalmans of Bengal, youths and adults alike, are indifferent to the present political movement; and, we are afraid, Bengal will not–cannot–take kindly to the cult of boycott, *Swadeshi*, *Khadri* and Gandhism.[64]

It was at this time that Das brought out his new weekly, with the significant title, *Banglar Katha*, 'Voice of Bengal'. The first edition made it clear that he was appealing to provincial sentiment: 'Whether Hindu, Musalman or Christian a Bengali is a Bengali for all that. He has a distinct temperament of his own and a distinct religion. He has a place in the world and a mission to perform. A Bengali must become a true Bengali'.[65] It was a line tailored to bhadralok tastes.

[60] *Subhas Chandra*, pp. 36–37.

[61] For biographical details see *An Indian Pilgrim or the Autobiography of Subhas Chandra Bose, 1897–1920* (Calcutta, 1948); S. C. Bose, *The Indian Struggle, 1920–1934* (Calcutta, 1948); H. N. Das Gupta, *Subhas Chandra* (Calcutta, 1946); H. Toye, *The Springing Tiger, A Study of a Revolutionary* (London, 1959).

[62] See e.g., *Servant*, 26 July 1921. Cf. *Dainik Basumati*, 30 Sept. 1921.

[63] The bhadralok resented the fact that most traders, including the Marwaris, had refused to join in the boycott of British goods in 1906. (GI, Home Public, A124–C, July 1906; and *ibid.*, B81, June 1907.)

[64] *Nayak*, 2 Aug. 1921.

[65] *Banglar Katha*, 30 Sept. 1921.

THE HARTALS

With their hold on the Congress again secure, C. R. Das and his party looked about for a new course of action. At the end of July the A.I.C.C. had given *swadeshi* precedence over other Congress activities,[66] and, although the Bengalis were unenthusiastic about the spinning campaign, they accepted the committee's direction, reasoning that the boycott of foreign manufactures would offer good opportunities for anti-Government demonstrations. They decided to concentrate upon Calcutta, for it was there that they could attract most attention.

Das chose Subhas Chandra Bose, the new hero of Bengali youth, to lead the first band of volunteers in the picketing of shops selling imported cloth. There were soon groups patrolling all the main trading areas.[67] At the same time Das' wife, Basanti Devi, toured the city exhorting Bengali women to demonstrate their support for the national struggle by offering their gold jewelery for the Swaraj Fund. There were house-to-house collections of rice for distribution to 'needy middle-class families'. Most exciting of all were the symbolic bonfires of imported cloth lit on the intersections of main thoroughfares to shouts of '*Bande Mātaram*' and '*Deshbandhu Dās ki jai.*'[68]

It was dangerous to offer such open encouragement to lawlessness in a city like Calcutta, but neither the Congressmen nor their allies, the Khilafatists, were in any mood to account discretion as the better part of valour. The behaviour of the volunteers became increasingly aggressive and shopkeepers complained of intimidation. The Marwari Chamber of Commerce appealed to Gandhi for protection,[69] but he was powerless to help them.

The movement reached its climax in November with the call from the A.I.C.C. for a campaign of civil disobedience.[70] On the 4th there was a fierce riot in Howrah, when the mob battered a police sergeant to death and was fired on as a result.[71] The tramway workers were already out on a month-long strike[72] and on the 17th,

[66] J. S. Sharma, *Indian National Congress. A Descriptive Bibliography of India's Struggle for Freedom* (Delhi, 1959), p. 479.

[67] *Subhas Chandra*, p. 40.

[68] GI, Home Political, Deposit 24, Oct. 1921.

[69] Sharma, *op. cit.*, p. 480.

[70] *Young India, 1919–1922, op. cit.*, pp. 933–936.

[71] BLCP, 21 Nov. 1921, Vol. V, p. 10.

[72] NP, Nov. 1921.

the day the Prince of Wales arrived in Bombay to start a goodwill tour of India, there was a total *hartāl* in Calcutta. All shops were closed and no public or private transport was allowed to move in the streets. The police lost control of the city to the volunteer brigades but they, in their turn, found that they were unable to manage the gangs of factory labourers who had been brought into the city from the outlying mill towns by the Khilafatists. Assisted by *gundās*, these gangs looted shops, molested pedestrians, and at Kalighat in South Calcutta fought a pitched battle with the police.[73]

The Government of Bengal saw the spectre of red revolution. The Prince of Wales was due in Calcutta in a month's time. Unless order could be guaranteed, his visit would have to be cancelled and the noncooperators conceded a complete victory, which could conceivably mean the end of British authority in the province. The time had come for action. On 19 November the Government declared the volunteer brigades illegal and prohibited public meetings in Calcutta. The offices of the Congress and Khilafat parties were raided.[74] With official approval the Bengal Chamber of Commerce and the British Indian Association formed a Citizens Protection League to supply armed assistance to the police.[75]

There was great excitement in the Bengal Congress. The Gandhians were afraid of further violence, and argued that civil disobedience should be suspended. C. R. Das himself was aware of the danger, but there could be no question of drawing back at that stage, for his followers' blood was up. 'We had been spoiling for a fight in Calcutta and the official notification therefore was thrice welcome to us', wrote Bose in *The Indian Struggle*.[76]

Das had to act carefully to prevent the situation getting out of hand. His tasks, as he saw them, were twofold: to get some control over the Khilafatists and to delay for as long as possible another mass demonstration. He persuaded both the Congress and Khilafat committees to appoint him as provincial dictator, and he then announced that only token resistance would be offered to the Gov-

[73] BLCP, 21 Nov. 1921, Vol. V, pp. 93–111; and *Statesman*, 18 Nov. 1921.

[74] H. N. Das Gupta, *Deshbandhu Chittaranjan Das* (Delhi, 1960), p. 66; and *Indian Struggle*, p. 94.

[75] BIA, Publications, Vol. XII; PP, 1924–5, [Cmd. 2361], Vol. X, p. 351; and B. N. Dutta Roy, *Sir N.N. Sircar's Speeches & Pamphlets* (Calcutta, 1934), p. iv.

[76] *Indian Struggle*, p. 94. See also *Subhas Chandra*, pp. 43–45.

ernment's ordinances.[77] Each day from 1 December small groups of volunteers were sent out to hawk *khādi* and to enlist support for a planned *hartāl* on the 24th, the day the Prince of Wales was due to arrive in the city. For a week the police made no move to interfere with the Congressmen, and Das' followers grew increasingly restive.[78] On the 8th, however, a group of women led by Basanti Devi were arrested and, as they refused to give bail, they were taken to the Presidency Gaol. Ronaldshay quickly intervened and had them released on the pretext of giving them 'time for further reflection',[79] but the damage had been done. There was an outcry at this 'victimisation of innocent women' and the volunteers began openly provoking the police.[80]

Ronaldshay called Das for an interview and offered to make concessions if the *hartāl* on the 24th were cancelled. He touched the Congress leader on the raw by insisting that in taking action against noncooperation he had followed the advice of the representatives of the people in the legislature. When Das protested that they were not the people's representatives, Ronaldshay replied that as Congress had not contested the elections it could not challenge their representative character.[81] It was a shrewd argument to use against a man who initially had supported council entry and who was now struggling to control the movement with which he had become involved instead. But Das was in no position to consider a compromise with the Government. 'He who rides a tiger is afraid to dismount'. His reply was that the *hartāl* would be enforced.

On 10 December Das and his chief lieutenants were arrested. In the following twelve days hundreds of noncooperators throughout Bengal were thrown into prison, and by the time the Prince of Wales arrived on Christmas Eve almost all resistance had been broken.[82]

THE LOSS OF CONFIDENCE

The arrests had been made just in time to avert a catastrophe in Calcutta. The noncooperation movement, which the politicians had

[77] *Indian Struggle*, p. 95.
[78] *Subhas Chandra*, pp. 45–46.
[79] Government press communique, *Amrita Bazar Patrika*,* 9 Dec. 1921.
[80] NP, Dec. 1921; and *Indian Struggle*, pp. 96–97.
[81] H. N. Das Gupta, *Deshbandhu Chittaranjan Das, op. cit.*, pp. 70–71.
[82] *Essayez*, p. 154.

laboured so hard to start, had gathered a momentum of its own and was now perilously close to running out of control. Andrews wrote to Tagore:

> Here is Christmas Day and I am on my way to the Congress, and the noise of battle and strife is already meeting me all along the way. Civil disobedience treads upon the very brink of violence the whole time; and yet there *are* things which are truly heroic—a new spirit infinitely beyond the servile spirit of the past.
>
> My own mind is torn. I *have* to speak out at Ahmedabad, but it is very difficult indeed to know what to say. I *must* speak against these veiled violences—these intimidations, social boycotts, burnings. . . . I think of Aurobindo Ghose saying: 'It is useless to speak: the people have gone mad'. Is silence best when one is tired out and one's faith dim?[83]

Gandhi was also perturbed by the course of events. He decided to shift the emphasis of the movement once more, this time to the refusal of taxes. This would divert attention from the cities, where nonviolence had failed, to the villages.[84]

In Bengal C. R. Das' party had never displayed enthusiasm for work outside the towns, but now its members were in prison. The Gandhians, who had escaped arrest through their disassociation with the recent violent provocations in Calcutta, could therefore take over the provincial Congress machinery and use it for a campaign among the peasantry. With the assistance of those Khilafat workers who were still at large, they began agitating against the payment of the *choukidāri* (village police) tax and land revenue. The peasants needed little urging, for economically they had had a bad year and politically a very active one. Indeed, they had their own ideas as to where the line should be drawn in the payment of revenue. To the dismay of the politicians, many peasants were soon refusing all rent, whether to the Government or to individual landlords. In some districts there were also outbreaks of violence against the zamindars.[85]

The bhadralok elite were appalled by these developments. That social disaster of which they had caught frightening glimpses during the political disturbances of 1906–1908 and 1918–1920 now seemed

[83] Andrews to Rathindranath Tagore, 25 Dec. 1921, quoted *Andrews*, pp. 178–179.

[84] *Young India, 1919–1922, op. cit.*, pp. 279–282, 947–952, and 1153–1156.

[85] NP, Jan. 1922.

imminent: an uprising by the rural masses which would destroy the economic and social dominance of the landed and educated classes. They feared that they would be overwhelmed by sheer weight of numbers and their culture swept away. The political movement had gone too far; Gandhi had stirred up a social revolution. In the early months of 1922 the Hindu bhadralok press was full of foreboding:

> The spirit of non-co-operation has spread into the lower stratum of society. The non-co-operation movement has assumed threatening proportions and the storm of unrest is blowing over the villages. Unless the leaders are released, it is difficult to say how long the movement will retain its non-violent nature. We are fearful of the future of our district from accounts which we are getting from the interior.
>
> *Tippera Guide*, Comilla, 24 January 1922

> If the proportion of private owners of land be taken to be 10 per cent., it would be much more in Eastern Bengal, then the campaign of non-payment of taxes would at once mean a fight between this 10 per cent. on one side and the 90 per cent. on the other. On one side will be skill, resource and accumulated strength and on the other shall be numbers to swamp the other side. And there will set in in the country a regular civil war.
>
> *Herald*, Dacca, 9 February 1922

> This is the great blunder made by the ruling class. If the masses can once lift their heads, then you, English ruling class, will sink and, along with you, we, the classes, will sink to the bottomless deep. Mahatma Gandhi is playing with the masses. These masses are beyond all reason and argument, all debate and dispute.
>
> *Nayak*, Calcutta, 11 February 1922

> *Playing with the Mob*
>
> A social revolution without political freedom will be injurious to a dependent country. Those who in their eagerness to build up the nation and systematise national strength are inciting the masses to agitate for political freedom, seem to forget that, if at their suggestion the masses succeed in humbling the power of the foreign ruler, they will not stop simply by completing the work wanted by the educated classes. Who will deny that if the ire of the masses is once roused against the social oppressions, etc., to which they have been subjected for centuries, it will consume the whole community like a volcanic eruption![86]
>
> *Atma Sakti*, Calcutta, 5 April 1922

[86] See also *Young India, 1919–1922, op. cit.*, pp. 981–983.

Gandhi was also losing confidence. The peasants seemed no more ready for *satyāgraha* than the townspeople had been. Worst of all, it was often the Congress workers who incited them to violence. On 5 February 1922, at Chauri Chaura in the United Provinces, a band of volunteers led a mob in an attack on a police station. The buildings were set alight and 22 policemen killed. Gandhi immediately called a meeting of the Congress Working Committee at Bardoli in Gujerat and announced that civil disobedience was to be suspended until such time as nonviolence could be ensured. Congressmen were instructed to concentrate on the constructive programme: spinning, a temperance campaign, village work, and the uplift of the depressed classes.[87] Justifying has action, Gandhi emphasised that Congress had failed in many places other than Chauri Chaura. 'In Calcutta Jamnalalji tells me there is utter disorganisation, the volunteers wearing foreign cloth and certainly not pledged to nonviolence'.[88]

The reaction in Bengal to Gandhi's decision was mixed. Many of the bhadralok elite were relieved that the dangers of mass politics had been recognised and that Congressmen had been directed to hold the people in check.[89] The politicians could rejoice in the knowledge that someone else had taken the difficult decision to suspend the movement—that Gandhi had leapt off the tiger first. There was nothing to be gained, however, in admitting even to oneself that one had stayed on more out of fear than of boldness, and among the political prisoners in the Alipore Central Gaol there was a display of anger at Gandhi's 'weakness'. What right had he to destroy the national movement for which they had sacrificed their freedom, simply because he had lost his nerve?[90] 'If you unmoored your boat and came rowing along to face the storm, why are you afraid now that the storm has burst?' demanded *Banglar Katha*.[91] This undoubtedly expressed the feelings of the vast majority of the lower-class bhadralok, whose enthusiasm had been brought to a peak by the previous months' exciting conflicts.

And what sort of a substitute for civil disobedience was the con-

[87] PP, 1st session, 1922, [Cmd. 1586], Vol. XVI, pp. 592–593.

[88] Jamnalalji was a Marwari, Seth Jamnalal Bajaj. Gandhi to J. Nehru, J. Nehru, *A Bunch of Old Letters*, 2nd ed. (Bombay, 1960), pp. 23–24. Cf. *Young India, 1919–1922, op. cit.*, pp. 993–1002.

[89] E.g., see *Amrita Bazar Patrika*, 14 Feb. 1922.

[90] *Indian Struggle*, p. 108.

[91] *Banglar Katha*, 17 Feb. 1922.

structive programme? If the volunteers were not to leave the movement in disgust, they had to be offered something more exciting than spinning or popularising prohibition. The Bengal Khilafatists were particularly angry for they had acquired a taste for mass action,[92] and some of their leaders had realised how much the community stood to gain from an attack on the existing social order. Finally, there was a general feeling that Gandhi's criticisms of Bengal's failure to preserve nonviolence were an insult to provincial honour. '. . . the Bardoli resolution is humiliating to the prowess of Bengalis'.[93] The press turned upon Gandhi, his 'Gujerati politics', and his *beniyā* supporters, the Marwaris. It was suggested that it was no coincidence that the latter favoured the constructive programme. 'How the Marwaris are profiting by the *khaddar* movement!'[94]

WHAT NEXT?

The Government of India considered that the time had come when it could safely strike at Gandhi. Previously it had been restrained by the knowledge that even if his arrest did not provoke outright revolt, it would almost certainly alienate the Moderates who might then withdraw their support from the reformed institutions, leaving the Government isolated and exposed to attack.[95] In its judgment the danger was past, for Gandhi had lost much of his influence. He was arrested at Ahmedabad on 10 March 1922, and the mildness of the protests against this action proved the Government's point.

Among the Bengal Congressmen a debate had begun on what should now be done. With all the leading nationalists in prison and the noncooperation movement in ruins, the outlook was bleak. The Gandhians insisted that the first essential was for Bengalis to recognise that the failure was their own. They had not heeded Gandhi's injunction to work with the masses, nor had they learnt self-control. The provincial Congress should now devote itself to the constructive programme. Its members should humble themselves and go out into the villages. 'Ours is a spiritual struggle and like true wor-

[92] See e.g., *Mohammadi*, 22 Feb. 1922.

[93] *Ibid.*

[94] *Hindusthan*, 14 July 1922. See also NP, Feb.–June 1922.

[95] For a full discussion of this see D. A. Low: 'The Government of India and the First Non-Cooperation Movement—1920–1922', *Journal of Asian Studies*, Vol. XXV, No. 2, Feb. 1966, pp. 241–259.

shippers we must purge ourselves of all failings and imperfections before we are privileged to enter the Temple of Liberty'.[96]

This view was contested by another section of the party which maintained that it would be retrograde for the province to continue with Gandhi. '. . . in view of the stage of attainment that the life of the Bengalis have reached, they will have to fall back if they have to follow the dictates of the Mahatma'. This group argued that Bengal had supported noncooperation in a temporary state of overexcitement, and that now that good sense was returning it would realise that it could gain its objectives only by terrorism. 'Bengalis cannot give up the creed of fire'. The *samitis* which had worked so heroically in the partition period should be revived.

> Forming these organisations is now the only work in the country; and, the more they become well established, the more will they be able to improve the country. The real thing is that the country must be free. . . . Many paths will come and go in order that the nation may gain experience, but it will not be possible for the nation of the Bengali to stick to the wrong path in their attempt to show reverence to an individual.[97]

C. R. Das offered a third course: to enter the legislative councils and destroy the reforms from within. The idea of council entry had never been discarded by a group among the Bengal noncooperators. As early as March, 1921, Bipin Chandra Pal had suggested that the Nagpur resolution should be reconsidered. Speaking as president of the Provincial Conference at Barisal, he warned his fellow Bengalis not to accept outside dictation, for this would destroy provincial individuality. Already, he said, a mistake had been made in asking lawyers to suspend practice, and there was a misconception about the legislative councils. Indians certainly did not want the British parliamentary system. 'But we are to some extent helpless in this matter. We are at the mercy of the stranger within our gates. Any British charlatan can, therefore, make any experiment with our fate and future. This is the tragedy of our present unfortunate position'.

The remedy, as Pal saw it, was to persuade the British to amend the preamble of the Government of India Act to include a promise of self-government for India at the end of ten years. To achieve this concession, Congress had to be willing to compromise with

[96] *Servant*, 18 Feb. 1922.
[97] *Nava Sangha*, Chandernagore, 23 July 1922.

the British and it had to reach a compromise quickly because it had promised the nation *swarāj* within twelve months. Moreover, the people had to be persuaded that *swarāj* had this limited meaning of gaining concessions from the British.

> It will spell disaster to our cause if we allow the masses to interpret this declaration in any other sense. That will be bound to create a reaction against the whole movement when the year is out, and they see that the British are still in possession of their country. . . . it will create deep and widespread discontent that may either lead people back to their old hopeless indifference and listlessness, or killing their faith in non-violent non-co-operation, drive them towards violent revolutionary ways as the only possible way to their political redemption.[98]

He was a foolhardy politician who would openly criticise Gandhi's programme in the early months of 1921, for the Mahatma was then at the height of his popularity; although there were many in the Bengal Congress who agreed with Pal, none would support him publicly.[99] He resigned in disgust from the B.P.C.C. and the A.I.C.C.,[100] and later entered the Indian Legislative Assembly at a by-election.

That there was no disagreement in principle between Pal and the C. R. Das group, however, was demonstrated in April, 1921, when the latter carried a motion in the B.P.C.C. reversing a decision of the Barisal conference to boycott local bodies.[101] These institutions were a source of local power—they had provided more than half the elected members of the Bengal Legislative Council at the 1920 general election—and the Das group saw no reason to leave them, as well as the Council, to the Moderates.

That Das also shared Pal's belief in the need for compromise to secure constitutional concessions was revealed after his imprisonment in December, 1921. The mass arrests in the second week of that month had offended the Moderates so seriously that the Government of India had decided that it would have to come to terms with the noncooperators to prevent the collapse of the Montagu-Chelmsford constitution.[102] It therefore sent emissaries to Gandhi

[98] B. C. Pal, *Bengal Provincial Conference Session, Barisal, 1921, Presidential Address* (Calcutta, 1921).
[99] The whole Bengali press was against him. (NP, Mar.–Apr. 1921.)
[100] GI, Home Political, Deposit 46, June 1921.
[101] *Navayuga*, 14 Apr. 1921; and *Herald*, 21 Apr. 1921.
[102] See D. A. Low, *op. cit.*, pp. 248–250.

and Das with the offer of a round table conference to discuss constitutional advance, on condition that the *hartāl* of 24 December was called off.

Das saw in this an opportunity to turn the noncooperation movement to positive gain and he was willing to accept the offer, with the proviso that all prisoners arrested for civil disobedience should be released immediately. He convinced the other inmates of the Alipore Gaol that he was right by pointing out the need for a demonstrable achievement by 31 December 1921, the day for which *swarāj* was promised.[103] He had less success with Gandhi, who mistrusted British intentions. The Mahatma challenged the Government to prove its good faith by stating what constitutional concessions it would make and by releasing immediately all political prisoners. This was asking too much, and the offer was withdrawn.[104]

There was general disgust in the Bengali camp at Gandhi's failure to take advantage of the opportunity,[105] and Das considered it a good time to reopen the question of council entry. He canvassed the idea among his fellow prisoners and soon had a group of supporters. When J. M. Sen Gupta was released from prison in January, 1922, he was charged with the task of talking with Motilal Nehru, a leading United Provinces Congressman who was known to favour council entry, and of organising support for the new scheme.[106] With the collapse of civil disobedience after the Bardoli resolution and Gandhi's arrest, the Das group was willing to put the idea to the public. Basanti Devi presided at the Provincial Conference held at Chittagong in April, 1922, and in her address she suggested that Congressmen should set out to capture all seats in local bodies and the Legislative Council.[107]

THE CASE FOR COUNCIL ENTRY

The case in favour of council entry which the Das group developed over the following eight months deserves close attention, for by providing an insight into their motives it will help to answer

[103] *Indian Struggle*, pp. 99–101.

[104] *Young India, 1919–1922, op. cit.*, pp. 911–918; and Jayakar, Vol. I, pp. 504–517.

[105] *Subhas Chandra*, p. 48.

[106] N. C. Banerji, pp. 172–173.

[107] *Bengalee*, 16 Apr. 1922.

the second of the two questions with which this chapter opened.

In the first place, they explained that they could not accept Gandhi's constructive programme because it was not suited to the provincial character. 'Not we alone, but Srijut Bipin Pal too has been saying from the beginning that Guzrati politics will not agree with the nature of the Bengalis'.[108] Council entry was Bengal's way, they insisted, but Gandhi and his adherents were too doctrinaire to admit provincial differences. They were also incapable of distinguishing between symbolism and reality in their own movement. C. R. Das observed:

> It is often stated that Khaddar alone will bring us Swaraj. I ask my countrymen to consider in what way it is possible for Khaddar to lead us to Swaraj. It is in one sense only that the statement may be said to be true. We must regard Khaddar as the symbol of Swaraj. But what would that symbol signify? To my mind such a symbol worship requires the spreading out of all non-co-operation activities in every possible direction.[109]

The aim of the noncooperation movement had been to destroy the system of government which made possible outrages like Amritsar. Despite all its achievements, it had failed to do this. British autocracy had been shaken but it had not been broken. Worst of all, it was still able to disguise the nature of its despotism behind the facade of the Montagu-Chelmsford institutions. 'The Reformed Councils are really a mask which the bureaucracy has put on', wrote Das. 'I conceive it to be our clear duty to tear this mask from off their face. To end these councils is the only effective boycott'. From the outside the noncooperators had succeeded in diminishing the prestige of the institutions 'and the country knows that the people who adorn the Council Chambers are not the true representatives of the people'. Nonetheless the Councils still existed, and Congress must now enter them and destroy them from within.[110]

That Das used this as his main argument is of great significance, for it shows that the noncooperators in Bengal were as concerned with the reformed institutions as were the Government and the Moderates, for opposite reasons. The Government considered it vital that it should never again have to rule without this institutional

[108] *Nayak*, 27 July 1922.

[109] Press statement by Das appended to *Report of the Civil Disobedience Enquiry Committee, 1922* (Madras, 1922), p. 134.

[110] *Ibid.*, p. 132.

support. The noncooperators were determined to force it to do so. 'I am aware of the large powers of veto which the Governors can exercise under the Reforms Act', wrote Das. 'Let them govern by veto till the time must come when they must either yield to our demands or withdraw the Reforms Act'.[111] The Moderates were concerned to maintain the reformed institutions as a means of justifying their political style. The noncooperators were resolved to prevent them from doing this. 'The Council has practically become a place for personal advertisement', warned *Nayak*. 'Let those who, boycotting it, are sitting silent, get up. It will not do to sit inactive'.[112] 'I warn my countrymen against the policy of allowing these Reformed Councils to work their wicked will', said Das. '. . . there is an apprehension in my mind. I desire to express it with all the emphasis that I can command, that if we allow this policy of drift to continue, the result will be that we shall lose the people who are with us today'.[113]

C. R. Das knew that the criterion by which the bhadralok judged its nationalist politicians was their skill in harrying the Government. He recognised that the noncooperators had lost their ability to do this with the collapse of civil disobedience, and for that reason they would be inviting defeat if they sat in the villages spinning yarn, and left the Moderates to goad the British in the Council. 'We are realising at every step that unless we can bring in a feeling of struggle against the bureaucracy, the non-co-operation movement will not live long', wrote *Banglar Katha*. 'The obstructionist policy in the Councils is a great instrument for fighting with the ruling powers'.[114]

This problem of coming to grips with the British, of keeping themselves actively in the public eye, worried the Bengal Congressmen throughout the remainder of 1922. While in prison they gave the Government as much trouble as they could by provoking their gaolers and inciting the ordinary criminals to riot. Their efforts were rewarded with a number of serious outbreaks of violence,[115] and the floggings the Government ordered in retaliation won them

[111] *Ibid.*

[112] *Nayak*, 13 July 1922.

[113] Presidential address, All-India Congress session, Gaya, 26 Dec. 1922, *Congress Presidential Addresses, 1911–1934* (Madras, 1934), p. 600.

[114] *Banglar Katha*, 22 Dec. 1922.

[115] GB, Jails, 4J–27(1–13), A8–24, Dec. 1922; and *ibid.*, 4J–50(1–7) of 1922, A3–11, Feb. 1923.

much public sympathy. They also had the satisfaction of seeing Sir Abdur Rahim resign his portfolio of gaols in protest against these punishments.[116]

When they were released in August, they organised rallies which brought young bhadralok men from all over Bengal to taste the political and other delights of Calcutta.[117] A chance for public service was provided early in October by disastrous flooding in Northern Bengal. The Government was in Darjeeling at the time, and, as in the Chandpur affair, was slow to act. Congress saw its opportunity and immediately despatched Subhas Chandra Bose and J. M. Sen Gupta to the disaster area to organise relief. Supported by a fund raised in Calcutta by Sir Prafulla Chandra Ray, the famous chemist, they enlisted more than 200 volunteers to rescue peasants and their livestock, and to distribute food, medicines, and clothing. As the floodwaters receded, they helped the villagers repair their devastated homes. With his indefatigable energy and outstanding organising ability, Bose in particular earned praise from all quarters for two months of invaluable work. Surendranath Banerjea, as Minister of Public Health, provided a pathetic contrast by making a one-day excursion through the area and returning to Darjeeling to collapse with pneumonia.[118]

THE COUNCIL ENTRY DEBATE

Throughout 1922 and the early months of 1923 there was a battle royal in the Bengal Congress over Council entry. When the Das group came out of gaol they found themselves for the first time since 1918 at a disadvantage in the B.P.C.C., which had been taken over in their absence by the Gandhians.[119] This party accused them of misinterpreting noncooperation by subscribing to 'the old Moderate fallacy that the sole end of political agitation is to embarrass the Government'. 'The object of the non-co-operator is not to annoy the officials or to obstruct their work temporarily',

[116] *Indian Struggle*, pp. 117–118; and BLCP, 28 Aug. 1922, Vol. IX, pp. 272–296.

[117] *Subhas Chandra*, pp. 52–53.

[118] *Ibid.*, pp. 53–54; NP, Oct.–Nov. 1922; J.T. Gwynn, *Indian Politics. A Survey* (London, 1924), pp. 236–256; P. C. Ray, *Life and Experiences of a Bengali Chemist* (London, 1932), pp. 236–256; BLCP, 21 Nov. 1922, Vol. X, pp. 141–182; and *Nation in Making*, pp. 376–377.

[119] N. C. Banerji, p. 173.

declared the *Servant*, '. . . it is his aim to so train up his countrymen by means of sacrifice and suffering as to be able at a given moment to stand completely aloof from all the various ramifications of the Government administration'. Council entry, whether to obstruct or cooperate, was a denial of this aim.[120]

Few of the Bengal newspapers favoured Gandhi's constructive programme, but initially they were no more enthusiastic about council entry, for it resembled too closely the Moderates' policy of cooperation on which they had been pouring their editorial scorn for the preceding eighteen months. C. R. Das knew that he had to have newspaper support if he were to carry the day. He revived *Banglar Katha*, which had been forced to cease publication in mid-1922 because of lack of staff,[121] and, after an abortive attempt to gain control of the Gandhians' main paper, the *Servant*,[122] he formed a company to produce a new English-language daily, *Forward*.[123]

Das also realised that a provincial political leader could no longer afford to restrict his activities to his home province. As his own actions at the Nagpur Congress session had emphasised, there had been a profound shift in the balance between national and provincial politics in 1920. Up until that time nationalist policies in each province had been an almost autonomous system. The power of nationalist leaders was regionally based, and their authority, though not their influence, was regionally restricted. They might advise or cajole their fellow nationalists in other provinces, but they could not dictate their internal policy or interfere in their internal organisation. A provincial leader with sound regional backing could comfortably disregard 'national' opinion. All this had been permanently changed in 1920. The old-style Congress, a federation of provincial grandees, had been destroyed by Gandhi's successful intrusions into provincial politics and his consolidation of the powers of the All-India Congress executive. As Das had acknowledged with his Nagpur decision, there were now two interdependent power structures, the national and the provincial, and to maintain his influence the nationalist politician had to gain a secure position in both.

[120] *Servant*, 24 Apr. 1922. Cf. *Ananda Bazar Patrika*, 18 Apr. 1922.
[121] *Banglar Katha*, 14 Dec. 1922.
[122] N. C. Banerji, p. 173.
[123] *Indian Struggle*, p. 117; and *Subhas Chandra*, p. 64.

On his release from prison in 1922, the time seemed opportune for Das to concentrate his effort at the national level. The provincial executive was out of his control, temporarily at least, and the all-India leadership was vacant because of Gandhi's imprisonment. At a meeting of the A.I.C.C. in Calcutta in November, 1922, Das supported Motilal Nehru in a resolution in favour of council entry, but their opponents had the matter postponed to the plenary session of Congress to be held at Gaya in the following month.[124] Das presided at Gaya, and in his opening address on 26 December 1922 he appealed for support for council entry.[125] His main opponent was the Tamil politician, C. Rajagopalachari, who successfully carried a counter resolution. Motilal Nehru and Das therefore decided to form a new party which would contest the elections. It was given the name Swaraj Party, and Das was elected leader. On 1 January 1923 he informed the new A.I.C.C. of their action and tendered his resignation from the Congress presidency. The prospect of the disintegration of Congress alarmed his opponents and they declined to accept the resignation. They also tried to persuade the council entry group to compromise, but Das and Nehru stood their ground. For the following six months the leaders of both groups toured the country seeking support for their views. By May Das' opponents had been forced into a minority on the A.I.C.C., and a special session of Congress in September recognised council entry as a legitimate line of action for Congressmen.[126]

In Bengal all the major newspapers had swung over to support the Swarajists by the middle of the year, and Das was slowly but surely winning recruits from among his opponents in the B.P.C.C. In August, he succeeded in replacing the Gandhian office-bearers with a group of neutrals, but the Gandhians refused to yield, and for a month there were two provincial executives claiming authority in Calcutta. The A.I.C.C. finally settled the dispute in favour of the new men.[127] When the B.P.C.C. was reelected toward the end of the year the Swarajists gained an outright majority, and C. R. Das resumed the presidency, with S. C. Bose as his secretary.[128]

[124] Jayakar, Vol. II, pp. 37–43.

[125] *Congress Presidential Addresses, 1911–1934*, *op. cit.*, pp. 587–600.

[126] Jayakar, Vol. II, pp. 47–155.

[127] *Subhas Chandra*, pp. 62–63; *Indian Struggle*, pp. 124–125; and *Dainik Basumati*, 16 Sept. 1923.

[128] *Subhas Chandra*, p. 65.

THE REACTION

C. F. Andrews wrote to Rathindranath Tagore on 11 August 1920:

> . . . these Indian leaders . . . are living from hand to mouth on every fresh excitement. Sadly enough, these false excitements, coming one after another, produce a morbid atmosphere, like drug or dram drinking. People cannot bear to be without them, and one excitement must follow another in quick succession. This means, in the long run, a terrible reaction and an appalling waste of energy.[129]

The reaction to the political excitements of 1920–1921 came in late 1922 and early 1923.

In some ways the Swaraj Party in Bengal benefitted from this, for the bhadralok's willingness to reconsider council entry was indubitably one manifestation of that reaction. Throughout 1922 a section of the Bengali-language press gave repeated warnings against the social dangers of Gandhi's methods, which depended upon a reawakening of the masses. 'Reawakening means the extinction of the middle classes. Are we ready to pay the price'.[130] Many, at least of the elite bhadralok, certainly were not, and they agreed that politics should be redirected into the old, safe channels.

In other ways, however, the reaction worked against C. R. Das and his party, and confronted them with some difficult problems of appeasement as they prepared for the Legislative Council elections to be held in November, 1923.

From leaders of the Hindu lower castes came complaints that the bhadralok politicians had run true to form in giving lip service to principles of social justice and then turning their backs the moment radical action was called for. Nirode Behari Mallick, a Namasudra representative in the Bengal Legislative Council, had voiced the general feeling of dissatisfaction in the 1922 budget debate: 'So far as mere sweet words are concerned, I admit that from the highest rulers of the province to the so-called Leagues, every one shows sympathy with the condition of the backward classes. But when the time for practical action comes, all sympathy evaporates'.[131] The *Raiyat Bandhu*, a Calcutta newspaper, was of the same opinion. In January, 1923, it advised its peasant readers that the nationalist

[129] Andrews MSS.

[130] *Atma Sakti*, 1 Nov. 1922. Cf. *Swaraj*, 14 July 1922.

[131] BLCP, 27 Feb. 1922, Vol. VII, No. 3, p. 27.

movement was not for them, 'but for those who have not to toil for their bread; who, seated in the midst of plenty, dream pleasant dreams, and who would live in the dirtiest lane of the town, rather than forego the charms of town life'.[132]

The Swaraj Party decided that it could safely ignore these complaints, for it considered that the lower castes were too poorly organised to exercise any decisive influence at the polls. Its judgment was borne out at the 1923 elections by the defeats inflicted by its high-caste candidates in Khulna and Bakarganj South, two Namasudra strongholds, on Nirode Behari and his brother Mukanda Behari Mallick, Vice-President and President of the Bengal Namasudra Association.[133]

Less easily disregarded were the fears expressed by many Hindu bhadralok that Congress had endangered Hindu society by allying with the Muslims during the noncooperation movement. 'The Congress has become an insignificant tail of the Khilafat conference', complained *Nayak* on 19 February 1923, and the 'Muhammadans are daily growing stronger and more united'.

> Within the next ten or twenty years they are sure to oust the Hindus from their leading position in Bengal, if they are intelligently guided, whether they secure communal representation or not. Our Babus can make very dexterous use of the catchphrases of international politics, such as 'mandate', 'franchise', 'proletariat', etc., but they do not understand their household matters. . . . The 2½ crores of Hindus of Bengal are scattered and feeble like flocks of sheep without a watcher by the side of their Muhammadan compatriots.

This conviction of the need to organise the Hindus against the rising power of the Muslims led to the formation in Bengal in 1923 of a number of communalist organisations, the most important of which was the Hindu Sabha,[134] supported by new vernacular newspapers which were aggressively anti-Muslim.[135] C. R. Das had little sympathy with the objectives of these bodies, and he offended their organisers by insisting that political and social security in Bengal

[132] *Raiyat Bandhu*, 19 Jan. 1923.

[133] PP, 1924, [Cmd. 2154], Vol. XVIII, pp. 524–525.

[134] NP, Aug. 1923.

[135] Commenting on one of these new papers, the *Sarathi*, S. K. Sahana, a Bankura landholder and local politician, noted in his diary: If it 'lasts it will be a valuable acquisition to the vernacular press—but the politics in it, I fear, will creat troubles soon'. (21 Aug. 1923, Sahana diaries.)

could be ensured only if the bhadralok were willing to admit the lower orders, Muslim as well as Hindu, to some form of partnership.[136] With this as his attitude he could not count upon electoral support from the communalists, but he could take heart from the fact that the Moderates had made themselves even more unpopular with these men because of their concessions to the Muslims in the Calcutta Municipal Act.

By 1923 the terrorists were again active in Bengal, working in groups modelled on the revolutionary *samitis* of the partition period and, in many cases, bearing the same names. They were composed mainly of young Hindu bhadralok and they had the support of the communalist Hindus.[137] Das personally disapproved of their activities, but some of his followers in the Swaraj Party, Subhas Chandra Bose among them, favoured violent methods,[138] and these men served as his liaison with the terrorists. The connection was later to prove an embarrassment to his party when it attempted to move toward cooperation with the Government, but in the short run it was a considerable electoral asset as it secured Hindu bhadralok sympathy.

While appreciating the continued importance of cultivating the Hindu bhadralok vote, Das realised that no party could hope to command a majority in the reformed Bengal Legislative Council unless it had Muslim backing. His position with the Muslims at the beginning of 1923 was not strong. Even at the height of the non-cooperation and Khilafat movements, the Hindu–Muslim alliance in Bengal had never been as close as it was in many other provinces, and in 1922 with Gandhi's retreat and the collapse of the Khilafat agitation it had disintegrated. The Muslims resented the contempt which many of the Hindu bhadralok elite displayed for the masses, and the growth of Hindu communalism convinced some of their leaders that their communal identity was endangered.[139]

At this time there was no enthusiasm displayed by the Muslim press for the idea of council entry, but Das was determined to gain the community's support for the Swaraj Party. The Moderates made his task easier by their reluctance to concede the Muslims' demands with regard to the Calcutta Municipal Bill, and the manner in which the Muslims finally achieved their victory over communal

[136] *Banglar Katha*, 7 Feb. 1923; and NP, 7 Apr. 1923.

[137] *Pundits and Elephants*, pp. 57–61.

[138] See Bose's 'Dreams of a Youth', originally published in May 1923, S. C. Bose, *The Mission of Life* (Calcutta, 1953), pp. 1–5.

[139] See NP, Jan.–Apr. 1923.

electorates convinced many of their leaders that the community's interests could best be secured by organising a solid Muslim bloc in the Council, which might then ally with other groups on its own terms.

There followed a vigorous intracommunal debate over council entry, which Das attempted to swing in his favour by campaigning in the Muslim centres of Eastern Bengal.[140] He made it clear that he was willing to negotiate terms with the Muslims as a community if in return they would support the Swaraj Party. On this basis discussions were begun in September, 1923, to settle the details of a Hindu-Muslim alliance in Bengal. These details were not completely settled until after the elections, but in the meantime many Muslim candidates had accepted the Swarajist label and the party had the general goodwill of the community in its election bid.

The communal and class dissensions that had appeared in 1923 were to have a disastrous influence on the political future of Bengal but, temporarily at least, C. R. Das had shielded his party from their most harmful effects and enabled it to contest the 1923 elections strong and united.

THE SWARAJIST ELECTION CAMPAIGN

The Swarajists approached the elections with many advantages. They were the heroes of the greatest anti-Government agitation India had ever seen and they proudly bore the new title of honour: prison graduates. They had symbols, such as the wearing of *khādi*, by which they could appeal to the new mass electorate, and they could offer themselves to the people as Mahatmaji's disciples. By contrast, the Moderates could be represented as 'Government men' and this had a ring of truth, for was it not a fact that they had been absent in Calcutta for the last three years on Government business?

Because of the time they had spent in their localities organising support for noncooperation, the Swarajists were known in person to the electors in a way few politicians in Bengal had ever been before. Moreover, they had at their disposal the reformed Congress organisation extending to the villages; and the volunteer brigades, although but a remnant of their former strength, were available for the hack work of election propaganda. By securing a sweeping

[140] *Progress*, 7 Aug. 1923.

victory in the local body elections in April, 1923, the Swarajists had secured an additional source of local power.[141]

Possibly even more important factors were the personnel and organisation of the party itself. In Chitta Ranjan Das it had a leader of outstanding ability—a politician with a flair for the dramatic and an acute sense of timing; a man who could command the unquestioning obedience of his followers and who could yet delegate power wisely. He was an excellent judge of men and had gathered a group of lieutenants who were scarcely less capable than himself: J. M. Sen Gupta, Subhas Chandra Bose, B. N. Sasmal, Nirmal Chandra Chandra, and Kiran Sankar Ray. Das was 53. His senior officers were all in their thirties or forties, with the exception of Bose who was 26. They were the ablest members of a young generation that acknowledged them as its leaders.

For the first time in Bengal there was a party that approached a general election with an unchallenged leader and a central organisation to nominate its candidates. It could furnish them with election workers and ample funds for campaigning, for it had its hands in many full pockets.[142] It could also provide electioneering expertise, for at least three of its members (Das, Bose, and Dr Bidhan Chandra Roy) had assisted British Liberal candidates in parliamentary elections while studying in England.[143] As a result, the party applied techniques new to Indian politics. These can be illustrated from Dr Roy's campaign in the 24-Parganas Municipal North constituency, where he gained a spectacular victory over Surendranath Banerjea.

At 41 Bidhan Chandra Roy was one of India's leading surgeons.[144] As a student he had had a brilliant career in Calcutta and London, and on his return to Bengal in 1911 he had divided his time between private practice and university teaching. In 1916, he had been elected to the Calcutta University Senate where he joined Sir Asutosh Mookerjee's group. It was P. C. Mitter's criticism of Mookerjee in 1922 that first gave Roy the idea of entering the Legislative Council.

[141] *Englishman*, 26 Apr. 1923.

[142] Simon Commission, Vol. VIII, pp. 143 and 150; P. C. Ray, *Life and Times of C. R. Das* (London, 1927), p. 198.

[143] H. N. Das Gupta, *Deshbandhu Chittaranjan Das* (Delhi, 1960), pp. 5–7; K. P. Thomas, *Dr B. C. Roy* (Calcutta, 1955), p. 63; and author's interview with Dr B. C. Roy, Calcutta, 2 Mar. 1961.

[144] For biographical details see Thomas, *op. cit.*; and obituary notice, *Statesman*,* 2 July 1962.

His ambition was encouraged by Surendranath Roy, who was looking for a candidate to set up against Banerjea to even the old score over his nonappointment as Education Minister.[145] He offered Dr Roy the support of his purse and his influence if he would contest the 24-Parganas Municipal North seat. Roy accepted the offer, reasoning that a victory against Banerjea would be an excellent start to a political career, while a defeat at his hands would be no disgrace.[146] C. R. Das recognised Bidhan Chandra's ability and gave him the Swarajist nomination for the constituency.

He opened his campaign in May, 1923, and during the following seven months spent most of his evenings and his Sundays among his electors. In the same period Banerjea visited the constituency twice only, for he was in Darjeeling throughout the summer. Roy had the help of the Congress volunteers, and Das personally supported him at a number of his meetings.

He offered the voters a choice between a representative who would devote himself to their service and one who was bound to the Government. In India there were only two parties, he said; the party of the few who supported the Government and profited from its every action, and the party of the many who suffered. 'I do not belong to the party of the Government'. On the other hand, Sir Surendranath Banerjea 'by accepting office . . . has identified himself with the Bureaucracy'.[147]

Socially, the 24-Parganas Municipal North constituency was a mixed bag. Lying on the outskirts of Calcutta, it comprised a number of satellite towns that had grown up around the jute mills along the Hooghly. Its centre was Barrackpur, which had a British cantonment and to which many bhadralok were attracted because of the excellent rail service to Calcutta. Between the towns were numerous villages.

Roy attempted to reach all classes of voters with his appeal. To the bhadralok he spoke of his keen interest in higher education and pledged himself 'to strive to preserve the position of the University and oppose any attempt to destroy the legitimate autonomy or in any way to reduce its status or utility as an institution for higher research'. He informed the mill operatives that he was opposed to 'the forces and resources of the State' being 'more readily placed

[145] Thomas, *op. cit.*, p. 88; and author's interview with Biren Roy, M.P., Calcutta, 10 Mar. 1962.

[146] Thomas, *op. cit.*, p. 88.

[147] *Ibid.*, pp. 91 and 94.

at the service of Capital than for due protection of the vital interests of labour'. He was careful to add, however, that he would set his face 'sternly against the fomenting of class war or the organisation of industrial strikes for the pursuit of political ends'. He would encourage 'healthy co-operation between capital and labour'. His final appeal was to the tenantry, whom he promised to protect against the tyrannies of zamindars and officials alike.[148]

In 1923, election day in Calcutta and the surrounding towns was a more exciting occasion than it had been in the past. There were noisy demonstrations by the supporters of the rival parties, and hundreds of motor cars plied the streets at the candidates' expense, bearing placards and carrying voters to the polls.[149] The results were announced on 30 November. In 24-Parganas Municipal North constituency Surendranath Banerjea had suffered a humiliating defeat, securing only 2,283 votes to Bidhan Chandra Roy's 5,689.[150] The new Swarajist daily, *Forward*, was jubilant: the Barrackpur contest 'represents the clash between the limitations of the real and the vision of an idea. The issue is plain and simple—Diarchy or a free and unfettered India with a soul and a nationality; a dead horse or a full manhood. Sir Surendra Nath represents Diarchy and, in his fall, was voiced the free will of the people'.[151]

Throughout the province the Swaraj Party had triumphed. In the Hindu constituencies its candidates had captured three-quarters of the seats and in the Muslim electorates, where there was considerable reluctance to acknowledge any but a communal allegiance, they had secured half. The Moderate party had been reduced to a rump and nearly all its leaders had been kept out of the Council.[152]

To what did the Swaraj Party owe its victory? Primarily to its success in spanning the two levels of politics—the old level of the sophisticated bhadralok and the new level of the mass electorate. The party had retained the confidence of the bhadralok because it was itself largely bhadralok in composition, but its members had also won a popular following through their district work. They had taken the old bhadralok Congress and refashioned it to meet the demands of mass politics. They had used symbols that did not of-

[148] *Ibid.*, pp. 92–93.

[149] GB, Appointment, 6R–220(1–5) of 1923, A87–91, July 1924.

[150] PP, 1924 [Cmd. 2154], Vol. XVIII, p. 521.

[151] *Forward*, 1 Dec. 1923.

[152] PP, 1924, [Cmd. 2154], Vol. XVIII, pp. 500, 503, and 522–534; Simon Commission Vol. VIII, p. 109; and *Statesman*, 1 Dec. 1923.

fend the bhadralok and yet could be understood by the masses. They had a watchcry which was simple and absolute: 'We want swaraj: we want freedom. Small rights will not satisfy us'.[153]

[153] Swaraj Party election manifesto, *Swadesh*, 29 Sept. 1923.

VII

REAPERS OF THE WHIRLWIND

STRATEGY AND ORGANISATION

Chitta Ranjan Das had brought his party triumphantly into the Legislative Council, but he had now to face new tasks. He had first to devise a strategy that would satisfy his party and enable it to retain the confidence of the electors. He had then to bind his following securely together so that the unity of the party would not be destroyed in the division lobbies. As he was well aware, neither task had been successfully accomplished by his predecessors in the Council.

In working the reformed institutions in Bengal, nationalist politicians were confronted with grave problems. In the first place, they had to serve two masters: the bhadralok, a politically experienced group with clearly formulated and exacting demands, and the new mass electorate, which was fractured and inarticulate. Secondly, the Legislature in which they had to work was divided by its constitution into groups responsible to separate communal and sectional electorates. There was thus no single 'bar' before which all members could be 'arraigned' for their actions in the Council, and no sense of a common allegiance. The Muslims who occupied 30 percent of the seats and the Europeans who occupied 14 percent (see Table 4) preferred their communal interests to wider considerations of general social welfare. These difficulties had proved too much for the Moderates. C. R. Das had now to wrestle with them.

Lord Lytton forced him into an immediate decision on strategy by calling him to Government House as soon as the election results were complete and offering him the ministerial portfolios as leader of the largest party. The Governor was holding open a door that Das dared not enter no matter how tempted he may have been. He had persuaded the bhadralok to tolerate Council entry by arguing that it was in the Council that the Government could best be fought, and the Swaraj Party was pledged to destroy dyarchy. Any hint from Das at that stage of willingness to cooperate with the British would have split his party and alienated its bhadralok support. In his reply to Lytton he nailed his colours to the mast of obstruction. 'The members of this party are pledged to do everything in their power, by using their legal rights granted under the Reform Act, to put an end to the system of diarchy. This duty they cannot discharge if they take office'.[1]

What did Das hope to gain by his policy of obstruction? He believed that if he could bring the working of the reforms to a standstill the British would be forced to come to him, cap in hand, with an offer of constitutional concessions. He would then be in a position to dictate his own terms. His belief was not unjustified, for since 1920 the British had been obsessed with the importance of keeping the reformed institutions working, and their fear of a collapse had brought them to Das and Gandhi in December, 1921, with the suggestion of a round table conference.

Successful obstruction would depend upon party solidarity, and as soon as the elections were over Das turned to this work. He had first to make good his promises to the Muslims. In this regard he could not afford to be niggardly for a considerable number of the 40 Muslim MLCs were as yet uncommitted, and some might join the Swaraj Party if it proved itself willing to give generously to their community. On the other hand, any suggestion of partiality for Hindu interests would almost certainly drive the existing Muslim members out of the Swaraj Party into a communal organisation.

Early in December, 1923, in discussions with a number of leading Muslims the terms of a Hindu-Muslim pact were settled, and these were accepted by a meeting of the Swaraj Council Party on 16 December. They were published two days later over the signature of S. C. Bose as Secretary of the B.P.C.C. 'It is resolved that in order to establish a real foundation of Self-Government in this province it it necessary to bring about a pact between the Hindu and the

[1] C. R. Das to Lytton, [16 Dec. 1923], *Pundits and Elephants*, p. 44.

Mahomedans of Bengal dealing with the rights of each community when the foundation of Self-Government is secured'. Representation in the Legislative Council was to be in proportion to population and through separate electorates. In local bodies, the majority community in each district was to have 60 percent of the seats and the minority community 40 percent. Fifty-five percent of government posts were to be reserved for the Muslims, and until that percentage was reached the community might supply up to 80 percent of all recruits. No resolution affecting the religion of any community was to be passed by the Legislative Council without the consent of three-quarters of the elected representatives of that community. There was to be no music in procession before mosques, and cow-killing was not to be interfered with.[2]

Das had paid a high price for the 21 Muslims who followed him into the Council.[3]

He had secured one flank. To secure the other he formed an alliance with a group nominally led by Byomkes Chakravarti, his old rival from the 1917–1920 period who had played but a minor role in politics since Das' triumph at Nagpur. However, Chakravarti had maintained his influence in Calcutta through his position in the Bengal Landholders' Association and the Bengal National Chamber of Commerce, and it was to represent the latter that he was returned to the Council in 1923. Immediately after the elections he had gathered around him a group of 24 MLCs—some former Moderates and others, renegade Swarajists—who shared little apart from the title Independent Nationalists and a common desire to hold office.[4] It was to this group that Lytton turned after Das had rejected his ministerial offer, but he found that Chakravarti would accept office only if all three Ministers were chosen from his party. As the Independent Nationalists would have to rely upon Moderate votes for a majority in the Council, Lytton refused to agree to this.[5]

[2] A. Karim, *Letters on Hindu-Muslim Pact* (Calcutta, 1924), pp. 2–3 and appendix A.

[3] There is a conflict of evidence on the exact composition and size of the parties at various stages in the second Council. The figures given in this chapter are the author's estimates based on division lists and the following sources: *Pundits and Elephants*, p. 46; *Reformed Constitution, 1927*, pp. 178–179; Simon Commission, Vol. VIII, pp. 103 and 109; *Statesman*, 1 Dec. 1923; and PP, 1924, [Cmd. 2154], Vol. XVIII, pp. 500, 503, and 522–534.

[4] *Reformed Constitution, 1927*, p. 178.

[5] *Pundits and Elephants*, p. 45.

With the prospect of office gone, the main bond uniting the group was destroyed and Chakravarti beat a hasty retreat to the Swaraj Party, whence five of his six Muslim followers had preceded him, attracted no doubt by the Hindu-Muslim pact. Displaying great tact, Das treated Chakravarti as the leader of a separate group while at the same time providing him with a new constituency to replace the Bengal National Chamber of Commerce seat of which he had been deprived because of the corruption by which he had secured his original election.[6] The remainder of Chakravarti's followers, most of whom rejected the Hindu-Muslim pact, remained outside the Swaraj Party, but he and Das were usually able to secure their votes on vital issues. Thus Das entered the new Council with its total of 139 members, supported by 46 Swarajists and 19 Independent Nationalists.

DOWN WITH THE MINISTERS

In search of Ministers Lytton had now to turn to the Moderates, a disorganized group of 30 MLCs who had no acknowledged leader. In these circumstances the only possible basis for selection was personality. Lytton's choices were Surendranath Mallick, an extremist in the first Council whose considerable influence in Calcutta had been increased by his appointment under Banerjea's regime as first Indian nonofficial Chairman of the Corporation;[7] Fazlul Huq, who now commanded a personal following of eight Muslim leaders; and Abdul Karim Ghuznavi, a former Imperial Legislative Councillor and a large landholder in Mymensingh.[8]

The Swarajists regarded Lytton's appointment of Ministers as a challenge—a challenge, moreover, that they were glad to accept for they knew that few of their electors drew any distinction between the personalities in the Government and the institutions of Government. For this reason, a successful personal attack on a Minister would be regarded as a success against the reformed institutions. They set out to knock down the Ministers, and Surendranath Mallick was selected as their first victim. A petition was filed contesting

[6] GB, Appointment, 6R–1(1–35), A105–139, July 1924; and *ibid.*, 6R–1 (1–9), A12–20, Nov. 1924.

[7] For biographical details see *Pundits and Elephants*, pp. 46–48; and *Nation in Making*, pp. 368–370.

[8] For biographical details see *Indian Year Book and Who's Who, 1939–40* (Bombay, 1940).

the legality of his return to the Council from the Calcutta South constituency, as a result of which a reelection was ordered. To oppose Mallick in the new contest the Swarajists and Independent Nationalists jointly nominated Surendranath Haldar, a barrister whose family had great influence in South Calcutta as the priests of the Kalighat temple. With the Swarajist election machine working for him, he was able to defeat Mallick comfortably and the Minister was forced to resign without having taken his seat in the Council.[9]

The attack on Huq and Ghuznavi was begun through the public press, which described the two Ministers as a pair of self-seeking opportunists.[10] The Swarajists' experience during the noncooperation movement had taught them the value of a well-conducted campaign of defamation, and with three major newspapers at their disposal, the English-language *Forward*, the Hindu-edited vernacular *Nayak*, and the Bengali Muslim *Mohammadi*, they were able to pillory every leading personality connected with the reformed institutions. Lytton and his Executive Councillors were represented as repressive autocrats; the President of the Legislative Council, Evan Cotton, was reviled as an enemy of Indian freedom—'the unworthy son of Sir Henry Cotton';[11] the Ministers were ridiculed for their every action; and the ordinary MLC who had the temerity to cast a vote for the Government was named in bold type in the centre of a black-bordered front page of the following day's papers.

The new Legislative Council was sworn in on 22 January 1924. The Swarajists made a striking impression. They came in a body, dressed uniformly in white *khādi*, bare-headed and clean shaven. They sat together in the centre of the opposition benches, and in the proceedings that followed showed a vigour and poise that was unusual in new members. They had a well-prepared party organisation, with a caucus and whips, including one for the Muslims.[12]

Their policy was to lop off the tall poppies—to hit at the main personalities opposing them—and their method was to misuse the constitutional machinery. In both ways they would earn bhadralok

[9] GB, Appointment, 18L–43(1–4), A31–34, Mar. 1924; and *Pundits and Elephants*, p. 48.

[10] E.g., *Mohammadi*, 28 Dec. 1923.

[11] *Nayak*, 26 Mar. 1924.

[12] J. G. Drummond, *The Working of the Bengal Legislative Council under the Government of India Act, 1919* (Cambridge University Ph.D. thesis, 1938–39), p. 127; *Reformed Constitution, 1927*, pp. 181 and 189; and *Indian Daily News*, 25 Jan. 1924.

applause and impede, if not wreck, the work of the institution.

Their first act was a mark of disrespect for the Governor: they absented themselves from the Council during his speech of welcome on 23 January.[13] They followed this with an attempt to criticise his appointment of Ministers by moving for the presentation of a formal address from the Council. Cotton ruled the motion out of order,[14] and this was the beginning of a running fight between the Swarajists and the President over points of procedure. Every possible ruling from the Chair was contested in an attempt to discredit Cotton and his office. There were rowdy demonstrations from the opposition benches, which frequently had vocal support from the visitors' galleries, and on a number of occasions the Swarajists walked out of the Chamber when they failed to get their way.[15]

The Ministers were subjected to a barrage of interjections whenever they addressed the Council, and frequent use was made of supplementary questions in an attempt to catch them off balance. When they voted with the minority, even on a reserved question, the Swarajists called for their resignations.[16] Those few items of legislation which the Government was rash enough to trust to the Council's tender mercies were obstructed or so mutilated as to ensure their withdrawal.[17]

The climax to the campaign came in March, 1924, with the Swarajists' attack on the Government's financial demands. On the reserved side they rejected every demand except that for police, and on the transferred side they refused grants to pay the salaries of the Education Department inspectorate, the Medical Department establishment, and the Ministers.[18] The contest over the last item was regarded by both sides as a major trial of strength, for the constitution would have to be suspended if no money was provided to pay the Ministers. The Swarajists were at pains to ensure that the electorate understood why they were opposing this grant. At public meetings and in the press they explained their motives,[19] and as a

[13] Drummond, *op. cit.*, p. 129.

[14] BLCP, 18 Feb. 1924, Vol. XIV, No. 2, pp. 35–36.

[15] E.g., *ibid.*, 24 Jan. 1924, Vol. XIV, No. 1, pp. 86–90; *ibid.*, 18 Mar. 1924, Vol. XIV, No. 5, pp. 61–62; *ibid.*, 24 Mar. 1924, Vol. XIV, No. 5, pp. 183–184; and *ibid.*, 26 Aug. 1924, Vol. XVI, pp. 45 ff.

[16] E.g., *ibid.*, 20 Feb. 1924, Vol. XIV, No. 2, pp. 126–150.

[17] Simon Commission, Vol. VIII, pp. 158–159.

[18] BLCP, Vol. XIV, No. 5.

[19] E.g., *Forward*, 18 Mar. 1924; and *Subhas Chandra*, p. 67.

result their rejection of the Ministers' salaries was acclaimed by the newspapers as a triumph for nationalism.[20]

March, 1924, also brought the Swaraj Party a victory outside the Legislative Council. In the elections for the Calcutta Corporation, reformed under Surendranath Banerjea's Municipal Act, it captured nearly three-quarters of the seats.[21] At the first meeting of the new Corporation C. R. Das was elected Mayor, and later Subhas Chandra Bose was appointed Chief Executive Officer. As a gesture toward the Muslims, the Deputy-Mayor was chosen from Calcutta's leading Muslim house: the Suhrawardys. He was 31-year-old Huseyn Shaheed,[22] who was to have a checkered association with the city's affairs throughout the following quarter century.[23]

Control of the Corporation provided the Swarajists with the power that was denied to them in the Legislative Council because of their policy of obstruction. They now had public funds at their disposal and jobs to distribute as patronage. They began by rewarding five party supporters with appointments as city aldermen, and, with an eye to the communal question, they found posts on the Corporation staff for 25 Muslims.[24] The business of the municipality furnished excellent opportunities for demonstrations of nationalist ardour. The Corporation's employees were outfitted in *khādi* and much publicity was given to the purchase of *swadeshi* goods in preference to imported equipment. Many of the city's streets and parks were renamed after the nation's heroes, and civic receptions were held for Congress leaders instead of British dignitaries as in the past. To gratify property holders, building rules were relaxed and, when it suited the party, tax arrears were disregarded. Popular support was gained by heavy expenditure on free primary schools and medical dispensaries in many parts of the city. A weekly journal —the *Calcutta Municipal Gazette*—was started to publicise the new regime's achievements.[25] The activities of the Swarajists in the Corporation were a perfect foil to their work of destruction in the Council and it served to consolidate their hold on Calcutta, still the key to political Bengal.

[20] E.g., *Telegraph*, 2 Feb. 1924.

[21] P. C. Ray, *Life and Times of C. R. Das* (London, 1927), p. 202.

[22] *Dainik Basumati*, 14 Apr. 1924; and *Indian Struggle*, pp. 135–136.

[23] For biographical details see *Who's Who in India, Burma and Ceylon, 1938* (Poona, 1938); and *Time*, 22 July 1957.

[24] *Dainik Basumati*, 14 Apr. 1924; and NP, 2 Aug. 1924.

[25] *Indian Struggle*, pp. 136–138; and *Reformed Constitution, 1927*, p. 162.

THE GOVERNOR IN POLITICS

Every Swarajist success in the Council or Corporation was galling for Lytton, for he had set out determined to prevent the party succeeding in its attempt to wreck the constitution. From the beginning he had regarded the affair as a fight in which he was personally involved, and he was fully prepared to come down into the political arena to grapple with Das and his followers. When in December, 1923, the Swarajists and Independent Nationalists rejected his offer of the ministerial portfolios, he had published a long press communiqué detailing his negotiations with them and explaining why he had finally chosen his Ministers from the Moderate party.[26] In his first address to the Council a month later he threw out a direct challenge to the Swarajists.

> I selected my new Ministers from among those who believed that the best way of achieving the end which is desired by all is not to refuse but to accept responsibility, not to destroy the foundations, but to build upon them, not to obstruct but to construct. . . . Throughout the sessions of this Council there will be only one main issue before you, namely, whether you will side with the party of obstruction or whether you will side with the party of construction.[27]

Once battle was joined in the Council, Lytton took an active part in advising his officers on tactics and supplying them with troops. He talked personally with MLCs in an attempt to persuade them to vote with the Ministers, and on one occasion he held a tea party at Government House for all non-Swarajists and lectured them on the need for party organisation.[28] Immediately before the Government submitted its demands for grants on 18 March, he appeared unheralded in the Council to warn the members that if they refused finance for the transferred items he would have no hesitation in closing down these departments, with the result that many public employees would be thrown out of work. He advised the MLCs to remember that it was they, not the Government, who would have to answer to the electors for such an unpopular move.[29]

There was an uproar in the press at what was variously described

[26] 23 Dec. 1923, GB, Appointment, 18L–43(1–4), A31–34, Mar. 1924.
[27] BLCP, 23 Jan. 1924, Vol. XIV, No. 1, p. 5.
[28] *Forward*, 2 Apr. 1924.
[29] BLCP, 18 Mar. 1924, Vol. XIV, No. 5, pp. 15–18.

as 'bluff' and an 'unconstitutional attempt to coerce the members',[30] but Lytton was convinced that his speech had had a salutary effect and had forestalled even more drastic cuts in the budget. Moreover, he considered that the refusal of the medical and education demands provided him with an excellent opportunity to teach the Swarajists a lesson. He promptly gave the school inspectors and medical staff six months notice of dismissal[31] and then published a press communiqué which said in effect: 'Look bhadralok at what the Swarajists are doing to your employment'.[32]

From Delhi and London the Viceroy and Secretary of State were watching Lytton's activities with growing uneasiness, for they were afraid that his provocative interventions in politics might aggravate what was already a serious situation. Both criticised his action in dismissing Government staff, and the Viceroy, Lord Reading, advised him to use his constitutional power to certify the funds required to pay the salaries.[33] Lytton refused, insisting that the politicians had to learn their responsibility to their electors.[34] In this case his gamble paid off, for there was deep concern expressed in the bhadralok press at the prospect of increased middle-class unemployment;[35] when the grants were resubmitted to the Council in August, 1924, they were restored without opposition.[36]

Of greatest concern to Lytton was the refusal of the Ministers' salaries, but he was determined not to accept this as a final verdict on dyarchy. Consequently, he allowed Huq and Ghuznavi to remain in office without pay and work to secure a majority at a revoting.[37] He even toyed with the idea of stretching his own powers of expenditure to authorise an interim payment for them, but Reading refused to permit this as it was strictly unconstitutional. He warned Lytton that he was running a grave risk by involving himself in politics in this manner, for he was playing into the Swarajists' hands by exposing himself to personal attack. The Viceroy explained to the Secretary of State, Lord Olivier: 'My objection . . .

[30] NP, 19 Mar. 1924.
[31] *Pundits and Elephants*, p. 49.
[32] 16 Apr. 1924, GB, Appointment, 2B–14(1–9), A78–86, July 1924.
[33] Reading, Vol. II, pp. 285–287.
[34] *Pundits and Elephants*, pp. 49–51.
[35] E.g., NP, 12 Apr. 1924.
[36] BLCP, 26 Aug. 1924, Vol. XVI, pp. 72–74.
[37] *Pundits and Elephants*, p. 51.

was intended to protect him against the risk of charges he might find it difficult to answer. These might seriously impair his position as Governor'.[38]

THE RAGGED SEARCH FOR A MAJORITY

While Lytton was arguing the point with Delhi, his Ministers were out in search of a majority. The officials gave them every assistance, relieving them of all administrative duties and interceding with MLCs on their behalf. Huq and Ghuznavi (in Lytton's words) 'worked their power of patronage for all it was worth'[39] and the vacant ministership was held out as an inducement to those with ambitions.[40] Their trump card, however, was communal. They made great play of the fact that the Hindu-dominated Swaraj Party was attempting to strike down a Muslim ministry. In reality this is a communal attack, they told their coreligionists, and all Muslims must unite to oppose the Hindus.[41]

The official members of the Government had already agreed that their best hope of breaking the Swaraj Party lay in encouraging communal divisions. Their experience in the first Montagu-Chelmsford Council had convinced them that the reformed institutions could be kept functioning by a series of tactical expedients. Admittedly communalism was an ugly weapon to use, but, as they hastened to point out, it was not they but the Swarajists who had declared total war. How could they be expected to fight clean when their opponents were breaking every rule of decent political behaviour?[42]

They were provided with a moral sanction for the use of communalism by their Muslim colleagues—Huq, Ghuznavi, and Executive Councillor Sir Abdur Rahim—who asserted that in the general interests of the Muslim community its representatives in the Legislative Council should be united against the Swaraj Party. These three men argued that C. R. Das had been able to inveigle Muslims into his party because of the factions that divided Muslim politicians.

[38] Reading, Vol. II, pp. 286–287.
[39] *Pundits and Elephants*, p. 52.
[40] *Baikali*, 26 Aug. 1924; and *Bengalee*, 28 Aug. 1924.
[41] *Pundits and Elephants*, p. 52.
[42] Chief Secretary, GB, to GI, 14 June 1924, GB, Appointment, 6R–92(1–10), A31–40, Dec. 1925.

Unless these could be overcome, they said, the community would remain weak and a liability to the Government.[43]

The best means of drawing off Das' Muslim followers was obviously to destroy their faith in the Swaraj Party's Hindu-Muslim pact. To this end a Muslim supporter of the Government, Khan Bahadur Musharruf Husain, MLC for Malda, had been persuaded early in the Council's first session to submit a resolution for the immediate implementation of the pact's provisions with regard to the employment of Muslims under the provincial Government. His motion called for the reservation for Muslims of 80 percent of Government appointments until such time as they occupied 55 percent of all offices.[44] Sir Abdur Rahim explained what the officials hoped to gain from this:

> It was felt in Government circles and among those who were anxious to defeat and destroy the Swarajist party that Mr C. R. Das would, by this resolution, be pushed into a tight corner; he would lose either his 20 Muhammadan followers, to all or to most of whom the Pact had been a strong inducement to join his party, or the support of the Nationalists without whose help he would never have secured a majority against the Government, but who would, on no account, accept the terms of the Pact. Khan Bahadur Mushruff Hossain received every sort of encouragement from the supporters of Government and also from individual members of Government to press his resolution.[45]

It was arranged that the motion should be put to the Council in the week preceding the voting on the budget, and during the debate every effort was made to force the Swarajists to commit themselves. Spokesmen for the Government and the European nonofficials expressed their support for the objects of the resolution and emphasised that it was merely a restatement of the terms of the Swarajists' own Hindu-Muslim pact. Here, they said, was an opportunity for the Hindu members of the Swaraj Party to prove their good faith.

From the speeches of the Independent Nationalists, who repudiated the pact, and the Muslim Swarajists, who revealed a painful conflict of loyalties, it was evident that Das was in a very tight corner. He could escape only by avoiding a division on the main question and he therefore moved for an adjournment of the dis-

[43] GB, Appointment, 4M–12(1–3), A70–71½, Nov. 1925.

[44] BLCP, 12 Mar. 1924, Vol. XIV, No. 4, p. 55.

[45] Minute, 27 July 1925, GB, Appointment, 4M–12(1–3), A70–71½, Nov. 1925.

cussion *sine die*. His excuse was that there had as yet been no time to place the pact 'before the country'. When the budget session was over he intended to tour Bengal to secure popular support for the agreement. Until this had been done, he said, any action in the Council was precipitate.

He succeeded in carrying his amendment,[46] but the damage was done. The Ministers were able to say to the Muslim MLCs: now you can see how you were misled with empty promises. The cry was taken up in the press.

> Had Mr C. R. Das really desired that the pact would be put into practice, he and his party would certainly not have proposed to postpone indefinitely the resolution of Khan Bahadur Musharruf Hossain. Mr C. R. Das has said that if the terms of the pact be not fulfilled after the attainment of Swaraj, the Musalmans will be quite entitled to realise their dues on the strength of the *lathi*. In the meantime the Hindus will become completely skilled in the use of the *lathi*, so that the Musalmans will never be able to realise their dues . . . . We ask our fellow-Musalmans to note the names of those Moslem members of Council who have voted against the resolution . . . .[47]

There were angry replies from the Hindu newspapers and bitter attacks on the British for their attempt to divide and rule.[48]

To consolidate their advantage, the Government's Muslim supporters began organising a communal party in the Council. At a meeting of the Central National Mahommedan Association on 24 April 1924, Khan Bahadur Abdus Salam, the Association's Honorary Secretary and MLC for Jessore North, argued that a party to unite all Muslim councillors was the logical corollary of communal electorates. Muslim politicians must 'shake themselves free from the shackles of Non-Moslem influences', he said. 'Otherwise, Moslem interests will become increasingly the football of Non-Moslems'.[49] The party's promoters ran into the old problem of 'personal jealousies and rivalries [which] bulk largely in Bengal Moslem Society',[50] but they were successful in persuading four Swarajist supporters in the Council to join their ranks, including

[46] BLCP, 12 and 13 Mar. 1924, Vol. XIV, No. 4, pp. 55–108.

[47] *Moslem Hitaishi*, 4 Apr. 1924.

[48] E.g., *Viswamitra*, 15 Mar. 1924; and *Sarathi*, 3 Apr. 1924.

[49] *Central National Mahommedan Association, Octennial Report, 1917–1924* (Calcutta, 1925), p. 61.

[50] *Ibid.*, p. 20.

two of the Suhrawardys, Dr Abdulla-al-Mamun and Huseyn Shaheed[51]—a considerable catch.

This was a great encouragement to the Ministers, for every vote would count when the demand for their salaries was resubmitted to the Council on 7 July. As the day approached, there was vigorous lobbying by both parties.[52] The Ministers played the communal issue for all it was worth, even invoking the authority of *mollās* to convince the Muslim MLCs that it would be wrong for them to vote with the Swaraj Party.[53]

By the end of June, Huq and Ghuznavi were confident that they had their majority, but once more the Swarajists outmanoeuvred them. On 3 July J. M. Sen Gupta made a successful application to the High Court for an injunction to prevent the President from resubmitting the salaries demand to the Council. Cotton and Lytton were furious at what they regarded as a personal affront, and, determined to avenge their honour, they prorogued the Council as soon as it assembled on the 7th and appealed against the Court's ruling. At this point Reading intervened, for he realised that nothing would suit the Swarajists better than a *cause célèbre.* To the intense annoyance of Lytton who wanted to fight out the case, he amended the Council rules to remove any doubt about the legality of a resubmission of demands.[54]

The Swarajists' strategem had secured them a month's grace, and in that time they had managed to tip the balance back in their favour—by a liberal application of silver, according to the Ministers.[55] The four Muslim members who had strayed into Salam's communal party had been shepherded safely back to the opposition fold. To clinch the issue, the party's English-language daily *Forward* published, on the morning of 26 August, the day that the new vote was to be taken, a copy of a letter carrying Fazlul Huq's signature which offered a bribe to an unnamed Rai Bahadur in return for his vote. Huq denounced the letter as a forgery, but it undoubtedly had some effect in securing a majority for the Swarajists. The new demand was rejected by 68 votes to 66.[56]

[51] *Ibid.*, p. 63.
[52] *Pundits and Elephants*, p. 52.
[53] *Dainik Basumati*, 21 May 1924.
[54] *Pundits and Elephants*, pp. 52–53; Simon Commission, Vol. IV, pp. 322–325; and NP, 2 Aug. 1924.
[55] *Pundits and Elephants*, p. 53.
[56] BLCP, 26 Aug. 1924, Vol. XVI, pp. 46–69.

The Ministers immediately resigned, and Lytton had no choice but to suspend the constitution. The Swarajists claimed a triumph. 'The Lord had given, the Lord has taken away, Blessed be the name of the Lord–so thinks the man in the street in regard to the withdrawal of dyarchy in Bengal', wrote *Forward*.[57]

Lytton was embittered by what had happened. He had come to regard the maintenance of the constitution as a matter of personal prestige, and its destruction was a severe blow to his pride. His actions throughout the preceding year had been subject to criticism from all parties: Swarajists, Moderates,[58] European nonofficials,[59] the Government of India, the Secretary of State, and British parliamentarians.[60] He had come out to India with a sentimental desire to do something big for Indians. 'It seemed that Fate was calling me, and perhaps I had an exaggerated idea of my own ability to steer the destinies of that country at a critical moment'.[61] Now that things had gone badly for him, he dismissed India as an alien society for which he could never hope to do anything. In his memoirs he wrote: 'Thoreau once said that it takes two to speak the truth–one to speak and another to hear. Truth in this sense is rare as between the British and the Indians, for the very terms in which their political controversies are conducted have very different meanings for each. Even, therefore, where sincerity and goodwill are present, it is easier to speak true than to hear true'.[62] In effect, Lytton now abdicated his idealistic aims and yielded the initiative to his I.C.S. officers who were on hand with a policy.

DAS' DILEMMA

Chitta Ranjan Das was also in trouble. He had successfully wrecked dyarchy in Bengal, but what had he gained? The British, he had always said, would be forced to come to terms. But would they? Lytton's communiqué suspending the constitution certainly gave no hint of any intention to negotiate. '. . . the people of Bengal have, through the action of their representatives, tempo-

[57] *Forward*, 9 Sept. 1924.
[58] E.g., IA Committee meeting proceedings, 2 and 4 Sept. 1924.
[59] E.g., European Association's proceedings, 4 Feb. 1924, reported in *Hindusthan*, 6 Feb. 1924.
[60] *Pundits and Elephants*, pp. 49–50; and *Statesman*,* 1 Apr. 1924.
[61] *Pundits and Elephants*, pp. 8–9.
[62] *Ibid.*, p. 1.

rarily lost the advantages which Parliament intended to confer upon them', he wrote. 'Until such time as the constitution is restored, the Legislative Council will be summoned only when required for the transaction of Government business'.[63]

Das had made a grave miscalculation. The British could continue to govern without the reformed institutions, and obviously intended to do so. What, then, was the difference between December, 1921, when they had been forced to sue for peace, and August, 1924? In 1921, they had been threatened with a collapse of the institutions throughout India, and, at the same time, they had faced a violent mass movement that was revolutionary in potential. In 1924, the institutional collapse was limited to Bengal and the Central Provinces, and there was no mass agitation to support it.

What was Das to do in these circumstances? Gandhi, who had been released from prison earlier in the year, was urging Congress to leave the councils and return to its work among the masses. His cry was taken up by his disciples in Bengal.[64] Das, however, knew that this programme would not be acceptable to the members of his party or to their elite bhadralok supporters, who had had more than enough of mass politics.[65] Here was the root of his difficulty. The Legislative Council as it had been reformed in 1919, with its entrenched representation for the Muslims and the Europeans, was a manifestly unsatisfactory institution for the Hindu bhadralok, but if they did not work within the political system constructed by the British they had either to engage in popular politics—which in Bengal meant inciting the Muslim and low-caste Hindu masses and thereby endangering bhadralok social dominance—or resort to terrorism, which could be beaten down by the British without great difficulty.

Das was on the horns of the dilemma forced upon his community by the British determination to extend the electorate and Gandhi's determination to bring the masses into the nationalist movement. Nor had his seven months in the Council assisted him in any way to overcome this difficulty for he had failed, just as the Moderates before him had failed, to devise a legislative strategy that would strengthen his hold on both sections of the electorate, bhadralok and non-bhadralok. He had done no more than to adopt the old bhad-

[63] 28 Aug. 1924, GB, Appointment, 18L–130(1–7), A3–9, Dec. 1924.
[64] *Forward*, 20 July 1924.
[65] *Ibid.*, 27 June 1924; and *Bijali*, 4 Apr. 1924.

ralok style of opposition to the Government and, by organising his followers efficiently, had scored a tactical success.

A LEADER BEING LED

Speaking at Gaya in December, 1922, in advocacy of council entry, Das had lightly dismissed the question of what should be done if dyarchy were destroyed and the British did not yield. Time enough to think of that should it ever happen, he had said. 'What do we do when it pours with rain? We turn our umbrella in the direction from which the water comes. It is the same way that we must turn the direction of our activities whenever the fulfilment of our national life demands it'.[66] When brought face to face with the issue in August, 1924, he had nothing more constructive to offer. In fact, he was losing his grip. His health had been broken by the exertions of the preceding five years, and the political situation in Bengal was going to pieces under him. The cracks that had appeared late in 1922, which the Swarajists had managed to paper over before the elections of 1923, were again visible.

Hindu-Muslim relations had deteriorated. The Swaraj Party's pact, that 'monstrous understanding' with the Muslims as it was described by a considerable section of the Hindu press, had offended many Hindu bhadralok, and there were dark predictions that it was 'the beginning of the end of his [Das'] influence with the Hindu community in Bengal'.[67] The Swarajists had found themselves in serious difficulties when Musharruf Husain's resolution was put to the Council, and, by moving for an adjournment, they had merely succeeded in giving offence to the Muslims without in any way pacifying their own community. The All-India Congress session at Cocanada in December, 1923, had refused to recognise any separate provincial agreement on the communal question on the ground that it might impede a later national settlement,[68] and although Das managed to get his pact ratified at the Bengal Provincial Conference at Sirajganj in June, it was clear that his authority was weakened.[69]

The Swarajists had made many enemies through their actions in

[66] *Congress Presidential Addresses, 1911–1934* (Madras, 1934), p. 598.

[67] *Bengalee*, 19 Dec. 1923; Cf. NP, 29 Dec. 1923; IA Committee proceedings, 29 Dec. 1923; and N. C. Banerji, p. 180.

[68] NP, Jan. 1924.

[69] NP, 14 June 1924.

the Calcutta Corporation. By using the municipality as a party patronage machine, they had antagonised those who were not provided for,[70] and even within the party there had been bickering over appointments. The outstanding instance was the three-cornered fight between S. C. Bose, B. N. Sasmal, and J. M. Sen Gupta for the highly paid position of Chief Executive Officer. Sen Gupta was relatively unconcerned at Bose's victory, but Sasmal was mortally offended;[71] a rift developed which was to split the Swaraj Party after Das' death.

By August, 1924, there were strong pressures within the Bengal Congress for lines of action of which Das disapproved, but he had no ready answer of his own and was forced back to talking vaguely of the delights of the indefinable *swarāj*. Addressing the first all-India meeting of the Swaraj Party in Calcutta, he said:

> It is asked 'what is the kind of Swaraj that you are striving for?' Some friends of mine are so anxious to have the details of Swaraj that in their attempt to define they lose sight of the real principle upon which the whole fight for Swaraj is based, and that is that we do not want any particular system of Government; we want the right to establish our own system of government.[72]

Das was bankrupt for ideas, and for the present he could offer little resistance to those who knew what they wanted.

The Hindu communalists had already dragged him into a dispute over temple management. Early in 1924 two Punjabi *swāmis*, Biswananda and Sachidananda, who had been active in the successful Akali movement in northwestern India, had come to Bengal to organise an agitation against what they described as the corrupt management of the main Hindu shrines.[73] They failed in an initial attack on the priestly hierarchy of the Kalighat temple,[74] but they then turned upon the *mohant* of Tarakeswar, a place of pilgrimage a few miles northwest of Calcutta. Their accusations of immorality and financial extortion from pilgrims caused a great stir in the Bengali press,[75] and Das' orthodox Hindu followers urged him to intervene. He was reluctant to do so, but his hand was forced by a

[70] E.g., see *Servant* and *Ananda Bazar Patrika*, 19 July 1924.
[71] *Subhas Chandra*, pp. 68–69.
[72] Quoted in P. C. Ray, *Life and Times of C. R. Das*, *op. cit.*, p. 114.
[73] *Statesman*, 27 May 1924.
[74] BIA, Publications, Vol. XIII.
[75] NP, 10 and 17 May 1924.

resolution at the Sirajganj Provincial Conference calling for *satyāgraha* at Tarakeswar to dispossess the *mohant*.[76]

In June, volunteers were enlisted and the two *swāmis* led a march on the temple. The *mohant* had brought in Gurkha *dārwāns* to protect his property, and there was violence when the demonstrators reached Tarakeswar. In the weeks that followed, the police intervened on a number of occasions to break up fights and remove pickets. There were many arrests and a few lives were lost, either through rioting or police firing.[77] Das had little control over the affair, but he was criticised by one faction for encouraging political interference in matters of religion and by another for not supporting the volunteers more wholeheartedly. When he succeeded in patching up a compromise between the *mohant* and the *swāmis* in September, he was accused by both parties of dishonesty and self-interest.[78] The episode served only to discredit him.

The terrorists' activities had also become an embarrassment. Their *samitis* were now overtly communal and at the same time they claimed the support of the Swaraj Party. Das dared not deny this, for terrorism was generally approved by the Hindu bhadralok. His difficulties were brought to a head by the execution of Gopinath Saha, a student who in an attempt to murder the Calcutta Commissioner of Police had mistakenly shot an English businessman. He had caused a sensation at his trial by expressing sorrow at having killed the wrong man. 'He was glad to pay with his life and hoped that every drop of his blood would sow the seeds of freedom in every Indian home'.[79] He was hanged—and the bhadralok had a new martyr.

A resolution was moved at the Sirajganj Conference expressing admiration for his patriotism and spirit of sacrifice, although at the same time discreetly reaffirming Congress' adherence to the principle of non-violence.[80] Das—a leader being led—spoke for the resolution. By doing this he protected his position with his own community, but his action offended the Muslims who were growing increasingly apprehensive of Hindu violence.[81] It also provided the provincial Government with the final argument it needed to per-

[76] *Indian Struggle*, pp. 143–145.
[77] BIA, Annual Report 1924–25.
[78] NP, July–Sept. 1924.
[79] *Indian Struggle*, p. 146.
[80] *Young India, 1924–1926* (Madras, 1926), p. 878.
[81] *Moslem Hitaishi*, 4 Apr. 1924.

suade the Government of India to arm it with extraordinary powers to deal with the terrorists.[82] After some months of careful preparation, it struck a coordinated blow at the revolutionary *samitis* throughout Bengal on the night of 24 October 1924. All the ringleaders were arrested, including S. C. Bose and two Swarajist MLCs, Anil Baran Ray and Satyendra Chandra Mitra.[83]

BACK TO THE COUNCIL

The Legislative Council did not meet between August, 1924, when the demand for the Ministers' salaries was rejected for the second time, and January, 1925. When it did resume, the Swaraj Party was without its leader, who was confined to a sick bed, and its two political détenus, Ray and Mitra, who were still in prison. What was worse, it could no longer rely upon its Muslim supporters, and it had made no progress toward a new policy. It was merely returning after five months for a repeat performance of obstruction.

It achieved an immediate success in rejecting a Criminal Law Amendment Bill with which the Government had hoped to replace the special ordinance under which the October arrests had been made,[84] but in February it failed to defeat a resolution moved by Sir Abdur Rahim for provision to be made in the budget for Ministers' salaries.[85] The Government had shrewdly held out the prospect of office to a number of groups but had not appointed Ministers before the vote was taken. In this way it had succeeded in dividing the Independent Nationalists from the Swarajists.[86]

When Lytton did make his choice early in March, the general opinion was that he had gained two friends and a host of enemies. His new Ministers were Moderates, Nawabaly Chaudhuri and a fellow zamindar from Mymensingh, Manmathanath Ray Chaudhuri, Raja of Santosh.[87] The Independent Nationalists had been disappointed once again, and Das appealed to them to stand with the Swarajists.[88]

[82] *Pundits and Elephants*, pp. 63–65.

[83] *Ibid.*, p. 66; Simon Commission, Vol. VIII, p. 103; *Subhas Chandra*, p. 74; and GB, Appointment, 18L–55(1–8), A20–27, May 1925.

[84] BLCP, 7 Jan. 1925, Vol. XVII, No. 1, pp. 15–27.

[85] *Ibid.*, 17 Feb. 1925, Vol. XVII, No. 2, pp. 3–42.

[86] *Mussalman*, 23 Jan. 1925; and NP, 28 Feb. 1925.

[87] NP, 21 Mar. 1925.

[88] *Forward*, 14 Mar. 1925.

Ten days of hectic lobbying followed during which it became evident that Fazlul Huq and his eight followers were available to the highest bidder. Huq suggested to the Government that it might consider the appointment of two more Ministers,[89] while at the same time he was negotiating with the Swarajists for a 'personal consideration'.[90] He kept both parties in suspense until the last day and then declared against the Ministers. His votes gave the Swarajists a majority of six, and on 23 March they once more rejected the demand for salaries.[91] Lytton had no hesitation in suspending the constitution, and this time he made it clear that he would not attempt to restore dyarchy until after the next general election, scheduled for late 1926.[92]

THE LAST BID

Das felt that the situation was slipping away from him. He dared not leave the Council again without a positive plan of action for his party, for it was obvious that he would lose his leadership to extreme elements unless he could keep his followers engaged. Nor was it simply a question of narrow political advantage. Das had realised, all too late, that he had to curb the tendency toward political and communal extremism if it was not to lead Bengal to disaster. Violence would beget violence, and the sharp hatreds of race, community, and class would tear into the fabric of provincial society.[93]

The horror of the situation for Das lay in the knowledge that it was partly the result of his own actions. A straight line could be traced from the boycotts and pickets, the strikes and *hartāls* of the noncooperation movement in 1921, through the negative campaign of destruction pursued by the Swarajists in the Legislative Council and Das' equivocal attitude to violence in the past year, to the extremes of terrorism and communalism which now characterised political life in Bengal.

If Das was to reverse the trend, he had to offer something constructive, but what could he offer? One possibility was cooperation

[89] *Reformed Constitution, 1927*, p. 172.

[90] *Bengalee*, 8 Apr. 1925; and Chief Secretary, GB, to GI, 28 Mar. 1925, GB, Appointment, 6R–92(1–10), A31–40, Dec. 1925.

[91] BLCP, Vol. XVII, No. 4, pp. 239–240.

[92] *Pundits and Elephants*, p. 80.

[93] *Forward*, 1 May 1925; and C. R. Das to Motilal Nehru, [13 June] 1925, quoted, Jayakar, Vol. II, p. 543.

with the British: to work with the constitution instead of obstructing it. Das knew that he would jeopardise his popularity with the bhadralok if he suggested this, but his position was already serious and he had to make some move. The risk would be worth taking if there were a reasonable chance of the British responding with an offer of constitutional concessions, for he would then be able to claim that Swarajist obstruction in the Council had achieved its purpose.

There were indications that the British might be willing to negotiate. In August, 1924, a committee had been appointed by the Government of India to examine the results of the reforms, and its published report emphasised the defects of dyarchy. Although the majority of the committee's members recommended no immediate constitutional advance, a minority minute of dissent entered a strong plea for a quick step forward.[94] The Viceroy, Lord Reading, was making preparations for a visit to England, and it was generally believed that he was going home to discuss the question of Indian reforms with the British Government.[95]

With the help of two European friends in Calcutta, Das arranged a secret meeting with Lytton at the Ramakrishna Mission at Belur and discussed the possibility of compromise.[96] Lytton had just returned from Delhi where he had gone to receive a briefing so that he could take over the Viceroyalty while Reading was in England. It seems likely that he had been empowered by the Viceroy to hold out the possibility of concessions to Das, if he were willing to dissociate himself publicly from the terrorists.[97] This was asking a lot of any bhadralok politician, but Das was ready to take the plunge, for he had to make some gain. On 29 March 1925 he published a bold renunciation of violence:

> I have made it clear, and I do it once again, that I am opposed on principle to political assassinations and violence in any shape or form. It is absolutely abhorrent to me and to my party. I consider it an obstacle to our political progress. It is also opposed to our religious teaching . . . . As a question of practical politics I feel certain that if violence is to take root in the political life of our country, it will be the end of our dream of Swaraj for all time to

[94] PP, 1924–5, [Cmd. 2360], Vol. X, pp. 1–214.
[95] Reading, Vol. II, p. 298.
[96] P. C. Ray, *Life and Times of C. R. Das*, *op. cit.*, pp. 219–220; and H. N. Das Gupta, *Deshbandhu Chittaranjan Das* (Delhi, 1960), pp. 118–119.
[97] *Pundits and Elephants*, pp. 79–80.

> come. I am, therefore, eager that this evil should not grow any further, and that this method should cease altogether as a political weapon in my country.[98]

This brought an immediate response from the Secretary of State, Lord Birkenhead. Speaking in the House of Lords on 31 March in a debate on the Bengal Ordinance, he welcomed Das' announcement and declared that it opened the way for the consideration of further constitutional advance for India.[99] This was encouraging for Das, but he needed something more definite. He therefore appealed to the British on 4 April for a clear statement of their position.[100]

He received no reply, which put him in an exceedingly difficult position. The Provincial Conference was to be held at Faridpur in four weeks time, and it was expected that he would face an attack from the pro-terrorist group.[101] He had hoped to be able to confront them with a definite British offer of constitutional concessions, thereby justifying his condemnation of violence. As it was, he would have to go empty handed. However, there could be no question of a withdrawal, and he decided for a bold line—he would make an outright offer of cooperation to the British. In his presidential speech on 2 May he again condemned terrorism and called upon the Congress to reaffirm its belief in constitutional methods. He was willing, he said, to work with the British if they would give real responsibility to the Indian people. The time had come for a change of heart.[102]

Das had staked everything on this offer and it was all-important to him that the British should respond. Waiting impatiently for the reply that had to come, he wrote to Motilal Nehru on 13 June:

> I do not know whether you will agree with me or not, but I believe something may come out of the Reading-Birkenhead conversations which are going on about India. I fear that you do not attach any importance to them. You may be right but something tells me that they will make some kind of proposal to us—whether it will be of any real value to us is another matter, but the Hindu-Mahommedan question must be settled before the year is out. . . .

[98] P. C. Ray, *Life and Times of C. R. Das*, *op. cit.*, p. 210.

[99] Parliamentary Debates, Great Britain, House of Lords, Fifth Series, Vol. LX, Cols. 850–851.

[100] P. C. Ray, *Life and Times of C. R. Das*, *op. cit.*, pp. 210–212.

[101] This expectation was fulfilled. See *Atma Sakti*, 1 May 1925; and *Dainik Basumati*, 6 May 1925.

[102] P. C. Ray, *Life and Times of C. R. Das*, *op. cit.*, pp. 247–256.

> The most critical time in our history is coming. There must be solid work done at the end of this year and the beginning of the next. All our resources will be taxed and here both of us are ill. God knows what will happen.[103]

No proposal came from the British, for they were playing this game with Das for party political advantage in England. The Conservative Government was concerned merely to build up a case in favour of Indian reform so that it would have an excuse to accelerate, if need be, the appointment of the statutory commission that was due to examine the Indian constitution in 1928. It was afraid that before then it might be defeated by the Labour opposition, and it did not want the Labour Party to have the opportunity of nominating the members of the commission.[104]

Das had gambled for the future of Bengal and had lost. His opponents gleefully shouted: Cooperator! 'The Swarajists are stumbling down the incline of constitutional co-operation so fast that the Liberals are already claiming them as members, even if wayward and fickle members, of their fold'.[105]

The clamour was silenced by Das' sudden death on 16 June.

DESPAIR

'The sky of Bengal is overcast with clouds. God has removed from Bengal her most notable leaders of men'. *Nayak* of 8 September 1925 lamented the death of five of Bengal's foremost public figures within 18 months: 23 May 1924, Asutosh Chaudhuri; 25 May 1924, Asutosh Mookerjee; 16 September 1924, Bhupendranath Basu; 16 June 1925, Chittaranjan Das; and 6 August 1925, Surendranath Banerjea.[106] Five leaders of two Hindu bhadralok genera-

[103] Quoted Jayakar, Vol. II, p. 543. The date (23 June) which Jayakar gives for this letter is obviously wrong.

[104] See Birkenhead to Reading, 10 Dec. 1925, Lord Birkenhead, *The Life of F. E. Smith, First Earl of Birkenhead* (London, 1959), pp. 511–512.

[105] *Mussalman*, 6 May 1925.

[106] Sir Asutosh Chaudhuri (b. 1860) was a former judge of the Calcutta High Court. He had played a radical part in the anti-partition agitation, and, as an outspoken opponent of noncooperation, had entered the Bengal Legislative Council in 1921. Bhupendranath Basu (b. 1859) was for 40 years a close, though not always amicable, associate of Surendranath Banerjea in the Indian Association. He was president of the Indian National Congress in 1916, and subsequently a member of the Council of India, London, Vice-Chancellor of Calcutta University, and a Bengal Executive Councillor.

tions dead and the leader of the new generation, Subhas Chandra Bose, imprisoned by the British at Mandalay. 'The most critical time in our history is coming', Deshbandhu had written three days before his death. 'God knows what will happen'.

The Hindu bhadralok were bereft of their leadership at the worst possible moment. There was no well-tested strategy to provide a guideline for the community's political future, and the politicians, the lesser men who remained, were divided and uncertain. The rifts in nationalist ranks and between the communities, which Das had struggled hard but unavailingly to heal, were wider than ever, and there was apprehension that they would result in violence. The Hindu bhadralok elite's fears of a social upheaval were sharpened by evidence of growing impatience among their own lower class at Congress' refusal to engage them in another struggle with the British, and by the Muslim politicians' renewed determination to form separatist organisations. These Muslim leaders were now talking of the need to organise the peasant 'masses' against the 'classes', and some were pointing to the legislature as an instrument with which Hindu power could be shattered in Bengal. The Hindu bhadralok politicians, for their part, were unsure of their ability to maintain control of this institution, particularly as they could not trust the British officials who apparently would not scruple to use religious or class divisions against them. The part the Government had played in the destruction of the Hindu-Muslim pact was sufficient warning. 'The sky of Bengal is overcast with clouds'. The mood was one of despair, and it gave rise to internal friction and extremism.

The Swarajists were attacked in the press as the creators of the trouble. They had dragged the Congress 'into the mire of the Councils' where communal dissension flourished.[107] With their western ideas of parliamentary politics, they had misled the educated classes and lost touch with the masses.[108] Their vaunted pact had merely aggravated communal tension. Busy as they were advertising themselves in the Council and lining their pockets in the Corporation, they had neglected all work in the mufussil. The District Congress organisation had fallen to pieces. Politicians such as these would never free India from foreign oppression.[109]

[107] *Ananda Bazar Patrika*, 13 Oct. 1925.

[108] *Servant*, 10 Aug. 1925.

[109] *Ananda Bazar Patrika*, 8 Oct. 1925; *Atma Sakti*, 16 Oct. 1925; and *Sanjivani*, 17 Sept. 1925.

A succession struggle had begun in the Bengal Congress. Gandhi was in Calcutta when Das died, and he stayed for some months to assist with the problems of transition. He urged the provincial Congress to accept J. M. Sen Gupta as its new leader,[110] but the other aspirants for the position brushed aside his advice. Sen Gupta would have to fight for the crown if he wanted it. His main rivals were S. C. Bose, B. N. Sasmal, and Byomkes Chakravarti. Bose, still in prison in Burma, was not an immediate threat; but he was maintaining his contacts and would have powerful support when he returned.[111] Chakravarti had an advantage in having never subscribed to the Hindu-Muslim pact, but he threw away his chance by declaring for 'responsive cooperation' with the British and calling for the unity of all parties, Moderates as well as Congressmen.[112] He was swimming against the tide, which was flowing toward separatism and extremism. The other contestants allied themselves with Hindu communal and terrorist groups, and adopted a defiant line toward the British.[113] At the B.P.C.C. elections in November, 1925, Sen Gupta defeated Sasmal; but his hold on power remained insecure, for his rivals continued to work against him.[114]

Nripendra Chandra Banerji, a former noncooperator returning to Bengal at this time after two years as editor of the *Rangoon Mail*, was appalled by the state in which he found provincial politics. He wrote:

> I went out on a tour to North Bengal towards the end of 1925: some of the sittings of the Bengal Provincial Congress Committee which I had attended had filled me with great misgivings about the internal discipline and strength of the Congress in Bengal and I wanted to judge for myself how the organisation was working in the districts. . . . I found an awful 'rot' in the rural centres of Congress: in many places the organisation had ceased to exist. In some others it was a fake and I found a local Muslim leader (who had been active on the Swaraj-cum-Khilafat front in 1921) wearing British cloth and not feeling he was doing anything anti-national![115]

The main concern of Hindu bhadralok politicians of all shades

[110] Subhas Chandra, pp. 90–91.
[111] S. C. Bose, *The Mission of Life* (Calcutta, 1953), pp. 19 ff.
[112] NP, 5 Dec. 1925; and *Dainik Basumati*, 11 Apr. 1926.
[113] *Bijali*, 13 Nov. 1925.
[114] *Ibid.*
[115] N. C. Banerji, pp. 202–204.

was now the protection of the interests of their community. There were demands in the Hindu press for the exclusion from Government appointments in Bengal of candidates from other provinces[116] and for the provision in the legislatures of communal representation for Hindus.[117] When the Government introduced a Tenancy Act Amendment Bill to the Legislative Council in December, 1925, every means was used by the Hindu bhadralok members to obstruct its passage. Their efforts were applauded by their fellow elite. 'In season and out of season Government indulge in vilification and denunciation of Bolshevism', observed the Burdwan *Pallivasi*. 'But is not the grant of occupancy right to a *korfa* raiyat, as contemplated in the Tenancy Bill, an application of the principle of Bolshevism?'[118] In the same month the Council refused leave to the Government to introduce a Municipal Bill that made provision for new taxation of property holders.[119] Official proposals for the extension of mass primary education in rural areas were also opposed by the Hindu bhadralok. 'If we enforce compulsory primary education on the peasants and compel them to give up tilling and thereby try to reform society by giving them newspaper education, it will be simply inviting ruin', wrote the *Atma Sakti*.[120] In all these matters, the interests of the caste-Hindus and the Muslims were in obvious conflict. This gave a boost to communalism in both camps.[121]

"THEY HAVE SOWN THE WIND"

Lord Lytton had been absent from Bengal officiating as Viceroy in the four critical months following the final suspension of the constitution in March, 1925. He had no desire to return. 'I began work again in Calcutta on August 9th, my 49th birthday', he wrote, 'and immediately experienced again that sense of suffocation from the fumes of insincerity, intrigue and selfishness of Bengal politics from which I had enjoyed such a welcome escape during the last four months among the hills of Simla'.[122] He had lost all enthusiasm

[116] *Amrita Bazar Patrika*, 10 Oct. 1925.
[117] NP, Mar. 1926.
[118] *Pallivasi*, 3 Feb. 1926. Cf. *Dainik Basumati*, 18 Sept. 1925; NP, 28 Nov. 1925; and BIA Publications, Vol. XIII.
[119] *Reformed Constitution, 1927*, p. 185.
[120] *Atma Sakti*, 15 May 1925.
[121] See e.g., NP, 9 Dec. 1925.
[122] *Pundits and Elephants*, p. 160.

for his work and would willingly let his subordinates have their way in managing the affairs of the province.

A few days earlier, Sir Abdur Rahim had again taken up his pen to remind his colleagues that they had unfinished business with the Muslims. He recalled the circumstances surrounding Musharruf Husain's Council resolution on Muslim recruitment of March 1924, and the Government's desire to drive a wedge between the Swarajist Hindus and their Muslim supporters. He continued:

> The political position remained uncertain and acute, and the best prospect of getting support for Government seemed still to lie in the Muhammadan quarters. At that time Messrs F. Haque and Ghuznavi were the Ministers and most members of the Government seemed to realise that one means of rallying the Muhammadans was to investigate the ways and means of removing their grievances regarding employment in public service. Mr Donald, who was then in charge of the Appointment Department, discussed the question with me at Darjeeling with the result that Mr Moberly, who was then the Chief Secretary, called upon the various departments of Government to supply facts and figures showing the progress made by Muhammadans in the service of Government. The information has now been collected, but I put off bringing the question before Government as it related both to the Reserved and Transferred Departments and the position of the latter, until the other day, remained uncertain.
>
> In the circumstances that I have narrated, it is our duty to review the entire position and to tell the Muhammadans how far we are prepared to admit the justice of their claims. I would go further and say that, having regard to what happened in connection with Maulvi Mushruff Hussain's resolution, we are pledged to that community to take steps at once to advance the position of the Muhammadans in the administration. For, the discussions on Mushruff Hussain's resolution amply showed that on the merits, the Swarajists as a body, the European non-officials and the Muhammadan ministerialists, constituting altogether a large majority of elected members, gave their support to it.
>
> This question, which has been an open sore on the body politic of Bengal for a long time, has now acquired as we all know, considerable dynamic political force and it is up to us to regard it from the point of view of statesmen and not of the appraisers of examination papers.[123]

[123] Minute, 27 July 1925, GB, Appointment, 4M–12(1–3), A70–71½, Nov. 1925.

There was an echo of Machiavelli in this argument. The Government is seriously in need of support. You suggest where that support may be found and the terms on which it might be obtained. You point out that the Government has already committed itself in some measure to meeting those terms. But the community you indicate as a likely source of support is your own, and the terms embody the essence of your community's ambitions. Moreover, it was you who manoeuvred the Government into the position of making the first guarded offers to your community, not only by arranging for a resolution to be moved in the Council and suggesting the line that the Government should take, but also, it is confidently asserted in some quarters, by having a hand in the original Hindu-Muslim pact which had made possible the whole machination.[124]

Rahim had played his cards well, and, although the British members of the Government had no illusions as to his object,[125] it suited their purpose to disregard his sleight of hand. They agreed with him that the Muslims should have a share of appointments in the services proportionate to their population 'to ensure that the general interests of the community shall not suffer and that the activities of Government as a whole shall be for the benefit of the whole population'. A meeting of the Executive Council in October, 1925, decided to instruct all departments to increase the tempo of Muslim recruitment,[126] and in December a communiqué was issued making public this order[127]—an action which in itself was a tacit admission of the Government's political motive. Its effect was to intensify communal ill-feeling.[128]

The British had given sufficient inducement to obtain Muslim support; however, this would be of no practical advantage unless the community had sufficient unity and political organisation to ensure the election to the Legislative Council of representatives who would vote consistently with the Government and not drift away to Hindu-dominated alliances as in the past. In the latter half of 1925 the Government decided to take a hand in this work of organisation.

[124] *Swaraj*, 1 Jan. 1924; and *Ananda Bazar Patrika*, 27 May 1926. This story was corroborated by Akram Khan, C. R. Das' chief Muslim negotiator, in an interview with the author (Decca, 14 Feb. 1962).

[125] *Englishman*, 10 Mar. 1925; and *Bengalee*, 12 Mar. 1925.

[126] GB, Appointment, 4M–12(1–3), A70–71½, Nov. 1925.

[127] *Ibid*., 4M–11(1–8) of 1925, A16–23, Feb. 1926.

[128] E.g., see *Dainik Basumati*, 21 Dec. 1925; and *Mohammadi*, 23 Dec. 1925.

The District Officers were instructed to throw their influence behind whichever local Muslim association was prepared to support the Government. They were to encourage other communal organisations to amalgamate with this chosen body and to bring all the community's affairs in the locality under its control. Those groups that insisted on maintaining their independence were to be removed from the Government's list of recognised organisations and thereby deprived of the opportunity to recommend candidates for public office, to assist in the preparation of electoral registers, to be represented at official functions, and to secure the hundred and one other minor forms of patronage normally dispensed by the Government.[129]

The operation was superintended by the Political Department in Calcutta, which had no hesitation in intervening directly if it saw an opportunity to secure a political advantage. For instance, in October, 1925, it received a report from the Dacca Divisional Commissioner regarding a new Islamia Anjuman that was seeking recognition in place of the District Moslem Association. The Commissioner advised against this, but the Political Department overruled him, for it was impressed by the aims of the executive committee of the new organisation.

> They say that the Anjuman proposes to take action to see that suitable Muhammadan candidates are nominated for election to all public bodies for which they are eligible and to prevent the loss of seats to Muhammadans by rivalries within their own community. They also propose to organise for the next Legislative Council election so that Muhammadan candidates may not be tempted to seek the support of the Swaraj Party. They say that the non-recognition of the Association by Government may lose them some support and ask that recognition may now be allowed.[130]

At the same time the Government was promoting *krishak* associations and cooperative societies,[131] and encouraging the Muslims to make common cause with other agricultural communities. The cry was taken up in the Muslim press and, as the general election approached in 1926, it became a regular item in its list of suggestions to candidates. 'Those who are ready to contest for the Council seats

[129] For an example of the application of this policy—in Midnapore District—see GB, Political, 8A–1(1–14), A393–406B, Aug. 1925.

[130] GB, Political, 8A–3, B55–56, Nov. 1925.

[131] *Ibid.*, 8A–6, B36–44, Dec. 1924; and *Ananda Bazar Patrika*, 29 Jan. 1926.

this year should bestir themselves to protect the agriculturalists in their respective constituencies', wrote the *Dainik Taraqqee* of 18 August 1926. 'The enormous sum of money that they spend for election should be employed to organise the agriculturalists and found co-operative banks'. That the advice did not go unheeded was shown by the apprehensive comments in the Hindu bhadralok papers. The *Barisal Hitaishi* of 14 July 1926 wrote:

> From the speeches delivered in the various mass meetings held at different places either jointly by the Muhammadans and the Namasudras or by the Muhammadans alone, it is apparent that the Namasudras and the Muhammadans are uniting against the upper classes. We should be careful of the Moslems whose motive in making alliance with the lower class Hindus is to oppress the upper class on the one hand and to convert the lower class Hindus into Muhammadanism on the other.

The Government had one more job to do. It had to extend the franchise. Even if the peasantry were organised and provided with 'loyal' leaders, their strength would be no asset to the Government until large numbers of them had the vote. The Montagu-Chelmsford reforms had enfranchised only the well-to-do cultivator in rural Bengal and, besides, it had given the urban electors a weightage of five to one.[132] Most of the witnesses before the Reforms Enquiry Committee of 1924 had insisted that this arrangement should be maintained because of the illiteracy of the rural masses. In 1925, the Government of Bengal undertook an enquiry in an attempt to prove them wrong. The Chief Secretary, Leonard Birley, wrote on 27 May:

> My own impression is that in Bengal too much is made of this theory of illiteracy. . . . It is the fashion to decry the electorate as ignorant and illiterate and some of the witnesses who gave evidence before the Committee even wanted to reduce the numbers of the electorate. It is in the interests of the middle class to depreciate the quality of the electorate and restrict the franchise to their class. It is in the interests of the cultivating class that the Bengal electorate should not be saddled with a reputation for illiteracy, which it possibly does not deserve.
>
> It is clearly in the interests of (1) democracy and of (2) the establishment of a system of party Government that the cultivating

[132] Simon Commission, Vol. VIII, p. 137, and Vol. XV, p. 358.

> classes should have as much representation as their conditions deserve.

Rahim fully agreed:

> I would even go further than Chief Secretary. Even if there is a great deal of illiteracy among the cultivating classes they should have the vote in Bengal and we should not countenance the attempt of any members of the middle class (Bhadralogue) to monopolise the franchise. Otherwise we should have to face even a greater political disaster in the future.[133]

The Divisional officers were instructed to report on the percentage of literate voters in sample electorates throughout rural Bengal. The figures were ready early in 1926, and they were a severe disappointment to the Government: in the Muslim constituencies 62 percent of voters were illiterate, and in the Hindu constituencies 47 percent. Birley's only consolation was that these figures could be used in support of the Government's campaign for extended primary education.[134]

"AND THEY SHALL REAP THE WHIRLWIND"

Writing to the Secretary of State, Lord Olivier, in 1924, Reading lamented the enmity existing between Hindus and Muslims. 'It is a menace to the peace of the country. Some, doubtless, think that this is to our advantage, but, if so, they fail to realize how grave the position might become if the feeling between the two communities continues to grow more antagonistic and fails to be alleviated by some compromise'.[135] From 1924 to 1926 the Government of Bengal used its powers to ensure that there was no such compromise in its province. Sir Abdur Rahim, a communalist to the core, called the pace, and he was aided and abetted by the British officials. It was a short-sighted and irresponsible policy that led Bengal into grave trouble in 1926.

Rahim's term on the Executive Council expired late in 1925; he was then free to play out his chosen role on a wider stage. His first act was one of outright provocation to the Hindus. Speaking in December as president of the All-India Muslim League session

[133] GB, Appointment, 6R–45(1), A16, July 1925.
[134] *Ibid.*, 6R–45(1–25) of 1925, A92–116, Mar. 1926.
[135] Reading, Vol. II, p. 306.

at Aligarh, the spiritual home of resurgent Indian Islam, he told his community that the time had come for an organised fight for Muslim rights. The political existence of the community was endangered by Hindu ambitions, he said, and the Muslims must resist their achievement with every weapon available. The Hindus were a menace to British and Muslims alike. If the British would willingly concede the Muslims' just demands, they would have the Muslim community as their ally in the coming battle.[136]

This raised a storm in the Hindu press throughout India,[137] but for Bengal it was just a beginning. Rahim entered the Legislative Council at a by-election in January, 1926, and took the lead of a Muslim group. Apart from the Swaraj Party, which had retained a few of its Muslim members, there were now no intercommunal groups remaining in the Council.[138] To encourage the trend, Abdul Gafur, MLC for Pabna and a former Swarajist, moved a resolution when the Council resumed in mid-February for the amendment of the Bengal Electoral Rules to provide for the representation of communities in proportion to their population. This displeased the Europeans and Anglo-Indians, whose representation in the Council was already far greater than their population entitlement. To save the situation, Rahim suggested an amendment to the resolution by the addition of the words: 'with just and proper representation of minorities and commercial interests'. The Swarajists objected to the admission of the amendment and, when the President overruled them, Sen Gupta led them out of the Chamber. The amended resolution was carried without a division and another nail was driven into the coffin of communal amity.[139]

Rahim's main work lay outside the legislature. His aim was to play on the existing state of communal tension so as to persuade the Bengal Muslims to organise an exclusively communal party under his leadership to contest the elections at the end of the year. The *Hanafi*, a Calcutta newspaper he had taken over, broadcast his message:

> Like the present Council the next Council also will trample on the religious and communal rights of the Musalmans if selfish and weak-minded members be elected from the Moslem constituencies

[136] 30 Dec. 1925, IAR, 1925, Vol. II, pp. 355–357.
[137] NP, 9 Jan. 1926.
[138] GB, Appointment, 18L–13(1–8), A38–45, Apr. 1926.
[139] BLCP, 18 Feb. 1926, Vol. XX, No. 1, pp. 129–146.

> through the influence of the Congress, solely dominated by the Hindus. It is, therefore, incumbent on the Moslem community to exert themselves beforehand and, independent of the Congress, to persuade every Moslem constituency to elect persons who have the interest of the community foremost in their minds.[140]

Rahim was assisted in his task by the fiercely communal tone that characterised all writing in the Muslim press at the time.[141] In March, there were also reports that *agents provocateurs* were in the province trying to foment strife between Hindus and Muslims.[142] Their task was all too easy, for the leaders of neither community were concerned to restrain them, and the Government, busy with arrangements for the annual move to the hills, failed to heed the signs of impending violence.

On 2 April 1926 the Arya Samaj held its annual procession in North Calcutta—with police permission and accompanied by the usual police escort. Led by a band, the procession wound its way two miles from Cornwallis Street to Harrison Road. It reached Dinu Miah's mosque at the time of the *āzān*, the call to prayer, preparatory to the four o'clock public worship. A Muslim ran out of the mosque and called for the music to be stopped. The Inspector of Police accompanying the procession instructed the Hindus to do as they were asked and all stopped playing except for one drummer who kept obstinately beating his drum. The Muslims in the mosque grew angry and began pelting the procession with debris. There was great noise and confusion. The crowd struggling in Harrison Road was quickly joined by men of both communities carrying *lāthis* and other weapons. The riot spread like wildfire through the neighbourhood, and a number of temples and mosques were desecrated.[143]

This was the start of a fortnight of fierce and bloody communal fighting throughout Calcutta, in which more than 50 people were killed and 700 injured. Shops were looted and burned, and temples, mosques, and gurdwaras were razed. The police could not cope with rioting on this scale; troops using automatic weapons and armoured cars were required to restore a semblance of order.

[140] *Hanafi*, 5 Feb. 1926.

[141] See, e.g., NP, 30 Jan. 1926.

[142] *Dainik Basumati*, 23 Mar. 1926.

[143] The account of the riots in this and the succeeding paragraphs is based on the following sources: 'Report of the Riots Enquiry Committee of the IA', IA Annual Report, 1926; Simon Commission, Vol. IV, pp. 104 and 112–115; and *Pundits and Elephants*, pp. 165–174.

The most sinister feature of the outbreak was the evidence of premeditation and organisation on both sides. There were Muslim and Hindu leaders who thought that their political cause could be advanced by a communal clash in Calcutta, and they had done their utmost to provoke violence. Once the fighting had begun, the newspapers were used to fan the blaze and inflammatory leaflets were circulated.

> Moslems, Beware!
> Otherwise the Hindus will eat you up.[144]

> Rise up, O Hindus! girding up your loins and stand up steadfast on the arena of the fight;
> On this holy plain of Kurukshetra either get killed or gain victory.
> Having given up trust in this or that; teach Shiva's teaching.
> Let all the higher and lower castes unite and exhibit the glory of the Hindus.[145]

Life in the city was apparently back to normal by 15 April, but extremists on both sides regarded this merely as a breathing space and a chance for reorganisation. On the 24th a drunken brawl in Cotton Street in Central Calcutta sparked off another fortnight's bitter civil war. A method of killing favoured in the first round—the imprisonment of victims in buildings which were then fired—gave way to the stabbing of individuals in back alleys by roving bands of the opposite community. Firearms made their appearance for the first time in Indian communal affrays, and the riotous mobs were swollen by up-country *gundās* imported by businessmen to protect their property. This time looting was more widespread and there were more deaths—seventy killed, four hundred injured.

Although order was restored in the city by 9 May, there were numerous clashes in other areas of the province and in Bihar throughout the following two months, and in the middle of July a dispute over the playing of music before a mosque again led to ten days of bloodshed in Calcutta. C. F. Andrews wrote to Rathindranath Tagore on 17 August:

> . . . for the last three or four months the Indian Press has not been interested in anything at all outside India. It has been too desperately engaged with these terrible riots and communal questions. Calcutta has been like an armed garrison city . . . . Every day came

[144] GB, Political, 12C–13, B484–485, Dec. 1926.
[145] *Dainik Bharat Mitra*, 12 Apr. 1926.

fresh news of outrages, murders, riots, and the flood of hatred ever mounting higher. Chitpur Road just by Dwarkanath Tagore house has been garrisoned night and day with soldiers with rifles and bayonets in charge of a European for over three months. No one's life has been safe.[146]

RAHIM'S SUCCESS

'The venom of the unreasonable demands of Rahim has spread through the whole social body', wrote the *Sandhya* of 5 April 1926. How long must the rioting go on to serve its purpose, demanded *Forward* at the end of the month. 'How long, the public ask, will it take to ensure the safe return of Sir Abd-ur-Rahim's thirty followers at the next elections? Is not the submerging of nationalism by communalism yet complete?'[147] Among the Hindu bhadralok it was generally believed at this time that the riots had been organised for political purposes by Rahim and his son-in-law, H. S. Suhrawardy,[148] who was known to have built up a following among the lower classes in Calcutta.[149] The Hindu press saw the danger of a solid Muslim communal bloc controlling the next Council through an alliance with the Europeans, and it urged its own politicians to take a leaf out of the Muslims' book and organise the Hindu community.[150] This aggressive line was widely approved. 'It is a good sign that the Hindus are no longer going to take lying the offensive spirit of the Muslims in every occasion', wrote a Bankura landholder, S. K. Sahana. 'I for one think that till the Hindus can convince the Muslims that they will get force for force, roughness for roughness & hooliganism for hooliganism from the Hindus, there is no hope of an abiding friendship—no friendship can last between persons differing in mentality, resources, strength, substance'.[151]

No suggestion of compromise would be tolerated. J. M. Sen Gupta as Mayor of Calcutta was bitterly attacked for appointing Muslim office-bearers in the Corporation, and especially for allowing H. S. Suhrawardy to remain as Deputy-Mayor.[152] At the Pro-

[146] Andrews MSS.
[147] *Forward*, 29 Apr. 1926.
[148] *Matwalla*, 1 May 1926; and BIA Publications, Vol. XIII.
[149] GB, Police, P.31–9(1–3), A26–28, Mar. 1926.
[150] *Amrita Bazar Patrika*, 7 May 1926.
[151] 9 Apr. 1926, Sahana diaries.
[152] *Ananda Bazar Patrika*, 15 May 1926.

vincial Conference at Krishnagar late in May there was an uproar when B. N. Sasmal, as president, criticised the terrorists. He was hounded out of the pandal, and in his absence the Hindu-Muslim pact was rescinded.[153] The old Swarajist leadership was obviously threatened by the extremists, and Sen Gupta decided that he must take a stand on the pact. At a meeting of the B.P.C.C. in June he managed to have the Conference's decision reversed, but this brought upon him the wrath of the Hindu press, which accused him of selling out Hindu interests to the Muslim communalists.[154] Congress unity in Bengal was shattered and the Hindu politicians wasted the remainder of the year in a futile faction fight.[155]

Everything was working in Sir Abdur Rahim's favour. The Bengal Congress was too involved with its internal disputes to be able to devote any time to the Muslims; besides, by allowing the Hindu extremists to gain the upper hand in its affairs, it had strengthened Rahim's case for Muslim unity. The riots had left a legacy of bitterness in Muslim hearts, and Rahim had only to remind his coreligionists of the role played in the disturbances by organisations such as the Arya Samaj and the Hindu Sabha to persuade them to eschew all contact with the Congress.[156]

His positive advantages were the possession of a programme—the domination of the Council by a Muslim party with the purpose of enacting legislation to improve the economic and social condition of the Muslim community—and the existence of pro-Government and anti-Hindu communal organisations throughout the mufussil. The Government had done its work well, and the consolidated district associations gave Rahim a firm foundation on which to build his election platform.[157]

He had still to contend with the factional rivalries among the Bengali Muslim leadership, but for the time being, at least, the bitter experience of the Calcutta riots had eradicated one old problem: the alliance of Muslim factions with Hindu parties in order to gain temporary advantages. Rahim knew the value of organisation, and well before the elections he had formed a Council party with a salaried organiser: Abul Kasem, a former Congress worker who had

[153] NP, 29 May 1926.

[154] Andrews to Rathindranath Tagore, 13 June [1926], Andrews MSS; and NP, 19 and 26 June 1926.

[155] *Amrita Bazar Patrika*,* 20 June 1927; and *Subhas Chandra*, pp. 91–96.

[156] E.g., see *Mussalman*, 4 June 1926; and *Khadem*, 4 Aug. 1926.

[157] GB, Political, 8A–5, B451–461, Sept. 1927.

long experience in political journalism and on representative bodies.[158]

Rahim also knew the value of communalism. He went to the electors with a simple religious appeal: 'Mussalmans! who are you going to vote for? For the servants of Rahim (Worshippers of God) or for the slaves of Rama (Hindus)'[159] The voters gave a clear answer. Of the 39 Muslim representatives returned to the new Council, only one was a Swarajist. The other 38 pledged themselves to work under the constitution in their community's interest.[160] Their resolve was applauded by the Government and by the European nonofficials, who assured them of their support.[161]

THE END OF AN ERA

The stage was set for a new act in the drama of Bengal legislative politics. Up to this time the Hindu bhadralok had played the leading role; now it was taken by the Muslims.

At first it was difficult to see what was happening, for the action was confused. Sir Abdur Rahim was appointed as a Minister in January, 1927, but had to resign because no Hindu would serve with him.[162] His successors, A. K. Ghuznavi and Byomkes Chakravarti, survived for only seven months, and their successors, Musharruf Husain and P. C. Mitter, for nine months.[163] Superficially, there seemed nothing novel in this; certainly the instability of the ministries was the result of the same communal divisions which had been a source of trouble ever since 1921.

There were new elements, however, that were to be of fundamental importance in provincial politics throughout the following twenty years. Because of the determination of the Muslims to stand apart from nationalist politics, there was a decisive shift in power in the Council away from the Hindu bhadralok. Henceforth the ministries were invariably led by Muslim politicians and supported in the Council by Muslims, low-caste Hindus, Europeans, Anglo-Indians, and a handful of 'responsivist' Hindu bhadralok members.

[158] *Dainik Soltan*, 11 Sept. 1926.

[159] Leaflet distributed in support of his party, GB, Appointment, 6R–77 (1–5) of 1927, A1–5, Feb. 1928.

[160] Simon Commission, Vol. VIII, p. 161.

[161] NP, Jan. 1927.

[162] GB, Appointment, 6R–19(1–11), A103–13, Feb. 1927.

[163] Simon Commission, Vol. I, pp. 206–207.

Moreover, despite their instability, these ministries pursued a common aim: the enactment of legislation to benefit the Muslim masses. Agrarian reform and the extension of education became the main planks on which all ministries were formed in Bengal up to 1947.

The Muslim politicians had made a discovery of profound significance: *they* had no need to serve two masters. If they dispensed with nationalism, they could also dispense with the Hindu bhadralok, for Muslim communal representation gave them an assured base from which to operate in the Council, and Muslim numerical superiority gave them power in the community at large. Moreover, any extension of the electorate and any development of general political awareness worked in their favour.

A solution had been found to the main problem involved in working the reformed institutions in Bengal, but for the Hindu bhadralok it was a disastrous solution. They had lost the initiative in politics, and until the province was partitioned twenty years later they were condemned to a course of frustrating opposition. In this period the legislature was used against them by the Muslims and the British, and their only recourse was to communalism and terrorism. It was the end of an era.

Epilogue

THE TRAGIC DECADES

AN EPITOME

On 12 February 1943 Shyama Prasad Mookerjee, Member for Calcutta University, rose before a packed Chamber of the Bengal Legislative Assembly to explain why he had resigned as Finance Minister in the Winter recess. He spoke for 45 minutes, and as he resumed his seat the House rang with cheers of '*Bande Mātaram*,' for his speech was a thoroughgoing indictment of British policies in Bengal.

His decision to join Fazlul Huq's Government at the end of 1941, he explained, had been prompted by the conviction that there should be an intercommunal ministry in Bengal. This was an ideal to which the British officials paid lip service, but in fact they exerted every effort to prevent the formation of any powerful alliance between Hindu and Muslim politicians. 'British rule thrives in the eyes of the outer world on constant strifes between Hindus and Muslims. And even a partial unity on the part of members belonging to these two great communities served as a nightmare to those bureaucrats who held in their hands the real powers of administration.'

When he took office, Mookerjee continued, he had discovered that the Governor of Bengal listened only to the advice of a coterie of reactionary I.C.S. officers, Bengal's 'Fourth Estate', who made a mockery of Responsible Government. Their policy 'was to ignore the claims of Indians to fuller political power, to hamper good government consistent with the true interests of the people and to weaken the forces of people's defence against enemy aggression'. The Governor and his official henchmen had obstructed the Ministry's efforts to secure a fair hearing for the political prisoners held without trial; they had refused to permit Bengalis to organise for the defence of their homeland when it was threatened with Japanese invasion in 1942; they had withheld information even from the Ministers on police and military outrages during the Quit India movement; they had discriminated against the Hindu community with the mass punishment of collective fines, and blocked all Cabinet discussion of the issue; and they still refused to put through the food procurement and price control which the Ministry recommended, and which alone could save lakhs of Bengalis from starvation in the famine that loomed over the province. Constantly he had protested against this oppression, Mookerjee declared, but 'true to the Hitlerian traditions' of the Government of Bengal, his written indictments were now proscribed literature. 'A Minister's accusation of autocratic misrule need not be replied to with facts and figures but must be suppressed under arbitrary rules–what grander conception could the British authorities hold before us of responsible Government in India?' His resignation was an appeal to all sections of the House for cooperation to put an end to 'the state of intolerable slavery'.[1]

This speech is a graphic illustration of the Hindu bhadralok's total loss of confidence in this period in the system of legislative politics, and their frustration at their inability to influence the major decisions on Bengal's future. Indeed, Shyama Prasad Mookerjee's career was an epitome of the main trends in Hindu bhadralok politics in the two decades after 1926: a virtual paralysis of the Bengal Congress; a progressive disillusionment with constitutional methods; and an overriding involvement with communal affairs.

Mookerjee started his career as many others in the preceding generation–including his father Sir Asutosh–had started, at the Bar and in university politics. He entered the legislature in 1929 as a Swarajist, but left the Congress in 1931 when he became convinced that its factional divisions and its inconsistent policy on council entry prevented it from offering an effective resistance to growing

[1] BLAP, Vol. LXIV, No. 1, pp. 25–35. Cf. S. P. Mookerjee, *A Phase of the Indian Struggle* (Kustia, 1942).

Muslim strength. From that time he devoted his political energies to the protection of Hindu interests, first in the legislature and the Calcutta Corporation, and later, as his constitutional efforts were frustrated, in extra-constitutional agitation. In the late thirties he joined the Hindu Mahasabha, and in the forties was its All-India president. With the Congress leaders imprisoned or in exile, he became the main spokesman of nationalism in wartime Bengal, and he voiced the growing apprehension of his fellow Hindu bhadralok that the Congress would throw Bengal to the wolves to save the rest of India from the Muslim League's Pakistan ambitions. He was the organiser of the Hindusthan National Guard which prepared at the end of 1946 to give battle to the Muslim irregulars who were threatening, after months of communal rioting, to plunge Bengal into outright civil war; and he put the finishing touch to two tragic decades by successfully pressing for the partition of Bengal to prevent its total incorporation in Pakistan.[2]

The detailed story of these years has yet to be told, but here we can do no more than write an epilogue to show the transformation of Bengal politics after 1926, and to give the full measure of the Hindu bhadralok's frustration.

THE FIRST LEGISLATIVE ATTACK

Between January, 1927, and December, 1936, when the last Council under the Montagu-Chelmsford constitution was prorogued, there were six ministries in Bengal, each headed by a Muslim and each primarily dependent upon the votes of elected Muslim and European members, and the nominated official group. For the first three years no ministry had stable support, for there was no politician who could unite the Muslim factions. Early in 1930, however, the solid Swarajist opposition bloc withdrew from the Council in response to an A.I.C.C. directive; thereafter, the Muslim MLCs could afford the luxury of opposition without seriously endangering their community's hold on ministerial power.

Both before and after 1930 the Ministers were provided with firm

[2] For biographical details see Balraj Madhok, *Dr Syama Prasad Mookerjee, A Biography* (Delhi, 1954); *Shyamaprasad Smaranika—A Souvenir* (Calcutta, 1959); and obituary notice, *Statesman*,* 25 June 1953. I am also indebted to B. D. Graham, 'Syama Prasad Mookerjee and the Communalist Alternative' (unpublished seminar paper, Australian National University, 1963).

backing by the officials and European nonofficials. Their rationale for this support is significant. The only 'lasting party divisions' in Bengal, they argued, were 'those of Hindu *versus* Muhammadan and of established Government *versus* Obstruction'. 'Hindu' and 'Obstruction' were virtually synonymous terms, and therefore the support of Muslim ministries was unavoidable. Although as a general principle such reliance on communalism was to be regretted, in the special circumstances of Bengal it contained the seeds of hope, for in this province another rough equation existed between 'Muslim' and 'tenant interests', and the only genuine line of political advance was toward 'a greater equality of influence of the two classes which are broadly represented by landlords and tenants'.[3]

With this logic the British in Bengal threw their weight behind the Muslim politicians' efforts at social engineering. These efforts to shift the balance of social and economic power by legislation were the most significant result—for the Hindu bhadralok a lamentable result—of the Muslims' newfound strength in the Council after 1926.

There were three areas in which they took action in the first decade: elementary education, local self-government, and peasant indebtedness. In 1929 a Rural Primary Education Bill was drafted, which had as its ultimate object the provision of free compulsory education throughout the province, administered by District School Boards and financed by an education cess. The measure was attacked in the Hindu bhadralok press as communalist-inspired.[4] It was evident that if it were passed the bhadralok would be forced to support a system that would mainly benefit the peasantry. Bhadralok children were already adequately provided with primary education in the existing state-aided private schools,[5] but the bill would require landholders to pay a considerable portion of the cost of establishing an extended system of public institutions. When the measure was introduced to the legislature the Swarajists succeeded in having it referred to a select committee,[6] from which it emerged

[3] Chief Secretary, GB, to Joint Secretary, Home Department, GI, 27 June 1927, *Reformed Constitution, 1927*, p. 186.

[4] See, e.g., *Modern Review*, Vol. XLVIII, Sept. 1930, pp. 348–349.

[5] For a comparison of Bengal's private school system with the public systems of other Indian provinces see Hugh Tinker, *The Foundations of Local Self-Government in India, Pakistan and Burma* (London, 1954), pp. 250–251, 256, and 350–351.

[6] BLCP, 5–9 Aug. 1929, Vol. XXXIII, pp. 109–138.

so truncated that the ministry withdrew it. It was reintroduced in August, 1930, and when, after heated debate, the Government refused to allow it to go to another select committee, the Hindu Minister, Kumar Shib Shekhareswar Roy, resigned, and 50 bhadralok Hindu members walked out of the Council in protest. The measure was enacted despite their opposition.[7]

The Muslim politicians and the Muslim press made no pretense about their determination to enhance their community's influence in educational administration at every level, nor did they hesitate to list the political advantages expected to accrue from this increased influence.[8] In February, 1931, the Government of Bengal appointed a large standing committee of British and Muslim educators and politicians to devise ways of advancing Muslim education,[9] and the provincial Education Department devoted a large part of its quinquennial review published two years later to an enumeration of the new facilities available to Muslims and the evidence of the community's eagerness to take advantage of them.[10]

The year 1932 brought the first of two bills introducing the communal reservation of seats on local bodies.[11] The principle of the legislation was attacked in the Hindu bhadralok press as 'anti-national' and a 'negation of democracy',[12] but there was not the thoroughgoing opposition there had been to the Primary Education Bill. For one thing, these bills provided for joint, not separate, electorates, and for another, seats were to be reserved for whichever community was locally in the minority. Such protection was now welcomed by many Hindu bhadralok, especially in Eastern Bengal where the Muslims' new electoral organisation and alliances with the Hindu peasantry had resulted in the Hindu bhadralok's loss of control of many local boards at the 1927 and 1931 elections.[13] At the same time, the Muslims had strengthened their position on the

[7] BLCP, Vol. XXXV, pp. 206–882.

[8] E.g., see Sir A. K. Ghuznavi's memorandum, Simon Commission, Vol. III, pp. 183–189.

[9] *Bengal Moslem Education Advisory Committee Report* (Alipore, 1935).

[10] M. R. Mitra and K. Zachariah, *Eighth Quinquennial Review on the Progress of Education in Bengal, 1927–1932* (Calcutta, 1933).

[11] Bengal Municipal Act Amendment Bill, 1932, and Bengal Local Self-Government (Second Amendment) Amending Bill, 1933.

[12] IAR, 1932, Vol. I, p. 323.

[13] *All Parties Conference, 1928. Report* (Allahabad, 1928), p. 47 and appendix C; M. Azizul Huque, *A Plea for Separate Electorate in Bengal* (Krishnagar, 1931), p. 8; and Tinker, *op. cit.*, p. 156.

Calcutta Corporation, and, with backing from the Europeans, they worked throughout the early thirties for an increased share of municipal appointments for their community.[14] The climax of their efforts was the election of Fazlul Huq as the first Muslim Mayor in 1935.

These were assaults on the superstructure of Hindu bhadralok political power. The legislation to relieve peasant indebtedness threatened the substructure of their economic power. Some of the rural credit in Bengal at that time was provided by non-Bengali traders, particularly Marwaris, and by itinerant Pathans; but the bulk of the moneylenders were Bengali Hindus. Their most lucrative opportunities were among the Muslim peasants of the rich jute and paddy lands of Eastern Bengal, and a number of private banking groups had been formed in the 1920's in Calcutta and Dacca to exploit this field. Apart from the professional bankers and village *mahājans*, and perhaps of more political significance, were a host of 'casual lenders'—landlords, shopkeepers, pensioners, men in the professions, and bhadralok families or widows with capital to spare—who found local lending a profitable supplementary source of income.[15] For the zamindars the chronic indebtedness of the tenantry had the added advantage of cementing their domination of rural society.

The objects of the Government's legislation in the early thirties were to reduce the peasantry's accumulated debt, and to furnish new sources of credit at lower rates of interest. To this end they established five state land-mortgage banks providing long-term capital on easy terms,[16] restricted the freedom of absentee moneylenders, imposed ceilings on interest rates,[17] and set up arbitration boards empowered to liquidate a portion of agricultural debts.[18]

The trading and banking interests lobbied hard against these measures, and the Hindu bhadralok politicians willingly lent their weight to the opposition, for they believed that this was simply the

[14] Simon Commission, Vol. VIII, p. 68; and IAR, 1934, Vol. I, p. 20.

[15] *Report of the Bengal Provincial Banking Enquiry Committee, 1929–30* (Calcutta, 1930), Vol. I, pp. 185 and 194–198; and N. C. Bhattacharyya and L. A. Natesan (eds.), *Some Bengal Villages. An Economic Survey* (Calcutta, 1932).

[16] BLCP, Vol. XLIV, No. 1, pp. 123–124.

[17] Bengal Moneylenders' Bill, 1932.

[18] Bengal Relief of Indebtedness Bill and Bengal Agricultural Debtors' Bill, 1935.

thin end of a wedge with which the Muslims hoped to crack open the existing structure of rural society. Their resistance in the Council was vigorous but unavailing, and it brought harsh reproaches from the Muslim and low-caste Hindu members. If every reasonable effort to secure social justice was to meet with such obstruction, then indeed (some said) the axe should be laid to the root of the system.[19]

CONSTITUTIONAL REFORM

This was bad enough, but worse threatened. Throughout this decade from 1927 the reform of the Indian constitution was under discussion, and each successive decision concerning Bengal seemed to the Hindu bhadralok to make more certain the ultimate domination of the political system by the Muslims.

In the first place, it was evident that any considerable extension of the franchise must inevitably swing voting power radically to the Hindu bhadralok's disadvantage, and, even if separate electorates were maintained, give the Muslims a stronger case for the enlargement of their legislative representation.[20] Consequently, from the mid-twenties the Muslims were agitating for universal adult suffrage and an end to urban weightage,[21] while the Bengal Government's Muslim-dominated reforms advisory committee supplied reasoned arguments sufficient to convince the various British commissions of enquiry that 'in the interests of democracy' the electorate should indeed be greatly enlarged.[22] Again Hindu bhadralok protests were ineffectual, and the pronouncements of their more extreme organisations merely reinforced the community's increasingly reactionary public image. 'Practically every man having a tolerable dwelling place has got a vote under the present constitution', wrote the Provincial Hindu Sabha with typical overstatement in 1930. 'To further extend the franchise, much less to grant adult suffrage will have the effect of giving votes to men who have nether

[19] See debates on Bengal Agricultural Debtors' Bill, Nov. and Dec. 1935, BLCP, Vol. XLVII, No. 1, pp. 76–171 and 205–476, and No. 2, pp. 17–367.

[20] Simon Commission, Vol. I, pp. 146–147, and Vol. II, p. 93.

[21] E.g., see Nawab Syed Nawabaly Chaudhuri's memorandum, *ibid.*, Vol. VIII, pp. 220–221; M. Azizul Huque, *A Plea for Separate Electorates in Bengal* (Calcutta, 1931); and statement issued by Bengal Presidency Muslim League, 3 Apr. 1932, IAR, 1932, Vol. I, pp. 312–313.

[22] Simon Commission, Vol. III, pp. 172–175.

[sic] political consciousness, education, sense of civic responsibility nor any stake in the country'.[23]

Even more important than the franchise was the apportionment of seats in any reconstructed legislature, and on this question there was no common ground between the communities in Bengal. The Muslims argued that their provincial majority entitled them to an enlarged representation, but at the same time they demanded the maintenance of separate electorates to shield them from the Hindu bhadralok's economic and educational superiority.[24] The Hindu bhadralok rejected both claims as absurd. The constitutional protection of a majority rightly had no precedent, and the extension of a community's representation on the grounds of self-confessed political incompetence was the negation of progress. In the interests of political development, it was the Hindus, with their enlightened and public-spirited nationalist leadership, who should be given the majority of seats.[25]

In the five years of intensive constitutional negotiation from 1928 to 1932, neither community would listen to any suggestion of compromise on these points; and for Bengal, as for the other provinces of British India, the deadlock was broken only by the direct intervention of the British Prime Minister. On 16 August 1932, Ramsay MacDonald published a Communal Award, which specified the number of seats each community would have in the new legislatures. In Bengal separate electorates were to be maintained, the Muslims were to take 48.4 percent of the seats, the Hindus 39.2 percent, and the Europeans 10 percent.[26] For the Hindu bhadralok this was calamitous. The Muslims had been given everything they had asked for, and in addition the British had cut a large slice of overrepresentation for themselves out of the Hindu's share. There was a storm of protest. 'The Award is a sentence of banishment passed upon the Hindus of Bengal from the legislature of the province', lamented N. K. Basu, moving an adjournment motion in the Council. The Muslim and European members responded with a hearty 'Amen'.[27]

[23] Statement for All-Parties Meeting, 31 Mar. 1930 (Sapru papers).

[24] E.g., see BLCP, 31 July 1928, Vol. XXX, No. 1, pp. 51–104.

[25] *Ibid.*; Bengal Provincial Hindu Sabha statement for All-Parties Meeting, 31 Mar. 1930 (Sapru papers); Bengal Hindu Manifesto, Apr. 1932, IAR, 1932, I, pp. 323–324; *Modern Review*, Vol. LI, June 1932, pp. 613–618.

[26] IAR, 1932, Vol. II, pp. 7, 234, and 236.

[27] BLCP, 23 Aug. 1932, Vol. XXXIX, No. 4, pp. 117–147.

For the Hindu bhadralok the Award had only one saving grace: it did not introduce separate electorates for the Hindu Depressed Classes[28] in Bengal, as in some other provinces. It did stipulate that they should have a minimum of ten seats in the reformed legislature, but they were left to secure these in open contests. This arrangement, however, did not survive. In September, 1932, Gandhi began a fast to protest the constitutional separation of the Depressed Classes from the Caste Hindus, and, to avert the tragedy of the Mahatma's death, an emergency conference of representatives of both sections thrashed out a compromise in less than a week. The untouchable leaders gave up their demand for separate electorates and were compensated with an increased representation through reserved seats in the general Hindu constituencies. In Bengal they were to have an additional 20 representatives in the new Legislative Assembly.[29]

The Hindu bhadralok were appalled, for the effect of this agreement combined with the Communal Award would be to reduce their percentage of legislative seats to 23, compared with the 48 percent they occupied in the existing Council. It was proposed that the new Bengal Legislative Assembly would have 250 Members, of whom 119 would be Muslims, 30 Depressed Class Hindus, and 25 British. Against this potentially hostile bloc of 174 votes, the bhadralok Hindus would be able to muster no more than 58 Members.

The announcement of the provisions of the Poona Pact (as the agreement was called) raised a furor in Bengal. How, it was asked, could fellow Indians expect the Hindu bhadralok to accept such a settlement, arrived at in haste by a body on which Bengal was unrepresented, and which, if implemented, would destroy nationalist strength in the province?[30] The only answer was a curt: like it or lump it! The Pact's signatories, under attack from many quarters, refused to reconsider any of its clauses, and their stand was sup-

[28] In constitutional discussions in the early thirties the expression 'Depressed Classes' was generally used for the Untouchables, but after the passage of the 1935 Government of India Act they were referred to as the 'Scheduled Castes'.

[29] IAR, 1932, Vol. II, pp. 237–253.

[30] IAR, 1933, Vol. I, p. 3, and Vol. II, p. 3; Protest circular signed by J. N. Basu, Profulla Tagore, H. N. Datta, Nalini R. Sarkar, T. C. Goswami, B. C. Chatterjee, and B. P. Singh Roy, 27 Jan. 1933 (Sapru papers); N. N. Sircar, *Bengal under Communal Award and Poona Pact* (Calcutta, 1933); and B. N. Dutta Roy, *Sir N. N. Sircar's Speeches and Pamphlets* (Calcutta, 1934).

ported by the A.I.C.C.[31] The British and the Muslims, well satisfied with the situation, insisted that it was none of their business, and the Bengal Depressed Class leaders rejected all suggestions of a local compromise with the retort that they were glad to take away from the bhadralok every seat they could.[32] Despite these rebuffs, the Hindu bhadralok politicians persisted with their efforts to have the Communal Award and the Poona Pact amended, but they succeeded only in hardening the lines of ill-feeling between high and low caste, and between Hindu bhadralok and Muslim.

The Government of India Act of 1935 was the testimony to their failure. To Bengal it applied the Communal Award and the Poona Pact without amendment. It enlarged the electorate by almost 600 percent, enfranchising four new Muslim voters to every three Hindus, and drastically reducing urban weightage. (Compare Tables 4 and 5.) The long-standing nationalist demand for autonomy and Responsible Government in the provinces was conceded, but for the Hindu bhadralok any sense of achievement was clouded by the knowledge that in Bengal it was the Muslims who would have the advantage of this accession of power.

THE SECOND LEGISLATIVE ATTACK

The first elections under the 1935 Act were held in January, 1937, and the Bengal Legislative Assembly was inaugurated on 7 April. There were two striking features of its composition: the absence of any single dominant party, and the number of its members, of whatever party allegiance, who claimed to represent the tenantry. There was, however, only one organised tenant group, and it was to the leader of this group that power fell. The leader was A. K. Fazlul Huq, and his organisation was the Krishak Praja Party, which he had founded in July, 1929, and which had gained experience in the old Council in pressuring the Ministers for more radical rural reform. Huq had brought off a personal *tour de force* at the 1937 elections by trouncing a former Minister and Executive Councillor, Sir Khwaja Nazimuddin, and he commanded a legislative following of 34.[33] His road to power was opened by Congress' indecision as to whether or not its members should accept

[31] Sapru to J. N. Basu, 10 Feb. 1933 (Sapru papers).
[32] BLCP, 14 Mar. 1933, Vol. XLI, No. 2, pp. 90–121 and 18–22 Dec. 1934.
[33] IAR, 1937, Vol. I, p. 4; and Coupland, pt. 2, p. 27.

TABLE 5

COMPOSITION OF BENGAL LEGISLATIVE ASSEMBLY AND COUNCIL AND ELECTORATES UNDER GOVERNMENT OF INDIA ACT, 1935

Legislative Assembly	Members[a]	Voters[b]
Elected:		
General urban[c]	12	385,347
General rural[c]	66	2,426,288
Muhammadan urban	6	55,538
Muhammadan rural	111	3,402,826
Anglo-Indian	3	8,525
European	11	14,175
Indian Christian	2	10,038
Commerce and industry	19	926
Landholders	5	1,951
Universities	2	1,479
Labour	8	313,400
Women	5	74,990
Totals	250	6,695,483
Legislative Council	**Members[a]**	**Voters[b]**
Nominated:		
By governor	6–8	
By legislative assembly	27	
Elected:		
General urban	2	5,733
General rural	8	4,477
Muhammadan urban	1	722
Muhammadan rural	16	2,961
European	3	5,717
Totals	63–65	19,610

[a] Government of India Act, 1935, 5th Schedule.

[b] Figures for 1937 General Election. (PP, 1937–38 [Cmd. 5589], vol. XXI, pp. 40–52).

[c] Of the 78 General Seats in the Legislative Assembly, 30 were reserved for the Scheduled Castes whose voters in 1937 numbered 821,119.

office, and his own party's possession of an electoral platform that was acceptable to a sufficiently large section of the Assembly as the basis of a ministerial coalition.

This platform is of great importance for it was the blueprint for an extended attack on Hindu bhadralok power in the succeeding five years. Its first salvo was its heaviest.

> In view of the fact that the land revenue system, known as Permanent Settlement and the land laws of Bengal have arrested the economic growth and development of the province and have ad-

versely affected the national outlook of the people, a committee of enquiry be immediately appointed to devise ways and means to get them replaced by a more equitable system and laws suitable to the needs and requirements of the people.

Compared with this, the other clauses were small shot, but well directed nonetheless. They included the amendment of the Bengal Tenancy Act to reduce rents and abolish landlords' customary exactions; the further reduction of peasant indebtedness and the encouragement of cooperative societies; the provision of universal primary education 'without taxation of the poor'; an administrative reorganisation of secondary and university education; and a reform of the Calcutta Corporation.[34]

Huq and his ministry went to work with a will on the implementation of this programme, and they had their predictable reward in a full measure of Hindu bhadralok ire. 'The Hindu Mahasabha records its strong protest against the openly communal and reactionary policy of the present Ministry in Bengal as evinced by its various legislative enactments and administrative measures calculated to curb the rights and liberties of the Hindus of Bengal and cripple their economic strength and cultural life'.[35] By the time Shyama Prasad Mookerjee moved this resolution on 30 December 1939, the Huq Ministry had honoured most of its initial promises. It had appointed a commission to examine the land revenue system, and, after the hearings, packed it with additional Muslim and Schedule Caste members to ensure that it recommended the abolition of the Permanent Settlement.[36] It had imposed severe restrictions on the zamindars' powers to enhance rents and recover arrears, and further limitations on moneylending.[37] Declaring that the reservation of seats in general constituencies had failed to satisfy Muslims, it had amended the Calcutta Municipal Act to provide an increased Muslim representation through separate electorates, at the same time giving seven bhadralok Hindu seats to the Scheduled Castes.[38]

In one field alone had the ministry's legislative performance failed to match its promises, in education, and yet it was in this field that it was most hotly attacked. The Hindu bhadralok were incensed at

[34] IAR, 1938, Vol. II, p. 219.

[35] IAR, 1939, Vol. II, p. 338.

[36] *Report of the Land Revenue Commission, Bengal* (Alipore, 1940).

[37] For details see Coupland, pt. 2, pp. 38–39.

[38] BLAP, 27 Feb. 1939, Vol. LIV, No. 2, pp. 14–67; and Coupland, pt. 2, p. 39.

what they believed was an insidious campaign to force Islamic elements into Bengali education. For the first time in its three-quarters of a century, the University of Calcutta had Muslim Vice-Chancellors from 1930 to 1934 and 1938 to 1942,[39] and, although Shyama Prasad's occupancy of the office in the interim had helped to redress the balance, it was believed that Muslim interests were being favoured at the Hindus' expense.[40] It was symbolic, many said, that the University administration should have bowed in 1938 to Muslim agitation for the removal of Hindu motifs from the University crest.[41]

Hindu bhadralok spokesmen claimed that there was evidence of similar official partiality for Muslim interests in the lower echelons of the education system. There were repeated complaints in the legislature and the press of communal discrimination in the distribution of scholarships and grants, and at the establishment of disproportionately large number of *maktabs* (Muslim primary schools) to the sacrifice of nondenominational schools, with the result that Hindu children 'had to read text-books which could not be acceptable to them'.[42]

The ministry's chief villainy in this field, however, was its Secondary Education Bill, under which control of higher schooling was to be transferred from the University of Calcutta to a Board of Secondary Education, composed of elected communal representatives and Government nominees. The idea was an old one,[43] and its resurrection in 1937 reawakened old Hindu bhadralok apprehensions. 'A grave crisis has arisen in the history of modern Bengal—a crisis of the most serious character', Sir Prafulla Chandra Ray, the famous chemist, told a protest meeting on 8 December 1937. 'The very cause of education is threatened. We must rise to a man throughout the province and record our strong protest against the

[39] *Hundred Years of the University of Calcutta* (Calcutta, 1957), pp. 426–427.

[40] E.g., see Pramathanath Banerjee's speech as President, All-Bengal College and University Teachers' Conference, 9 Apr. 1939, IAR, 1939, Vol. I, p. 24.

[41] BLAP, 26 Aug. 1937, Vol. LI, No. 3, pp. 601–646; IAR, 1937, Vol. II, p. 468, and 1938, Vol. I, p. 11.

[42] S. P. Mookerjee, 15 Dec. 1939, BLAP, Vol. LV, No. 3, pp. 189–206.

[43] The formation of a Board of Secondary Education had been recommended by the Calcutta University Commission in 1919, and an attempt by Lord Lytton's Government to act on this recommendation had caused trouble in 1921. (See above, pp. 193–194.)

sinister attempt and the sinister motive behind it'.[44] 'Ugly, communal and official', was one bhadralok Hindu member's characterisation of the bill on its stormy introduction to the Legislative Assembly in August, 1940.[45]

PROBLEMS OF CONTROL

This delay of three years in taking legislative action is significant, for it was the result of difficulties experienced by Fazlul Huq in maintaining control of his support in the Assembly. His ministerial coalition, as originally formed, was based on the Krishak Praja Party, the Muslim League, the Scheduled Caste Party, and a few independent Hindu bhadralok members, in addition to which it normally had the votes of the European group. The alliance was almost immediately subjected to strain by the demands of the more militant wings of the Praja and Scheduled Caste parties for drastic rural reform, and by the manoeuvres of the Congress legislative group to entice these radicals into opposition.[46] The Ministry's legislation failed to satisfy them, and within a year Huq had lost the regular support of half the Praja Party and almost the whole Scheduled Caste group.

This left him heavily dependent upon the Europeans and the Muslim League, and his ability to resist pressures for open communal favouritism was proportionately reduced. He was disinclined to yield to these pressures, however, for he knew that blatantly communal legislation might unite the dissident Hindu bhadralok Members and possibly even drive the Scheduled Caste groups into a formal alliance with Congress. For this reason he stalled on the Secondary Education Bill when faced with Scheduled Caste demands for an enlarged representation on the board of control, and bhadralok Hindu threats of a boycott. He had less success in avoiding trouble in other areas. On 25 August 1938, a member of the coalition party, Mian Abdul Hafeez, moved a resolution for the reservation of 60 percent of all Bengal Government appointments for the Muslims and 20 percent for the Scheduled Castes, and this motion was carried against the votes of the Ministers.[47] Although

[44] IAR, 1937, Vol. II, p. 17.
[45] Atul Sen, 22 Aug. 1940, BLAP, Vol. LVII, No. 5, p. 83.
[46] BLAP, 1937, Vol. LI.
[47] BLAP, Vol. LIII, No. 4, pp. 272–298.

Huq was able to delay action for almost a year, the party finally forced him to implement the resolution in a slightly modified form.[48]

Whatever craft he displayed in the legislature, Huq could hardly escape being branded as a communalist, and in his extramural activities he seemed to care little for his reputation. Toward the end of 1937 he had accepted M. A. Jinnah's invitation to rejoin the Muslim League, and in his appearances on public platforms as a League politician he displayed few of the inhibitions that restrained him in the provincial legislature. His speech of welcome to the Calcutta special session of the League on 17 April 1938 was no more immoderate than usual:

> Gentlemen, we are passing through times which are extremely critical for the Muslims of India. On the one side we find the Congress with all its might, organisation and resources, determined to crush and subdue the Muslims and on the other side we find the Hindu Mahasabha with all its communal bigotry, characteristic intolerance, narrow political outlook, and unholy intentions, devoting its energies to the frustration of Muslim hopes and the suppression of the legitimate rights and liberties of the Muslim community. . . . Let us prepare to fight, if need be on a double front and with our backs to the wall. If Panipat and Thaneswar must repeat themselves, let the Muslims prepare to give as glorious an account of themselves as did their forbears . . . . May the all-merciful God guide these deliberations on the right lines and may your decisions bring nearer the day of Islam's deliverance in India.[49]

His last sentence was an oblique reference to the alleged oppression of Muslims under Congress provincial Governments, an issue on which the League was to stir up bitter controversy in the following eighteen months, with Huq in the role of chief prosecuting counsel.[50] There was undoubtedly an element of constitutional irregularity in this public attack by the head of one provincial Government on the actions of others, but a more immediate threat to constitutional procedures in Bengal was posed by the increasingly frequent use of *hartāls* and mob violence to influence the deliberations of the legislature.

It was, of course, Congress that had developed the *hartāl* as an

[48] IAR, 1939, Vol. I, pp. 32e–32f.

[49] IAR, 1938, Vol. I, pp. 377–381.

[50] See Huq's open letter to President, Bengal Hindu Sabha, 7 Nov. 1938, IAR 1938, Vol. II, p. 23; and Coupland, pt. 2, Chap. XVII.

agitational technique, but it was Huq's party that gave it this new application in Bengal. When his ministry was threatened with a vote of no confidence in August, 1938, the Calcutta branch of the Muslim League called upon all Muslim shopkeepers to close their stores for a day and join protest demonstrations. Congress MLAs were picketed in their houses, and some were assaulted on the streets. Many slept in the Assembly on the night preceding the vote, fearing violence from the mob. When the motion was defeated amid unruly scenes, Huq immediately left the Chamber to announce his victory to the thousands of Muslims waiting outside and to receive their tumultuous acclamation.[51]

The opposition had no hesitation in applying the same methods, and it was soon commonplace for disagreements in the Bengal legislature to provoke street fighting in Calcutta. This aggravated the existing state of communal ill-feeling; tension mounted steadily until in August, 1940, there was a serious outbreak of Hindu-Muslim rioting, which marked the beginning of ten months of widespread violence. Huq and the Muslim League were accused by the Hindu politicians of a calculated reign of terror, and the Chief Minister, in his turn, pointed a finger of accusation at Shyama Prasad Mookerjee and the Hindu Mahasabha. Face to face in the Assembly, these two firebrands denounced each other as wicked, irresponsible men whose evil ambitions were tearing asunder Bengal society.[52]

STRANGE BEDFELLOWS

In December, 1941, Fazlul Huq reconstructed his Government to include S. P. Mookerjee as Minister of Finance. There has been no more startling event in modern Indian political history than the reconciliation of these two apparently irreconcilable men. The sudden about-face was the result of Huq's break with the Muslim League in protest against Jinnah's persistent attempts to interfere in provincial affairs,[53] and his ability, with this regained freedom from communal associations, to persuade large sections of the Krishak Praja and Scheduled Caste parties to rejoin him in a coali-

[51] BLAP, 8 Aug. 1938, Vol. LIII, No. 2, pp. 6–42; and IAR, 1938, Vol. II, pp. 6–7, 118, and 120–121.

[52] E.g., see BLAP, 9 Apr. 1941, Vol. LIX, No. 6, pp. 204–219.

[53] B. Shiva Rao to Sapru, 22 Oct. 1941 (Sapru papers); and Coupland, pt. 2, pp. 29–30.

tion with the Congress Forward Bloc[54] and a group of 'Nationalist Hindus' led by S. P. Mookerjee.

Mookerjee justified his action in joining hands with a man whom he had so recently reviled as a public enemy on the grounds that Hindu interests could be protected only if there were an intercommunal ministry. He was aided in his self-defence by the ill-concealed distaste of the European group at the formation of a viable Muslim-bhadralok Hindu coalition, and the Muslim League's denunciation of Huq in his new role as a tool of the Hindu Mahasabha.[55]

Mookerjee's association with the ministry was short-lived for, as we have seen, it was less than a year later that he departed, cursing the system and all who worked within it. Despite this, he could claim an important achievement for his brief term of office: he had called a halt to the legislative attack on the Hindu bhadralok. It was certainly true that after December, 1941, Fazlul Huq's Government produced no new social legislation, and even the Land Revenue Commission's recommendations for rural reforms were shelved.[56] Similarly, the only injuries inflicted by the two Muslim League ministries that held power in the four years after Huq resigned as Chief Minister in March, 1943, were the imposition of a tax on agricultural income[57] and a renewed effort to pass the Secondary Education Bill. It was too late in the day, however, for any Hindu bhadralok jubilation, for irreparable damage had been done to their power in the twenty years that the Muslims had had control of the legislature.

CONGRESS FACTIONALISM

It is evident from what we have written that the Muslim politicians' decision in the mid-twenties to stand aloof from the Hindu bhadralok nationalists and to concentrate upon economic and social reform, marked a decisive shift in political power in Bengal. It is also evident that there was good reason for men like Shyama Prasad Mookerjee to feel a deep sense of communal grievance and to lay the blame at the door of the British, who had consistently

[54] On the formation of the 'Forward Bloc' see below, p. 308.
[55] Coupland, pt. 2, p. 30.
[56] BLAP, 15 Mar. 1943, Vol. LXIV, No. 3, pp. 237–264.
[57] Bengal Agricultural Income Tax Bill, 1944.

supported the Muslims in the legislature and who had reconstructed the constitution to give them increased strength.

Even so, there remains the question as to why the Hindu bhadralok had failed to offer an effective legislative opposition, especially in view of the opportunities provided by Muslim factionalism. The short answer is that the Bengal Congress was as much troubled by factionalism as any of the Muslim parties. 'Is not the Congress being rapidly reduced to a magnified edition of that shameful spectacle, the Calcutta Corporation during the last few years?' asked Jawaharlal Nehru disgustedly in August, 1934. 'Might not the dominant part of the Bengal Congress be called today "the society for the advancement of Mr Nalini Ranjan Sirkar" . . . . And the other part probably a similar society for a similar laudable object?'[58] Some of the trouble undoubtedly stemmed, as Nehru believed, from personal rivalries and ambitions which had split the provincial Congress after C. R. Das' death in 1925 and which were never resolved. They gave rise to incessant public squabbling over elections to party office, and to seats in the Calcutta Corporation and the provincial legislature–squabbling which drew frequent rebukes from the local press.[59]

Beneath the faction fights, however, were fundamental disagreements over political strategy, for the Hindu bhadralok politicians were faced, from the late twenties, with problems to which there were no simple solutions. What was the best counteraction to the Muslim-British domination of the legislature? How could the Muslims be dissuaded from using mob action to enforce their will on the Hindu minority? Were the bhadralok Hindu Congressmen still justified in compromising their community's interests in the hope of a renewed nationalist alliance? Was Gandhian nonviolence appropriate for Bengal, or could more be achieved by terrorism or revolution? Could the Bengal Congress afford to maintain its conservative social policy while the franchise was extended and the Muslim politicians bid for the support of the new Scheduled Caste voters? What institutions could be developed to provide a secure

[58] Nehru to Gandhi, 13 Aug. 1934, J. Nehru, *A Bunch of Old Letters*, 2nd ed. (Bombay, 1960), p. 117.

[59] *Forward*, 8 June 1926; *Amrita Bazar Patrika*, 20 June 1927; IAR, 1927, Vol. I, pp. 56–62; Andrews to Rathindranath Tagore, 13 June [1926], Andrews MSS; N. C. Banerji, pp. 207–210; and *Modern Review*, Vol. IL, May and June 1931, pp. 620 and 729.

basis for mass agitation? Was obedience to the dictates of the All-India Congress executive compatible with provincial interests?

There were no easy answers and very little agreement. Yet the pressure for both answers and action was strong, for a growing section of Congress support in Bengal was becoming increasingly frustrated at the failure of the nationalist movement to achieve anything worth while.[60] The lower-class Hindu bhadralok in particular were extremely impatient. They had eagerly enlisted in the non-cooperation movement in 1920–1921 on the promise of imminent *swarāj*, only to see Gandhi throw up his hands in horror at the height of the agitation in 1922, and the elite Swarajists retreat to the security of the legislative councils in 1923. The remaining years of the decade had produced nothing more satisfying than communal rioting and increasingly brash demands by the Muslims for a lion's share of the government clerical jobs that were the lower-class bhadralok's mainstay. With their economic position disintegrating as the world depression strangled Bengal's export trade,[61] they could have little sympathy for the elite's legislative struggle to protect the interests of capital, nor for its elegant hesitations over the hazards of mass agitation. The lower-class bhadralok wanted action. They wanted men who would (in the *Amrita Bazar Patrika's* words) 'lead the scattered forces of Nationalism to the onward march, leaving the so-called leaders to fight out their freedom's battle in the gilded council chambers'.[62]

Despite this trend of opinion, there was still a sizeable section of Bengal Congress politicians who maintained that participation in elective institutions was important, at the very least for self-defence; but, given the communal composition of the Legislative Council and their own enfeebling disunity, they could achieve nothing to justify their stand. Consequently, they were unable to resist the popular All-India Congress decision of December, 1929, against council entry, and had to be satisfied with work in the Calcutta Corporation and other local bodies in their subsequent four years of exile from the legislatures. A few, like Shyama Prasad, thought it a gross error to hand the Muslims control of the Council on a platter, and they left the party. More defections followed when the Bengal Congress was forced by the A.I.C.C. to acquiesce in the

[60] N. C. Banerji, pp. 202–204 and 212 n.
[61] *Census of India*, 1931, Vol. V, pt. 1, pp. 11–15.
[62] *Amrita Bazar Patrika*, 20 Jan. 1927.

Poona Pact.[63] The presence of these splinter groups only served to weaken still further Hindu bhadralok opposition in the legislature when the Swaraj Party did return in 1934.

VIOLENCE

The ideals of liberal constitutionalism had almost no remaining influence on Hindu bhadralok political thinking in the late twenties and the thirties. Popular opinion favoured the overthrow of the British by terrorism or a revolutionary uprising, and communal organisation–including organised violence if need be–to protect Hindu bhadralok interests against the Muslim onslaught. Those Congressmen who wished to remain influential and yet continue to engage in legislative or local politics found it expedient to give no discouragement to the rumours (many well founded) that they were 'front men' for one or other of the rival terrorist groups, which now had powerful networks extending over much of rural as well as urban Bengal. These organisations were notoriously communalist,[64] and this tendency was encouraged by the Hindu Sabha, which advocated gymnastic and military training for Hindu youth and the formation of Hindu vigilante parties to combat 'Muslim outrages' in rural districts.[65]

Other politicians, inside and outside Congress, were experimenting with new agitational organisations–youth and students leagues, political sufferers conferences, trades unions, teachers associations, national militia–and with radical watchcries, borrowed in most cases from contemporary extremist movements in Europe. The most prominent of these men was Subhas Chandra Bose, whose attractive personal attributes–his youth, his eloquence, his former close association with Chitta Ranjan Das, and his recent three years imprisonment for terrorist complicity–were reinforced by a keen sensitivity to prevailing Hindu bhadralok moods. In his speeches, writings, and actions he skillfully wove together the main strands of the community's political beliefs and aspirations. He evoked their pride of region and culture.[66] He encouraged their elite, activist

[63] IAR, 1934, Vol. II, pp. 260 ff.; and *Statesman*,* 15 Jan. 1937.

[64] See Motilal to Jawaharlal Nehru, 30 Dec. 1926, J. Nehru, *A Bunch of Old Letters*, *op. cit.*, p. 55.

[65] IAR 1927, Vol. I, pp. 416–423; and 1929, Vol. I, p. 395, and Vol. II, p. 338.

[66] E.g., see his presidential address to the Bengal Provincial Conference, 30 Mar. 1929, IAR, 1929, Vol. I, pp. 374–377.

philosophy of politics, and offered it a purpose in a catchword 'Socialism', which he was careful never to define. He applauded heroic acts of violence—the glory of self-immolation for the nation[67]—and he provided paramilitary organisation and parades to appeal to the Hindu bhadralok's romantic militarism.[68]

Violent words led to violent deeds. When the A.I.C.C. called for civil disobedience in 1930, the Hindu bhadralok were ready to offer resistance to the British on an unprecedented scale. To the now routine *hartāls* and picketing were added forays against rural police parties, the sabotage of telegraph, rail, and steamer facilities, mail raids, gaol riots, and bomb and revolver attacks that cost dozens of government officials their lives. The most spectacular episode, the Chittagong Armoury Raid of 18 April 1930, secured for the terrorists a large quantity of arms and ammunition. This led to months of almost open warfare in the Chittagong District, and running gun battles between the police and the revolutionaries elsewhere as the arms were distributed throughout Bengal. In Midnapore the Congress established a parallel Government, with its own administration, arbitration boards, and police force, and, with the assassination of three successive District Magistrates, British authority in the area temporarily collapsed. Rebukes from non-Bengali Congressmen at such flagrant violations of the nonviolence creed were disregarded, and when Gandhi himself called a halt to civil disobedience he was publicly denounced by Subhas Chandra as a self-confessed political failure.[69] The violence continued in Bengal until the mid-thirties.

The British replied in kind. When civil disobedience was launched in 1930, they promptly outlawed the Bengal Congress and all its affiliated organisations, confiscating its records and arresting its leaders. With the aid of the Muslims they succeeded, where in the past they had always failed because of united bhadralok opposition, in carrying a bill through the provincial legislature constituting special tribunals to enable them to detain political suspects without due process of law.[70] In the next four years all nationalist meetings and demonstrations were broken up by the police or the military, frequently with violence, and well over 10,000 young Hindu bhad-

[67] S. C. Bose, *The Mission of Life* (Calcutta, 1953), and *Indian Struggle.*
[68] N. C. Banerji, pp. 210, 215–216, and 220.
[69] 9 May 1933, IAR, 1933, Vol. I, p. 22.
[70] Bengal Criminal Law Amendment Bill, 1930.

ralok followed the politicians to prison.[71] Punitive police were stationed in areas where the terrorists were most active, and the local bhadralok Hindu community were collectively fined to pay for their maintenance. Additional restrictions imposed on bhadralok Hindu youths, such as curfew and the carrying of identity cards, failed to stop the terrorist attacks, and in some parts of Eastern Bengal, where the Muslim majority could be relied upon for support, the local British residents took the law into their own hands with reprisals against Hindu bhadralok families.[72] The appointment as Governor in 1932 of Sir John Anderson, a senior British Civil Servant with experience in counterinsurgency in Ireland, was followed by an overhaul of the Government's intelligence system and the movement to Bengal of seven battalions of British infantry, who were deployed to hunt down the revolutionary bands and restore British rule in the countryside. By 1934 the back of the resistance was broken.

THE FRUITS OF VIOLENCE

The effects of this period of violence and counterviolence on the subsequent course of Bengal politics were profound. In the first place, Congress organisation was seriously weakened by the confiscation of documents and the imprisonment of officeholders. Almost all leading Bengal Congressmen went to gaol in the early thirties, and most had only a few years of restored freedom before being reincarcerated in the forties for their opposition to the British war effort or their involvement with the 'Quit India' revolution of August, 1942. As a consequence, the Bengal Congress could offer ill-sustained opposition to the Muslim parties, which suffered no comparable disruption; and during the war years the Hindu bhadralok had to rely almost wholly on the Hindu Mahasabha for the defence of their communal interest.

Another, less predictable, result of the imprisonments was the conversion to Marxism of many of the terrorists during their gaol years, which threw them into contact with Communists and gave them leisure for discussion and reading. They left prison in the late

[71] IAR, 1932, Vol. II, p. 6, and 1933, Vol. II, p. 6.

[72] The most serious case occurred in Chittagong on 31 Aug. 1931. See IAR, 1931, Vol. II, p. 14, and 370–378; N. C. Banerji, p. 253; BLCP, 1 Feb. 1932, Vol. XXXVIII, No. 1, pp. 122–143, and 16 Aug. 1932, Vol. XXXIX, No. 3, p. 91.

thirties determined to give a new ideological direction to the Hindu bhadralok's authoritarian activism. They did succeed in adding a half-dozen new parties to fracture still further Hindu bhadralok political unity, and to complete the spectrum of extremism in Bengal.

A third consequence of these upheavals was the reinforcement of the ideal of violence in Hindu bhadralok political thinking. The Civil Disobedience and Quit India agitations provided thousands of Hindu bhadralok youths with a thrilling means of expressing their nationalist fervour, and, having 'courted imprisonment' or in many cases suffered it, they felt a bond of comradeship with the terrorists, whose reckless and often fatal exploits with revolver and bomb had made them the new folk-heroes of Bengal. The seal was set on this romance of violence by Subhas Chandra Bose's daring escape in 1941 from house arrest in Calcutta, to journey across Central Asia and join the Axis in raising an Indian National Army to fight the British.

For Bengal's economy and administration this decade of disruption was disastrous. With all their energies concentrated on the struggle for political survival, the British administrators and their Indian subordinates had time for no more than gestures of regret at the development schemes, long planned and long postponed. Because of the provisions of the Permanent Settlement, the bhadralok elite's sustained resistance to enhanced property levies, and an abnormally low yield from income and export taxes in the late twenties and the thirties because of a depression in the jute and tea trades, Government revenues in Bengal were inadequate even to keep pace with the demands on the established services. What little there was had to be eked out to cover the greatly extended activities of the law enforcement agencies, with the result that public services in Bengal remained rudimentary, even by comparison with British India's other provinces.[73] This incidentally reduced the scope for bhadralok employment.

The subordinate services in Bengal were understaffed and underpaid, and the province was an unpopular choice for recruits to the I.C.S., who generally preferred the more prosperous and politically stable provinces.[74] The burden of constant political and communal

[73] See Sir John Anderson's memorandum on the state of the Bengal administration, written for King George V, 10 June 1932, J. W. Wheeler-Bennett, *John Anderson, Viscount Waverly* (London, 1962), pp. 129–132.

[74] See Lord Casey, *Personal Experience, 1939–1946* (London, 1962).

trouble told on service morale, as on personal health,[75] and when, with the outbreak of war in 1939, leave was suspended and I.C.S. recruitment from Britain stopped, many men cracked under the strain.

> In the ordinary course of events, the administration of a country does not break down [wrote R. G. Casey, Governor of Bengal, in appealing to the Viceroy for aid in 1945]. The worst that happens is that it deteriorates, wrong decisions are made on a series of levels, and the speed of achievement does not keep pace with the oncoming problems. However, in Bengal, worse may befall. The food problem is always with us, and if the administration is unable to cope with it . . . you may get what happened in 1943, which is as near a breakdown as no matter.[76]

What happened in 1943 was one of the great disasters of the twentieth century: a famine of colossal proportions in which a million and a half people died in Bengal.[77] Its basic cause was the loss of the normal rice imports from Burma because of the Japanese occupation, combined with a devastating cyclone in West Bengal and poor harvests in many parts of India in 1942. That year had imposed staggering additional burdens on the Bengal administration. The advance of the Japanese into Assam and the arrival of thousands of British and American troops had choked the Calcutta port facilities and the transport system of Eastern Bengal. Further dislocation had resulted from the compulsory evacuation of strategic areas of the province, the influx of refugees from Burma and Assam, and bombing raids on Calcutta itself. Finally, the Quit India uprising of August had again snapped the overextended line of British authority in many districts. The Bengal Government had no resources left to deal with the food shortage, with its ugly consequences, maldistribution and profiteering, and the summer of 1943 brought hideous tragedy. For the Hindu bhadralok, forced to be helpless witnesses to the agonising death of thousands upon thousands of their fellow-countrymen, the breakdown was an indictment on the alien Government and its Muslim associates who, in their view, had reduced the Hindus to political impotence.

[75] In this period two successive Governors died in office: Lord Brabourne in February, 1939, and Sir John Herbert in December, 1943.

[76] Casey to Lord Wavell, 1 Mar. 1945, Lord Casey, *Personal Experience, 1939–1946*, *op. cit.*, pp. 213–214.

[77] *Famine Enquiry Commission: Report on Bengal* (New Delhi, 1945).

OUTSIDE ANIMOSITY

Two brush strokes only remain to complete the canvas of the twenty years after 1926. One was the Hindu bhadralok's growing conviction in this period that outsiders bore an animus toward Bengal, or, at the very least, were callously indifferent to its interests.

> I see from the papers that you are promoting still another pact, one between the Hindus and the Mahommedans [wrote N. K. Basu, a Bengal MLC, in an open letter to Madan Mohan Malaviya dated October 13, 1932]. . . . I am afraid that like similar other previous settlements, this one may also be arrived at without any consideration of the circumstances in Bengal. Non-Bengalees are apt to forget the contributions, moral and material, that Bengal has been making for the benefit of All India for over a century. They arrive at agreements without any consultation with Bengal, and rely upon political hysteria to force them down her throat. Bengalee Hindus have demonstrated that they are still willing to undergo privations and sacrifices for the sake of Indian Nationalism, but I am venturing to bring to your mind that it would be a blunder to ignore them altogether, and decide upon their political extinction behind their backs.[78]

Basu's outburst was provoked by the refusal of those responsible for the Poona Pact to make any concession to Hindu bhadralok objections to its Bengal provisions, and this was certainly the chief source of his community's grievance against outsiders in the early thirties. There were, however, a variety of other provocations to confirm the Hindu bhadralok in their belief that Bengal was being ill-used.

For years the provincial Government, Legislative Council, political parties, and press had joined in protesting against the financial settlement between the various governments of British India, in which arrangement they believed that Bengal was unfairly treated;[79] but their main reward was the accusation that they were so narrowly provincial that they could not appreciate the nation's wider interests. This charge of parochialism against Bengalis was very frequently heard, and it was one among a number of criticisms that

[78] IAR, 1932, Vol. II, pp. 287–288.

[79] See above, Chapter V. Also Anderson to the King, 10 June 1932, J. W. Wheeler-Bennett, *John Anderson, Viscount Waverly*, *op. cit.*, pp. 129–132; and *Modern Review*, Vol. XLIII, Mar. 1928, pp. 363–364, and Vol. XLV, Mar. 1929, pp. 394–396.

raised bhadralok hackles in the thirties. There was always some eminent personage or outstation journal shaking a finger of admonition at them for their factionalism or their inconstancy to Gandhian ideals–scolding them one day for their improper involvement with the legislatures, and the next for their shameful toleration of terrorism.

The most unpopular critics, and among the most vocal, were senior Congressmen, for the 1930's saw the development among the Hindu bhadralok of an antipathy toward the All-India Congress Working Committee. It was widely criticised in Bengal as an autocratic body, intolerant of public opinion, insensitive to varying regional needs, and unreasonably dogmatic about political methodology. Its frequent interventions in the provincial Congress' faction fights were a persistent irritant, and the preference normally displayed by the majority of its members for the 'Khadi Group', the Gandhian faction which had least popular Hindu bhadralok support, was particularly unwelcome.

Three of its actions in the late thirties completed its discredit in Bengal. The first was the decision in 1937 that only the first two stanzas of 'Bande Mataram' should be sung at nationalist functions, because of the Hindu communalist overtones of the rest of the song. This was regarded as a gratuitous insult to Bengal's culture and historic contribution to the nationalist movement, and for many Hindu bhadralok it became a point of honour thereafter to begin public meetings with a recital of the complete song as originally written by Bankim Chandra Chatterjee.[80]

The Working Committee's second unwelcome act was its decision in favour of Bihar in a Bengali-Bihari controversy over access to government employment. Educated Biharis had long resented the invasion of their white-collar jobs by Bengal bhadralok, and, after the grant of provincial autonomy, they had taken their case to the Congress executive. In January, 1939, the Working Committee accepted a report on the problem from Rajendra Prasad (a Bihari, as the Bengalis were quick to point out) which recommended the 'preferential treatment of the people of the province' for employment in government services and for places in educational institutions.[81]

[80] Gandhi to J. Nehru, 18 Nov. 1937, J. Nehru, *A Bunch of Old Letters*, *op. cit.*, p. 258; and IAR, 1939, Vol. I, p. 383.

[81] *All India Congress Committee. Bengali Bihari Question* (Allahabad, 1939).

The same month brought a more celebrated incident: the clash between Subhas Chandra Bose and Gandhi over the presidency of the National Congress. Bose had held this office in 1938 and he was reelected in January 1939 for a second term, against Gandhi's opposition. Unwilling to accept the continued leadership of a man with ideas so antagonistic to his own, Gandhi persuaded all but two of the Working Committee to refuse to serve with Bose, and he was forced to resign. His successor as President was Rajendra Prasad, who gave the Bengal seats on the Congress executive to the factions opposing Bose. Bose's reply was the formation of a 'Forward Bloc' inside Congress to 'rally all radical and anti-Imperialist progressive elements in the country',[82] and the organisation of protest demonstrations against A.I.C.C. decisions. This gave the Working Committee an excuse for further action. They debarred Bose from all Congress office for three years on the ground of 'grave indiscipline', and, alleging financial malpractice, they disbanded the B.P.C.C. and handed control of its affairs to an ad hoc committee, from which all of Bose's supporters were excluded.[83]

The ejection, by such dubious means, of their most eminent politician from national and provincial office, and the arbitrary dismissal of the elected provincial committee, was definite proof for many Hindu bhadralok of how insensitive the rest of India had become to Bengal's sentiments and interests. It strengthened their conviction that outsiders could not be trusted to deal fairly with Bengal.

THE SECOND PARTITION

This conviction was to play its part in the last and most tragic episode of these decades: the partition of Bengal. The possibility of a new partition of the province became a live issue in 1940, when Fazlul Huq moved the Pakistan resolution at the All-India Muslim League Session at Lahore.[84] With this resolution the League redefined its constitutional objective as the creation of independent sovereign states in the Muslim majority areas of northwestern and northeastern India. 'The problem in India is not of an inter-communal character, but manifestly of an inter-national one, and it must be treated as such', explained the chief proponent of the

[82] IAR, 1939, Vol. I, p. 30.
[83] Coupland, pt. 2, p. 91; and IAR, 1939.
[84] 23 Mar. 1940, IAR, 1940, Vol. I, p. 312.

scheme, Muhummad Ali Jinnah. '. . . the only course open to us all is to allow the major nations separate homelands by dividing India into "autonomous national States" '.[85]

For the Hindu bhadralok this was the threat of the ultimate disaster: the incorporation of Bengal, in whole or in part, into an avowedly Muslim state. Their reaction was understandably sharp. 'Mr Jinnah is a poor copy of Lord Curzon', declaimed N. C. Chatterjee, Working President of the Bengal Hindu Mahasabha. 'Between us and the Pakisthanists there shall be war and nothing but war. For us the Rubicon is crossed and we should not in the Holy Land of Hindusthan allow such fantastic and mischievous ideas to be preached any further. The evil should be nipped in the bud'.[86] 'Mr Jinnah's Pakistan scheme will remain embodied in pamphlets and reports and so long as 28 crores of Hindus remain alive, it will not operate in any part of Hindusthan', thundered Shyama Prasad.[87] Such strident talk suggested that the Hindu bhadralok were in fact deeply concerned that they might not be able to prevent Pakistan. On the one hand, they could not fully trust the Congress High Command to protect their interests, and on the other they feared that the Bengal Muslim League–possibly with British support–would be able to force the issue on its own account.

Initially their fears of Congress betrayal seemed groundless, for all leading Congressmen rejected the suggestion of a partition of India out of hand. The idea had immense appeal to the Muslims, however, and in the early forties Jinnah went from strength to strength as its promoter. It became increasingly clear that further constitutional advance would be almost impossible unless some concession were made to the Pakistan idea. In an attempt to break the deadlock, a veteran South Indian nationalist, C. Rajagopalachari, opened a correspondence with Jinnah in 1944, which led him to propose that a plebiscite, on the issue of continued association with or separation from 'Hindusthan', should be held after the war in those contiguous districts of northwestern and northeastern India which had a Muslim majority. To the horror of the Hindu bhadralok, Gandhi gave his blessing to this proposal.[88]

[85] 22 Mar. 1940, *ibid.*, p. 309.

[86] N. C. Chatterjee, *Hindu Politics. The Message of the Mahasabha* (Calcutta, 1945), pp. 2–3.

[87] 1 Mar. 1941, IAR, 1941, Vol. I, p. 46.

[88] IAR, 1944, Vol. II, p. 129.

The Bengal Congress immediately sent a delegation to urge the Mahatma to reconsider his decision. The application of Rajagopalachari's scheme, they explained, would result in the total dismemberment of Bengal. Three-quarters of the existing province, with its richest resources and more than half of its Hindu population, would be given to the Muslims, and the remaining segment would have to be added to Bihar or Orissa.

> Bengal leaders are emphatic that it would be very difficult for the people of Bengal who had struggled with good results against the Curzonian partition three decades ago, to yield to any kind of partition now or in the future as Bengal, situated as at present, is culturally and linguistically one single homogeneous unit, perhaps the largest in India. It is, however, affirmed that Bengal accepted the principle of self-determination, but it should be applied on the linguistic and cultural basis. . . .[89]

A united Bengal, defined by language and culture, had always been a basic tenet of Hindu bhadralok political faith, but now a cloud had risen to darken even this horizon. The Muslims had gained such an ascendency in provincial politics that they were talking of an independent sovereign Bengal, under their domination.

In March, 1943, Fazlul Huq's coalition ministry had been forced out of office by the Governor, Sir John Herbert, acting, it was generally believed, on the instigation of the European legislative party.[90] Its place had been taken by a Ministry led by Sir Khwaja Nazimuddin and backed by the Europeans, an enlarged Muslim League legislative group, and a majority of the Scheduled Caste Hindus whom the Namasudra leader, J. N. Mandal, had united into a new party with the avowed object of assisting the Muslims in 'undermining the foundations of vested interest and privileges'.[91] Fazlul Huq, it will be recalled, had deserted the Muslim League in 1941, and Jinnah now gloated over his downfall, claiming it to be a triumph for the League's ideals. 'Bengal has set an example from which others may learn. The League is now the voice of the people, the authority of the Millat, and you have to bow before it, even though you may be the tallest poppy in the Muslim world'.[92] Nazi-

[89] 11 July 1944, *ibid*., p. 180.

[90] A. K. Fazlul Huq, *Bengal Today* (Calcutta, 1944); and V. P. Menon, *The Transfer of Power in India* (Princeton, 1957), pp. 150–151.

[91] J. N. Mandal to Liaqat Ali Khan, n.d., *Times of India*, 9 Oct. 1950. (I am indebted to B. D. Graham, University of Sussex, for this reference.)

[92] Speech, Muslim League, New Delhi, 24 Apr. 1943, IAR, 1943, I, 280.

muddin, with the immediate problems of government in mind, was rather less eager to give his victory so aggressively communal an interpretation, and he took office with an expression of general goodwill and an appeal for support to the 'leader of the Hindu Community', S. P. Mookerjee. He received a terse reply: 'Hindus of Bengal have no confidence in your Ministry'.[93]

There was no longer any ground for compromise. Bitterly resentful of the communal injuries they had suffered and fearful of what the future would bring, the Hindu bhadralok distrusted the Muslim's every word and action. They were fighting with their backs to the wall and believed it would be fatal to be caught off guard. As World War II slowly receded from India and talk of an early end to British rule became general, tension mounted steadily in Bengal and communal affrays became an almost everyday affair.[94] There were ugly threats from extremists on both sides of massive retaliation if their opponents attempted to impose their will, and equally ugly rumours of violent preparations.

Meanwhile, the British were trying to form a coalition Government in New Delhi to which they might hand interim power, and to assemble a constituent body to draft a constitution for a united independent India. The Muslim League refused to be drawn into any arrangement that might jeopardise Pakistan, and in April, 1946, Jinnah threatened violence if the British persisted: 'so far as Muslim India is concerned, the conception of a United India is impossible. If any attempt is made to force a decision against the wishes of Muslims, Muslim India will resist it by all means and at all costs'.[95] He had his answer from Shyama Prasad Mookerjee: 'The time has gone when we shall be satisfied with nominal denunciations on paper of the mischievous principle of Pakistan'.[96]

The lines of battle were drawn, and Bengal was to be the ground. At the end of July the Muslim League made its declaration of war:

> Whereas Muslim India has exhausted without success all efforts to find a peaceful solution of the Indian problem by compromise and constitutional means . . . the time has come for the Muslim nation to resort to direct action to achieve Pakistan and assert their just rights and to vindicate their honour and to get rid of the present

[93] IAR, 1943, Vol. I, pp. 56 and 57.

[94] See the comment by the District Magistrate, Dacca, on communal tension in 1944, Lord Casey, *Personal Experience, 1939–1946*, *op. cit.*, p. 202.

[95] 7 Apr. 1946, IAR, 1946, Vol. I, p. 192.

[96] 14 June 1946, *ibid.*, p. 208.

> slavery under the British and contemplated future Caste-Hindu domination.[97]

A few days later H. S. Suhrawardy, who had formed a new Muslim League Ministry in Bengal in April, 1946, added the threat of 'the declaration of complete independence by Bengal and the setting up of a parallel Government' should power be handed to Congress in Delhi. 'We will see that no revenue is received by such central Government from Bengal and consider ourselves as a separate state having no connexion with the Centre'.[98] Jinnah named 16 August as 'Direct Action' day, and Suhrawardy declared the date a public holiday in Bengal. What followed is too well known and too horrible to describe in detail. The 'Great Calcutta Killings', which started on 16 August 1946, set off four months of virtual civil war in eastern India, in which thousands of Indians were butchered by their fellows, and complete villages and urban *pārās* were razed to the ground.[99] News of the slaughter in Bengal provoked similar atrocities elsewhere, and for a time it seemed as though the fabric of Indian society might be torn to shreds. Above the holocaust, the inflexible voice of M. A. Jinnah was to be heard proclaiming that the only way to stop the violence was to concede Pakistan.[100]

By January, 1947, the two communities in Bengal had fought each other to a standstill, and the Hindu bhadralok had been forced to a bitter conclusion: the partition of Bengal was preferable to its total incorporation in a Muslim state. When the British announced in February that they would leave India within fifteen months, the Bengal Congress and Hindu Mahasabha both appealed for the division of the province.

> Partition of Bengal alone will offer a peaceful solution of the grave communal problem confronting the province. This will give the two major communities in Bengal full freedom to develop their own culture and tradition in the areas where they are in predominant numbers; both are sure to recognise soon that it will be to their mutual interest to guarantee full protection to the respective minorities in the two (proposed) provinces.[101]

[97] Muslim League Council resolution, 29 July 1946, *ibid.*, Vol. II, p. 177.

[98] V. P. Menon, *The Transfer of Power in India* (Princeton, 1957), p. 294.

[99] For an eyewitness account of the rioting see F. Tuker, *While Memory Serves* (London, 1950).

[100] IAR, 1946, Vol. II, pp. 16–60.

[101] S. P. Mukherjee, 19 Mar. 1947, IAR, 1947, Vol. I, p. 48. See also pp. 37, 38, 47, 53–54, and 241–242.

It was a tragic irony, and proof of how heavily the Hindu bhadralok had fallen, that it should now be the Muslim and Scheduled Caste leaders who were defending the ideal of an undivided Bengal. 'I have always held the view that Bengal cannot be partitioned. I am in favour of an united and greater Bengal', declared H. S. Suhrawardy on 8 April 1947.[102]

By then communal killings had started again in Calcutta and other parts of nothern India, forcing the Congress and the British finally to admit that there was no way out but Pakistan. On 9 May the Congress Working Committee conceded the principle of a divided India, with the qualification that the Punjab and Bengal should be partitioned,[103] and on 3 June the British provided a formula for the operation. Each provincial legislature of British India was to vote on which country the province would join, Pakistan or Hindusthan. In the Punjab and Bengal the representatives of the Muslim majority and non-Muslim majority districts would vote separately on the issue, and the boundary lines between the two new states would be established by boundary commissions.[104]

The Bengal Legislative Assembly met in two sections on 20 June 1947 to decide the province's fate. Two questions were put to the members. To the first—should Bengal be partitioned?—the bhadralok Hindus answered yes, and the Muslims and many of the Scheduled Caste Hindus, no. To the second—which constituent assembly should draft the constitution?—the bhadralok Hindus replied: the existing (Indian) assembly, and the Muslims and some of the Scheduled Caste Hindus: a new (Pakistani) assembly.[105]

Ten days later the boundary commission was appointed to score a line across the heart of Bengal, which, with inevitable tragedy for the Hindu bhadralok, would trace the old scar of Lord Curzon's bisection. The British had advanced the date of their departure to 15 August 1947, and, in the hope of averting trouble, the commission's award was kept secret until the 17th. It gave all the Muslim majority districts, with the exception of Murshidabad and part of Nadia, to Pakistan, leaving in India only a third of Bengal's land and people, and only a slightly more than half its Hindu popula-

[102] *Ibid.*, p. 55. Cf. J. N. Mandal's statement, 21 Apr. 1947, and Nazimuddin's, 22 Apr. 1947, *ibid.*, p. 59.

[103] *Ibid.*, p. 64.

[104] *Ibid.*, p. 72.

[105] BLAP, 20 June 1947.

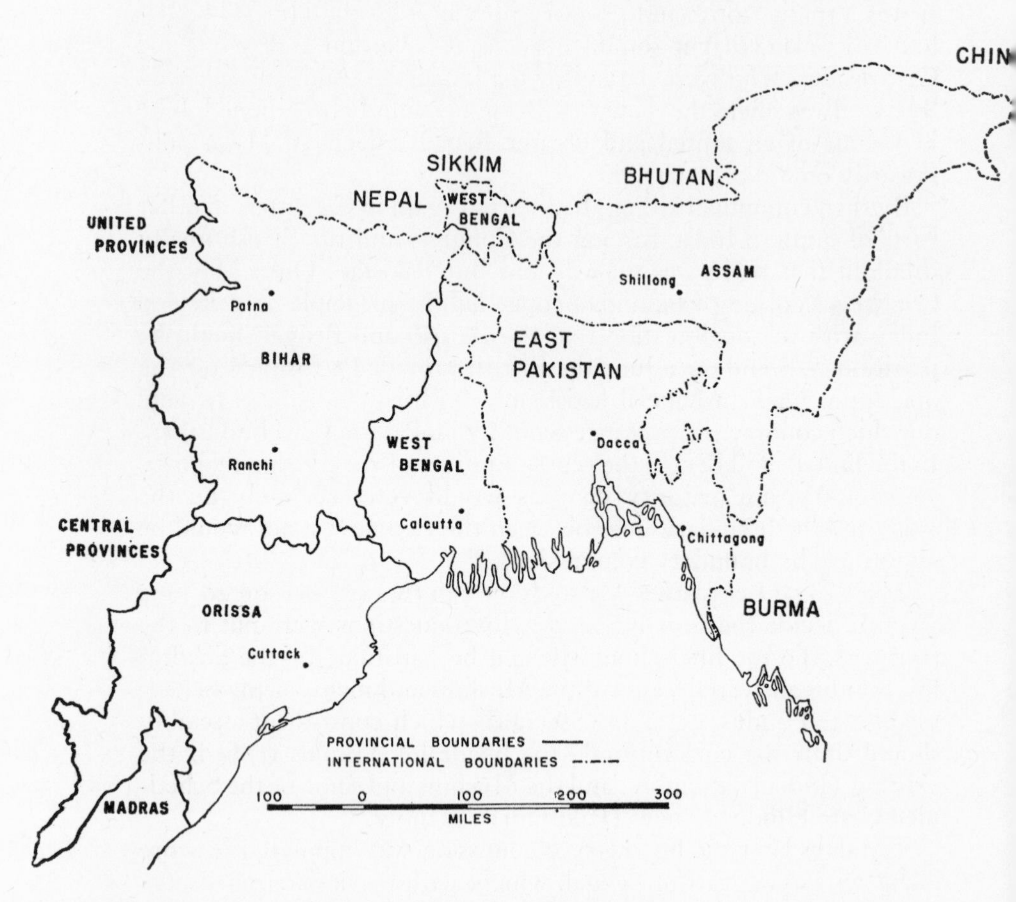

MAP 4. Partitioned Bengal, 1947

tion[106] (see Map 4). The new frontier cut across the great waterways and the railway system. It separated the port and industrial complex of Hooghly-side from its rich sources of raw materials in the Ganges Delta and the Brahmaputra Valley. It divided the two cultural worlds of the bhadralok, their city from their countryside —that land of broad rivers and green paddy extolled in story, poem, and song: Eastern Bengal.

[106] "Bengal Boundary Commission. Report", *Gazette of India*, Extraordinary, 17 Aug. 1947, pp. 1059–1062.

The Hindu bhadralok had been saved from what they regarded as a calamity: permanent Muslim domination. They had been restored to power in part of their former domain and they still had Calcutta, but the cost was so great and their losses so heavy that they could look to the future only with anguish. They could not accept the partition of Bengal as a settled fact, certainly not while millions of Hindus remained in the east, but they were helpless to change the situation. Their frustration was worst when they looked back upon their history. Outsiders, wrote the *Statesman* on 24 June 1950,

> do not fully appreciate how full West Bengal is of discontent with present conditions. It is not only that people are deeply conscious of the plight of the East Bengal Hindus. They are constantly aware also of past glories and present potentialities. They do not forget either that Calcutta was long the country's capital or that Bengalis took the lead in the freedom movement. Once they swayed the destinies of India; now they cannot even determine their own.

CONCLUSION

In Bengal in the last quarter of the nineteenth century there was a small but keenly ambitious group of nationalists whose immediate objective was to extend their countrymen's share of administrative and political power, and whose ultimate ambition was to participate in the development of a system of parliamentary self-government in India. These men were sustained in their constitutional ideal by the British Whig tradition, and they were encouraged in their efforts to organise and publicise by the sympathy of a section of British Indian opinion. At the same time, they were discouraged by the most powerful group within the Indian Civil Service, whose antagonism to their aspirations was climaxed by the partition of Bengal in 1905.

In resisting this measure the Bengal nationalists, their number now greatly increased, obtained agitational experience. They acquired an understanding of the opportunities and difficulties of any movement which seeks popular support, and they were forced to acknowledge the political relevance of class and communal divisions in Bengali society. By pitting themselves against the British they gained greater self-confidence, balanced by a more realistic measure of British power.

Their agitation achieved its main purpose with the reunification of Bengal in 1912, but it had other legacies. One was a profound distrust of the political objectives of the British Indian Government and equally profound scepticism of any political strategy that was dependent for its success on British cooperation. A second was the emergence of the Bengal Muslim leadership as an independent political elite who could not be denied their claim to separate recognition. A third was a new opportunity for Bengal politicians to participate in representative institutions and a renewed willingness to do so on the part of a section of the nationalist leadership.

The years from 1913 to 1920 furnished the political elites, bhadralok Hindu and Muslim, with experience in working within a legislative system, and early in that period high expectations were raised of institutional reforms that would give greater power to Indians. The nationalists framed constitutional demands and secured their endorsement by the Muslim leaders, but the British were reluctant to respond; when they did, they gave such guarded promises that the nationalists doubted their sincerity. The uncertainty was prolonged by protracted constitutional enquiries, which coincided with the economic and social dislocation accompanying the end of World War I. Social unrest and political impatience spawned agitation and, fearing a general revolution, the British vacillated between repression and reform. By their uncertainty they opened the way for the emergence of a charismatic national leader, Gandhi.

The structure of Bengal's political system in 1921 was fundamentally different from that of the preceding decade. There was now a large representative legislature responsible to an extended electorate, and there was a revolutionary nationalist agitation with all-India leadership and mass support. In both spheres–institutional and agitational–the Hindu bhadralok politicians were confronted with serious problems of organisation and control. Conversely, the Bengal Muslim politicians were presented with new opportunities for mobilising support, and the Hindu-Muslim nationalist alliance –which had been forged in 1916 in common idealism and which had been held together into the twenties by common expediency– shattered as the divergence of Muslim and bhadralok Hindu political interests was revealed. By the mid-twenties an influential section of the Bengal Muslim leadership was determined to turn the separatist tendencies of their community to political gain, and a hard-pressed provincial Government encouraged their efforts in the hope of securing tactical advantages in its own political defence.

The crucial year was 1926. The communal violence that resulted from the mutual provocations of extremist Hindu bhadralok and Muslim politicians aided the latter's efforts to reorganise the Muslim electorate, and in the following year the Hindu bhadralok lost control of many local bodies and the provincial legislature. Taking allies from the European and low-caste Hindu communities, the Muslims mounted a sustained attack in the 1930's on Hindu bhadralok political power at all levels–in the civil service, the legislature, the universities, the Calcutta Corporation, other local bodies, and educational boards–and upon their dominance of the rural economy.

Hindu bhadralok resistance was weakened by the provincial Congress' acquiescence in national party directives regarding the legislature inappropriate to Bengal, and by the imprisonment for long periods of nearly all their leaders. Unable to hold their own in constitutional politics, the community increasingly sought extreme solutions through terrorist and revolutionary violence, Hindu communalism and, finally, Marxism. Retaliation by the British and the Muslims was correspondingly extreme, and the 1940's brought such wide-scale violence that all groups were finally prepared to agree to a partition of Bengal on communal lines.

THE ELITE AND THE INSTITUTION

The problem the Hindu bhadralok faced from the beginning, a problem which they never solved and which played its part in the tragic finale to this story, was the problem of a caste elite whose economic and political strength rested on its successful participation in imported, liberal institutions–the bureaucratic, educational, legal, and legislative systems–which were by their nature 'open ended' (that is, the basis for recruitment was ability, not birth) and which therefore tended to create an open society. The Hindu bhadralok were proud of their achievement, but they also valued their high-caste status. They wished to develop the adopted institutions, which had served them so well in the nineteenth century, and yet they were concerned to preserve the social order, with its ascribed advantages for themselves. They knew that further institutional development would bring increasingly insistent demands from the lower orders for accommodation: for the wider opening of the doors of schools, colleges, and offices to non-bhadralok. They were understandably apprehensive of the social effects of such accommodation, and uncertain of their own ability to control the pace and direction of change.

Their problem was a real one, and they were right to emphasise the importance of maintaining stability. As S. N. Eisenstadt has observed, this has proved to be a crucial issue in all modernizing societies:

> The institutionalization of change, or the development and crystalization of new institutional settings requires the internal transfor-

> mation of the societies or groups within which it occurs. The capacity for such internal transformation is manifest in structural frameworks or cultural symbols that enable some groups to mobilize new forces and resources without necessarily destroying the existing structure. In modernizing societies, internal transformation is especially critical because modernization requires not only a relatively stable new structure but one capable of adapting to continuously changing conditions and problems.[1]

Throughout the nineteenth century the bhadralok had shown a remarkable capacity for internal transformation. They had been able 'to mobilize new forces and resources' without destroying the existing social structure because, despite the British presence, they had exercised sufficient control over the development of new institutions to provide continually expanding opportunities for their society without threatening their own sense of security.

There is no reason to think that with the coming of the twentieth century the bhadralok had lost this capacity to adapt to changing conditions and problems, despite their self-doubts as reflected in Hindu revivalism. But to maintain this capacity they had to have continuing institutional opportunities to match their widening range of skills and expectations. They also required some control of this institutional development to give them security.

At that stage the development of a parliamentary system in Bengal offered an opportunity to provide this exceptionally talented and ambitious group with the political scope it demanded, and an arena in which it might resolve the main problem of change then confronting it: the non-bhadralok's demands for accommodation. There were two requirements for the success of a parliamentary system in this context. One was a guarantee of power, immediate or imminent, within the system which would make profitable the investment therein of political resources. The other was the formation of territorial–not communal–electorates, which initially were restricted and hence manageable by the bhadralok, but which would be extended progressively, thereby forcing them to appeal to ever-widening sections of society in order to maintain their power. If it was clear from the outset that this was to be the course of development, the bhadralok politicians would be encouraged, at the very

[1] S. N. Eisenstadt, 'Transformation of Social, Political, and Cultural Orders in Modernization', *American Sociological Review*, Vol. XXX, No. 5, Oct., 1965, p. 659.

least, to develop techniques of communication with non-bhadralok, and in time the elite might be persuaded to open its ranks wider to aspiring individuals or groups from below. It might be assisted in creating an open society.

The positive significance of the bhadralok's experience with the Bengal Legislative Council from 1913 to 1920 has already been suggested: it demonstrated their capacity to work within a parliamentary system should one be developed and reinforced their interest in such a development, as was shown by their support for council entry through the twenties. The negative significance of that experience was that the bhadralok were discouraged, on the one hand, from committing themselves fully to the institution because of the lack of power vested in it and the absence of any guarantee that it would be given power, and, on the other, from making the effort to establish political contact with non-bhadralok by an extremely narrow franchise and separate communal electorates. They were given no indication of the way in which the franchise or the system of representation would be developed, and were unprepared for what happened in 1921: the enfranchisement of a million new voters of whom the majority were rural illiterates. Their politicians' appeals during the preceding constitutional hearings for the maintenance of a reasonably restricted franchise 'in order to secure competent voters and manageable electorates'[2] were disregarded, as was their opposition to communally segmented constituencies. The combined effect was to make their position in the new legislature extremely insecure.

This coincided with the transfer to the elected MLCs of their first real power through the appointment of responsible Ministers, and a promise of more power in the future. If the Hindu bhadralok could not control the institution, there was therefore the serious possibility of its being used by non-bhadralok to wrest from them command of other institutions that were vital to their interests. As a consequence, the development of a parliamentary system became a menace to the Hindu bhadralok position instead of an opportunity to maintain that position in a changing society.

The effect was to cut the ground from under the feet of the liberal secularists and to enhance the influence of the Hindu revivalists, who had always argued that the introduction of foreign

[2] *Evidence taken before the Reforms Committee (Franchise)* (Calcutta, 1919), Vol. II, p. 383.

legislative institutions would sap the strength and destroy the integrity of Hindu society. Before the Parliamentary Join Select Committee on the Government of India Bill in 1919, all witnesses could justifiably assert that caste played an insignificant part in Bengal politics, by contrast with Madras or Maharashtra;[3] by 1923, however, Bengali high-caste men had formed defensive communal *sabhās*, and, as the feared legislative attack from below developed over the next decade, these organisations won steadily increasing influence and respect. This was one manifestation of a general trend in Hindu bhadralok politics from the mid-1920's toward exclusive and authoritarian styles, of which we see other examples in the revival of the terrorist secret societies, and the following that Subhas Chandra Bose gained with his call for disciplined youth to be the storm troopers of national freedom.

PROBLEMS OF COMMUNICATION

Why, it may be asked, did such a talented and experienced group as the Hindu bhadralok find the prospect of a mass electorate so alarming? Basically because of their difficulties of communication with the non-bhadralok, a problem the seriousness of which they had been forced to recognise by their failure to secure mass support for the anti-partition agitation.

In the first place, they had virtually no institutional contact with the lower orders. Their own highly developed network of institutions was in this respect a disadvantage to their politicians, for it involved them in complex commitments within the community and set styles of associational behaviour which inhibited their development of non-bhadralok contacts.

This was one facet of the general problem of the culture gap between bhadralok and non-bhadralok. The bhadralok's nineteenth-century experience of cultural adaptation and innovation had not been shared by other strata of Bengali society, and in consequence there were many commonplace bhadralok concepts that were incomprehensible to the non-bhadralok. Among these were basic elements of nationalist thought such as imperialism, nationality, statehood, and independence. The problem the bhadralok faced was by no means unique, but it was none the less thorny for that. Very crudely, it was the problem of thoroughly literate men trying to

[3] PP, 1919 (203), Vol. IV.

make themselves understood by the unlettered, of a written tradition confronting an oral tradition.

With his rebuke of Gandhi in 1921—'the mind, surely, is not of less account than a length of cotton thread spun on the wheel'[4]—the poet Rabindranath Tagore voiced the Bengali intellectual's vexation at the Mahatma's consuming preoccupation with *khādi*, but Gandhi understood as did few of the Hindu bhadralok the indispensability of symbolism in the creation of a mass movement in India. Here again, however, the Hindu bhadralok were in difficulty: what politically emotive symbols could be used in Bengal that would be universally or even generally acceptable? The nationalists had had some success during the anti-partition agitation with Tagore's attractive idea of adapting the *rākhi bandhan*, a thread ceremony from northern India, to symbolise the brotherhood of all Bengalis; but their attempt to identify the Bengali Motherland with the bloody Sakta figure, Ma Kali, had provoked Muslim enmity.

The presence of a Muslim majority in Bengal was, of course, the crux of the Hindu bhadralok's problem of symbol manipulation, but even within Hindu society their scope was limited. Only a minority of bhadralok Hindus worshipped Visnu whereas the vast majority of the Hindu peasantry in Bengal were Vaisnavas. Bengal had a great bhakti tradition but, in contrast with Maharashtra, for instance, this tradition was not a bond between the high and low castes, for in modern Hindu bhadralok mythology bhakti was identified as one of those popular, emotional developments that had weakened medieval Hinduism and paved the way for foreign conquest. Similarly, unlike the Arya Samaj in the Punjab which had carried its message of religious reform to low- as well as high-caste men, Bengal's major Hindu reform movement, the Brahmo Samaj, had had no significant impact outside bhadralok society. In religion, as in other aspects of their culture, the Hindu bhadralok had little in common with their inferiors.

TOWN AND COUNTRY

Earlier it was emphasised that the bhadralok were not simply an urban group—that they maintained rural contacts and often a rural home. At first sight this would appear to have given them an

[4] 'The Call of Truth', 29 Aug. 1921, Rabindranath Tagore, *Towards Universal Man* (London, 1961), p. 267.

advantage in recruiting political support from the peasant masses, but it must be recalled that the bhadralok had always striven to maintain their distance from the *chota lok*, the hoi polloi. They were at pains to make it clear that though they lived 'with' the people they were not 'of' them. They expressed sympathy for the condition of life of those who tilled the soil, but it was the patronising sympathy of superiors for their social inferiors.

Moreover, there could be no close identity of economic interest between one rural group—the peasants—who laboured, and another—the bhadralok—who shared in the products of that labour through their ownership of much of the land and their control of much of the ready cash necessary to finance cultivation. Economics could not provide a satisfactory channel of mass communication for the Hindu bhadralok politicians. If the rural economy became a political issue, it was less likely to produce a sympathetic dialogue between bhadralok and non-bhadralok than a hostile confrontation. This was a fact which the Hindu bhadralok politicians understood and which made them consistent opponents of Gandhi's no-tax campaigns.

One of the most striking contrasts in Bengal politics in this period was between the disadvantages under which the Hindu bhadralok laboured in rural politics and the opportunities they had in the cities, particularly in Calcutta. Whereas in the countryside they were a small, scattered minority, in the towns they formed a sizeable proportion of all residents. Movement within the towns and between them was made relatively easy by road, rail, and river transport, and political ideas circulated freely in the newspapers and journals produced there. In the towns were the symbols of British authority—the flags and the government buildings on which they flew, the clubs and churches, and the Englishmen themselves with their uniformed attendants busy with the ceremonials of Empire—all offering ready targets for attack. Here, too, enmity against the foreign rulers could be reinforced with enmity toward the foreign economic exploiters: the British businessmen and their accomplices, the 'Hindustani *beniyās*', familiar and unpopular urban figures in Bengal. In the towns, particularly in Calcutta, there were occupational groups that could be readily mobilised for political agitation, and the nationalists found that it was urban violence which most concerned the British in Bengal, for it most directly threatened their administrative, commercial, and communications centres.

Calcutta posed great problems of control for the imperial rulers, but in compensation it also gave the Hindu bhadralok some headaches. It was so much bigger and apparently so much more important than anything else in eastern India, the political scope which it offered seemed so great, that many a bhadralok politician was tempted to disregard all else. Calcutta could become a world in itself, demanding special political techniques, and giving in return its special rewards and its peculiar experience. But Calcutta was not all in all. The great mass of Bengal's population and a large part of its wealth, including much bhadralok wealth, was in that difficult rural hinterland that the Hindu bhadralok politicians were always inclined to neglect. It was this neglect which left them so vulnerable to attack in the legislature, once the peasants were enfranchised.

Calcutta's advantage to the agitational politician was its volatility. A stamping ground of the opportunist and the footloose, it could always be relied upon to furnish a mob on immediate demand, and its clearly marked ethnic, religious, and economic divisions were ready-made channels for the direction of violence. The problems of controlling this violence once it was started have been emphasised, but there was another, equally serious, problem: the enmities generated by disturbances in Calcutta influenced mufussil society. Rural Bengal could not be insulated against urban Bengal. In consequence, the Hindu bhadralok were always liable to find that an apparently successful city manoeuvre provoked an unpleasant backlash in the countryside where their control was so much less secure.

THE LOWER-CLASS BHADRALOK

The opportunities and difficulties of urban politics were closely paralleled by the opportunities and difficulties the Hindu bhadralok politicians had with their own lower class. From our discussion of the 1905–1908 and 1921–1922 agitations, it will be apparent that the great advantage to the politicians of the underprivileged and discontented lower-class bhadralok was their availability as a reservoir of numbers that could be readily tapped whenever there was a need to demonstrate 'popular' support or whenever workers were required for a special effort.

The lower-class bhadralok responded readily to straightforward nationalist appeals and to Sakta symbolism. Their nationalist ardour and their careless disregard of the dangers of British or Muslim retaliation lent vigour to any agitation in which they were involved. On the other hand, their disinclination to heed the cautions of their leaders once their enthusiasm was aroused made them somewhat of a liability on those occasions when the politicians saw the need to restrain nationalist agitation to forestall a threatened social upheaval. With their limited political vision they could not appreciate the destruction that might be wrought by inflamed communal hatreds, nor were they as quick as the elite to sense a threat to landed property and capital.

What they were always on their guard against was any threat to their means of access to schools and colleges, and their insecure hold on clerkships, subordinate government appointments, teaching posts, and the like. These inferior white-collar jobs were, of course, the primary objectives of aspiring non-bhadralok, and for sheer self-preservation the lower-class bhadralok were determined to resist every concession to ambitious outsiders. The vernacular press was the watchdog of their interests, and the effect of its work was to restrict severely the freedom of the elite politicians to meet the demands of the leaders of other communities for a more equitable share of education and professional employment.

The vernacular press also spoke for the lower-class bhadralok when it questioned the integrity of that section of the elite which was closely associated with the British in the upper echelons of the administrative and legal systems, particularly of that select band of English-speaking politicians who were involved with the legislatures. What sort of nationalists were these, it was asked, who would work with the British in imperialist institutions? This criticism came naturally from a group such as the lower-class bhadralok which had no share in the exclusive politics of the councils and which envied the advantages enjoyed by those who did. Nonetheless, it was an extremely effective criticism which had the council members always on the defensive, for its logic was simple and hard to dispute. The style of Bengali nationalism since the days of Curzon's partition had been one of uncompromising opposition to the British, and council entry could never quite be made to fit this style.

It is a fact—and the point is of crucial importance—that the inflexible stance the Hindu bhadralok politicians had adopted, or been forced to adopt, in the first decade of the twentieth century seriously impeded their ability to manoeuvre thereafter. They were held prisoner by their own angry words and actions, and were always liable to be called to account by their own followers if they showed an inclination to be less angry. The most deleterious consequence was that they so narrowly restricted their grounds for compromise with the British that they were unable to secure the institutional concessions so essential for the development of their community. Their own intransigence encouraged intransigence in others. The difficulties experienced by Surendranath Banerjea in his relations with Carmichael from 1913 to 1916 and by Chitta Ranjan Das in his efforts to negotiate with Lytton in the year before his death clearly demonstrate this.

MUSLIM SEPARATISM

If we can detect inflexibility in Hindu bhadralok political attitudes, we can certainly detect the same in the attitudes of the Muslims, and we must take account of this in considering the problems of communal accommodation and institutional development.

It is a striking fact that throughout this period of almost half a century the Bengal Muslim politicians unflaggingly asserted their community's right to a separate political existence. The strategies of Muslim politics were not constant, the type of Muslim politician with influence varied, and the political system underwent radical changes. But this determination to maintain a distinct political identity was throughout the basic factor in Muslim thinking. The suggestion that the community should take its place simply as one religious and cultural group in a diverse Indian nation was never entertained, and we must ask why.

If we phrase the answer in the most general terms we can say that it was in the character of Islam itself. 'An independent political community as the arena of religious activity is part of the very genius of Islam', Wilfred Cantwell Smith has observed. 'The existence of such a community is not something peripheral; it lies close to the heart of the faith'.[5] This attitude was reinforced for the Indian Muslims by their own history. The memory of imperial rule was cherished by the community, and if the ambition to rule again was not universal, a determination never to submit to former subjects, the Hindus, was certainly widespread.

It is not difficult in this context to understand the Bengal Muslim

[5] W. C. Smith, *Islam in Modern History* (New York, 1959), p. 211.

politicians' distrust of the Congress. The domination of the nationalist organisation in Bengal by Hindu bhadralok, their equivocation over liberal, secularist principles, and, from the time of the partition, their recurrent appeals to Hindu symbolism, all served to convince the Muslims that Congress rule would mean Hindu rule.

This apprehension was a negative spur to separatism. More positive encouragement was derived from the fact that there were ambitious men with social influence—landholders, lawyers, government officials, teachers, and scholars—who could convert that influence to political power so long as the community had a recognised political existence. Under the consultative system prevailing at the turn of the century, the influence of these men was underwritten by their nomination as Muslim representatives in the legislative councils, and when election was introduced in 1909 their position was again guaranteed through separate communal electorates. By 1919, the distinct political organisation of the Muslim community was a fact that neither Congress nor Edwin Montagu could deny, however much they may have desired to do so; and the massive extension of the franchise under the constitution of that year provided new opportunities for power for the politicians whose communal influence enabled them to sway large numbers of men.

For the Bengal Muslim politician the great advantage of the maintenance of separate electorates under the Montagu-Chelmsford constitution was that it reduced the demands on his technical initiative which mass politics would otherwise have made. Although we must not underestimate the problems created for him by the divisions of class, status, sect, region, and language in Bengal Muslim society, it is evident that the religious definition of his constituency greatly simplified his task of mass communication. He had to hand a ready-made organisation in the local communal *ānjumāns*, which, by contrast with the voluntary associations with which the Hindu bhadralok were involved, cut across the dividing lines of class and status, associating landholders, professional men, and merchants with peasants. Moreover, as a political Defender of the Faith, the Muslim politician could rely on the traditional structure of communal authority: the institutions and symbols of religion. He could enlist the *mollās* to speak on his behalf to the regular gatherings of the Faithful. Mosques could serve as political as well as religious centres, and festivals could provide opportunities for patronage and a display of zeal. From the community's universal pride in a great past, the politician could draw stirring exhortations for a great achievement in the future.

If history united the Bengali Muslim community, so too did its enmity toward the Hindu bhadralok. In search of an object of denunciation the communalist politician did not, like the nationalist, have to resort to the remote and relatively unfamiliar figures of the British raj. He had an excellent target for attack in that dominant Hindu minority that supplied the landholders and their agents, the moneylenders, the lawyers, the tax collectors, and other government officials with whom every Bengal Muslim, rural or urban, was forced to have dealings. To charge this group with tyranny and to call for united backing to break its power was a sure way to arouse popular enthusiasm. And if anger ran to violence, it was the privileged Hindu minority that was likely to be hurt most seriously.

For a Muslim politician to deny the encouragement to separatism which the 1919 constitution gave, with its communal electorates and its enfranchisement of Muslim peasantry, was to fly in the face of an opportunity for power. This was an error into which Fazlul Huq was almost led by his collaboration with the Hindu bhadralok nationalists in the Lucknow Pact years. In the twenties he had only a shadow of his former influence as he struggled to devise a new method suitable to the changed conditions. Success came when he realised that the rural economy was excellent ground on which the Muslim politician might recruit mass support, and he was given his chance of power when in 1937 another four million peasants were enfranchised. Many of these were Scheduled Caste Hindus, and the Muslim politicians—with Huq in the van—were now able to broaden the base of their support, while still asserting their separatist tenets.

Their aim was to dominate all of Bengal, but here the logic of their position worked against them. Partition, which many of them did not desire, was the logical result of their separatist endeavours.

THE BRITISH OBJECTIVE

The undertow of Hindu and Muslim communalism in Bengal was very strong, and there were too few men in either community with the single-hearted determination necessary to resist it. There were equally few among the British.

As a small minority community with very large economic interests in Bengal, the British nonofficials were always separatist in their political thinking. They advocated separate communal electorates for others so that they might secure them for themselves. They allied with communalist politicians against the nationalists to protect their own communal interests. The British officials also had interests to protect and, as we have seen, they were not beyond the encouragement of communal differences to secure tactical advantages on occasions when they were particularly hard pressed. That it was their job to maintain British rule in Bengal and that they would seek allies against their nationalist opponents is obvious enough, but we would be mistaken to think that this in itself provides a full explanation of their actions.

The British officer's task, by his own definition, was not simply to rule Bengal but to rule it well. He had been entrusted with power and he had to use that power wisely to secure the people's welfare. He had, among other things, to decide which groups should receive his encouragement and which should be discouraged. One community which most of the I.C.S. regarded as in no need of encouragement was the Hindu bhadralok, which they identified not unfairly as an economically exploiting and politically aggressive group, possessed of a consuming ambition to dominate all provincial affairs. Its particular objective was to get control for its own ends of the British-imported institutions. To prevent such 'hijacking', as well as to protect the interests of other communities, the British officials stressed the need to maintain constitutional safeguards—built-in barriers to bhadralok ambition—and to develop the strength of others who might serve as a counterweight.

To argue as the nationalists did (and as we have done here) that the best hope for Bengal's future lay in recognising the creative capacity of the bhadralok, in fostering their liberal tendencies through the provision of extended institutional opportunities, and in encouraging their efforts at accommodation by assisting them to establish contact with non-bhadralok, was to provoke the retort from the I.C.S. that if this was not special pleading it certainly revealed a lamentable ignorance of the hard realities of Bengal political life.

What this argument in fact did was to offend the I.C.S.'s cherished vision of their role in India. In their own eyes it was not the bhadralok but themselves who were the creative elite, and their great contribution was to give justice and order. For India to progress, materially or morally, it had to be held stable, and stability could be assured only if the I.C.S.—that dedicated, disinterested, and incorruptible band of men—maintained firm and impartial control. For India's sake their power must not be sapped by social changes, nor must their initiative be lost to any Indian group, however able or ambitious. This philosophy had its classic expression in J. F. Stephen's famous article in the *Nineteenth Century* of 1883 entitled 'Foundations of the Government of India'.[6] Its principle underlay the institutional adjustments of Minto's viceroyalty, as well as those of Curzon's. It was on this ground that Bengal was partitioned in 1905 and reunited in 1912. It was with this logic that Reginald Craddock and the District Administration Committee of 1914 rebuked the wayward Government of Bengal, and the hydra's longevity was well attested by Percy Lyon's unsuccessful tussle with it in September, 1916.

The upheaval resulting from World War I moved some influential British public men to suggest that there might be utility in encouraging Indians to initiate changes in their polity and ultimately to take charge of their own affairs, a lead that was followed by Edwin Montagu with his declaration that he would build the machinery to make this possible. For the I.C.S. the illusion of indispensability was shattered: 'the Indian civil servants were very sorry that their day was done'.[7] Forced to participate in a constitutional reconstruction of which they disapproved, the Bengal officials tried to salvage something from the wreckage of their paternalist ideals and came up with the idea of forming a mass, peasant electorate which the bhadralok would be unable to control and which might, in time, throw up genuinely popular leaders. That this was a hazardous venture they hastened to admit, but then they were 'frankly dubious as to the working of [Montagu's] scheme' in its entirety, and could see no safe way of preventing the Hindu bhadralok 'oligarchy' from snatching power to the eternal detriment of the mass of the people.[8]

This much they were determined to do, and so they were led in the twenties into the devious manoeuvres required to destroy C. R. Das' Hindu-Muslim pact, and then to the wider task of aiding the

[6] *Nineteenth Century*, Vol. LXXX, July–Dec. 1883, pp. 541–568.

[7] W. S. Marris, I.C.S., in conversation with Montagu, 6 Dec. 1917, Montagu, p. 88.

[8] J. H. Kerr, Chief Secretary, GB, to Secretary, Home Department, GI, 15 Oct. 1918, *Government of India's Despatch of March 5th, 1919, and Connected Papers* (Calcutta, 1919), p. 194.

Muslims to get full value from their separate electorates through better organisation of the voters. In the thirties British official and nonofficial votes in the legislature sustained a succession of shaky coalition governments pledged to break Hindu bhadralok economic power, and in the forties their support was available for the Muslim League.

The basic objective of British policies in Bengal throughout this half-century was to combat Hindu bhadralok exclusiveness, but the tragic effect of those policies was to reinforce that very characteristic. By their actions the British gave encouragement to the separatists, and when they finally yielded power it could only be to the opposing governments of a divided Bengal.

GLOSSARY

ānjumān Communal assembly or association. In Bengal applied only to Muslim organisations.

bābu In Bengali a title of respect for an English-speaking Hindu. Applied derogatorily by the British to semi-educated bhadralok clerks, and by extension to any bhadralok.

Bande Mātaram 'Hail to the Mother'. The title of a song in Bankim Chandra Chatterjee's novel *Anandamath*, which was adopted in Bengal as the anthem of nationalism during the anti-partition agitation.

beniyā Merchant, trader, trading caste.

bustee Urban slum, consisting of a chaotic jumble of squalid huts to which narrow winding footpaths normally provide the only approach.

crore Ten millions.

dacoity Gang robbery. A dacoit is a member of a robber gang.

dārwān Gatekeeper.

durbar Court, audience, or levee of a king or man of rank.

gundā Gangster.

hartāl Suspension of work or business as a mark of protest.

khādi, *khaddar* Cloth hand-woven from hand-spun thread.

kriskak Peasant, farmer.

lakh One hundred thousand.

lāthi Long stick, sometimes tipped with metal, used as a weapon.

mahājan Moneylender, banker, merchant.

mohant Head of a temple.

mollā Muslim lawyer or learned man, who, in the absence of a priesthood in Islam, customarily expounds the teachings of the Koran to the faithful.

mufussil The country, or towns in the country, as opposed to the *sadar*, the principal town. Its usual application in

Bengal is to the country in general as distinct from Calcutta.

pandal — Temporary structure of cloth or basketwork supported on posts, to give shelter to an assembly.

pārā — Urban neighbourhood.

pardā — Veil, screen, or curtain which conceals the women of a Muslim family from the gaze of men. The *parda* quarters are the area of the house from which men are excluded.

raj — Rule, dominion, ruling power, ruling family, kingdom, principality.

sabhā — Assembly or place of assembly.

samiti — Association.

satyāgraha — Passive resistance. A coinage of Gandhi's from:
satya = truth
āgraha = firmness.

swadeshi — Of one's own country. Hence, the encouragement of indigenous manufactures to the exclusion of imported articles.

swāmi — Hindu holy man.

swarāj — Self-government, freedom.

thānā — Police station, or the area under its authority.

zamindar — Hereditary landholder.

INDEX

Addy, Amulya Dhone, 195–196
Ahimsa, 148
Ahmed, Emaduddin, 59
Ahmed, Wasimuddin, 181
Ahmedabad, 224, 227
Akali movement, 260
Ākhrās, 30
Ali, Syed Nasim, 195
Aligarh, 45, 274–275
Alipore Central Gaol, 226, 230
All-India Congress Committee (A.I.C.C.), 139, 221, 284, 291, 300; call for *hartāl*, 142; discusses noncooperation, 165–166; calls for civil disobedience, 221, 302; B. C. Pal resigns from, 229; Calcutta meeting, 235; Working Committee, 226, 307–308
Americans, 305
Amritsar: Jallianwala Bagh affair, 142, 143, 145, 231; Congress session at, 144–145
Amrita Bazar Patrika, 48, 135
Anderson, John, 303
Andrews, Charles Freer, 165; on Jallianwala Bagh, 142; on noncooperation, 150, 151, 165, 167, 212, 217, 218–219, 236; on Khilafat movement, 157; as labour arbitrator, 214–219; on civil disobedience, 224; on Calcutta rioting, 277–278
'Anglicisation', criticism of: by Gandhi, 149, 164; by Extremists, 149; by Bengali press, 149, 163; by C. R. Das, 163–164
Anglo-Indians, 280; in Calcutta, 3; legislative representation, 128, 184, 275, 292
Armenians, 3
Arya Samaj, 276, 279, 322
Assam, 27, 40, 184, 215–218, 305
Associations: Hindu bhadralok, 12, 208, 321; Muslim, 157–158, 208, 272–273, 279, 327; Namasudra, 158–160
Azad, Abul Kalam, 156–157, 167

Bābus, 133, 237; Deakin on, 25; British jibes at resented, 33; as bhadralok elite, 56, 163, 164; in Midnapore, 211*n*
Backward classes. *See* Hindu lower castes
Bahadurabad, 217
Baidya, 6, 134
Bajaj, Seth Jamnalal, 226 *and n*
Bakarganj, 206, 237
Bande Mātaram, 307
Banerjea, Jitendralal, 219–220
Banerjea, Surendranath, 63, 79, 135, 141, 147, 326; Calcutta Corporation boycott, 29; in anti-partition agitation, 29–31; as Moderate, 34; attitude to Bengal reunification, 46–47; reenters Bengal Legislative Council, 55–56, 57–60, 61–62; education and early career, 66–68; opposition leader in Bengal Legislative Council, 68–71; demand for constitutional reforms, 86–87; defeated in Imperial Legislative Council election, 90; on Montagu declaration, 99; on Hindu-Muslim unity, 113, 129–130; and Lucknow Pact, 133–134, 136; in dispute over Congress presidency, 135–136; control of Indian Association, 137–138; President, National Liberal League, 140; on noncooperation, 151; on Hindu conservatism, 154; on masses, 160; attacked by Extremists, 162; appointed Minister, 173–174; Calcutta Corporation reforms, 174–175, 194–197, 247, 250; in 1920 elections, 175; press criticism of, 176–177, 183; on legislative factions, 180–181; party

organisation, 183–184; nepotism, 194; and North Bengal floods, 233; 1923 election defeat, 241–242; death, 266 *and n*
Banerji, Nripendra Chandra, 268
Banglar Katha, 206 *and n*, 213, 220, 234
Bankura, 192, 237*n*
Baqr-Id, 115, 119
Bar associations, 12, 58, 135
Bardoli resolution, 226–227, 230
Barisal, 64, 228, 229
Barrackpur, 68, 241
Basanti Devi, 221, 223, 230
Basu, Bhupendranath, 47, 55, 60, 194, 266 *and n*
Basu, N. K., 289, 306
Belur, 264
Bengal: area in 1900, 2; climate and topography, 4; population in 1900, 4; Hindu and Muslim majority areas, 5; urban population, 5. *See also* Government of Bengal
Bengal Chamber of Commerce, 110; legislative representation, 19, 38, 54, 106*n*, 182, 185; as pressure group, 43; address to Montagu and Chelmsford, 108; on Montagu-Chelmsford Report, 109; forms Citizens Protection League, 222
Bengal Joatdars and Raiyats' Association, 157
Bengal Landholders' Association, 246
Bengal Moslem Education Advisory Committee, 286
Bengal Namasudra Association, 158 *and n*
Bengal National Chamber of Commerce, 246, 247
Bengal Provincial Congress Committee (B.P.C.C.): dispute over Congress presidency, 135–136; controlled by Indian Association, 137; struggles for control of, 139, 219–220, 233, 235; on noncooperation, 166; in Charmanair affair, 199; B. C. Pal's resignation from, 229; resolution on local government, 229; elections, 268; on Hindu-Muslim Pact, 279; S. C. Bose faction expelled from, 308
Bengalee, 67, 68, 135
Bengali: nineteenth-century development of, 10–11; Muslim literature in, 44
Besant, Annie, 135–136, 137, 147
Bhadralok: in Calcutta professions, 3; as dominant elite, 5–14; urban and rural networks, 11–12, 322–323; estimated numbers in 1900, 13*n*; as status group, 12–14; open or closed elite debate, 14–18, 318–320; class divisions, 32–33; elite, 154; voluntary associations, 12, 208, 321, 327; attitudes to mass politics, 152–155, 321–324
Bhadralok lower-class, 267; in anti-partition agitation, 32, 162; economic condition, 32–33; press appeals to, 56, 162–163; support for Gandhi, 162, 164–165; impatience with Congress, 300; role in politics, 324–325
Bhowanipur, 135
Bihar, 27, 145, 184, 307, 310; part of Bengal, 2; separated from Bengal, 40; rioting in, 115, 119, 277; peasant unrest in, 155
Birkenhead, Lord, 264–266
Birley, Leonard, 273–274
Biswananda, Swami, 260–261
Bogra, 58
Bombay, 155, 222
Bose, Subhas Chandra, 240, 301–302, 321; on C. R. Das, 208; in noncooperation movement, 220–222; flood relief, 233; Secretary, B.P.C.C., 235; attitude to terrorists, 238; and Hindu-Muslim Pact, 245–246; in Calcutta Corporation, 250, 260; imprisoned, 262, 267, 268; clash with Gandhi, 302, 308; formation of I.N.A., 304
Boycotts, 30, 31, 152, 208–209, 212, 220, 221, 263, 295
Brabourne, Lord, 305*n*
Brahmaputra, 1, 314
Brahmins, 6, 59
Brahmo Samaj, 134, 322
Bright, John, 87
British: in Calcutta, 1, 43–44; antipathy towards bhadralok, 24–25, 329; response to Moderates' reform proposals, 87–88, 96–98, 131–132; bhadralok distrust of promises, 98–99. *See also* Europeans
British Indian Association, 58, 133; rival of Indian Association, 67; in 1920 elections, 175; Lytton's speech to, 189; forms Citizens Protection League, 222
Buckland, P. L., 110
Buddhism, 16
Burdwan, Bijay Chand Mahtab, Maha-

rajadhiraja of, 48, 59, 100, 185–186, 190
Burdwan, 7, 53, 269
Burma, 268, 305
Burra Bazar, 1, 120, 122, 220
Bustees, 3

Calcutta, 48, 49, 51, 53, 58, 59, 60, 64, 65, 66, 105, 107, 120, 121, 134, 176, 188, 199, 204, 217, 239, 240, 260, 304, 315; description of, 1–4; port, 1–2, 305, 314; commerce in, 1–2, 155, 287; British in, 3, 43–44; Bengali area of, 3; in Bengal's urban population, 5; dialect, 10; as centre of renaissance, 10–11; ratepayers' associations, 12; rioting in, 32, 122–124, 130, 155–156, 222–223, 276–278, 279, 312, 313, 323–324; capital of India moved from, 40; legislative representation, 55, 104, 185; Indian Association's activities in, 57; Urdu speakers in, 119, 125, 157 *and n*; armed police, 124; Extremists' support in, 139, 164; Congress special session at, 144–145, 153, 166; Tagore's speeches in, 150; Gandhi in, 150; Andrews in, 151; Abul Kalam Azad returns to, 156; high castes in, 160; noncooperation movement in, 185, 207, 208–209, 226; *hartāls* in, 185, 221–223, 296–297; labour agitation in, 213, 221; youth rallies in, 233; A.I.C.C. meeting in, 235; Swarajists' strength in, 250; Lytton returns to, 269; H. S. Suhrawardy's influence in, 278; Muslim League session in, 296; bhadralok strength in, 323–324
Calcutta Agricultural Association, 157
Calcutta Bar Library, 135
Calcutta Corporation, 12, 284, 299; legislative representation, 19, 38, 53, 54; Curzon's reform of, 26; S. N. Banerjea's boycott of, 29, 67, 68; S. N. Banerjea's reform of, 174–175, 194–197, 238, 247, 250; Marwari representation on, 195; Muslims in, 195–197, 278, 287, 318; communal electorates for, 195–197; Congress in, 251, 259–260, 267, 300; Krishak Praja Party's reform of, 293
Calcutta High Court, 2, 8, 65, 134, 191, 192, 208–209, 216, 256, 266*n*
Calcutta Improvement Trust, 79
Calcutta Municipal Gazette, 250
Calcutta Review, 192
Calcutta Trades Association, 38, 54, 108
Calcutta University. *See* University of Calcutta
Camac Street Club, 151
Canning, Lord, 87
Capital, 43
Carmichael, Lord, 43, 46, 63, 78, 85, 95, 174, 326; appointed Governor of Bengal, 41–42; as Governor of Madras, 42; political contacts, 47–49, 51, 61–62; and Dacca Nawab, 51; and I.C.S. subordinates, 51–52; and legislature, 52, 60–61; and Moderates, 55–56, 68–70; policy on terrorism, 73–75, 77; criticised by Craddock, 73–74, 94; concedes to Government of India, 79–81; on Defence of India Act, 88; own verdict on achievement, 94; compared with Ronaldshay, 96; and Muslims, 49, 51, 117–118; leaves Bengal, 118; compared with Lytton, 188
Casey, R. G., 305
Caste associations, 158 *and n*
Central National Mahommedan Association, 116, 125–126, 127, 255
Central Provinces, 167, 258
Chakravarti, Byomkes, 135, 138, 139, 144, 147; leads delegation to Government, 122; in dispute over Congress presidency, 135–136; constitutional demands, 136–137; in Home Rule League, 137; opposed to noncooperation, 167; in 1923 elections, 246; Independent Nationalist Party Leader, 246–247; in Congress succession struggle, 268; appointed Minister, 280
Chandpur affair, 184–185, 214–219
Chandra, Nirmal Chandra, 240
Charmanair affair, 198–200
Chatterjee, Bankim Chandra, 148
Chatterjee, N. C., 309
Chaudhuri, Asutosh, 266 *and n*
Chaudhuri, Hafizar Rahman, 58–59
Chaudhuri, Jogesh Chandra, 58–59
Chaudhuri, Kisori Mohan, 89
Chaudhuri, Promothanath, 151
Chaudhuri, Rahmatjan, 198–200, 201
Chaudhuri, Syed Nawabaly, 183–184, 196; contacts with officials, 51, 126–127, 130; political strategy, 125–129; criticism of Abul Kalam Azad, 157; appointed Minister, 173–174, 262; press criticism of, 176
Chauri Chaura, 226
Chelmsford, Lord, 97, 101, 108, 116, 125

Chitpur Road, 278
Chittagong, 27, 201, 215, 220, 303 *and n*; Hindu majority in, 5; legislative representation, 38, 54, 91; growth, 46 *and n*; noncooperation movement in, 175, 184–185, 216–219; Provincial Conference in, 230; armoury raid, 302
Chota Nagpur, 2, 27
Christians, 128, 292
Citizens Protection League, 222
Civil Disobedience Movement, 302–303, 304
Cobban, Alfred, 14
Cocanada, 259
Colleges. *See* Education
Commerce, 101, 119, 122, 287–288, 323, 327; British, 1, 106, 107; Indian, 1; nineteenth-century bhadralok in, 7; legislative representation, 38, 54, 128, 292; Marwaris in, 120; recession in, 155, 212–213, 300, 304
Commerce, 43
Communal Award, 289, 291
Communal electorates, 103, 238–239, 244, 275, 281, 286, 288–292, 319–320, 327–328; Morley's opposition to, 36–37; Minto's advocacy of, 36–37; for Muslims, 50, 103–104, 126–128; opposed by nationalists, 55; Hindu bhadralok opposition to, 160; for Europeans, 110, 329; in Lucknow Pact, 114 *and n*; Montagu-Chelmsford Report on, 118; for Calcutta Corporation, 195–197, 293; in Hindu-Muslim Pact, 246; advocated for Hindus, 269
Communal rioting. *See* Rioting
Communists, 303–304
Congress, 50, 58, 86, 87, 122, 151, 165, 172, 185, 188, 196, 198, 212, 250, 266*n*, 283, 284, 291–292, 295, 318; formation, 21; Surat split, 34; opposes communal electorates, 37; in mass politics, 60; S. N. Banarjea in, 67; Extremists reenter, 97, 133; and Lucknow Pact, 98, 113–114; S. P. Sinha's presidency, 118; and Montagu-Chelmsford reforms, 121, 141, 145; dispute over presidency, 135–136; Extremists' control of, 136–142, 144, 164; Amritsar session, 1919, 144–145; Calcutta special session, 1920, 144–145, 166; Nagpur session, 1920, 144–145, 167–168, 204–205, 206, 219, 234, 246; Extremists withdraw from, 162; criticism of, 163, 214, 296; accepts noncooperation, 165–168; Moderates withdraw from, 173; I.C.S. supporters of, 187; criticism of I.C.S., 190; in Charmanair affair, 199–200; in 1923 elections, 203; News Service, 206; reorganisation, 206–208, 234, 237, 242; appeals to Muslims, 207–208; boycotts, 208–209; fund raising, 210; labour agitation, 212–219; Bengal factions, 219–220, 259–260, 267, 268, 278–279, 283, 299–301, 307, 308; party offices raided, 222; Ahmedabad session, 1921, 224; council entry debate, 227–235; Calcutta youth rallies, 233; flood relief, 233; Gaya session, 1922, 235, 259; Cocanada session, 1923, 259; rescinds Hindu-Muslim Pact, 279; forms provincial Governments, 296; *hartāls*, 296–297; Forward Bloc, 298, 308; difficulties in legislatures, 299–301; terrorist connections, 301; new agitational organisations, 301–302; outlawed, 302; organisation weakened, 303; *Bande Mataram* decision, 307; Bengali-Bihari decision, 307; S. C. Bose's presidency, 308; Bengal distrust of high command, 309; accepts partition, 312–313; intransigence in Bengal, 325–326. *See also* All-India Congress Committee, Bengal Provincial Congress Committee *and* Provincial Conference
Constitutional Club, 183–184
Constitutional Party, 197–198
Contai, 211–212
Cornwallis Street, 276
Cotton, Evan, 183, 187–188, 248–249, 256
Cotton, Henry, 21, 23, 187, 248
Cotton Street, 277
Council entry, 161, 166, 168, 245, 300, 325; debate, 227–235; accepted by Congress, 235; rejected by Congress, 300
Cow killing, 115, 120, 195–196, 246
Craddock, Reginald, 85, 330; on S. N. Banerjea, 73–74; on Carmichael, 73–77, 94; on bhadralok, 74–75; on Bengal politics, 80–81; on Bengal administration, 91–92
Crewe, Lord, 49, 74, 76, 78, 79, 80; reunifies Bengal, 39–41; selects Carmichael, 40–41; on Bengal politics, 42–47
Criminal Investigation Department (C.I.D.). *See* Police

Cumming, J. G., 100
Curtis, Lionel, 97, 107
Curzon, Lord, 78, 95, 174, 309, 310, 313, 325, 330; ideal of administrative efficiency, 26; reform of Calcutta Corporation, 26; university reforms, 26–27, 191; Bengal partition, 27–29; resignation, 35; S. N. Banerjea's opposition to, 67

Dacca, Khwaja Salimulla, Nawab of, 59, 126, 173–174; welcomes partition, 45; patronage of, 46, 65; political strategy of, 49–51, 117–118; criticism of, 63–65; death, 113, 118
Dacca, 27, 46, 64, 65, 134, 216; population, 5, 46 *and n*; as capital of Eastern Bengal and Assam, 45; High Court for, 46; commerce in, 287
Dacca Ismalia Anjuman, 272
Dacca University, 46, 192, 292
Dacoity, 70–71, 72–73, 198, 215, 216, 217
Darjeeling, 233, 241, 270
Das, Chitta Ranjan, 138, 139, 144, 262, 301, 326; political debut, 134–137; in dispute over Congress presidency, 135–136; Bhowanipur speech, 135, 163–164; constitutional demands, 136–137; rivalry with Gandhi, 147, opposed to noncooperation, 167–168; at Nagpur Congress, 168, 246; in 1923 elections, 203; as noncooperation leader, 204–209, 212–214, 217–224; forms Swaraj Party, 204, 235; publishes *Banglar Katha*, 206 *and n*, 220, 234; criticism of, 212 219, 255; leadership challenged, 219–220; Congress reorganisation, 219–220; appointed provincial dictator, 222; interview with Ronaldshay, 223; arrested, 223; advocates council entry, 228–235; negotiations with Government of India, 230; publishes *Forward*, 234; Gaya speech, 235, 259; criticises Hindu communal organisations, 237–238; Hindu-Muslim Pact, 238–239, 245–246, 253–256, 330; political ability of, 240; support for B. C. Roy, 241; enters Bengal Legislative Council, 244–247; refuses to form ministry, 244–245; Mayor of Calcutta, 250; difficulties with legislature, 257–259; death, 260, 266–267, 268, 299; on *swarāj*, 260; and Tarakeswar *satyāgraha*, 260–261; and terrorists, 261, 264–265; offer of cooperation to Government, 263–266; meeting with Lytton, 264
Das, Mrs. C. R. *See* Basanti Devi
Das, Satish Ranjan, 181–183, 184, 197–198, 201, 217, 218*n*
Datta, Akhil Chandra, 91
Datta, Narendranath. *See* Vivekananda, Swami
De, K. C., 215–216
Deakin, Alfred, 25
Defence of India Act, 80, 82–83, 85, 88, 91
Delhi, 79, 88, 95, 126, 252, 253, 264, 311, 312; as new capital of India, 40, 106; assassination attempt in, 62–63
Depressed classes. *See* Hindu lower castes
Dey, Lal Behari, 7
Diehards, 140
Dinajpur, 58
Dinu Miah's Mosque, 276
District Administration Committee, 77, 82, 92, 330
Donald, J., 270
Doveton College, 66
Dufferin, Lord, 22–23
Duke, William, 52, 53–54, 70–71, 97
Durga Puja, 119
Dutt, Aswini Kumar, 30, 162
Dutt, K. B., 89
Dyarchy, 170 *and n*, 191, 242, 245, 252, 257, 264
Dyer, Reginald, 145

Eastern Bengal and Assam: new province, 28–29; communal violence in, 32; legislature, 38; Fuller, Lieutenant-Governor of, 39; Muslims in, 45–46, 50; Lyon, Chief Secretary of, 52
Education, 249, 252, 269, 274, 281, 318, 325; in Calcutta, 2–3, 250; English-language, 7, 8; and bhadralok, 8, 9 *and n*, 15, 289; exclusive system of, 9, 285 *and n*; student accommodation, 11–12; students' associations, 12; competition for, 15, 33; of Muslims, 44, 45, 46, 116; of Bengal Legislative Council members, 59, 175; Government of India and Bengal system, 75, 77, 78; ministry, 170, 174, 192, 241; secondary, 193; school boycott, 208–209; Muslim reforms of, 285–286, 298; Krishak Praja Party's reforms of, 293–295; in Bihar, 307. *See also* National Educa-

tion Movement, University of Calcutta *and* University of Dacca
Eisenstadt, S. N., 318–319
Elections, 103; 1912–1913, 56, 57–60; 1916, 89–90; 1920, 175–176; 1923, 200–201, 203, 236, 237, 242–243; 1926, 263, 272–273, 278, 280; 1937, 291
Elliott, C. A., 25
Elphinstone, Mountstuart, 87
Englishman, 43
Eurasians. *See* Anglo-Indians
European Association, 108, 110
European Defence Association, 62, 78
Europeans, 99, 101, 205, 298, 303, 310, 323; in Bengal, 3, 43–44; legislative representation, 19, 38, 110, 128, 131, 133, 184, 244, 258, 275, 289–292; attitude to transfer of capital, 43; London lobby, 43; animosity to Hardinge, 62; attitude to legislatures, 62–63, 106, 110; criticism of Carmichael, 77–78; opposition to Montagu-Chelmsford reforms, 106–112; associations, 108; appeal to Moderates, 110–111; distrusted by bhadralok, 111–112; Calcutta Corporation representation, 195–197; on Hindu-Muslim Pact, 254, 270; criticism of Lytton, 257; support for Muslims, 278, 280, 284–285, 287, 295, 298–299, 310, 317, 331 on communal electorates, 328–329. *See also* British
Executive Council, Bengal, 170*n*, 174, 181, 186, 253, 266*n*, 274, 291; members of, 36, 51, 52, 100–101, 105, 173, 190; formation, 37; and legislature, 38, 54, 128; salaries, 179; in joint consultation with Ministers, 188, 190; press criticism of, 248; on Muslims in government service, 271. *See also* Government of Bengal
Extremists, 90, 161, 170; appeals to bhadralok lower-class, 32–33, 162–164; leave Congress, 34, 46–47, 162; Morley on, 35; boycott of Morley-Minto legislatures, 55–56, 132, 143, 144, 153; criticism of Moderates, 72, 84–85, 89, 131–133, 141; reenter Congress, 98; on constitutional reform, 132–133; capture Bengal Congress, 136–142; on Montagu-Chelmsford reforms, 139, 140, 142–145; candidates for election, 166; attitude to noncooperation, 170; in Bengal Legislative Council, 175, 180, 181, 183, 247
Famine, 1943, 283, 305
Faridpur, 198, 210, 217, 265
Forward, 234, 248
Forward Bloc, 298, 308
Franchise Committee, 102, 104, 110, 125–127, 141
Fraser, Andrew, 24, 27
Fuller, Bampfylde, 39
Functions Committee, 102, 125–126

Gafur, Abdul, 275
Gandhabaniks, 7*n*
Gandhi, 170, 218–219, 238, 239, 245, 258, 290, 299, 307, 309–310, 317; advocates noncooperation, 145–146; criticism of, 147, 148, 150–151, 220, 225, 226–227, 228–229, 230, 231, 302, 322; Congress reorganisation, 147, 206, 234; on alien institutions, 149; in Calcutta, 150, 268; and mass politics, 153, 206; on Khilafat movement, 156–157; on untouchability, 161–162; supported by lower-class bhadralok, 162, 164–165; attack on 'Anglicisation', 164; outmanoeuvres Bengal Congressmen, 165–168; begins personal noncooperation, 166; Calcutta victory, 166; charisma, 171; halts civil disobedience, 196, 226, 300, 302; imprisoned, 196, 227, 230; on boycott, 208; constructive programme, 209; opposes social boycott, 210*n*; on labour agitation, 214; Bengal Congress supporters of, 219–220; no-tax campaign, 224–225, 323; refuses to negotiate with Government of India, 229–230; clash with S. C. Bose, 308
Ganga, 1, 314
Gaya, 235, 259
George V, 39–40
Ghose, Aurobindo, 148, 224; in anti-partition agitation, 30, 32, 162; defended by C. R. Das, 134; leaves politics, 144
Ghose, D. C., 180
Ghose, Motilal, 48–49, 90, 135, 136–137, 143
Ghose, Rashbehari, 135
Ghuznavi, Abdul Karim, 252–253, 270; appointed Minister, 247, 280; Swarajist attack on, 248–250; on Hindu-Muslim Pact, 252–254
Goalundo, 215, 218
Gokhale, G. K., 147
Golden age myth, 16
Gourlay, W. R., 94, 101

Government, Local. *See* Local Government *and* Calcutta Corporation
Government of Bengal, 27, 63, 65, 186, 231–232, 276; composition of, 51–52, 94–95, 170 *and n*; and terrorism, 72, 92, 261–262, 302–303; on Montagu-Chelmsford Report, 101–102; on franchise, 102–104, 288, 330; and legislature, 103–104, 105, 126–127, 171–172, 175, 180, 202–203; and Muslims 117*n*, 118, 270–273, 317, 329–331; and 1918 Calcutta riot, 121–122, 124; Nawabaly Chaudhuri to, 127; criticism of, 176–177, 282–283; revenues, 177–179, 189, 249–250, 304, 306; and Chandpur affair, 184, 215–218, 233; and noncooperation movement, 185, 205, 209; joint consultation in, 186–188; dispute with Calcutta University, 191–194; on Midnapore local government, 212; and labour agitation, 213–218; fears revolution, 222; orders prison floggings, 232–233; and Northern Bengal floods, 233; and Hindu-Muslim Pact, 253–256, 267, 274, 330; attack on Swaraj Party, 270; survey of literacy, 273–274. *See also* Executive Council, Bengal, and Ministers
Government of India, 2, 53, 90, 101; favours communal electorates, 37; moves to Delhi, 40; on partition of Bengal, 45, 50; Lyon offends, 52, 93–94; criticism of Carmichael, 73–77; 93–94; and Bengal terrorists, 73–77, 262; and Calcutta University, 78, 192; passes Defence of India Act, 80; opposed by Carmichael, 88; on Bengal administration, 91–92; and Moderates' reform proposals, 87–88, 96–98, 131–132; Montagu's criticism of, 100, 169; on Bengal franchise, 103; and 1918 Calcutta riot, 121, 124; passes Rowlatt Act, 141; on Bengal Muslim legislative representation, 126–127; appoints Sedition Committee, 140–141; on Nagpur Congress, 167; revenues, 177–178, 189; on Bengal Executive Council, 190; and noncooperation movement, 205–206; arrests Gandhi, 227; proposes round table conference, 229–230, 245, 258; criticism of Lytton, 257; appoints Reforms Enquiry Committee, 264
Government of India Act, 1919, 104, 110, 142, 228, 321, 328
Government of India Act, 1935, 291, 292
Government service, 269, 304–305; bhadralok in, 7, 9*n*, 325; Muslims in, 9*n*, 46, 117*n*, 246, 254, 270, 295–296, 300; communal rivalry for jobs in, 196; Hindu lower castes in, 9*n*, 295–296; in Bihar, 307
Gujerat, 148, 150, 226, 231
Gujeratis, 3
Gymnasiums, 30

Hafeez, Mian Abdul, 295
Haldar, Surendranath, 248
Hanafi, 275–276
Hardinge, Lord, 77, 80; reunifies Bengal, 39–41, 47; unpopularity with Calcutta British, 43, 62; on Bengal Muslims, 46; assassination attempt against, 62–63, 73, 74; scheme of reforms, 97
Harijans. *See* Hindu lower castes
Harrison Road, 276
Hartāls, 263; against Rowlatt Act, 142, 145; in Eastern Bengal, 217; in Calcutta, 221–223, 296–297; in Civil Disobedience movement, 302
Herbert, John, 305*n*, 310
Hindu lower castes, 195, 196, 258, 273, 299, 328; legislative representation, 104, 128, 290–292, 310; Gandhi on, 146; criticism of bhadralok, 158–160, 236–237, 288; associations, 158–160; industrial labourers from, 212; in 1923 elections, 237; support for Muslims, 280; Calcutta Corporation representation, 293; on Land Revenue Commission, 293; in government service, 9*n*, 295–296; on 1947 partition, 313
Hindu Mahasabha, 284, 298, 303, 309; criticises Huq ministry, 293; attacked by Huq, 296, 297; accepts 1947 partition, 312–313. *See also* Hindu Sabha
Hindu-Muslim Pact, 245–246, 247, 259, 268; of C. R. Das, 238–239; Government attack on, 253–256, 267, 274, 330; rescinded, 279
Hindu raj, 115, 125, 196, 327
Hindu revivalists, 143–144, 319, 320–321; opposition to liberal secularists, 15–18, 30, 32; attitude to parliamentary institutions, 19–20
Hindu Sabha, 237, 279, 288–289, 301, 321. *See also* Hindu Mahasabha
Hindusthan National Guard, 284
Hogg, G. P., 199–200, 217

Home Rule League, 137
Hooghly, 1, 155, 241, 314
Howrah, 1, 155, 221
Huda, Syed Shamsul, 51, 64, 117*n*, 118, 187
Hume, A. O., 21
Huq, Abul Kasem Fazlul, 130, 135, 138, 252–253, 263, 270; education and political debut, 64–65; criticism of Government, 91; criticism of British, 112; and Muslim League, 113–114, 124–125, 296, 297, 308, 310; political strategy of, 118; and 1918 Calcutta riot, 121–122, 124; and Lucknow Pact, 136, 328; peasant organisation by, 157–158; Krishak Praja Party leader, 158, 291–298; on leadership, 165; appointed Minister, 247; Swarajist attack on, 248–250; on Hindu-Muslim Pact, 253–254; accused of bribery, 256; Chief Minister, 282, 310; Mayor of Calcutta, 287; and S. P. Mookerjee, 297–298
Husain, Musharruf, 254, 255, 259, 270, 280

Imperial federation, 86, 97
Independent Nationalist Party, 246–247, 248, 251, 254, 262
India, Government of. *See* Government of India
India Office Advisory Committee, 183, 188
Indian Association, 133, 266*n*; and S. N. Banerjea, 29, 67, 197; agitation for Bengal reunification, 47; on Legislative Council regulations, 55; in legislative elections, 57–58; 89, 175; A. C. Mazumder's address to, 83; control of Bengal Congress, 137, 139, 141; Extremist attempt to capture control of, 137–138
Indian Civil Service (I.C.S.), 61, 87, 106, 149, 205, 257, 304–305; size, 2; object of bhadralok ambition, 8; liberals in, 21–23; paternalism, 23–25; 329–330; view of institutional development, 24; distrust of bhadralok, 24–25; opposed to Morley's Executive Council reforms, 36; S. N. Banerjea dismissed from, 66, 134, 174; Lyon's demands on, 93; Ronaldshay on, 95; distrusted by bhadralok, 99; distrust of Montagu, 100; confidence in Ronaldshay, 100–101; opposition to Montagu-Chelmsford reforms, 101–102, 169, 189–190; attitude to parliamentary institutions, 105, 316; salaries, 177; support of Congress, 187; S. C. Bose resigns from, 220; criticised by S. P. Mookerjee, 282
Indian Councils Act, 1861, 19, 22–23
Indian Councils Act, 1892, 19, 23
Indian Councils Act, 1909, 37–38
Indian Moslem Association, 116
Indian National Army, 304
Indian National Congress. *See* Congress
Indian Reforms Committee, 188
Indian Statutory Commission, 266
Inflation, 33, 119, 155, 177, 212–213
Ironside, W. A., 109

Jainism, 3, 148. *See also* Marwaris
Jallianwala Bagh, 142, 143, 145, 216
Jamuna River, 217
Japanese, 283, 305
Jayaswal, K. P., 78
Jenkins, James, 40
Jessore, 255
Jews, 3
Jinnah, Muhammad Ali, 296, 297, 308–309, 310, 311–312
Joint family, 11
Joint Select Committee, 104, 105, 160, 178–179, 321

Kakina, Mahendra Ranjan Ray Choudhuri, Raja of, 58–60
Kalami, Madrasi agitator, 119, 122
Kali, 30, 322
Kalighat, 222, 248, 260
Kasem, Abul, 57, 279–280
Kayasthas, 6, 59
Kerr, J. H., 101, 102, 177–178, 182
Khādi, 146, 204, 220, 223, 227, 231, 239, 248, 250, 322
Khalifa, 65, 113, 119, 196. *See also* Khilafat movement *and* Panislamism
Khan, Syed Ahmed, 45
Khilafat movement, 196, 237, 238, 268; Gandhi supports, 146; organisation, 156, 165–166, 167, 207–208; Hindu bhadralok opposition to, 156–157; Andrews on, 157; and 1920 elections, 175; in Bengal, 209, 221–222, 227; labour agitation, 213; offices raided, 222. *See also* Khalifa *and* Panislamism
Khulna, 237
Krishak Praja Party, 158, 291–293, 295, 297–298

Krishnagar, 279
Kurukshetra, 277

Labour, 241–242; in Calcutta, 3, 119; legislative representation, 128, 292; agitation, 155, 184–185, 212–219; effects of economic recession on, 212–213
Lahiri, Naresh Chandra, 207
Lahiri, Pravash Chandra, 207
Lahore, 308
Landholders, 101, 104, 107, 108, 125, 158, 237*n*, 242, 247, 250, 262, 269, 285, 304, 323, 327; status, 6; in nineteenth-century Bengal, 6, 32; associations, 12, 208, 246; communal proportions among, 44 *and n*; legislative representation, 37, 38, 54, 59, 128, 292; Carmichael's contacts with, 48; Eastern Bengal Association, 58; delegation to Viceroy, 67; opposition to Land Alienation Bill, 79; opposition to Calcutta Improvement Trust, 79; in Politics, 153; Gandhi on, 146; in 1920 elections, 175–176; opposition to taxation, 178; in anti-partition agitation, 209; caste role, 209*n*; rents withheld from, 224–225; as moneylenders, 287; Krishak Praja Party's attack on, 292–293; Muslim attack on, 328. *See also* British Indian Association
Land Revenue Commission, 292–293, 298
Legal profession, 12, 59, 134, 175, 208–209
Legislative Assembly, Bengal: composition, 290–292; parties in, 291–292, 295, 297–298; 310; *hartāls* to influence, 296–297; Muslim control of, 298; Congress difficulties in, 299–301; partition vote, 313
Legislative Council, Bengal, 22–23, 51, 88, 110–111, 149, 153, 160, 170 *and n*, 172, 174, 181–182, 190, 205, 223, 230, 238, 280–281, 302, 317, 320–321, 325; opened to bhadralok, 12; composition of, 18–19, 37–38, 53–54, 59, 126–129, 175–176, 292; reforms of Calcutta Corporation, 26, 195–197; Carmichael's attitude to, 52–53; rules redrafted, 53–54, 105; electorates, 54, 128, 129, 291–292; Moderates in, 54–56, 131, 244; boycotts of, 55, 89–90, 175, 205, 208; election to Imperial Legislative Council, 59–60; Carmichael's inaugural address to, 60–61; S. N. Banerjea as opposition leader in, 68–71; parties in, 77, 179–180, 183–184, 246–247, 255–256, 275; political influence of, 90, 170, 201; Secretaries, 105, 180; President, 105, 187–188; Lucknow Pact provisions for, 114 *and n*; Krishak Praja Party in, 158, 291; Namasudra demand for representation in, 159; Ronaldshay's speech to, 172; financial resolutions in, 178–182, 306; and noncooperation movement, 184, 198–200; and Chandpur affair, 184–185; Lytton's speeches to, 188, 190–191, 202; criticism of Asutosh Mookerjee in, 192; and Charmanair affair, 198–200; Swarajists in, 244–245, 248–249, 262–263, 284; attack on Hindu-Muslim Pact in, 254–256
Legislative Council, Eastern Bengal and Assam, 38, 51, 53, 58
Legislature, Imperial, 2, 82, 86, 87, 90, 125, 197, 229, 247; composition, 18; Bengal representation in, 59–60, 110; S. N. Banerjea's experience in, 68
Legislatures, 56, 149; nationalists attitudes to, 17, 19–20, 169, 316; I.C.S. liberals' attitudes to, 21–23; nineteenth-century development of, 22–23; Morley-Minto reforms of, 35–38; Muslims' position in, 50; Carmichael's attitude to, 52–53; B. C. Pal on, 84–85, 228–229; Moderates' proposals for reform of, 85–87; Montagu-Chelmsford reform proposals for, 101; Europeans' attitudes to, 106–107; C. R. Das on, 231–232; bhadralok loss of confidence in, 283; opportunities in development of, 319–320
Liberals. *See* Moderates
Libraries, 12
Literacy, 3, 273–274
Local Government, 134, 149, 230, 246, 317; bhadralok in, 12, 18, 286–287; representation in Bengal Legislative Council, 19, 38, 53, 54, 55, 89, 91, 175–176, 229; Ripon's reform of, 22, 24–26; Curzon's reforms of, 26; Decentralisation Commission on, 37; criticisms of, 56; elections, 58, 210–211, 239–240, 250, 286–287; Europeans advocate development of, 108; ministry, 170*n*, 174–175; Banerjea's reforms of, 194–197; in Midnapore, 210–212; B.P.C.C. resolution on, 229; Congress in, 239–240,

300; Muslim reforms of, 286–287
London, 1, 8, 22, 36, 43, 51, 66, 142, 151, 240, 252
Lothian Commission, 95, 100
Lucknow Pact, 86, 98, 124, 125, 128, 130, 133, 328; provisions, 114 *and n*; rejection in Bengal, 114–117, 130; Central National Mahommedan Association on, 126; S. N. Banerjea on, 133–134, 136; Fazlul Huq on, 136
Lyon, Percy, 95, 97, 330; on nationalism, 52, 92–93; retires, 118
Lytton, Lord, 198, 326; appointed Governor of Bengal, 187; liberal ideals, 187–188; extends joint consultation, 188–189; speeches to legislature, 188, 190–191, 202, 251; criticism of, 189, 248, 251–253; administrative difficulties, 189–191, 202; dispute with Asutosh Mookerjee, 191–194; on Charmanair affair, 200; chooses Ministers, 244–245, 246, 247; struggle with Swarajists, 244–245, 248, 251–257; suspends dyarchy, 257–258, 263; meeting with C. R. Das, 264; officiates as Viceroy, 264, 269

MacDonald, Ramsay, 289
McLeod, Norman, 63
Machiavelli, 271
Madras, 135, 321
Maharashtra, 321, 322
Mahishyas, 211 *and n*
Mahmudabad, Raja of, 135–136, 137
Mahtab, Bijay Chand. *See* Burdwan, Maharajadhiraja of
Maitra, J. N., 199
Malaviya, Madan Mohan, 306
Malcolm, John, 87
Malda, 254
Mallick, Mukanda Behari, 158–159, 237
Mallick, Nirode Behari, 236, 237
Mallick, Surendranath, 185, 247–248
Mandal, J. N., 310
Mandalay, 267
Marwaris, 226*n*; in Calcutta, 3, 119–120; opposition to anti-partition agitation, 31, 220 *and n*; legislative representation, 104; Muslim enmity towards, 119–120, 122; violence against, 122; Calcutta Corporation representation, 195; support for Gandhi, 219; press criticism of, 220, 227; Chamber of Commerce, 221; as moneylenders, 287
Marxism, 14, 303–304, 318
Mazumder, Ambika Charan, 83, 89, 91
Meah, Lal, 199
Mehta, Pherozeshah, 147
Meston Committee, 177–178, 189
Midnapore, 210–212, 302
Migrants: in Calcutta, 1, 3, 119; bhadralok outside Bengal, 7–8, 33, 307; and disturbances, 123–124, 212
Ministers, 170*n*, 171, 251, 284, 320; Ronaldshay's selection of, 172–173; press criticism of, 176–177, 183, 248; salaries, 179, 204 *and n*; 249–250, 252–253, 256–257, 262–263; difficulties in legislature, 179–180, 183–184, 200–201; and non-cooperation movement, 186; joint consultation with Executive Council, 186–188, 190; Lytton's selection of, 244–247; Swarajists' attacks on, 247–250. *See also* Government of Bengal
Minto, Lord, 35–38, 67, 330
Mitra, Satyendra Chandra, 262
Mitter, Pravas Chandra, 184, 240; in Congress presidency dispute, 135–136; appointed Minister, 173–174, 179, 280; press criticism of, 176; conflict with Asutosh Mookerjee, 192–194; on dyarchy, 200
Moberley, A. N., 270
Moderates, 97, 101, 142, 161, 166, 174, 227, 231–232, 238, 239, 246, 247, 251, 262, 268; split with Extremists, 34; Morley on, 35–36; attitude to Bengal reunification, 46–47; reenter Bengal Legislative Council, 54–56, 61–62; in legislative elections, 57–60, 89–90, 175, 200–201, 204, 242; oppose Government in legislature, 65–66, 77; difficulties in Morley-Minto legislatures, 69, 83–86, 131, 170; attitude to terrorism, 71–72, 83–84; criticised by Extremists, 84–85, 131–133; constitutional demands, 85–87, 93, 131–133, 317; effects of Legislative Council participation, 90; Europeans' appeal to, 110–111; on Hindu-Muslim unity, 129–130; challenged by new men, 134; lose control of Congress, 136–142; control of Indian Association, 137–138; on Sedition Committee report, 141; on Rowlatt Act, 141; conference on Montagu-Chelmsford Report, 141; in Montagu-Chelmsford legislatures, 168, 171–172, 173, 197, 200–201, 205, 244, 258; press

criticism of, 176–177; and noncooperation movement, 182–183, 185–186, 229; and Chandpur affair, 184–185; British supporters of, 188; in voluntary associations, 208; in local government, 229; criticism of Lytton, 257
Mohammadi, 248
Mollās, 44–45, 123, 209, 256, 327
Moneylenders, 23, 33, 104, 287, 323; victims of political dacoities, 72*n*; Gandhi on, 146; Krishak Praja Party's attack on, 293; Muslim attack on, 328
Montagu, Edwin, 101, 105, 141, 182, 186; appointed Secretary of State, 98; 1917 declaration, 98–99, 107, 115, 118, 330; distrusted by I.C.S., 100; criticises Government of India, 100, 169; Indian visit, 101; in Calcutta, 108, 116, 125, 137; Muslim representations to, 116, 125; on communal electorates, 116–117, 327; influence on Lytton, 187; on Indianization, 188; resignation, 189
Montagu-Chelmsford Report, 108, 109, 121, 130; proposals, 101; reception in Bengal, 101–102, 119, 140, 158–159; on communal electorates, 104, 117, 118; Congress session on, 141
Mookerjee, Asutosh, 65, 78, 191–194, 240, 266, 283
Mookerjee, Shyama Prasad, 294, 311; as Finance Minister, 282–283, 297–298; career, 283–284; attacks Huq ministry, 293; attacked by Huq, 297; leaves Congress, 300; on Pakistan, 309, 311, 312
Morley, John, 35–38, 55, 76, 87
Municipalities. *See* Calcutta Corporation *and* Local Government
Murshidabad, 313
Muslim League, 120, 127, 133, 157, 284, 295, 311, 331; Carmichael's speech to, 49; and Lucknow Pact, 86, 98, 113–118, 125; and Montagu-Chelmsford Report, 121; Huq as president, 124; Aligarh session, 1925, 274–275; Calcutta special session, 1938, 296; attack on Congress Governments, 296; *hartāl*, 297; criticism of Huq, 298; ministries, 298; Lahore session, 1940, 308–309; legislative representation, 310; calls for Direct Action, 311–312
Muslims, 99, 118, 131, 133, 153, 160, 199, 237, 238, 269, 282, 302, 305, 310, 315, 316, 322, 324–325; Bengal majority, 4–5, 28, 123; attitude to 1905 partition, 31; hostility to anti-partition agitation, 31–32; education, 32, 44, 45, 46; legislative representation, 37, 38, 54, 103–104, 114 *and n*, 126–129, 183–184, 198, 244, 245–246, 258, 281, 288–292, 327; nineteenth-century revivalism, 44–45; economic situation, 44, 287–288; anger at reunification of Bengal, 44, 46, 51, 63–65; in professions, 45; favoured by Eastern Bengal and Assam Government, 45–46; Carmichael's contacts with, 49; political strategies, 49–51, 65, 113–119, 124–130, 156, 173–174, 238–239, 267, 274–281, 298–299, 317–318, 326–328; Lyon's sympathy for, 52; in Rajshahi, 58–59; delegation to Viceroy, 67; and 1914–1918 war, 113, 145; factions, 113, 119, 124–125, 157 *and n*, 179, 253–254, 255, 279, 284, 299; on Hindu raj, 115, 125, 196, 327; representations to Montagu and Chelmsford, 116; in government service, 9*n*, 117*n*, 246, 254, 270–271, 295–296; attitude to Montagu-Chelmsford Report, 119; enmity towards Marwaris, 119–120, 122; 1918 Calcutta riot, 119–122, 155–156; techniques of violence, 123–124, 129; addressed by Gandhi, 147; associations, 157–158, 208, 272–273, 279, 327; in legislative elections, 176 *and n*, 280; local government representation, 195–197, 286–287; and Swaraj Party, 204, 245–246, 248, 250, 253–256, 259, 262, 270, 272; Congress appeals to, 207–208; Namasudra enmity towards, 210; as industrial labourers, 212; apprehension of Hindu communalism, 238; debate council entry, 238–239; legislative party, 255–256; electoral organisation, 271–273; legislative programme, 285–288; educational reforms, 285–286, 293–295; on Land Revenue Commission, 293; and Hindu lower castes, 299
Mutiny, 22, 205
Mymensingh, 27, 51, 217, 247, 262

Nadia, 313
Nagpur, 144–145, 162, 167–168, 204, 205, 206, 219, 234, 246
Nakhoda Mosque, 122
Namasudras, 273, 310; opposition to anti-partition agitation, 31; association,

158–160, 237; enmity towards Muslims, 210; legislative representation, 236–237
Naoroji, Dadabhai, 147
Nashipur, Ranajit Sinha, Maharaja of, 60
National Education Movement, 30, 135, 152, 209, 212
National Liberal League, 139–140, 173
Nawabaly Chaudhuri. *See* Chaudhuri, Syed Nawabaly
Nayak, 149, 248
Nazimuddin, Khwaja, 291, 310–311
Nehru, Jawarharlal, 299
Nehru, Motilal, 230, 235, 265
Newspapers. *See* Press
Nilkantha, 56 *and n*
Noakhali, 175
Noncooperation movement, 144, 164, 172, 181, 258, 300, 317, 324; Gandhi's plans for, 145–146; Bengali criticism of, 146–162, 173, 210, 212, 225, 228–229; popular support for, 165, 167; accepted by Congress, 165–168; endorsed by C. R. Das, 168; strength, 170–171; and legislatures, 175, 180, 184, 198–200, 205; press support for, 183; in Chandpur affair, 184–185, 214–219; *hartāls*, 185, 217; Gandhi halts, 196, 203, 226; in Bengal, 204–227; Muslim participation in, 207–208, 209, 210, 221–222, 238; in Faridpur, 210; in Midnapore, 210–212; labour agitation and, 212–219; mass arrests, 223; no-tax campaign, 224–225; constructive programme, 226, 227–228, 231; prison riots, 232–233

Olivier, Lord, 252–253, 274
Orissa, 2, 27, 40, 310
Oudh, 135

Pabna, 58, 181, 207, 275
Padma, 184, 215
Pakistan, 284, 308–313
Pal, Bipin Chandra, 67, 89, 144, 231; in anti-partition agitation, 30, 32, 162; as Extremist, 34; criticises Morley-Minto reforms, 84–85, 90; defended by C. R. Das, 134; absent from Bengal, 135; rivalry with Gandhi, 147; opposes noncooperation, 147, 148, 166, 167, 228–229; resigns from B.P.C.C. and A.I.C.C., 229
Pal, Radha Charan, 180
Panipat, 296
Pan-Islamism, 65, 113. *See also* Khalifa *and* Khilafat movement
Parliamentary institutions. *See* Legislatures
Parsons, Talcott, 14
Partition of Bengal (1905), 78, 85, 313, 325, 330; Government discussion of, 27–29, 45; agitation against, 29–35, 89, 117, 134, 150, 151–153, 208, 209, 220 *and n*, 228, 316, 324; Hindu bhadralok attitudes to, 29, 31, 34; Muslim attitudes to, 31–32, 45; criticised by Morley and Minto, 39; annulled, 40, 330; Muslim attitude to annullment, 46, 51; Moderates' attitude to annullment, 46–47; S. N. Banerjea leads opposition to, 67; European anger at annullment, 106
Partition of Bengal (1947), 281, 284, 308, 310, 312–314, 318, 328, 331
Passive resistance. *See Satyāgraha*
Paternalism, 23–25, 95, 329–330
Pathans, 287
Peasant associations, 157–159, 272–273, 291
Peel, Lord, 189
Permanent Settlement, 75, 177, 292–293, 304
Police, 63, 73, 92, 102, 198, 207, 210, 221, 249, 261, 276, 283, 302–303; C.I.D., 34, 152; terrorist attacks on, 72–73, 302; criticism in legislature, 91, 181–182; in Calcutta, 122, 124, 222; in Charmanair affair, 198–199; in Chandpur affair, 215–216; arrest Basanti Devi, 223; attacked at Chauri Chaura, 226
Poona Pact, 290–291, 300–301, 306
Prasad, Rajendra, 307–308
Presidency College, 8, 64, 134
Presidency Division, 53, 57, 104
Presidency Gaol, 223
Press, 67, 74, 75, 91, 105, 135, 201, 257, 306; in Calcutta, 3, 43, 323; nineteenth-century development of, 10; circulation increased by anti-partition agitation, 31*n*; criticism of bhadralok elite, 32, 325; appeals to lower-class bhadralok, 32, 162–163; censorship, 34, 39; of Calcutta Europeans, 43, 63, 77, 107–109; on Carmichael's appointment, 47–48; Carmichael on, 48; criticism of Moderates, 56, 84–85, 162–163, 185; on legislatures, 56, 89, 90, 183, 232, 300;

on Calcutta Improvement Trust, 79; on Ronaldshay's appointment, 95; on British duplicity, 98; on Montagu's declaration, 99; on Lucknow Pact, 114–115; communal enmity in, 115–116, 119, 120–121, 159–160, 197, 220, 237 *and n*, 238, 255, 259, 275–276, 277, 294; and communal rioting, 119, 124, 276–278; on Marwaris, 120, 220; criticism of S. N. Banerjea, 133, 196–197; on C. R. Das, 135, 205, 255; on Congress presidential dispute, 136; support for Government, 156; criticism of Montagu-Chelmsford reforms, 159–160; criticism of Ministers, 176–177, 183; criticism of Government of Bengal, 179; on noncooperation, 183, 236; on Chandpur affair, 185, 216, 218; on Charmanair affair, 199; noncooperators' use of, 206; criticism of Gandhi, 220; criticism of council entry, 233–234; on Swaraj Party, 235, 248, 249–250, 259, 266, 267; criticism of Lytton, 251–252; on Tarakeswar *satyāgraha*, 260–261; on peasant associations, 272–273; criticism of Abdur Rahim, 275, 278; criticism of Hindu-Muslim Pact, 279; on Muslim educational policy, 285–286, 294; criticism of Congress factions, 299, 300

Professions, 179 *and n*, 287, 327; Hindu bhadralok in, 7, 44 *and n*; legal, 12; competition for jobs in, 32–33; Muslims in, 44 *and n*, 45; and politics, 153; in Contai, 211

Provincial Conference, 137; 1917, 135, 163–164; special session, 1918, 140; 1919, 168; 1920, 165; 1921, 228–229; 1922, 230; 1924, 259, 260–261; 1925, 265; 1926, 278–279

Punjab, 114, 142, 260, 313, 322

Quit India movement, 283, 303, 304, 305

Rahim, Abdur, 196, 262; appointed to Bengal Executive Council, 100, 173, resigns Gaols portfolio, 233; on Hindu-Muslim Pact, 253–254; on Muslims in government service, 270–271; on franchise, 274; Muslim separatist strategy of, 274–280; press attacks on, 275, 278; appointed Minister, 280

Rahman, Fazlul, 119, 122

Rai, Lajpat, 147

Rajagopalachari, C., 235, 309–310

Rajshahi, 58–60

Rākhi bandhan, 322

Ramakrishna Mission, 264

Ranchi, 156

Rangpur, 58

Rasul, Abdul, 78

Ray, Anil Baran, 262

Ray, Girija Nath, 58

Ray, Kiran Sankar, 240

Ray, Mahendranath, 89

Ray, Prafulla Chandra, 233, 294–295

Ray, S. N., 211*n*

Ray, Shib Shekhareswar, 160, 286

Ray Chaudhuri, Raja of Santosh, Manmatha Nath, 262

Ray Choudhuri, Raja of Kakina, Mahendra Ranjan, 58–60

Reading, Lord, 252–253, 256, 264–266, 274

Reforms Enquiry Committee, 264, 273

Rhodes, C. W., 182

Rioting, 284, 300, 311; in Eastern Bengal, 32; in Calcutta, 32, 122–124, 276–278, 279, 297, 312, 313, 317, 323–324; in Rajshahi, 59; in Bihar, 115, 119; in Faridpur, 210; at Tarakeswar, 261

Ripon, Marquess of, 21–23, 24–26, 87

Ronaldshay, Lord, 177, 182, 202; appointed Governor of Bengal, 95; on administration, 95–96; on Montagu's declaration, 99–100; appointments to Government of Bengal, 100–101, 172–173; and 1918 Calcutta riot, 121, 124; and legislature, 172, 181, 182–183; on noncooperation movement, 172; on joint consultation, 186; and Asutosh Mookerjee, 192; interview with C. R. Das, 223

Round Table, 97

Rowlatt, S. A. T., 140–141

Rowlatt Act, 141–142

Rowlatt Committee, 109, 140–141, 173

Roy, Bidhan Chandra, 240–242

Roy, Surendranath, 57, 89, 178–179, 180, 241

Russian Revolution, 155

Sachidananda, Swami, 260–261

Saha, Gopinath, 261

Sahana, Satya Kinkar, 237*n*, 278

Saktas, 16, 322, 324. *See also* Kali

Salam, Abdus, 255, 256

Salimulla, Khwaja. *See* Dacca, Khwaja Salimulla, Nawab of
Samitis, 321; in anti-partition agitation, 30, 31, 33; suppression of, 152; terrorist, 228, 238, 262
Santals, 79
Santiniketan, 150
Santosh, Manmathanath Ray Chaudhuri, Raja of, 262
Sapru, Tej Bahadur, 171–172, 183, 198, 201, 202
Sarathi, 237*n*
Sarkar, Kumud Nath, 207
Sarkar, Nalini Ranjan, 299
Sarkar, Nilratan, 61
Sarkar, Rishindranath, 192
Sarvadhikary, Devaprasad, 57, 197
Sasmal, Birendra Nath, 211–212, 240, 260, 268, 279
Satyāgraha, 148, 149, 168, 226, 260–261
Scheduled Caste Party, 295, 297–298
Scheduled castes. *See* Hindu lower castes
Schools. *See* Education
Secularists, 320; debate with Hindu revivalists, 15–18; parliamentary ideal of, 19–20; attacked by Hindu revivalists, 30, 32; Morley's attitude to, 35–37
Sedition Committee, 109, 140–141, 173
Sen, Baikunthanath, 136, 138
Sen Gupta, Jatindra Mohan, 240, 256, 275; imprisoned, 185; noncooperation leader in Chittagong, 216; favours council entry, 230; flood relief, 233; and Calcutta Corporation, 260, 278; in Congress succession struggle, 268; on Hindu-Muslim Pact, 279
Servant, 220
Shah, Habib, 119–122, 123
Shahabad, 115
Shibchar, 198
Simla, 99, 269
Simon Commission, 266
Sinha, Maharaja of Nashipur, Ranajit, 60
Sinha, S. P., 36, 61, 86, 87, 92, 100, 118, 141
Sirajganj, 259, 261
Siva, 56*n*, 277
Smith, Wilfred Cantwell, 326
Socialism, 302
South Africa, 145
Southborough Committee, 102, 104, 110, 125–127, 141
Statesman, 43
Stephen, J. F., 330
Stephenson, H. L., 105
Stewart, F. H., 78
Students associations, 12, 134. *See also* Education
Subarnabaniks, 7*n*
Subjects Committee, 104, 110, 141
Suhrawardy family, 176, 179; Abdulla-al-Mamun, 78, 256; Huseyn Shaheed, 250, 256, 278, 312, 313
Surat, 34, 46
Swadeshi, 30, 31, 151–152, 166, 209, 220, 221, 250
Swarāj, 152, 217, 243; Gandhi on, 146; Andrews on, 150; B. C. Pal on, 229; C. R. Das on, 231, 260, 264
Swaraj Fund, 207, 210, 219, 221
Swaraj Party, 283, 300; in 1923 elections, 171, 203, 204, 236–243; formation, 235; and terrorists, 238, 261–262; in local government, 239–240; personnel, 240; struggle with Lytton, 244–245, 248, 251–257; and legislatures, 244–250, 262–263, 284, 301; and Muslims, 245–246, 247, 253–256, 259, 270, 272, 275, 279, 280, 285–286; control of press, 248; control of Calcutta Corporation, 250, 259–260, 267; press criticism of, 266, 267

Tagore, Dwarkanath, 278
Tagore, Rabindranath, 212, 214, 224, 277; on Hindu revival, 30, 32; leaves politics, 144; on noncooperation, 150, 151, 322
Tarakeswar, 260–261
Taylor, A. J. P., 152
Tea planters, 38, 54, 215–217
Terrorism, 55, 79–80, 94, 161, 198, 258, 279, 281, 299, 307, 318, 321; in anti-partition agitation, 30, 33–34; British repression of, 33–34, 46, 261–262, 302–303; resurgence in Bengal, 70–73, 238; Government of India on, 88; Ronaldshay on, 95–96; Sedition Committee on, 140–141; Hindu bhadralok attitudes to, 149, 153, 228; and Swaraj Party, 238, 261–262; C. R. Das on, 264–265
Thaneswar, 296
Thoreau, Henry, 257
Tilak, Bal Gangadhar, 147
Tipperah, 51, 103
Trade. *See* Commerce

Trade unions, 30, 213–214, 216, 217–219, 301
Turkey, 113, 119, 145, 196
Twenty-Four Parganas, 241

United Provinces, 116, 155, 184, 226, 230
University of Calcutta, 66, 241, *266n*, 317; location, 3; foundation, 8; politics, 8, 191–194, 240, 283; legislative representation, 19, 38, 54, 55, 57, 128, 282, 292; Curzon's reform of, 26–27; lecturers' appointments in, 78; dispute with Government of Bengal, 191–194; Commission, 192; Muslim Vice-Chancellors of, 294
University of Dacca, 46, 192, 292
Untouchables. *See* Hindu lower castes

Vaisnavism, 16, 148, 322
Vincent, William, 127
Vivekananda, Swami, 142–143, 148
Volunteer brigades, 30, 208–209, 210, 221–222, 239, 241
Voters: 1916, 54; 1920, 128, 129; 1937, 328

Waddell, P. H., 206
Wales, Prince of, 222
Walsh, Pakenham, 217
War, 1914–1918, 317, 330; outbreak, 80, 86; Government of India's policy on, 88; Indian contributions to, 97; social effects of, 122, 155; economic effects of, 177, 212–213
War, 1939–1945, 283, 284, 303, 304–305
Wares, D. H., 103
Watson-Smyth, R. M., 85, 110–111
Wheeler, Henry, 100, 105, 185; appointed to Bengal Executive Council, 94–95; in legislature, 181–182; press criticism of, 183; in Chandpur affair, 217
Weber, Max, 13–14
Wedderburn, William, 21, 23

Yule, George, 21

Zamindars. *See* Landholders
Zetland, Marquess of. *See* Ronaldshay, Lord